ALEXANDER FAMILY

Migrations from Maryland

Wesley E. Pippenger

HERITAGE BOOKS
2018

HERITAGE BOOKS

AN IMPRINT OF HERITAGE BOOKS, INC.

Books, CDs, and more—Worldwide

For our listing of thousands of titles see our website
at
www.HeritageBooks.com

Published 2018 by
HERITAGE BOOKS, INC.
Publishing Division
5810 Ruatan Street
Berwyn Heights, Md. 20740

International Standard Book Number
Paperbound: 978-0-7884-5837-8

CONTENTS

LIST OF FIGURES v

PREFACE vii

ABBREVIATIONS USED ix

EARLY ALEXANDER FAMILY 1

JOHN ALEXANDER of Eredy 2

WILLIAM ALEXANDER of Eredy 4

WILLIAM ALEXANDER I 6

WILLIAM ALEXANDER II 7
   MOSES ALEXANDER 9
     JOHN ALEXANDER 10
       Sheldon Family 10
       Death of John Alexander 11
       JOHN SHELDON ALEXANDER 15
         WILLIAM ALEXANDER 18

JOHN BEVANS ALEXANDER 23
   William Whitfield Alexander 24
     John Joseph Alexander 26
     Charles Newton Alexander 27
     Mary Ann (Alexander) Guy 28
     Sarah Elizabeth (Alexander) McCain 30
     George Washington Alexander 33
     Thomas Jefferson Alexander 34
   Elizabeth Ann (Alexander) Davis Vint 35
   Susan Jane (Alexander) Dukes 36
   James Newton Alexander 38

ELEANOR TULL (ALEXANDER) THACKER 40

MOSES LISTON ALEXANDER 43

ELIZABETH ANN (ALEXANDER) JACKSON 46

WILLIAM BENJAMIN ALEXANDER 47
   Maxwell and McCue Families 56
   Catling Family 57
   Thomas Woodward Alexander 57
   Mary Ann (Alexander) Fauber 59
   Emma Jane (Alexander) Whitlock 60
   Sarah Margaret (Alexander) Whitlock 60
   Charles William Alexander 62
   Alice Cornelia (Alexander) McCormick 63
   Moses Harvey Alexander, Sr. 65
   Bettie Lee (Alexander) McCormick 68

JAMES WASHINGTON ALEXANDER 71
   Sarah Catherine (Alexander) King Eynon Barker 78
   Martha Mae (Gover) Alexander Gilliam 82
   Louis Fry Alexander 85
   Annie Amelia (Alexander) McLaughlin 85

Nina Lee (Alexander) Pippenger 91
Emma Leola (Alexander) Teft 94
Henriette Catherine (Alexander) Barrett 95
Bertha Irene (Alexander) O'Neill 96

REUBEN ALEXANDER 99
David Alexander 104
John Henry Alexander 106
Robert Ellis Alexander 111
David Stickley Alexander 112

ANDREW ALEXANDER 116
Elias Alexander 116
Adam Alexander 119
Abraham Alexander 120

ELIZABETH (ALEXANDER) WALLACE 121

JAMES ALEXANDER 123

FRANCIS ALEXANDER 127
Henry Alexander, Sr. 127

SAMUEL ALEXANDER 128
James Alexander, Sr. 129
Martin Alexander 130
Francis Alexander 132
Andrew Alexander 134

JOSEPH ALEXANDER 136
James Alexander 136
Amos Alexander, Jr., Mayor of Alexandria, Virginia 140
Hezekiah Alexander 142
John McKnitt Alexander 144

JOHN ALEXANDER 146

JANE (ALEXANDER) McKNITT 147

UNCONNECTED LINES 148
Benjamin Alexander 148
Henry Alexander 148
John Alexander of Talbot County, Maryland 149
John Alexander of Lincoln County, Tennessee 149
Thomas Alexander of Talbot County, Maryland 149

SELECTED BIBLIOGRAPHY 151

INDEX 155

LIST OF FIGURES

Figure 1 - Estate inventory for John Alexander in Northumberland County, Va., filed 1769 12
Figure 2 - Record copy of will of John Alexander in Northumberland County, Va., 1757 14
Figure 3 - Bond and consent for Sarah Alexander to marry Richmond Walton in 1807 17
Figure 4 - Marriage bond for William Alexander and Anna Bibbins [Bevans], Albemarle County, Va. in 1803 . . . 21
Figure 5 - Family Records for the children of William Alexander and Ann Bevans (Rockingham Co., Va.) 22
Figure 6 - Parental consent from William Alexander for his son John Bevans Alexander to marry in Augusta County in 1823 24
Figure 7 - Joseph Minger, father of Abigail (Minger) Alexander 24
Figure 8 - (l to r) Sarah E. Alexander McCain, Charles N. Alexander, John J. Alexander, George W. Alexander, Thomas J. Alexander, Samuel P. Alexander in 1929 27
Figure 9 - Samuel R. McCain 30
Figure 10 - Elizabeth Ann (Alexander) Davis Vint 35
Figure 11 - Parental consent for marriage of William Thacker to Eleanor Tull Alexander, 1823 42
Figure 12 - Parental consents for marriage of Moses L. Alexander to Nancy Hamilton, 1835 45
Figure 13 - William Benjamin Alexander and granddaughter Edith Whitlock 47
Figure 14 - James Franklin Alexander 48
Figure 15 - Furniture store operated by the William B. Alexander family, located in Waynesboro, Va., about where Maple Avenue ends at Main Street, c.1890's. (left to right) Charles W. Alexander, Thomas W. Alexander, William B. Alexander 49
Figure 16 - Alexander Family homestead in Waynesboro, Va. The structure had a canon ball embedded in the right chimney during the Civil War. 49
Figure 17 - William Benjamin Alexander 49
Figure 18 - Bible record, William B. Alexander Family, Marriages 50
Figure 19 - Bible record, William B. Alexander Family, Births 51
Figure 20 - Bible record, William B. Alexander Family, Baptisms 52
Figure 21 - Bible record, William B. Alexander Family, Deaths 53
Figure 22 - William B. Alexander Family Home, at 703 W. Main St., Waynesboro, Va. 55
Figure 23 - Marriage bond for William B. Alexander to Sarah Ann Maxwell, 1844 55
Figure 24 - Thomas Woodward Alexander 57
Figure 25 - Elmo Gibson Alexander 58
Figure 26 - Emma Jane (Alexander) Whitlock 60
Figure 27 - Charles William Alexander 62
Figure 28 - Charles William Alexander in 1882 63
Figure 29 - Alice Cornelia (Alexander) McCormick 63
Figure 30 - Stables of Moses Harvey Alexander, situated on the corner of Lafayette Avenue, Marshall, Mo. . . . 64
Figure 31 - New House of Moses Harvey Alexander, Marshall, Mo., before 1893 64
Figure 32 - Moses Harvey Alexander, Sr. 65
Figure 33 - Moses Harvey Alexander, Jr. 66
Figure 34 - Moses Harvey Alexander, Jr. and Elizabeth Lee Alexander c.1900 67
Figure 35 - Horatio Thompson McCormick 70
Figure 36 - Bettie Lee Alexander 70
Figure 37 - Emma Whitlock with Caroline Alexander and Betty Whitlock 70
Figure 38 - Pair of photographs believed to be James Washington Alexander (by Hutchings) and wife Mary (Rice) Gover (by D.P. Thompson). 71
Figure 39 - Letter from James Washington Alexander to his Brother William Benjamin Alexander, 1844, page 1 74
Figure 40 - Letter from James Washington Alexander to his Brother William Benjamin Alexander, 1844, page 2 75
Figure 41 - Letter from James Washington Alexander to his Brother William Benjamin Alexander, 1844, page 3 76
Figure 42 - Letter from James Washington Alexander to his Brother William Benjamin Alexander, 1844, mailing cover 77
Figure 43 - John Eynon and wife Sarah Catherine Alexander, with baby Esther Maude Eynon (Taken by R.W. Harris of Pleasanton, Kansas) 78
Figure 44 - (left to right) Samuel T. Barker, a neighbor, Omer Brown, Jr., Sarah Catherine (Alexander) Eynon Barker, two neighbors, Jessie (Brown) Bruce 78
Figure 45 - Lorene Estelle King 79

Figure 46 - Ernest Carlee Brown 79
Figure 47 - Jessie Brown Bruce 79
Figure 48 - Gay Lee Brown and Barbara Dell Brown 79
Figure 49 - (l to r) Lester King, Ernest King, and Frank King 80
Figure 50 - Gilliam Family, children Emma, Mary and Walter with their father Edward Marshall Gilliam (taken in Marceline, Mo.) 82
Figure 51 - Sisters (l to r) Nina Lee (Alexander) Pippenger, Emma Leola (Alexander) Teft, Annie Amelia (Alexander) McLaughlin, and their sister-in-law Inez Ellen (Barker) King Alexander 83
Figure 52 - (l to r) Ralph E., Mary L., and Walter H. Gilliam 83
Figure 53 - (l to r) Mary L., Edward M., Emma P., Ralph E., Sallie E., Martha Mae, and Walter H. Gilliam in 1908 83
Figure 54 - (l to r) Martha Mae "Mattie" Gilliam (step-daughter of J.W. Alexander), Ralph Edward Gilliam, Emma Pauline Gilliam, Eulalia Gilliam [McClintock], Walter Harvey Gilliam, Edward Marshall Gilliam, Mr. Duncan (a farm worker). 84
Figure 55 - Rex Wilford McClintock and Sallie Eulalia Gilliam in 1982 84
Figure 56 - Mary Louise Gilliam Baggett in 1944 84
Figure 57 - Charles Peake McLaughlin and wife Annie Amelia Alexander, 1895 85
Figure 58 - Charles Peake McLaughlin 89
Figure 59 - Annie Amelia Alexander McLaughlin 89
Figure 60 - Robert Henry Searcy 89
Figure 61 - Norman Eugene McLaughlin 89
Figure 62 - Alexander and Pippenger Family Reunion, Kansas City, Mo., 1936 90
Figure 63 - Nina Lee Alexander 91
Figure 64 - Nina and John Pippenger 93
Figure 65 - Nina and John Pippenger in 1960 93
Figure 66 - Clyde Delose Teft 94
Figure 67 - Emma Leola Alexander, wife of Clyde Delose Teft 94
Figure 68 - Ray Teft, age 4 94
Figure 69 - Henriette Catherine Alexander Barrett 95
Figure 70 - John Barrett and "Retta" Alexander in 1924 95
Figure 71 - Henriette Catherine Alexander Barrett 95
Figure 72 - Bertha Irene Alexander 96
Figure 73 - Bertha and Jim O'Neill 96
Figure 74 - Alberta O'Neill and Bill Corteville 97
Figure 75 - McLaughlin Family 97
Figure 76 - Bond for Reuben Alexander to marry Sarah Smith in 1810 99
Figure 77 - David Alexander Bible, Page 1 - Marriages 100
Figure 78 - David Alexander Bible, Page 2 - Births 101
Figure 79 - David Alexander Bible, Page 3 - Births 102
Figure 80 - David Alexander Bible, Page 4 - Deaths 103
Figure 81 - Residence of David Alexander, south of Harrisonburg, Va. on Route 11 (Roller House) 104
Figure 82 - Residence of David Craun Alexander, Highway 42 106
Figure 83 - David Craun Alexander 107
Figure 84 - Eva Blanch Craun and Rudolph Bell Alexander 109
Figure 85 - Marshall Huffman Alexander 109
Figure 86 - Residence of Robert E. Alexander, Grottoes, Va. 111

PREFACE

For some time I have delayed in preparing a genealogy for this part of my family—the biggest reason being that I could not learn anything about the ancestry of the last wife of my ancestor, James Washington Alexander, who apparently married five times. We have not known many details about James' last wife Mary, by whom he had a daughter, and our ancestor, named Nina Lee Alexander. As will be seen later, Mary was apparently an orphan at an early age, lived with perhaps more than one family, resided with a Rice Family after which she later called herself, married Walter Gover (a man we can not place), and had a child Mattie—all before she married Mr. Alexander. Records show her as Mary Reece, but several family members recalled how Reece was only how she pronounced the Rice surname.

Also, it seemed doubtful that a group of seven brothers and sisters Alexander in Somerset County, Maryland were really the issue of a Rev. James Alexander as had been claimed by some researchers for several decades. Recent research has linked the group of seven children to John Alexander of Eredy, County Donegal, Ireland, and his son William Alexander.

There are quite a few researchers that follow the Alexander Family out of Somerset County, Maryland. Because of this, I have primarily followed only my direct line that removed from Maryland to Virginia, through John Sheldon Alexander, and have not pursued his siblings' descendants past about 1800.

Time has not helped reveal many clues in some areas, and for the most part a great many people who once corresponded with me through the mail about this history have since died.

Wesley E. Pippenger
Tappahannock, Virginia

ABBREVIATIONS USED

b.	born	m.	married
bapt.	baptized	MDSA	Maryland State Archives
Bk.	Book	men.	mentioned
bur.	buried	n.d.	no date given
c.	circa or about	n.p.	no place given
Cem.	Cemetery	op. cit.	source cited above
cert.	certificate	p. or pp.	page or pages
Co.	County	prov.	proved
comp(s).	compiler(s)	q.v.	see elsewhere
d.	died	rem.	removed
d.inf.	died in infancy	res.	resident of or resided
d.y.	died young	s/o	son of
div.	divorced	twp.	township
d/o	daughter of	VHS	Virginia Historical Society
ed.	Editor	w/o	wife of
fol.	folio	wid/o	widow of
ibid.	same as preceding source	wit.	witness or witnessed
inv.	inventory of estate		

* * *

A plus sign "+" before the numbering system means this person's history is carried forward in his or her own sketch elsewhere in the work.

The letter "a" following a generation indicates an adopted child.

It is assumed that locations are in the state of Virginia unless otherwise noted.

EARLY ALEXANDER FAMILY

As a well-known surname, the Alexander Family's history is perhaps most published by those who claim descent from the Earls of Stirling, founding fathers from Menstrie and Stirling Castle, located in the region surrounding Edinborough, Scotland.

Clues to the precise ancestry of our branch of the Alexander Family were for some time all but plenty, yet the strongest paths led us to Maryland, where William Alexander and his wife Ann Bevans claimed as their birthplace.

In the writings of Emma Jane (Alexander) Whitlock, we were directed to find our Alexander roots in Eastern Shore Maryland; an area which includes, among others, Talbot, Dorchester, Somerset and Worcester Counties. Many by the surname Alexander also settled in an area now split between Chester County, Pennsylvania and Cecil County, Maryland, and were known as the "New Munster Alexanders." We now know that the New Munster Alexanders descended from Somerset County, Maryland.

After discovering enough coincidences to make it most probable that our branch of the Alexander Family was from Somerset and Worcester Counties in Maryland, a closer look proved this was indeed the case. In the late 1600s, a William Alexander had, among other children, sons Moses and Liston Alexander. Moses was known to be a blacksmith, and possibly a clockmaker—a craft very similar to the fine furniture making known of our Alexanders of Virginia. Our William Alexander and his wife Ann Bevans had a son named Moses Liston Alexander. This was my key to the puzzle.

Though the Alexanders of Somerset and Worcester Counties in Maryland were land owners, none were found there by the time the 1800 Federal census was taken. It is possible that they removed to the south through Accomack County, Virginia on their way into Western Virginia, or to the north through Cecil County, Maryland. Elizabeth (Dunavant) Alexander of Waynesboro said to me several times that William Alexander came up the James River as far as Scottsville in Albemarle County.

The Alexander and Bevans families were neighbors in Maryland, and intermarried more than once. The Catling Family also was a neighbor, and had ties through land purchases into Augusta County, Virginia. We will see that these three families, Alexander, Bevans, and Catling were closely interrelated, and continued to interact for many years to come.

JOHN ALEXANDER of Eredy
(c.1589-after 1665)

For many years researchers of the Alexander Family in Maryland based their conclusions on an article found in the *Pennsylvania Genealogical Magazine*,[1] which proposed the Reverend James Alexander of Scotland, and late of County Donegal, Ireland was the earliest known ancestor of this branch of the Alexander Family. If this were to be true he would have been the progenitor of a vast number of Alexander branches known to have roots in Eastern Shore, Maryland. However, in a rare, two-volume history of the Alexander Family, it is strictly stated this Reverend James Alexander *died without issue with his wife*.[2]

More recent research ties the family group to John Alexander of Eredy, County Donegal, Ireland.[3] Dr. Alvah M. Stafford, in his unpublished work "Alexander Notebooks,"[4] stated:

> The Alexander pioneers who settled in Somerset County, Maryland were: Andrew, Francis, James, John, Samuel and William. It is reasonably certain that they all came from Ulster, in the North of Ireland, and were of pure Scottish blood. It must be concluded that several of the Alexanders recorded here were brothers, if not, they were undoubtedly a cousinal relationship between them. Probably some of these Alexanders were of County Donegal—possibly from the Parish of Raphoe.

John Alexander of Eredy was perhaps born c.1589 in Kintyre, Scotland, and died after 1665 in Eredy, Ireland. Eredy is in Raphoe Parish of County Donegal, Ireland, and a short distance southwest of Londonderry. Alexander appears to have been a tenant farmer in County Donegal on land owned by Sir James Cunningham.[5] In 1613, Cunningham granted legal tenures on his land in Donegal among 39 persons, with the portion of Moyegh called Eredy being divided among 9 settlers, one being this John Alexander.[6] It was not until 1629 that he recovered title to his Donegal lands.[7] It has been said that John Alexander of Eredy previously resided in Magheracoltan which belonged to the Hamilton family in Tyrone County, Ulster, Ireland, before he secured lands on County Donegal.

John Alexander of Eredy, is recorded in the first census of Ireland, taken in 1659. By 1662, he is found in Taghboyne Parish in County Donegal where he is assessed 4 pounds 18 shillings. He had several holdings of land in Taghboyne, Raymoghy, Raphoe and Conleigh parishes. On the Hearth Tax Roll for Raymoghy Parish in 1663, he was styled "John Alexander of ye Dukes Land."

Some have claimed that John Alexander of Eredy was a son of Archibald Alexander who died in 1621 and married 1589 to Elizabeth Alexander, daughter or Robert Alexander, Burgess of Stirling. Historian Rogers states that this Archibald Alexander had only one son, a James Alexander,[8] and thus disproves the claim.

Much research continues around the world to show that one John Macallister, Tutor of Loup in Kintyre, assumed the surname Alexander. He was "granted a bond of manrent [sic] to the House of Hamilton, where he worked for them in return for his protection, as well as for all of Clan Macalister," and "took the English equivalent of Alexander for his family name of Macallister, and became one of the extended family of the House of Hamilton." Thus, John Macallister became John Alexander of Eredy. Researchers of Clan Hamilton propose that John Alexander of Eredy married a daughter of Robert Hamilton. Also, it may be that John [Mcalister] Alexander is a son of Charles Macalister of Kintyre, Scotland.[9]

---

[1] Pennsylvania Genealogical Magazine (Philadelphia, Pa.: The Genealogical Society of Pennsylvania), Vol. XVI (October 1948), pp. 85-90.

[2] Rev. Charles Rogers, Memorials of the Earl of Stirling and of the House of Alexander (Edinburgh, 1877), Vol. 2. Rogers presumed that the Alexanders living in *Eredy* were connected to Clan MacAlister, as was Lord Stirling. This conflicts with Sir Robert Douglas who states in his Peerage of Scotland (1813), Vol. 2, p. 535 this line is likely a branch of the Clan Macdonald.

[3] Recent researchers on this line have included Helen Smith of Waco, Tex., Lee Parker, and Jack Wells.

[4] Copy at the Charlotte-Mecklenburg Public Library, Charlotte, N.C., in the Carolina Room.

[5] Rogers, Vol. 2, pp. 61-62. Sir James Cunningham [Cuninghame] who d. 1623, was closely related to Sir William Alexander of Menstry, afterward Earl of Stirling from whom he borrowed money to initially purchase the lands in Donegal. Cunningham defaulted and Sir William Alexander foreclosed in 1618.

[6] Rogers, Vol. 2, p. 61. James Cunningham let his Eredy lands to William Arnett, Andrew Arnett, John Alexander, John Gutchine, Peter Stevenson, John Hamilton, Edward Homes and George Leich. The date of the lease was 1 MAY 1613.

[7] Rogers, Vol. 2, p. 63.

[8] Rogers, Vol. 1, pp. 22-23.

[9] Sarah Alexander Culton, A Documentary of Scotch-Irish Alexander Family History: The People, Places and Events Before 4000 B.C. to 2005 A.D., Third Edition (Colville, Wash.: By the Author, 2005), pp. 150, 161, 178. Much of this work covers lineage from Adam and Eve before concentrating on the Alexander Family and its connections in Scotland and Ireland. Unfortunately, not many statements of claimed fact are referenced and are not easily verified. The compiler states John Macalister, later John Alexander of Eredy, was a son of Charles Macalister, brother of the 4th Chief Alexander MacAlister in Kintyre, Scotland.

Probable children of John Alexander of Eredy:[1]

a.   Archibald Alexander, of Taghboyne Parish, County Donegal, Ire. in 1661-1663, d. 31 MAR 1689, m. Elizabeth Mackey, d. 30 JAN 1715, age 78 years; both bur. Balleighan, Taghboyne Parish.[2]

b.   Robert Alexander, of Meyboy, and afterwards of Drumquin,[3] on the Subsidy Roll of 1661 in Errigal Parish, County Londonderry, near Raphoe. Name of wife unknown.

c.   John Alexander, Jr., of Clonmany Parish in 1665, perhaps married twice.[4]

d.   [Rev.] Andrew Alexander, ministered in County Coleraine, d. 1641, m. Dorthea Caulfield daughter of Rev. James Caulfield.[5]

+   e.   WILLIAM ALEXANDER,[6] of Raphoe Parish, County Donegal, Ireland, b. c.1614 in Eredy, d. c.1666. The 1665 list is the last Hearth Tax Roll for Raphoe Parish, County Donegal, Ireland on which is found William Alexander.

---

[1] All five sons appear on the 1665 Hearth Tax Money Rolls for various parishes in Ireland. These rolls have been transcribed and are found on-line at several locations, one being *Ancestry.com*.
[2] Rogers, Vol. 2, p. 88.
[3] Ibid., p. 86.
[4] Ibid., pp. 64, 66. This John Alexander , Jr. is likely the father of Rev. James Alexander, Presbyterian minister at Raphoe Parish from 1677 until his death in 1704. The will of Rev. James Alexander shows his only heir as his wife Mariam Shaw, so placing him as the father of the seven brothers and sisters in Maryland is incorrect.
[5] Also see Burkes Peerage, "Alexanders of Antrim, Armagh, Carlow and Donegal."
[6] Rogers, Vol. 2, pp. 94, 96.

WILLIAM ALEXANDER of Eredy
(c.1614-c.1666)

William Alexander is known to be the fifth son of John Alexander of Eredy,[1] and was born c.1614 in Raphoe Parish of County Donegal, Ireland. The 1665 list is the last Hearth Tax Roll for Raphoe Parish, County Donegal, Ireland on which is found William Alexander. It may be that at this time he removed to Scotland with his wife and nine children. It is quite possible he never set foot in America.

One researcher claims this William Alexander was a prisoner at Newgate and/or died in the Battle of Rullion Green,[2] which was fought November 28, 1666 in Scotland as the culmination of the brief Pentland Rising of the local government. This same researcher claims that William's widow and nine children migrated to Lancaster County, Virginia to avoid religious persecution.[3] Another version of the story is that the group of seven brothers and their mother landed on Manhattan Island.[4] In Lancaster County there was indeed a William Alexander, who could be the right age to be eldest of the seven brothers, and who was indentured for 5 years to Robert Beverley in 1667.[5] The name of William Alexander's wife is unknown.

Proposed children of William Alexander of Eredy, with proposed birth years:

+ A. WILLIAM ALEXANDER I, b. 1646, m. Ann Liston, removed to Somerset Co., Md.

+ B. ANDREW ALEXANDER, b. 1648, m. Ann Taylor, removed first to Somerset Co., Md. then Cecil Co., Md.

+ C. ELIZABETH ALEXANDER, b. 1650, m. Matthew Wallace [Jr.], removed first to Somerset Co. then Cecil Co., Md.

+ D. JAMES ALEXANDER, b. 1652, m. Mary (   ), removed to Cecil Co., Md. Some have speculated he was the same who removed to Accomack Co., Va., and m. Mary (   ), widow of William Burton (d. 1696).

+ E. FRANCIS ALEXANDER, b. 1655, m. Rebecca (   ), resided in Somerset Co., Md.

+ F. SAMUEL ALEXANDER, b. 1657, m. Mary Taylor, resided first in Somerset Co., Md., then removed to Cecil Co., Md.

+ G. JOSEPH ALEXANDER, b. 1659, m. Abigail McKnitt, resided in Cecil Co., Md.

---

[1] Rogers, Vol. 2, pp. 94, 96. This William Alexander is likely the father of Rev. James Alexander, Presbyterian minister at Raphoe Parish from 1677 until his death in 1704. The will of Rev. James Alexander shows his only heir as his wife Mariam Shaw, so placing him as the father of the seven brothers and sisters in Maryland is incorrect.

[2] Culton, p. 184.

[3] Also see Alexander Kin, Vol. 2, p. 362, in a citation taken from the Ramsey Papers in the Estes Kefauver Library of the University of Tennessee, Knoxville, Tenn., in an 1844 letter from J.G.M. Ramsey of Mecklenburg, N.C. to Rev. William Henry Foote of Petersburg, Va., stating: the Alexanders were "... originally from Scotland. The policy and edicts of the Stuarts drove many of them into exile ... found a temporary refuge in Ireland, Ulster County, I believe, whither seven brothers of the name of Alexander fled ... before they bid adieu to civilization ... to baptize their children ... The minister came but just as he concluded the service ... an armed soldiery entered the ship, arrested the minister and incarcerated him ... The seven brothers ... rescued the "preacher" ... precise date of emigration I have not been able to ascertain ... believed to be near the end of the seventeenth or about beginning of the eighteenth century ..."

[4] Jethro Rumple, The History of Presbyterianism in North Carolina (Richmond: The Library of the Union Theological Seminary in Virginia, 1966), p. 270. The compiler recounts the following story: "Among the families so changing homes, was one named Alexander, from Scotland. This family consisted of seven brothers and their mother. Having determined to leave Ireland and seek a new home in America, before their departure they sent to Scotland for their old minister to baptize their children and give them his blessing. When this was all done, on the evening before sailing, while on shipboard, a posse of armed enemies arrested the minister and lodged him in jail. As the night drew near the determined mother of the seven Alexanders [brothers, as there were also two daughters], who had been covenanting for her grand-children, ordered her sons, in terms which had never been disobeyed, to rescue the minister, and take him along with them to America. Before morning the minister was on board, and, having no family ties to prevent, he sailed with them to America. The emigrants landed on Manhattan Island, and a part of them settled there, from whom descended William Alexander, a Major General in the Revolution, commonly known as Lord Stirling [sic Sterling]." The fact there was a group of seven brothers is established; however, the group settled in Somerset Co., Md. and there is no evidence they left descendants in New York. It has been established that the line of William Alexander, Lord Stirling is related no closer than back 12 generations before they have a common ancestor with the Maryland line.

[5] Lancaster Co., Va. Orders, Bk. 1666-1680, p. 42, court held 10 JUL 1667, first entry "William Alexander, Servant to Robert Beverley comeing into this Countrey without Indenture and appearinge at this Cort., is ordered to serve five yeres from his arrivall." If this William Alexander was bound to serve Beverley for 5 years in Virginia, he is unlikely the same William Alexander who in 1670 was transferred a cattle mark in Somerset Co., Md. (see reference later).

+   H.   JOHN ALEXANDER, b. 1662, m. Mary Barbary, resided in Somerset Co., Md.

+   I.   JANE ALEXANDER, b. 1665, m. John McKnitt, removed to Somerset Co., Md., then Cecil Co., Md.

Note: The focus of this genealogy is to follow the William Alexander line that moved into Virginia. Because of this, the descendants of the children above are not generally followed forward past 1800, except the line of William Alexander I.

A. WILLIAM ALEXANDER I
(c.1646-bef.1707)

Possibly the earliest record of this branch of the Alexander Family in Somerset County, Maryland is of William Alexander I who was first assigned property there c.1666 by Thomas Strawbridge.[1] It seems most certain that William Alexander was born c.1646 in Eredy, County Donegal, Ireland, and was surely a son of William Alexander of Eredy, Raphoe Parish, County Donegal, Ireland. It is probable that he married Ann Liston, daughter of the Reverend William Liston of Letterkenny, Ireland[2] and his wife Victoria.

On November 9, 1670, William Alexander I was transferred a cattle mark from Thomas Strawbridge in Somerset County.[3]

By an indenture dated November 5, 1687, William "Allexander" purchased a 100-acre parcel located at the headwater of the Wicomoco Creek called *Hunting Quarter* from Cornelius Anderson for the consideration of 5,000 pounds of tobacco.[4] On November 28, 1689 he was listed as a resident of Somerset County.[5]

In September 1690, William Alexander I witnessed a deed of gift from Reverend Thomas Wilson to his sons Ephraim and Thomas Wilson.[6]

William also owned a 100-acre tract called *Hogg Quarter*, which was at the head waters of Wicomoco Creek and surveyed April 25, 1689.[7] From the 1732 will record of William Alexander II, we know that his father William Alexander I, passed a tract of land known as *Trouble* to the son—that which he had possessed from Thomas Strawbridge, some time after October 13, 1677.

On November 28, 1689, William Alexander I and his son William Alexander II signed an address of loyalty in defense of the Protestant religion while residents of Somerset County, Maryland.[8]

By a meeting held November 8, 1692, William Alexander "of Wiccocomoco" was appointed to appear in court to assist the justices in laying out and dividing Somerset County into parishes,[9] as was also his neighbor Matthew Wallace,[10] who was probably his brother-in-law.[11]

William Alexander I died before 1707 without leaving a probate record.

There is only one known child of William Alexander I and Ann Liston:

+ A1. WILLIAM ALEXANDER II, b. c. 1674, m. Catharine Wallace, and died in 1735 in Somerset Co., Md.

---

[1] Somerset Co., Md. Deeds, Liber B1, fol. 16.

[2] Frederick A. Virkus, Compendium of American Genealogy, Vol. VI, p. 248. Also, we find wills from the Diocese of Raphoe, for Rev. William Liston of Letterkenny, 1695, and Victoria Liston of Letterkenny, 1698.

[3] Archives of Maryland (Baltimore: Maryland Historical Society, 1883), Vol. LIV.

[4] Somerset Co., Md. Deeds, Liber MA3, fol. 879.

[5] Clayton Torrence, Old Somerset on the Eastern Shore of Maryland (Richmond: Whittet & Shepperson, 1935), p. 349.

[6] Torrence, p. 232.

[7] Maryland Rent Rolls, Liber 9, fol. 156; Alice Norris Parran, Register of Maryland's Heraldic Families, 1634-1935 (Baltimore: H.G. Roebuck & Son, c.1935-1938), Vol. 2, p. 64.

[8] Torrence, p. 349.

[9] Ibid., p. 153.

[10] Ibid.

[11] Pennsylvania Genealogical Magazine (Philadelphia, Pa.: The Genealogical Society of Pennsylvania), Vol. XVI (Oct. 1948), p. 86.

A1. WILLIAM ALEXANDER II
(c.1674-1735)

William Alexander II, a (tobacco) planter, son of William Alexander I and Ann Liston, was probably born in Somerset County, Maryland about 1674, as he was age 50 in 1724.[1] About 1695 he was married, probably in Somerset County, to Catharine Wallace,[2] thought to have been the daughter of Matthew Wallace, Jr. and his wife Elizabeth Alexander, who was actually both William's mother-in-law and aunt. Catherine (Wallace) Alexander died c.1732/5.[3] William Alexander II sold land of his neighbor Matthew Wallace when Wallace moved to Cecil County, Maryland in 1707. William Alexander II and his wife Catharine Wallace are believed to have been members of the Manokin Presbyterian Church of Somerset County, Maryland.

William Alexander II is known to have owned tracts of land *Trouble*, *Daintry*, *Hunting Quarter* (which he received from his father) and *Raphoe*, the latter 200-acre tract of which had been surveyed on May 20, 1689 and located on the South branch of the Rokiawakin River in Somerset County. Of his early property called *Raphoe*, we find this a coincidental link (but not a family link) to the Reverend James Alexander of Scotland who died November 17, 1704 in Raphoe, County Donegal, Ireland. The tract *Raphoe* was located on the Manokin River.

By indenture dated April 17, 1703, William Alexander II purchased a parcel of land called *Daintry* from Jonathan Raymond, which was situate on the southwest side of the Chesapeake Bay.[4] In 1728 he re-patented the *Daintry* tract as a parcel of 300 acres.

On May 18, 1709, William Alexander II was witness to the will of John Persons of Wicomico Hundred in Somerset County, proved April 1, 1712.[5]

By 1723, William Alexander II was an elder of Manokin Presbyterian Church of Princess Anne, Somerset County, Maryland,[6] as was John McKnitt (c.1660-1714), his uncle by marriage to Jane Alexander, who resided on a tract called *The Strand* in Somerset County, Maryland.[7]

On July 1, 1724, a William "Elexander" was listed on the tax list for Wicomico Hundred of Somerset County.[8]

The 1730 tax list for Somerset County, Maryland shows William Alexander II as head of household #472 in Wicomico Hundred, along with a James Alexander, presumably his son.[9]

William wrote two wills in Somerset County, one dated March 7, 1732[10] that was proved June 18, 1735, and the latter (after the death of his son James Alexander) dated March 27, 1734/5[11] which was proved July 19, 1735.

In his first will, William Alexander II provided for his son Samuel Alexander to receive 300 acres of land which was part of two separate patents on the east and west side of Mr. Thomas Gillie's mill, yet stipulated that *in case my son Samuel should depart this life without issue* then 150 acres shall descend to his son James and his heirs and assigns. Samuel outlived James. Further, Moses Alexander was to receive 200 acres in two tracts being where Moses was living at the time of the will in 1732, and another where William Alexander I had lived. The *youngest son Liston* received a tract called *Trouble* which was about 250 acres, containing a 90-acre parcel William Alexander II had bought of *Griffith Jones*,[12] and lying *where my now dwelling plantation is*. The 1732 will was witnessed by John Caldwell, John Crawford and William Dulaney.

---

[1] Maryland Bk. IR1, fol. 26, planter; also see *Maryland Historical Magazine*, Vol. XXIII No. 2 (January 1928), p. 102.

[2] Somerset Co., Md. Deeds, Liber CD21, fol. 151.

[3] Virginia W. Alexander and Charles C. Alexander, <u>Alexander Kin</u> (Columbia, Tenn.: Privately Printed; 1964), Vol. 1, Chapter III.

[4] Somerset Co., Md. Deeds, Liber GI reverse, fol. 52.

[5] <u>Maryland Wills</u>, Liber 13, fol. 424; <u>Maryland Calendar of Wills</u>, Vol. III, p. 227.

[6] Alethea Helen Whitney, <u>A History of the Manokin Presbyterian Church, Princess Anne, Maryland, 1672-1980</u> (Denton: The Baker Printing Company, 1981), pp. 4, 12.

[7] Whitney, p. 4.

[8] Wilmer O. Lankford, <u>They Lived in Somerset County, Maryland 1700-1725</u> (Princess Anne: Manokin Press, 1991), p. 3.

[9] The 1730 Tax List, Somerset Co., Md., copy located at the Research Center for Delmarva History and Culture, Salisbury State University, Salisbury, Md.

[10] MDSA, Somerset Co., Md. Wills (Original), Box 4, folder 83.

[11] Somerset Co., Md. Wills, Liber 21, fol. 450.

[12] MDSA, Somerset Co., Md. Deeds, Liber IK, fol. 100, indenture roughly 13"x20" per page, dated 25 NOV 1720, between Griffith Jones of Albemarle Co., N.C., gentleman, and Mary his wife on the one part, and William Alexander, Junior, of Somerset Co., Md., planter, on the other part. Albemarle Co., N.C. was created in 1663 as one of the state's three original counties, but no longer existed by 1739, being in the extreme northeast corner of the state, bounded by Norfolk and Princess Anne counties in Virginia. The parcel of land William Alexander II purchased was originally part of a tract called *Waley's Chance*, situated on the east of the Chesapeake Bay and south side of the head of the Wicocomoco River. Waley was seized of the parcel in April 1687 by Michaell Judd of Baltimore Co., Md., subsequently possessed by Edward Day in 1695, and seized by George Godard, late of Somerset Co., dec., then adjacent to a parcel formerly surveyed for Thomas [Strawbridge] dated 1 JUN 1685. George Godard was seized of estate of inheritance in fee simple of two tracts called *Waley's Chance* and *Windsor*, by deed dated 6 JUN 1704. The two tracts were conveyed to Griffith Jones who renamed in part *Monmouth*. Further, for 50 pounds sterling, Griffith Jones discharged part of *Monmouth* to William Alexander II. Samuel Alexander signed the subject indenture on behalf of Griffith Jones <u>NOT</u> William Alexander II, after a letter of power of attorney dated 4 NOV 1720 was recorded in Somerset Co., Md. at Liber IK, fol. 99.

William's second will of 1734/5 was succinct, yet made approximately the same provisions as the earlier one—that Liston Alexander got plantation *Trouble*, James Alexander received a tract called *Daintry*, and Moses Alexander got a tract called *Hogg Quarter*. Witnesses of the second will were Benjamin Cottman, Thomas Talbot, John Griffin, and Robert [Landall?].

We have no information about dates of death or grave locations for either William Alexander II or his wife Catharine Wallace.

Known children of William Alexander II and Catharine Wallace:

+ A11.   MOSES ALEXANDER, a blacksmith, b. c.1697 in Md., m. Elizabeth (Robertson) Weatherly, and d. post 1748, probably in Somerset Co., Md.

A12.   MARY ALEXANDER, b. c.1695, m. John Mills.[1]

A13.   SAMUEL ALEXANDER, b. c.1699, single. In 1730, Samuel was head of household #473 in Wicomico Hundred of Somerset Co., Md., as reflected in the tax list taken that year.[2] He inherited 300 acres from his father in 1735.

A14.   JAMES ALEXANDER, b. c.1701, a planter, single. In 1730, James was living in household #472 of his father William, as reflected in the tax list taken that year.[3] He inherited part of the tract *Daintry* from his father in 1735, and died that year Somerset Co., Md. In his will dated 30 MAR 1735, James, *sick and weak*, provided for his land on the west and south side of the branch known as Thomas Gillie's mill to go to his brother "Listian," and the residue to his sister Agnes Alexander.[4]

A15.   LISTON ALEXANDER, the youngest son, b. c.1703, inherited the tract called *Trouble* from his father, but died without issue.[5] On 29 JUL 1737, was filed in Somerset Co., Md., *the account of Listian Alexander, surviving executor of the Last Will and Testament of William Alexander, late of the County aforesaid*, wherein legacies of the estate were paid to children.[6] When Liston died in 1738, he left his dwelling plantation and land adjoining thereto (being part of 2 tracts *Trouble* and *Daintry* [sic "Dentry"]), to his brother Moses Alexander (with caveat to sister Agnes), and a horse bridle and saddle to a cousin Alexander Mills.[7]

A16.   AGNES ALEXANDER, b. c.1705. Determining her age is an important fact in shuffling through errors of her placement by other genealogists. The way she was mentioned in her father's 1735 will as Agnes Alexander, it is presumed by this compiler that she was single. Because some genealogists have claimed this Agnes Alexander was married to her cousin William Alexander, son of Elias and Sophia (Alexander) Alexander, it might seem possible that she was at one time Mrs. Agnes (Alexander) Alexander, wife of William Alexander. There are generally two beliefs: (1) she was the wife of John Laws (1715-1790), judge of Sussex Co., Del. Court of Common Pleas, who was a son of William Laws and Sarah Bevans, or (2) [though seemingly incorrect], she married her cousin William Alexander, who d. 1772 in Cecil Co., Md. The evidence supports that Agnes married John Laws, and in the most conclusive piece of this evidence that I find (Somerset Co., Md. Deeds) states on 24 MAY 1749, that John Laws and his wife sold to Thomas Pollitt, 170 acres which was part of tracts *Daintry* and *Trouble*, that Moses Alexander deeded to his sister Agnes Alexander, "now wife of John Laws." It is believed that both John and Agnes (Alexander) Laws died in Sussex Co., Del.

---

[1] Maryland Calendar of Wills, Vol. 7, p. 115, Somerset Co., Md. The will of John Mills, dated 20 FEB 1729/30, proved 19 NOV 1734, mentions wife as Mary Alexander, and children: Rebecca, Hannah, Mary, Esther, and Robert Mills, and heirs (part of land lying in Virginia), Alexander Mills and Nathaniel Mills. Overseer of the will was John Caldwell.
[2] 1730 Tax List, Somerset Co., Md., copy located at the Research Center for Delmarva History and Culture, Salisbury State University, Salisbury, Md.
[3] Ibid.
[4] MDSA, Somerset Co., Md. Wills (Original), Box 4, folder 82, proved 18 JUN 1735. Also filed Liber TD, fol. 399; and Liber EB9, fol. 174.
[5] Given name clearly spelled "Liston" in the 1735 will of his father William Alexander II, although subsequent land deeds are transcribed as "Listian," or "Listen." No trace of a Liston family so far has been found in eastern Maryland, but it may be from France and they were later residents of Delaware.
[6] MDSA, Somerset Co., Md. Accounts, Liber 14, fol. 350-352, signed by Nehemiah King. Mentions James Alexander has died, and his balance is left to Elizabeth Alexander.
[7] MDSA, Somerset Co., Md. Wills (Originals), Box 5, folder 28, dated 20 MAR 1737/8, proved 23 JUL 1738, court copy filed Liber TD, fol. 897, and Liber EB9, pp. 203-04. Witnessed by Thomas Phillips, David Polk, and Thomas Talbot.

A11. MOSES ALEXANDER
(c.1697-post 1748)

Moses Alexander, son of William Alexander II and Catharine Wallace, and grandson of William Alexander I and Ann Liston, was born c.1697, probably in Somerset County, Maryland. He was a blacksmith[1] and possibly a clocksmith.

Moses Alexander received a tract of land known as *Hunting Quarter* from his father William Alexander II, but also resided on a parcel known as *Hogg Quarter*.[2]

From clues in a property deed, we know that his wife's name was Elizabeth. It later becomes obvious that Elizabeth was Elizabeth (Robertson) Weatherly,[3] widow of James Weatherly II.

A deposition in 1724 gives Moses' age as 27, and occupation as blacksmith.[4]

The 1730 tax list for Somerset County shows Moses Alexander as head of household #474 in Wicomico Hundred, having his brother Samuel Alexander, and father William Alexander II as close neighbors.[5]

The 1733 tax list for Somerset County shows Moses Alexander in Nanticoke Hundred with 2 slaves and 200 acres of land, with James Weatherly and Benjamin Billings as members of his household. In June 1736, Moses Alexander, son of William Alexander II, sold to his brother Liston Alexander for 5 shillings all of his interest in the lands of William Alexander I: 380-acre *Hungary Neck* being a part of *Trouble* and part of tract *Daintry*. In 1738, Moses Alexander sold to his sister Agnes Alexander 150 acres of *Daintry* with part of *Trouble*.

The 1739 tax list shows Moses Alexander in Wicomico Hundred with slaves Tom and John.

The 1744 tax list for Somerset County, shows Moses Alexander as head of household #852 in Wicomico Hundred, and with him are living his son John Alexander, a William Haith (possibly a relative), son Samuel Alexander, and a slave named Sevin.[6]

In 1748, Moses Allexander [sic] appears as head of household #636 on the tax list for Wicomico Hundred in Somerset County, and with him is residing a Samuel Allexander. It is not clear at this time whether the Samuel Allexander is indeed his son, or perhaps his brother.

In 1749, Moses Alexander conveyed to his son Samuel Alexander, the tract *Hunting Quarter* and other lands in Somerset County.

No evidence has been found about the deaths of Moses or Elizabeth, so it may be that they left Somerset County, and possibly removed to the adjacent Dorchester County, Maryland.

Known children of Moses Alexander and Elizabeth (Robertson) Weatherly:

A111.   SAMUEL ALEXANDER, a wheelwright, b. c.1712, inherited the tract *Hunting Quarter* from his father in 1738. On the 1744 tax list, Samuel is residing in household #852 of his father in Wicomico Hundred.[7] On 21 MAR 1750 he sold 100 acres of *Hunting Quarter* to John Dorman,[8] and a deed mentioned his grandfather William Alexander II, as witnessed by Wm. Stoughton and Henry Bullard.

A112.   WILLIAM ALEXANDER, b. c.1714. No further information.

A113.   MARY ALEXANDER, b. c.1716, received a young mare in her grandfather William Alexander II's will of 1735. No further information.

+   A114.   JOHN ALEXANDER, b. c.1717, d. 1767 in Northumberland Co., Va., m. (1) Mary Sheldon, m. (2) Sarah ( ).

A115.   ELIZABETH ALEXANDER, b. c.1718, received a young heffer in her grandfather William Alexander II's will of 1735. No further information.

---

[1] *Maryland Historical Magazine*, Vol. XXIII No. 2 (June 1928), p. 102, age 27 in 1724 per I.R.L. No. 1, fol. 25.

[2] Somerset Co., Md. Deeds, Liber IX, fol. 174.

[3] MDSA, Somerset Co., Md. Accounts, Liber 18, Folio 241-2. The second account of Moses Alexander and Elizabeth his wife who was executrix of the Last Will and Testament of James Weatherly, late of Somerset Co., mentions payments to Mary, Sarah and Elizabeth Weatherly, Mr. Robert Twillor (possibly for his wife's share of inheritance?), and mentions children of deceased: James, Anne, Elizabeth, Mary, Sarah, John and Rachel Weathorby [sic].

[4] *Maryland Historical Magazine*, Vol. XXIII No. 2 (June 1928), p. 102, age 27 in 1724, per Liber I.R.L. No. 1, fol. 25.

[5] 1730 Tax List, Somerset Co., Md., copy located at the Research Center for Delmarva History and Culture, Salisbury State University, Salisbury, Md.

[6] 1744 Tax List, Somerset Co., Md., copy located at the Research Center for Delmarva History and Culture, Salisbury State University, Salisbury, Md.

[7] Ibid.

[8] Somerset Co., Md. Deeds, Liber O22, fol. 172.

A114. JOHN ALEXANDER
(c.1717-1767)

This John Alexander, eldest son of Moses Alexander and Elizabeth Robertson, was probably born c.1717, as he was married by the time of his father's will in 1738.

In 1744, John Alexander was listed on the tax list for Wicomico Hundred of Somerset County, Maryland, and living in household #852 of his father Moses Alexander.[1]

John Alexander was a blacksmith, as confirmed in an inventory of the contents of his estate taken June 15, 1767,[2] which itemized his smith's tools and a residue of 50 pounds of iron. It is probable that he was a learned man, as his estate inventory included *some old books*, and a *fine hat*.

It appears John Alexander was married twice. We know that his wife was named Mary—most certain to be Mary Sheldon, daughter of John Sheldon,[3] by whom he had son John Sheldon Alexander. Preliminary research lead us to examine records of the Gray Family of Somerset County, as it appears the wife of John Sheldon was Mary (   ), who died c.1768,[4] widow of Westcot Gray,[5] son of Joseph Gray (d. c.NOV 1724).[6]

Some time before 1765, when he wrote his will, John Alexander was married to Sarah (   ), and she is named as his Executrix. An alarming statement in his will speaks to his former wife, so it appears either Mary Sheldon died or, based on what is in the statement, the couple was separated (see later).

Sheldon Family

Westcot Gray was a planter of Somerset County, Maryland and was born August 29, 1694.[7] He died c.1729 in Somerset County,[8] where his will was filed. He was the son of Joseph Gray (d. 1724) by his first wife Elizabeth.[9] In his will, Wescot Gray mentioned his wife Mary and children Sarah, Rebecca, Joseph and William. In June 1729, Mary Gray, the executrix of Westcot Gray, filed an estate inventory on which William Freeman and William Porter signed as next of kin.

On June 18, 1729, William Freeman of Somerset County, attorney in fact to Philip Jones and Mary his wife, granddaughter and sole heir of Joseph Freeman, deceased, conveyed to Mary (   ) Gray of the same place, widow, for £10, the tract called *Mt. Hope*, which had been granted September 14, 1675 to Henry Smith who sold it to Joseph Freeman who died intestate by means of which the land fell to William Freeman, his heir and son and father of Mary. William Freeman also died intestate and his widow Mary was his sole legatee.[10]

On December 27, 1730, John Sheldon and Mary his wife, executors of Westcot Gray, filed an account of the estate.[11] Thus we see that John Sheldon had married the widow. They filed another account on March 24, 1737/8, which showed payment of the widow's thirds but no further distribution.[12] John Alexander and wife Mary Sheldon resided in Wicomico Hundred, Worcester County, Maryland. John Sheldon witnessed the will of Hugh Porter, gentleman, of Somerset County, made December 15, 1731, and proved November 22, 1732.[13]

On June 26, 1733, John Sheldon gave cattle to his children-in-law, William Gray and Sarah Gray, son and daughter of Westcot Gray, for love and affection.[14] On October 17, 1737, Margaret Maginnis, spinster, gave to Mary Sheldon, daughter of John Sheldon and Mary his wife, for love and affection, all her goods and estate at her decease.[15] On March 14, 1741, Sarah Gray, spinster, sold to John Sheldon all bonds, bills, etc. due to her and bequests which her father Westcot Gray left her.[16] On April 6, 1743, Nehemiah Dorman who married Sarah, daughter of Westcot Gray, acknowledged that his wife had received all legacies from John Sheldon who had married Mary, executrix of Westcot

---

[1] 1744 Tax List, Somerset Co., Md., copy located at the Research Center for Delmarva History and Culture, Salisbury State University, Salisbury, Md.
[2] Northumberland Co., Va. Records, Liber 7, fol. 330.
[3] Worcester Co., Md. Accounts, Liber 44, fol. 326.
[4] Worcester Co., Md. Wills, Liber JW3, fol. 181.
[5] Somerset Co., Md. Deeds, Liber MFY, fol. 234.
[6] Edward C. Papenfuse, et al. A Biographical Dictionary of the Maryland Legislature, 1635-1789, 2 vols. (Baltimore: Johns Hopkins University Press, 1979), Vol. 1, p. 371.
[7] Letter, Leslie Dryden (Hyattsville, Md., 25 JAN 1990).
[8] Somerset Co., Md. Wills, Liber CC2 No. 19, fol. 719; dated 5 MAR 1729, prov. 22 APR 1729.
[9] Letter, Leslie Dryden (Hyattsville, Md., 25 JAN 1990).
[10] Somerset Co., Md. Deeds, Liber 17, fol. 147.
[11] Maryland Accounts, Liber 11, fol. 81.
[12] Somerset Co., Md. Accounts, Liber DD4, fol. 117.
[13] Maryland Calendar of Wills, Vol. VI, p. 245.
[14] Somerset Co., Md. Deeds, Liber 18, fol. 87.
[15] Somerset Co., Md. Deeds, Liber 19, fol. 211.
[16] Somerset Co., Md. Deeds, Liber 20, fol. 234.

Gray.[1]

A John Sheldon purchased an 80-acre tract called *The Fork* which was part of *Freeman's Discovery*, from McKemmey Porter, on June 3, 1738 in Worcester County, Maryland. Much later, a portion of *Freeman's Discovery* was sold by John Sheldon Alexander on April 7, 1796 to William Corbin.[2]

In 1739, John Sheldon patented 305 acres in Worcester County, called *Providence*, and the next transaction of record for the parcel was when on April 7, 1796 it was sold by John Sheldon Alexander and wife Leah [or Sarah] Fleming to William Corbin.[3]

In 1747, John Sheldon patented *Sheldon's Addition* in Worcester County, and the next transaction for the parcel was on October 6, 1797 when Betty Broadwater of Accomack County, Virginia conveyed it to William Corbin of Worcester County.[4]

On August 6, 1751, John Alexander and wife Mary Sheldon sold 446 acres of *Addition to Hog[g] Quarter* in Somerset County to William Jones.[5]

On August 25, 1756, John Sheldon resurveyed *Freeman's Discovery* and *Mt. Hope* for 268 acres.[6]

John Sheldon died by December 22, 1758 when his widow Mary filed a bond as his administratrix; John Alexander was one of her securities. Coventry Parish records show that John Sheldon died November 24, 1758. Mary filed an account of his estate on January 26, 1763, but no distribution was shown.[7]

Mary Sheldon died by February 12, 1768 in Worcester County, when her will was filed by Betty Corbin, her executrix.[8] She left bequests to her children Sarah Dorman, Ann Murray and Betty Corbin and her grandsons William Corbin and Peter Corbin. Her daughter Mary (Sheldon) Alexander is presumed to have died by this time. In the account of her estate, a payment was made to John Dorman, and it is uncertain whether this was her son-in-law.[9]

Something which may be coincidental, but quite odd and yet unexplained, is that there is an estate inventory of a John Sheldon, deceased, dated November 20, 1767, filed in Augusta County, Virginia. An account was claimed against the estate by the administrator William Beard for final doctor bills and expenses of the funeral and coffin.[10]

Known children of John Sheldon and wife Mary (   ):

1. Mary Sheldon, m. (A114.) JOHN ALEXANDER, *q.v.*
2. Sarah Sheldon, m. [John?] Dorman.[11]
3. Ann Sheldon, m. [James] Murray.
4. Betty Sheldon, m. (1) 12 AUG 1750 to Peter Corbin in Coventry Parish of Somerset Co., Md., m. (2) to James Broadwater, will dated 16 SEP 1795, proved 18 MAY 1801 in Accomack Co., Va.[12] Later, Betty Broadwater was residing in Accomack Co. and conveyed all her right to several land tracts to William Corbin.[13]

Death of John Alexander

John Alexander left a will in Northumberland County, Virginia, dated July 27, 1765, which was proved June 8, 1767.[14] It is rather brief, but bequeaths to his son John Sheldon Alexander *one lot of land lying in Snow Hill Town, Worcester County, Maryland*; and one Negro woman named Brigett and her child James. The testator specifies that his son [John Sheldon Alexander] *should not be possessed with his Negroes till he arrives to the Age of Twenty-one*. The will further provides for his son to go to his friend Solomon Tousan [Townsend] in Worcester County *and be bound to a house Carpenter and house Joyner*. Apparently that was not done (or if so, not for long), as we know John Sheldon Alexander removed to Albemarle County, Virginia.

The 1765 will of John Alexander names his wife as Sarah Alexander, and instructs that *I so doe Disinherit a child as **my former wife had** in my [abstinance], called Ann, with one shilling sterling*. Sarah Alexander was executrix, and

[1] Worcester Co., Md. Deeds, Liber A, fol. 72.
[2] Ruth T. Dryden, Land Records of Worcester County, Maryland, 1666-1810 (San Diego: By the Author, 1987), p. 241.
[3] Ruth T. Dryden, Worcester Co., Md. Deeds, p. 500.
[4] Ruth T. Dryden, Worcester Co., Md. Deeds, p. 560.
[5] Somerset Co., Md. Deeds, Liber O22, fol. 187.
[6] Ruth T. Dryden, Worcester Co., Md. Deeds, p. 415.
[7] Maryland Accounts, Liber 49, fol. 89.
[8] MDSA, Maryland Wills, Liber 36, fol. 392, dated 2 FEB 1767, filed 12 FEB 1768; also see Maryland Inventories, Worcester Co., Liber 95, fol. 323, dated 16 FEB 1768, which lists next of kin as Sarah Dorman and James Murray.
[9] MDSA, Maryland Accounts, Liber 66, fol. 224, filed 24 JAN 1772.
[10] Augusta Co., Va. Wills, Bk. 3, 1761-1767, p. 365.
[11] Maryland Inventories, Liber 81, fol. 78, estate of Absolom Hobbs of Somerset Co., Md., when Charity Dorman (daughter of Matthew Dorman who d. 1740) was the administratrix for the estate of her deceased husband William Gray (d. 1760) and mentioned next of kin as Mary Sheldon and Sarah Dorman.
[12] Accomack Co., Va. District Court Wills, 1800-1806, pp. 152-3.
[13] Worcester Co., Md. Deeds, Bk. S, fol. 172.
[14] Northumberland Co., Va. Records, Bk. 7, p. 84, dated 27 JUL 1765, prov. 8 JUN 1767.

the will was witnessed by Thomas Airs and Mary Enser. An estate inventory was filed in 1769.[1]

Only known child of John Alexander and his <u>first wife</u> Mary Sheldon:

\+ A1141. JOHN SHELDON ALEXANDER, b. c.1755, prob. in Somerset Co., Md., d. after 1822, prob. in Augusta Co., Va.,[2] m. Leah [or Sarah] Fleming.

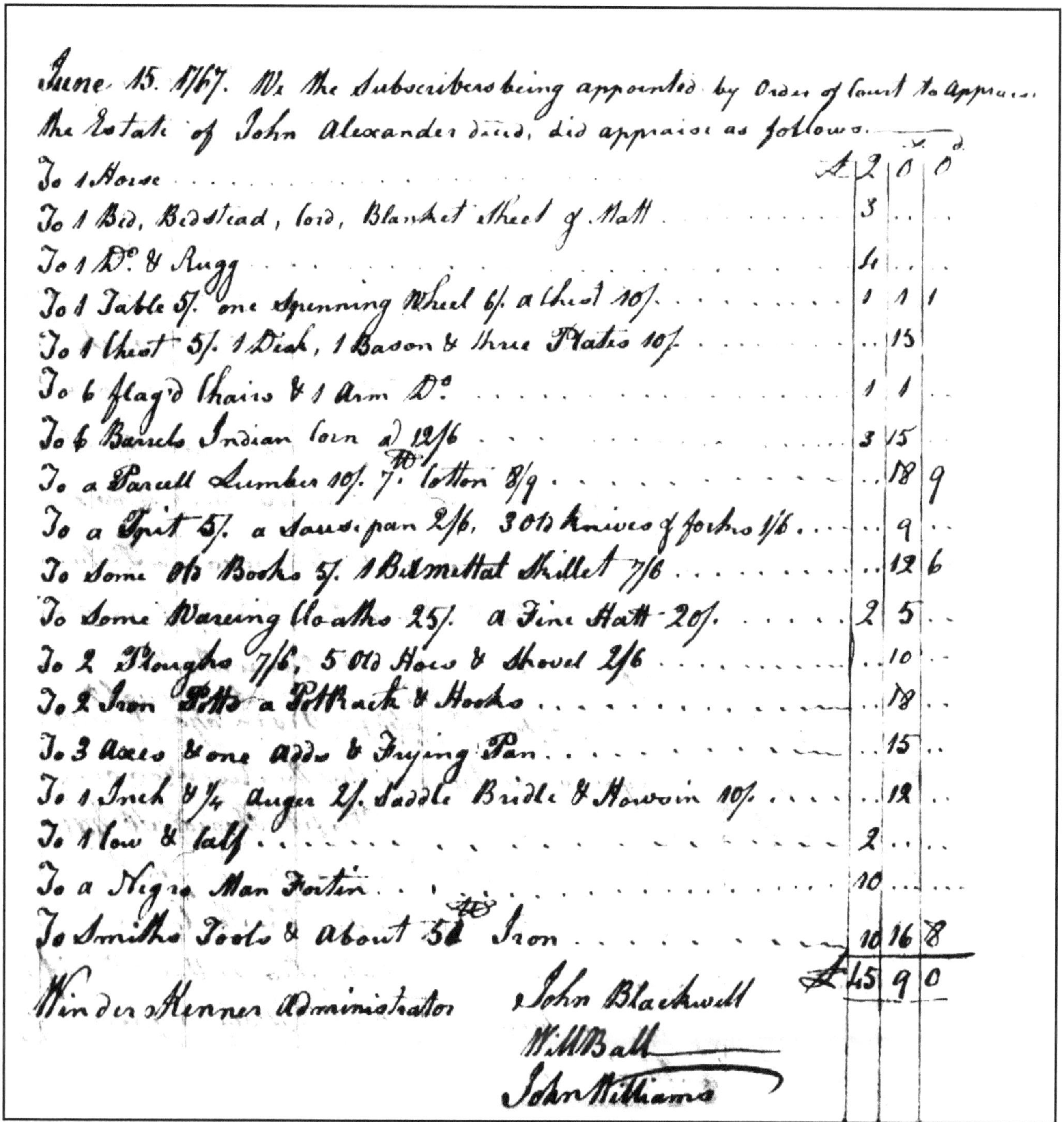

June 15. 1767. We the Subscribers being appointed by Order of Court to apprais the Estate of John Alexander decd, did appraise as follows.

	£	s.	d.
To 1 Horse	2	0	0
To 1 Bed, Bedstead, Cord, Blanket Sheet & Matt	3	..	..
To 1 Do. & Rugg	4	..	..
To 1 Table 5/. one Spinning Wheel 6/. a Chest 10/.	1	1	1
To 1 Chest 5/. 1 Dish, 1 Bason & three Plates 10/.	..	15	
To 6 flag'd Chairs & 1 Arm Do.	1	1	..
To 6 Barrels Indian Corn at 12/6	3	15	
To a Parcell Lumber 10/. 7 lb. Cotton 8/9	..	18	9
To a Spit 5/. a Saucepan 2/6, 3 old Knives & forks 1/6	..	9	..
To Some old Books 5/. 1 Bellmettal Skillet 7/6	..	12	6
To Some Wareing Cloaths 25/. a Fine Hatt 20/.	2	5	..
To 2 Ploughs 7/6, 5 old Hoes & Shovel 2/6	..	10	..
To 2 Iron Potts a Pott Rack & Hooks	..	18	..
To 3 Axes & one Adds & Frying Pan	..	15	..
To 1 Inch & 1/4 auger 2/. Saddle Bridle & Howsin 10/.	..	12	..
To 1 Cow & Calf	2	..	..
To a Negro Man Fortin	10	..	..
To Smiths Tools & about 56 lb Iron	10	16	8
	£45	9	0

Winder Kenner Administrator

John Blackwell
Will Ball
John Williams

Figure 1 - Estate inventory for John Alexander in Northumberland County, Va., filed 1769

[1] Northumberland Co., Va. Records, Bk. 7, pp. 330-1, filed court term 13 MAR 1769.
[2] Augusta Co., Va. Wills, Bk. 13, p. 74, bill of sale from John S. Alexander, formerly of Albemarle Co., but now of Augusta, his personal property to Richmond T. Walton, dated 2 JUL 1819. A deed of trust is recorded 15 MAY 1822, in Will Bk. 14, p. 20.

The will of John Alexander was presented to court by his widow Sarah Alexander, Executrix. Winder Kenner was granted letters of administration after he gave security.[1] The whereabouts of the Negroes mentioned in the will, after distribution was made, is unknown, i.e. Negro woman Brigett and her child James, and Negro man Fortan.

---

[1] Northumberland Co., Va. Orders, Bk. 1767-1770, p. 73, court term 8 JUN 1767.

(84)

In the name of God amen, I John Alexander of Northumberland County being very
Sick and weak but in perfect Sence and memory, Doe make my will as followith ——
First, I Give my Soul to God who gave it me Desiring Pardon for all my Sins, and my
body to be Decently buried at the Discretion of my Executors hereafter mentioned. ——
Impr. I Give and bequeave to my Son John Shildon Alexander, One Lott of Land lying in
Snow hill Town in Worsister County, also one Negro Woman named Brigett and her Child
James, to him and his heirs Lawfully begotton of his body, and for the want of such heir to
return to my well beloved Wife Sarah Alexander. ——
My will and Desire is that my said Son Should goe to my friend Solomon Townsan in
Worsister County in Maryland, also my Will is that my said Son Should be bound to
a house Carpenter and house Joyner, Also my Will is that my Son Should not be ——
posposed with his Negrows till he arives to the Age of Twenty one years. ——
Item, I also doe Disinheit a Child as my former Wife had in my abstience ——
Called Ann, with one Shilling Sterling. ——
Item, I Give and bequeave to my well beloved Wife Sarah Alexander one Negro man
Named Fortan, to make Sale as she Shall think proper, and all my Personal Estate
to make use as She thinks proper ——
I also do appoint my well beloved Wife my whole and Sole Executrix of this my Last
will and Testament in manner, I have hereunto set my hand and affixed my Seale
this 27th day of July 1765. ——

Teste. Thos. Airs   John Alexander (Seal)
        Mary Enser

           —At a Court Held for Northumberland County the 8. day of June
               1767. —
This Last will and Testament of John Alexander deed was Presented in Court by
Sarah Alexander the Executrix therein Named, who refused to take on her the burthen
of the Execution thereof, And being proved by Thomas Airs & Mary Enser Witnesses thereto
was Admitted to Record, And on the motion of Winder Skenner Gent. who made Oath
thereto according to Law, Certificate is granted him for obtaining Letters of
Administration with the will Annexed on the sd. Decdt. Estate in due form ——

                                         Teste.
                                              Thos. Jones C. Cur.

Figure 2 - Record copy of will of John Alexander in Northumberland County, Va., 1757

14

A1141. JOHN SHELDON ALEXANDER
(c.1755-post 1822)

John Sheldon Alexander, born c.1755, probably in Somerset County, Maryland (he was under age 21 in his father's 1765 will). He was a son of John Alexander and Mary Sheldon. John S. Alexander was married to Leah [or Sarah] who was perhaps a Fleming, born about 1757. I have speculated that she was Leah Fleming, daughter of William Fleming, who in 1783 was taxed for the tract *Fleming's Loss* in Somerset County, Maryland—the same property that was sold on August 27, 1788 by John S. Alexander and his wife Leah [or Sarah] to John Harris, Jr. On February 25, 1780, John Sheldon Alexander and wife Leah sold to Joshua Townsend, Lot #6 in Snow Hill Town, Worcester County, Maryland.

John S. Alexander was on the 1783 tax list for Pocomoke Hundred of Worcester County, Maryland, with properties that included 30-acre *Fleming's Discovery*, and a household that included two white males and three white females. He owned part of a tract called *Daintry* as late as 1788, and was enumerated on the 1790 Federal census for Worcester County. On April 15, 1788, John S. Alexander and wife Leah [or Sarah[1]] of Worcester County sold a parcel of land in Somerset County to Michael Dorman.[2] On August 27, 1788, John S. Alexander and his wife Leah, of Worcester County, sold 175 acres in two tracts *Middle Town* and *Fleming's Loss*, for £50, to John Harris, Jr. of Somerset County.[3] He is listed on the 1790 Federal census for Worcester County, Maryland.[4]

On April 7, 1796, John Sheldon Alexander and wife Leah, of Worcester County, conveyed to William Corbin several land tracts: *Sheldon's Addition*, *Freeman's Discovery*, *Mt. Hope*, *Mill Lot*, and *Providence*. Again, his wife appears in handwriting as *Leah*.[5]

On October 6, 1797, Betty (Sheldon) Broadwater, of Accomack County, Virginia, conveyed to William Corbin all her right to *Sheldon's Addition*, *Freeman's Discovery*, *Mt. Hope*, *Mill Lot*, *Sandhill* and others.[6]

John S. Alexander removed from Maryland to Albemarle County, Virginia, c.1797, perhaps along with Eleanor "Nelly" (Tull) Bevans and her second husband Joshua Merrill Catling. The Alexanders are listed on the 1800 tax list for Albemarle County, Virginia.[7] In 1803, William Alexander and wife Ann, formerly Bevans, appointed John S. Alexander as their attorney to settle sale of the *Warwick* tract of land in Worcester County, Maryland.[8] On February 20, 1804, John S. Alexander, of Albemarle County, conveyed part of the *Warwick* tract to Rowland Bevans of Worcester County, Maryland.[9]

John S. Alexander and his wife are listed on the 1810 Federal census for Augusta County with an elder female (age 10 to 16), a younger daughter (under age of 10), two elder males (between ages 16 and 26) and 2 younger males (under age 10).[10] I propose John S. Alexander has living with him one of his sons who has three young children, and this may be Asa Alexander who also appears on the 1820 Federal census for Augusta County. He is also found to be taxed for personal property in 1820 in Augusta County, but not thereafter.

John S. Alexander and his wife are listed on the 1820 Federal census for Waynesboro in Augusta County, Virginia (page 3, alphabetized), and, besides themselves (each over the age of 45 years), have a female between the ages of 16 and 26 years.[11] He is taxed as a white tithable on the personal property list for 1821 in Augusta County, but not thereafter. John S. Alexander died after May 1822, probably in Augusta County, Virginia,[12] some time after joining Richmond T. Walton in transferring personal property to Nicholas C. Kinney in order to secure a debt.

Children of John Sheldon Alexander and wife Leah [or Sarah] Fleming:

+ A11411.   WILLIAM ALEXANDER, b. 16 FEB 1778, probably in Pocomoke Hundred of Worcester Co., Md., d. 8 JUN 1854 in Port Republic, Rockingham Co., Va., m. 5 JAN 1803 in Albemarle Co., Va. to Ann Bevans, daughter of John Bevans and Eleanor "Nelly" Tull of *Warwick* tract in Worcester Co., Md.,

---

[1] Transcriptions often cite Leah as the wife of John S. Alexander, but upon actual study, this may indeed be Sarah. We know the signature on an 1807 consent for daughter Sarah to marry Richmond Walton reads "Sarah Alexander." It has not been determined if John married twice.

[2] Somerset Co., Md. Deeds, Liber O29, fol. 361.

[3] Somerset Co., Md. Deeds, Liber O29, fol. 410.

[4] 1790 Federal Census, Worcester Co., Md., NARA film M637, roll 3, p. 153, no township listed.

[5] Worcester Co., Md. Deeds, Liber R, fol. 112.

[6] Worcester Co., Md. Deeds, Liber S, fol. 172.

[7] Virginia Genealogist, Vol. 3, p. 4.

[8] Albemarle Co., Va. Deeds, Liber W, fols. 146-47.

[9] Albemarle Co., Va. Deeds, Liber W, fols. 147-48. The same day a deed is made from John S. Alexander of Albemarle Co. to Kitturah Milburn of Worcester Co., Md. for part of *Warwick* tract.

[10] 1810 Federal census, Augusta Co., Va., John Alexander, 2-0-2-0-1 // 1-1-0-1-0.

[11] 1820 Federal census, Augusta Co., Va., Waynesboro, John S. Alexander, 0-0-0-0-0-1 // 0-0-1-0-1.

[12] Augusta Co., Va. Wills, Bk. 13, pp. 74-5, bill of sale from John S. Alexander, *late of Albemarle, now of Augusta*, for his household goods and furniture to Richmond T. Walton, dated 2 JUL 1819, witnessed by Isom Walton [brother] and Andrew Robison. A deed of trust is recorded 15 MAY 1822, in Will Bk. 14, p. 20. Also see Augusta Co., Va. Deeds, Bk. 14, p. 20, dated 15 MAY 1822, where Richmond T. Walton and John S. Alexander convey to Nicholas C. Kinney their personal property in order to secure a debt of $35.30.

b. 10 JUN 1783 in Worcester Co., d. 25 NOV 1872 in Waynesboro, Augusta Co., Va., bur. Riverview Cem. there. William served with his brothers Reuben, Asa and Samuel Alexander in the War of 1812.

+ A11412. SARAH ALEXANDER,[1] b. prev. to 1783 (as reflected on the 1783 tax list for Pocomoke Hundred of Worcester Co., Md., and the 1790 Federal census); m. 27 JAN 1807 by bond in Albemarle Co., Va. to Richmond Terril Walton.

+ A11413. REUBEN ALEXANDER, b. between 1784 and 1794 (not listed on 1783 tax list), m. 23 JUL 1810 in Albemarle Co., Va. to Sarah Smith, daughter of John M. Smith.

A11414. Daughter ALEXANDER, b. prev. to 1783, as reflected on the 1783 tax list for Pocomoke Hundred of Worcester Co., Md., and the 1790 Federal census for Maryland.

A11415. SAMUEL ALEXANDER, **possibly** m. by bond of 11 JAN 1808 in Augusta Co., Va. to Sally Helms.[2] Samuel served as a private in Capt. Robt. McCullough's Co. of Light Infantry (Gray's) in the 7th Virginia Militia in the War of 1812.[3] As such, his military papers in the National Archives indicate he commenced service 29 AUG 1814 at Camp Carter near Richmond for a term of 2 months at a pay rate of $8/month. He ended his service 21 FEB 1815 and was allowed 5 days to travel to his home. No further information.

A11416. ASA ALEXANDER, b. between 1776-1794, m. 8 MAY 1817 in Staunton, Augusta Co., Va. to Jane Kennedy, daughter of Stuart Kennedy.[4] Asa served in the 7th Reg. of the Virginia Militia (Gray's) during the War of 1812, and as a private was in the infantry commanded by Capt. Robt. McCullough, stationed at Camp Carter near Richmond.[5] The attendance records on file at the National Archives indicate Asa was present at Camp Carter on 6 NOV 1814, but sick. For the period 29 OCT to 28 DEC 1814 he was paid at the rate of $8/month. His service ended 21 FEB 1815, and it was recorded that Asa was allowed 5 days traveling time to return to his residence from Camp Carter, though the station was 100 miles from the mustering ground. Asa Alexander heads a household on the 1820 Federal census for Augusta County, with a young wife and a young son and young daughter. We have no further information about this family, so it is likely they left the area.[6] Probable children:

A114161. Son ALEXANDER, b. 1817-1820.
A114162. Daughter ALEXANDER, b. 1817-1820.

A11417. NANCY ALEXANDER, b. in 1794 [1810/1820 Federal census], m. by Rev. Conrad Speece as recorded on a bond 20 NOV 1823 in Augusta Co., Va. to William R. Grass, son of Frederick Grass, as witnessed by Frederick Grass and Erasmus Stribling.

---

[1] Notes in possession of Jared Craun Alexander, name a daughter Sarah Alexander.

[2] It is uncertain whether Sally Helms' husband Samuel Alexander was a son of this John Alexander of Albemarle Co.

[3] Also see Virginia Auditor of Public Accounts, Virginia Militia in the War of 1812 (Baltimore: Genealogical Publishing Co., 2001), Vol. 1, p. 343; the pay roll shows private Samuel Alexander served for 5 months and 28 days.

[4] City of Staunton, Va., Marriage Bonds.

[5] Also see Virginia Militia in the War of 1812, Vol. 1, p. 343; the pay roll shows private Asa Alexander served for 5 months and 28 days.

[6] The 1830 Federal census for Mill Creek twp., Hamilton Co., Ohio, has a household headed by Asa Alexander with 0-2-1-0-0-1-0-0 // 2-0-1-0-1-1-1, and it is feasible this is the same family. They are not found here on the 1840 Federal census.

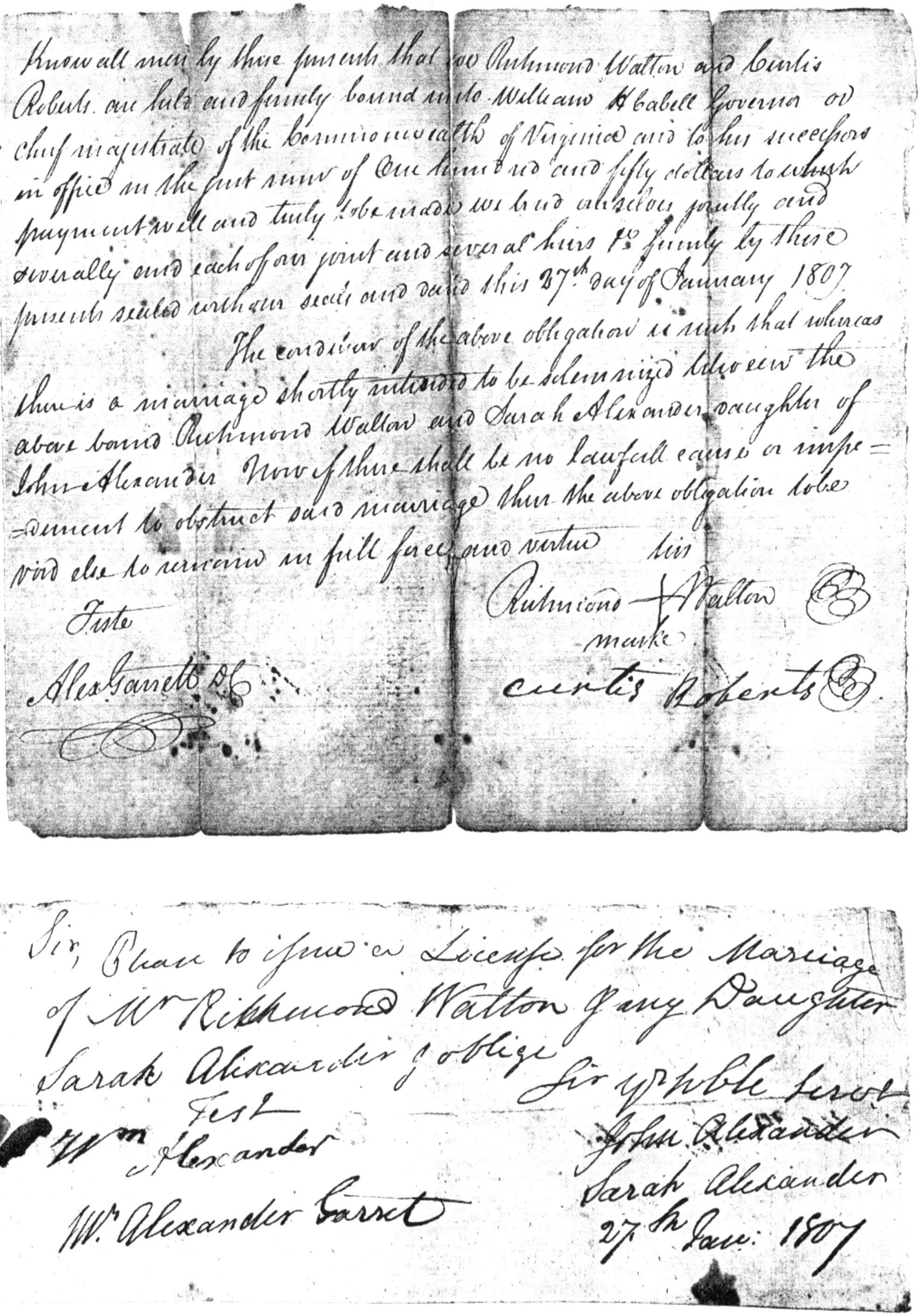

Know all men by these presents that we Richmond Walton and Curtis Roberts are held and firmly bound unto William H Cabell Governor or chief magistrate of the Commonwealth of Virginia and to his successors in office in the just sum of One hundred and fifty dollars to which payment well and truly to be made we bind ourselves jointly and severally and each of our joint and several heirs &c firmly by these presents sealed with our seals and dated this 27th day of January 1807

The condition of the above obligation is such that whereas there is a marriage shortly intended to be solemnized between the above bound Richmond Walton and Sarah Alexander daughter of John Alexander Now if there shall be no lawfull cause or impediment to obstruct said marriage then the above obligation to be void else to remain in full force and virtue

Teste
Alex Garrett &c

his
Richmond X Walton
mark

Curtis Roberts

Sir, Please to issue a License for the Marriage of Mr Richmond Walton & any Daughter Sarah Alexander & oblige

Test
Wm Alexander

Wm Alexander Garret

Sir yr hble servt
John Alexander
Sarah Alexander
27 th Jan: 1807

Figure 3 - Bond and consent for Sarah Alexander to marry Richmond Walton in 1807

A11411. WILLIAM ALEXANDER
(1778-1854)

My direct ancestor, William Alexander, was born on Monday, February 16, 1778[1] in Maryland, probably in Somerset County. He was a son of John Sheldon Alexander and Leah Fleming. A family tradition without strong evidence as recorded in notes made and left by the late Lottie H. Fauber claimed that Mr. Alexander was sometimes a fisherman and hauled produce by water, on the James River and/or the Chesapeake Bay.[2] We do not have any evidence that he was involved in the businesses of his sons who were actively making furniture and coffins or involved with the undertaking business.

In 1803, about the time the United States of America was entering negotiations with France for the Louisiana Purchase, William Alexander was married on January 5th in Albemarle County, Virginia to Ann Bevans, daughter of John Bevans (the record is written "Bibbins").[3] Members of our family had heard a story that Ann was of Bibbins Point, Maryland, while other relatives recorded that she was of Bibbins Landing. Neither location has been identified. It has been suggested that Bibbins Point may have been the name of a plantation. It took many years of research to determine that the maiden name of Ann was really not Bibbins, rather Bevans. On the Albemarle County marriage bond is the only place where Ann's maiden name is spelled as "Bibbins." In other official documents we find the name spelled Bevans or Bivins, and it seems apparent that Bevans is an old Maryland family name. The surname is easily spelled several ways phonetically. For the sake of consistency, I will use the spelling "Bevans," since it is the spelling most commonly found on official documents pertaining to Ann Alexander and her immediate ancestors of Worcester County, Maryland.

The bondsman for the marriage of William and Ann was a Mr. Joshua Catling. It is known that Mr. Catling was related to Mr. Alexander by marriage at a later date, but it is not known for certain if the two were related in 1803.

Ann Bevans was born January 10, 1783 in Worcester County, Maryland. In 1797, as Ann Bevans was now an orphan, she appointed Rowland Bevans as her guardian with intent to look after her interest in the *Warwick* tract.[4]

Ann's father John Bevans was married to Eleanor "Nelly" Tull. He lived on a tract of land called *Warwick* in Somerset County, Maryland, and died before December 2, 1783, when James Tull and Nelly Bevans were his estate administrators in Somerset County, Maryland. John's widow Nelly Bevans married second to Joshua Merrill Catling. In September 1797, Joshua Merrill Catling and his new wife Nelly sold her interest in her father's *Warwick* tract to Thomas Milbourn of Worcester County, Maryland, and soon left Maryland for Albemarle County, Virginia where it is presumed she died. Eleanor was born c.1751 in Somerset County, Maryland, and was a daughter of Jonathan Tull (c.1719-1787) and Mary Fountaine of Somerset County, Maryland.

John Bevans was a son of Thomas Bevans of Worcester County, Maryland, and a grandson of Rowland Bevans who is claimed to have been captain of the ship *Desire*, which arrived May 9, 1667 in Boston, Massachusetts. Rowland Bevans first married on December 27, 1670 in Somerset County, Maryland to Margaret Price, and married second on August 4, 1672 in Somerset County to Mary Dewry. There are many researchers of the Bevans Family, so further data will not be presented here.

Ann Alexander died at the age of 89 years, 10 months and 15 days on November 25, 1872 at the home of her son William Benjamin Alexander on Main Street in Waynesboro, Augusta County, Virginia. She was buried[5] in the old Presbyterian Church Cemetery of Waynesboro, but her grave along with others of the immediate family, was later removed to Riverview Cemetery of Waynesboro (Block 58, grave 8-B) by Edith (Whitlock) Chambers. A small note announcing her death appeared in the *Staunton Vindicator* newspaper on December 13, 1872, and asked that the Rockingham County papers copy the story. I found no article in the available newspapers for neighboring areas in Rockingham County.

In the writings of Lottie H. Fauber we found that she recorded the following:

William's father died leaving his Virginia estate to his son William. About this time there was much talk about the rich valley beyond the hills, the Valley of Virginia later known as the Shenandoah Valley. William made trips to the valley and found it so rich, and with a strong desire to settle there, he leased his estate on the

---

[1] His date of birth is recorded in a record book of coffins made by his son William Benjamin Alexander, and in 1991 in the possession of Elizabeth (Dunavant) Alexander of Waynesboro, Virginia (copy in possession of the author). Birth and death dates for William Alexander and his wife Ann are also found in the Bible record of the Charles William Alexander Family.

[2] There was record of a William B. Alexander, fisherman, who was involved with Chapman's Ferry of Alexandria, Va., and with fishing operations of Charles Co., Md. I believe, however, that this person was William Brown Alexander, a son of Charles Alexander, who was born in Alexandria and later moved to Saline Co., Mo. He was buried in Macpelah Cemetery of Lexington, Mo.

[3] Marriage bond dated 3 JAN 1803, with Joshua Catling as security. Records of the Albemarle Co., Va. Orphan's Court indicate Ann Bibbins was an orphan of John Bibbins (presumed deceased). Bibbins is a poor spelling for the surname known on the Eastern Shore as Bevans or Beavens.

[4] Worcester Co., Md. Orphans Court Proceedings, 1797-1799 [Book LH8], pp. 26-7. In Ann's appointment she notes she is "gowing out with my Mother and other friends unto the Western part of this Country, [immediately] and cannot have opportunity to wait untill a Court to [choose] a guardian...

[5] Riverview Cemetery, Waynesboro, grave marker: ANN ALEXANDER / Died / Nov. 25, 1872. / Aged / 89 Yrs. 10 Mo. & 15 ds. / *Asleep in Jesus.*

Potomac [Northumberland County?, W.P.] to a land company for a period of ninety-nine years and came to the valley and settled at a place later known as Port Republic, and here he raised his family.

The land company started to develop the Potomac estate, and thus the city of Alexandria, Virginia was born. When the lease expired during my grand-father's lifetime[1] he was visited by numerous lawyers insisting that he take steps to reclaim this land but he refused to do so saying, 'People who bought the land and built homes did so believing they had clear title to the land', and he would not do anything to rob them of their homes.

I have found absolutely nothing to support any connection of our branch of the Alexander Family to that of Alexandria, Virginia—in fact it is quite clear that there is no relation as long as the family has been in America.

On August 29, 1814 in Albemarle County, William Alexander enlisted in the company of Captain Edmund Davis during the War with Great Britain (War of 1812). The company was later commanded by Captain Robert McCullough. On February 15, 1815, after 177 days of service, William was discharged due to blindness at Camp Carter, Virginia and was allowed 5 days travel time to return to his home.[2] By affidavit dated October 5, 1871, Isaac Hoy of Augusta County, testified he served a term of 6 months with William Alexander in Captain McCullough's company and that William was honorably discharged at McCullough's Mills. Also found in Ann Alexander's widow pension is an affidavit from Selah Holbrook[3] who attested to the fact that William and Ann had lived together as husband and wife since he knew them in 1820 until his death in 1854, and that the couple raised a family.

By reason of the Military Bounty Land Act of September 28, 1850,[4] the father William Alexander had been awarded bounty land located in Saline County, Missouri, described as *West ½ of Northwest 1/4 Section 8, Township 50, Range 21*, as filed at the land office in Clinton, Missouri.

The parcels of land were situated in *the County of Saline in the State of Missouri; that is to say the east half of the north east quarter of Section Seven (7) and the east half of the north east quarter of Section (17) Seventeen and all in Township Fifty (50) of Range (21) Twenty one containing in all 160 acres more or less agreeable to Government Survey.*

William Alexander of Rockingham County, appointed George W. Allen of Saline County, Missouri (probably in Marshall) to be his attorney and to locate his warrant #10513 for 80 acres. After lengthy correspondence with lawyer George W. Allen, son William B. Alexander ultimately sold the bounty land grant parcel on March 14, 1860 to a Mr. Davidson. This sale was witnessed by Willis Jackson, son-in-law of William Alexander, on October 4, 1851.

On March 24, 1855, Ann Alexander (whose name is spelled Anna Bevins) completed application for a widow's pension based on her husbands military service. On April 11, 1871, she employed lawyer Alfred Chapman of Alexandria, Virginia to request an increase in the pension amount, after which a pension of $8.00 a month was granted.

The family of William Alexander was enumerated on the 1840 Federal census for Port Republic, Rockingham County. They were enumerated in District 56 there on the 1850 Federal census.

In papers where Ann Alexander applied for a widow's pension based on this service, we have seen that William Alexander died June 9, 1854 in Port Republic, Rockingham County. The date of his death is written in several family records, but the location of death is only found in the pension papers. Despite intensive searching, the location of his grave has not been determined.

Beginning in June 1856, Ann Alexander had an account with the business of her son William B. Alexander. Normal entries are found for the purchase of fabrics, shoes, etc. The same record notes she traveled to New Hope, Virginia about May 1867.

On the 1860 Federal census for Rockingham County, the widow Ann Alexander is shown residing with her son-in-law and daughter, William Thacker and Eleanor Tull Alexander. On the 1870 Federal census for the city of Waynesboro,[5] Augusta County, we find her residing in the home of her son William Benjamin Alexander.

An additional important clue found in Mr. Alexander's military papers was that he claimed his brothers Asa, Reuben and Samuel Alexander, who fought in the same company has he, were a reference to support the fact of his military service. No further information is found about brothers Asa and Samuel, as they may have left the Augusta County area.

In December 1989, I discovered a Bible-like record for the children of William Alexander and Ann Bevans, in the possession of Jared Craun Alexander of Weyers Cave, Virginia. At last, this gave us a possible birth date for our ancestor James Washington Alexander, though the day may easily be correct, the year is presumably incorrect.

---

[1] Lottie Fauber's grandfather would be William Benjamin Alexander, 1820-1901.

[2] The papers for the widow's application for pension by Ann Alexander, at the National Archives, lead one to believe that William Alexander was honorably discharged due to his age and number of dependent children; however, in the writings left by Emma Jane (Whitlock) Chambers, she noted he was discharged due to blindness. Also see Virginia Militia in the War of 1812, Vol. 1, p. 343; the pay roll shows private William Alexander served for 5 months and 28 days.

[3] Selah Holbrook was living in Port Republic in 1837 when his daughter Judith was married to Benjamin F. Kemper. He was a blacksmith, and with his son, J.H. Holbrook, made sickles for Cyrus McCormick who used them in his first reaper.

[4] War of 1812, Pension Records, Bounty land references to numbers 10513-80-50 and 5824-80-55.

[5] Basic City was earlier a part of what is now Waynesboro, in Augusta Co., Va.

Known children of William Alexander and Ann Bevans:

+ 1. JOHN BEVANS ALEXANDER, b. 22 NOV 1803 in Henrico Co., Va., m. Ann W. Roberts.

+ 2. ELEANOR "Ellen" TULL ALEXANDER, b. 26 DEC 1805, m. William Thacker.

   3. MARY SHELDON ALEXANDER, b. 20 JUL 1809, d. 4 AUG 1850, bur. in Riverview Cem. of Waynesboro.[1] No further information.

   4. THOMAS S. ALEXANDER, b. 29 JUN 1810, d.y. No further information.

   5. MARGARET ALEXANDER, b. c.1814 (age 36 in 1850) in Va. No further information.

+ 6. MOSES LISTON ALEXANDER, b. 4 APR 1815 in Va., m. Nancy Hamilton.

+ 7. ELIZABETH ANN ALEXANDER, b. 4 APR 1818 in Va., m. Willis Jackson.

+ 8. WILLIAM BENJAMIN ALEXANDER, b. 20 JUL 1820, m. Sarah Ann Maxwell.

+ 9. JAMES WASHINGTON ALEXANDER, b. 23 MAR 1821/3 in Va., m. possibly five times, his last wife being my ancestor, Mrs. Mary (Rice) Gover, perhaps the widow of Walter Gover.

For the remainder of this section, the numerical system will be abbreviated.

---

[1] Riverview Cemetery, Waynesboro, grave marker: MARY S. / ALEXANDER / Born / July 20, 1809 / Died / Aug. 4, 1850. / *Asleep in Jesus*.

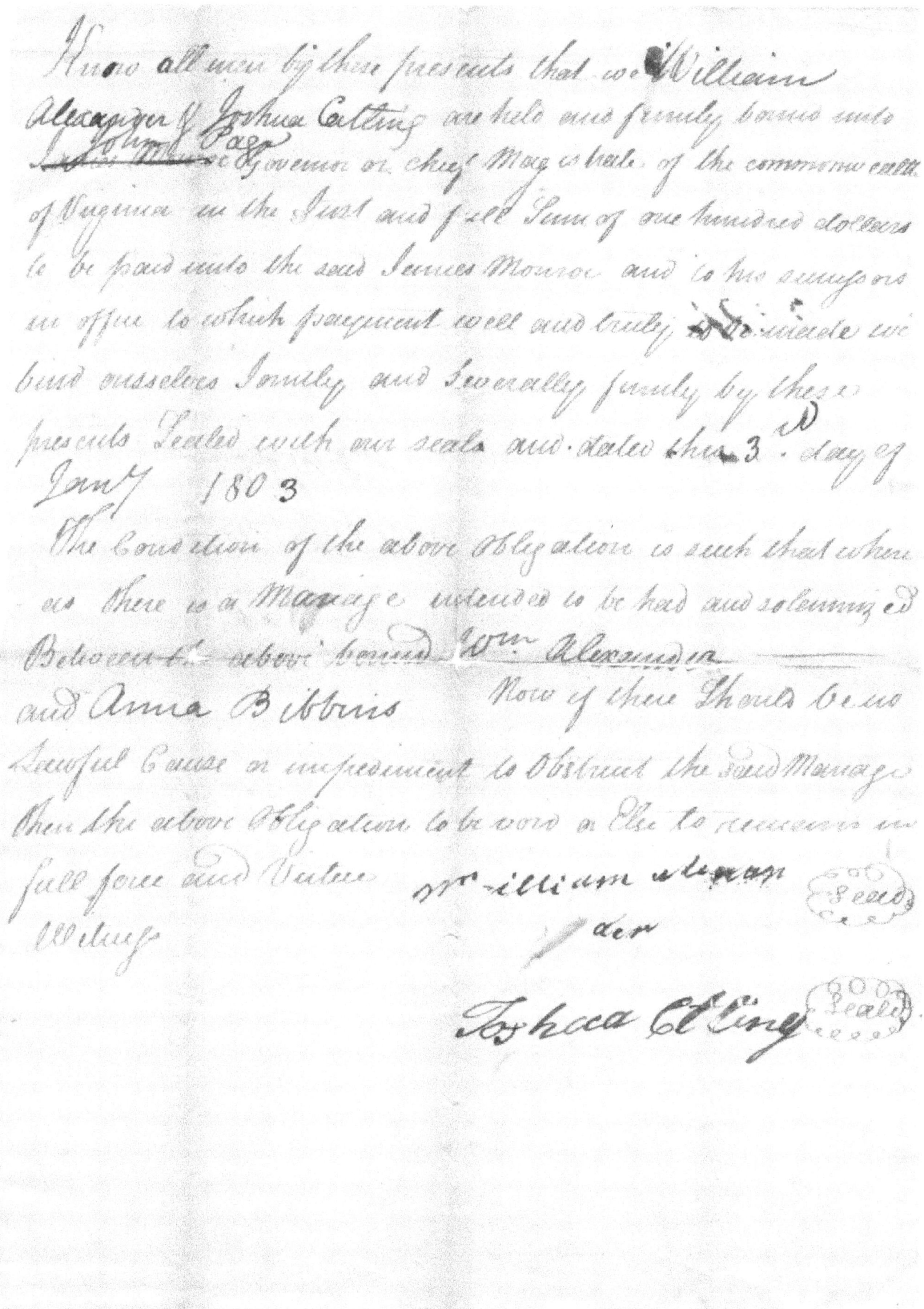

Know all men by these presents that we William
Alexander & Joshua Catting are held and firmly bound unto
_____ Page ___ Governor or chief Magistrate of the commonwealth
of Virginia in the Just and full Sum of one hundred dollars
to be paid unto the said James Monroe and to his successors
in office to which payment well and truly ~~to be made~~ we
bind ourselves Jointly and Severally firmly by these
presents Sealed with our seals and dated this 3ᴰ day of
Jan'y   1803

The Condition of the above Obligation is such that when
as there is a Marriage intended to be had and solemnized
Between the above bound Wᵐ Alexander _____
and Anna Bibbins   Now if there Should be no
Lawful Cause or impediment to Obstruct the said Marriage
then the above Obligation to be void or Else to remain in
full force and Virtue
Witness   William Alexan   {Seal}
                                       der

                              Joshua Catting   {Seal}

Figure 4 - Marriage bond for William Alexander and Anna Bibbins [Bevans], Albemarle County, Va. in 1803

21

GEO W STEELMAN. A. E. SHORE.

CLYDE MILLS,

DEALERS IN GRAIN

AND MANUFACTURERS OF FLOUR, MEAL AND FEED.

PRIDE OF YADKIN IS OUR SPECIAL BRAND.

ALL QUOTATIONS SUBJECT TO MARKET FLUCTUATIONS IMMEDIATE ACCEPTANCE AND SHIPMENT.

SHIPPING AND TELEGRAPH STATION, DONNAHA.

Shore, N.C. ______ 190__

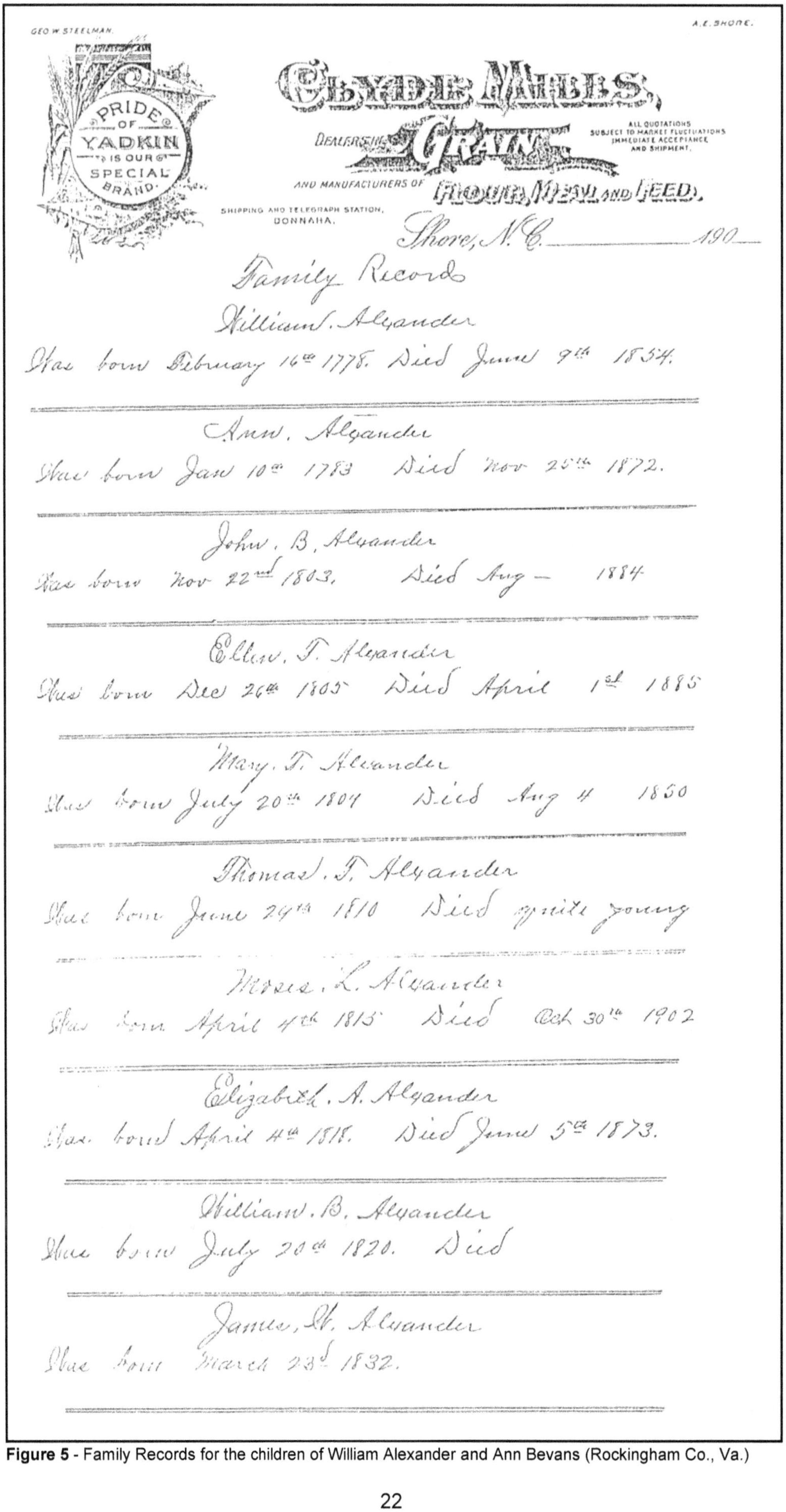

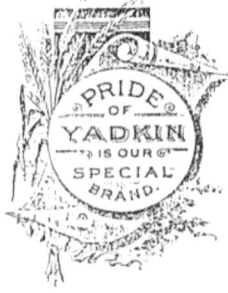

Family Record

William. Alexander

Was born February 16th 1778. Died June 9th 1854.

Ann. Alexander

Was born Jan 10th 1783 Died nov 25th 1872.

John. B. Alexander

Was born nov 22nd 1803. Died Aug – 1884

Ellen. T. Alexander

Was born Dec 26th 1805 Died April 1st 1885

Mary. T. Alexander

Was born July 20th 1807 Died Aug 4 1850

Thomas. T. Alexander

Was born June 29th 1810 Died quite young

Moses. L. Alexander

Was born April 4th 1815 Died Oct 30th 1902

Elizabeth. A. Alexander

Was born April 4th 1818. Died June 5th 1873.

William. B. Alexander

Was born July 20th 1820. Died

James, W. Alexander

Was born March 23d 1832.

Figure 5 - Family Records for the children of William Alexander and Ann Bevans (Rockingham Co., Va.)

1. JOHN BEVANS ALEXANDER
(1803-1884)

I t was for quite some time during our research into the Alexander Family that not much was known about John Alexander, other than that he was known to have lived in Rockbridge County, Virginia. John Bevans Alexander, son of William Alexander and Ann Bevans, was born in Henrico County[1], in December 1803. He was a farmer.

John was married November 6, 1823 in Augusta County, by Rev. Willson, to Ann W. Roberts. We find in the records of the Circuit Court of Augusta County that on October 27, 1823, Mr. William Alexander of Port Republic signed a statement giving consent for his son to marry "Anne" Roberts. The statement was witnessed by Stephen Harnsberger and John Dunmore. The bondsman, in addition to the groom, was David Parsons.

This family was enumerated in District 51 (page 387) for Rockbridge County on the 1850 Federal Census. On July 18, 1860, they were enumerated in District 6 (#231/231, p. 248) of Rockbridge County, and on August 25, 1870 and in 1880 they were residing in Walker's Creek Township on the census.

Not much is known at this time about Ann W. Roberts, but we do know from the Federal census records that she was born about 1806 in Virginia, and that she died sometime after 1873. A record of John Alexander's death appears in the vital records of Rockbridge County. He died August 20, 1884 of diarrhea at Walker's Creek. Correspondants who assisted the compiler on this family included Anna Mae (Dukes) Knight and Homer Gerold White.

Known children of John Bevans Alexander and Ann W. Roberts:

11. JOHN FRANKLIN "Frank" ALEXANDER, b. 22 AUG 1835 in Augusta Co., Va., m. (1) 6 SEP 1866 by W.W. Trimble in Brownsburg, Rockbridge Co. to Barbara Ann Silvy, daughter of John Silvy and Elizabeth Flemmings.[2] Barbara A. Alexander died 11 APR 1876 of dropsy at Walker's Creek, age 26y 1m.[3] Frank m. (2) on 17 FEB 1885 at the residence of Samuel Miller in Rockbridge Co., by Rev. J.M. Schreckhire, to Mary M. Palmer, daughter of Jacob Palmer. Frank served in Company G of the 58th Virginia Regiment for the Confederate army during the Civil War, and was reportedly wounded at the Battle of Fredericksburg on 13 DEC 1862[4]. Frank, a shoemaker by trade, may have had a mailing address of Zack, in Rockbridge Co. He died 16 JUN 1922 in Walker's Creek, Rockbridge Co. According to his death certificate he was bur. the next day in Emanuel Cem. (grave has not been located),[5] at Zack, Va. Child:
    111.   LUCINDA MAE ALEXANDER, b. c.AUG 1868 in Rockbridge Co.

+   12. WILLIAM WHIT(E)FIELD ALEXANDER, b. 4 DEC 1836 in Rockbridge Co., was m. (1) to Abigail A. Elizabeth Minger.

+   13. ELIZABETH ANN "Lizzie" ALEXANDER, b. c.JAN 1842 in Rockbridge Co., m. (1) to Campbell Robert Davis, then m. (2) to William Vint.

+   14. SUSAN JANE ALEXANDER, b. 6 FEB 1845 in Rockbridge Co., m. there to William Henry Dukes.

    15. Possibly BARBARA ANN ALEXANDER, a child appearing as aged 20 on the 1870 Federal census, b. Va.

+   16. JAMES NEWTON ALEXANDER, b. 23 JUN 1851 in Rockbridge Co., m. Martha Jane Patterson.

    17. Unknown Male child.

---

[1] Birthplace provided from his death record in the Rockbridge Co., Va. Probate Court.
[2] Elizabeth Silvy gave consent in 1866 for her daughter Barbara Ann to marry John F. Alexander.
[3] Rockbridge Co., Va. Death Register.
[4] Injury information from Homer White of Lane, Kan.
[5] Commonwealth of Virginia, Certificate of Death, #16651, informant J.R. Reese.

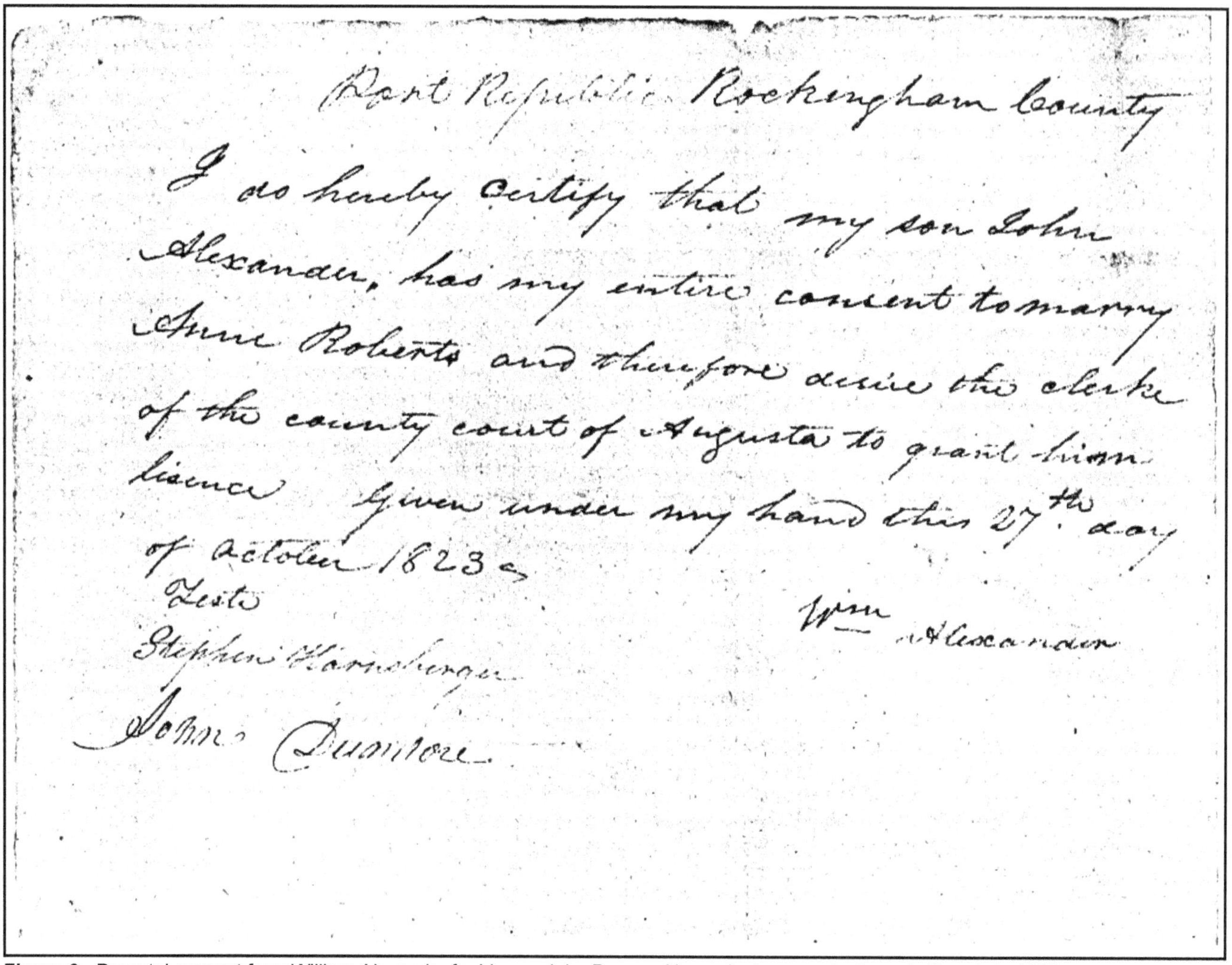

Port Republic Rockingham County

I do hereby cirtify that my son John Alexander, has my entire consent to marry Anne Roberts and therefore desire the clerke of the county court of Augusta to grant him licence Given under my hand this 27th day of October 1823

Teste

Wm Alexander

Stephen Harnsberger

John Dunmore

Figure 6 - Parental consent from William Alexander for his son John Bevans Alexander to marry in Augusta County in 1823

12. William Whitfield Alexander
(1836-1917)

William Whitfield Alexander, often known as "W.W." Alexander, was born December 4, 1836 in Cedar Grove Mills, Rockbridge County, and was the second child known to John Bevans Alexander and Ann W. Roberts.

He was first married at the home of William Minger in Putnam County, West Virginia, on August 27, 1857, to Abigail Ann Elizabeth Minger, daughter of Joseph, by Rev. Thomas Harmon. The middle name for Mr. Alexander has been found as Whitfield, Whitefield, or even Winfield.

He served in Company E of the 141st Ohio Volunteer Infantry during the Civil War. From the military records we learn that W.W. Alexander stood about 6 feet tall, had a fair complexion, and had blue eyes with light hair.

On June 22, 1860, this family was enumerated on the Federal census for District 3 (page 331) in Putnam County, West Virginia. William moved to Ohio where he resided until April 1865 when he moved his family to Boone County, Indiana. After the birth of at least two children, the Alexander moved on to Kansas about 1869. Mr. Alexander was a farmer by occupation.

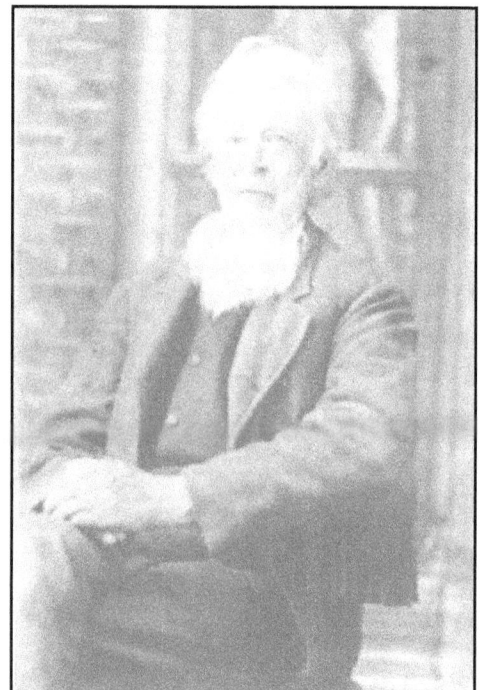

Figure 7 - Joseph Minger, father of Abigail (Minger) Alexander

Abigail, who was born in Rockbridge County, Virginia on September 23, 1841, died in Linn County, Kansas on August 28, 1887. She was buried in the Greeley Cemetery, Anderson County, Kansas.[1] Her original, vertical, white stone cemetery marker was later replaced by a large flat and domed slab which covers the length and width of the plot.

After the death of Abigail, W.W. Alexander married second on February 21, 1889 at Greeley, Anderson County, Kansas to Mrs. Millie (Loveless) Fogle, widow of George Fogle. Millie, a daughter of John H. and Susan Loveless, was born in October 1836 in Ohio, and died October 1, 1909 in Linn County, Kansas. She was buried on Sunday, October 3, 1909 in the Greeley city Cemetery, Greeley, Kansas. According to May (Alexander) Amyx, the home of W.W. burned after Millie died, and nearly all his possessions were destroyed.

Mr. William W. Alexander married third on April 3, 1913 in Garnett, Anderson County, Kansas to Mrs. Amanda Elizabeth (Potter) Hendrix. It is known that Amanda had married Mr. Joseph A. Hendrix on December 13, 186 _, and that he died August 13, 1907 and was buried in the city cemetery at Greeley, Kansas. His cemetery stone reflects that his birth date was November 7, 1836. Amanda, a daughter of Uriah Potter, was born May 24, 1849, and died April 3, 1926. She was buried in the city cemetery at Greeley, Kansas. In 1980, May (Alexander) Amyx decribed:

> I remember when the house burned; grandfather Alexander married his third wife soon after he rebuilt. I never met her. There was an old stone tool shed, blacksmith shop on the place and an old smoke house made of stone that stood by the house, and a cider and wine press were housed there too. It was a lovely farm home with a white picket fence around the front of the place.

On the 1900 Federal census, the family of W.W. Alexander was enumerated in the city of Parker, Linn County, Kansas. On the 1910 Federal census he was enumerated in Liberty Township of that county, and had his sister Susan J. Dukes as a member of his household.

William W. Alexander, a farmer, died on Tuesday, May 8, 1917 near Parker, Liberty Twp., Linn County, Kansas, and was buried on May 10, 1917 in the city cemetery at Greeley, Kansas.[2] Correspondants who assisted the compiler on this family included Otto Alexander, Kenneth Alexander, Flossie (Alexander) Sullins, and Barbara Underhill.

Children of William Whitfield Alexander:

+ 121. JOHN JOSEPH ALEXANDER, b. 21 APR 1858 in Putnam Co., Va. (now W.Va.), m. (1) to Fannie Eva Jones, and (2) to Sarah Martha Reid. He d. 20 SEP 1929.
  122. WILLIAM OTTERBEIN "Willie" ALEXANDER, b. 16 JUL 1860 in Putnam Co., Va., d. 10 JUL 1866 in Boone Co., Ind. No further information.
  123. JAMES FRANKLIN ALEXANDER, b. 1 DEC 1861, d. 14 JAN 1862 in Gallia Co., Ohio. No further information.
  124. ANDREW JACKSON ALEXANDER, b. 14 FEB 1863 in Gallia Co., Ohio, m. 23 AUG 1882 to Sarah Egger [or Eggen]. The family was listed on the 1900 Federal census for Parker, Linn Co., Kan. Andrew, a farmer, d. 16 SEP 1900. Sarah was listed on the 1910 Federal census for the city of Parker (sheet 3) in Liberty Twp., Linn Co., Kan. Sarah E. Alexander d. 31 JAN 1912 in Parker and was bur. in Highland Cem. there. Children:
    1241. BELLE ALEXANDER, b. 12 AUG 1884 in Linn Co., Kan., m. Henry Bowman. Belle d. 24 OCT 1914 in Linn Co., and bur. in Highland Cem. of Parker, Kan.
      12411. GOLDIE BOWMAN.
      12412. CHARLES BOWMAN.
    1242. NORA ALEXANDER, b. c.FEB 1887 in Kan. (age 13 in 1900), m. 16 NOV 1909 in Kansas City, Kan. to John Copeland, and lived in Hoisington, Kan. She d. before 1917. Children:
      12421. CATHERINE COPELAND.
      12422. WINIFRED COPELAND.
    1243. CHARLES L. ALEXANDER, b. c.FEB 1890 in Kan. (age 10 in 1900), m. Juanita Day, and d. in Colo.
    1244. ETHEL W. ALEXANDER, b. c.FEB 1896 in Kan. (age 4 in 1900), d. c.1920 and bur. in Highland Cem. of Parker, Kan. She m. Fred S. Amyx, b. 1895, d. 1918 and bur. in Highland Cem. Child:
      12441. FREDA S. AMYX, b. 1918, d. 1920, bur. in Highland Cem.
    1245. Infant female, b. 15 AUG 1900.
+ 125. CHARLES NEWTON ALEXANDER, b. 2 JAN 1865 in Gallipolis, Gallia Co., Ohio, m. 1 JAN 1893 to Emma Diehm. Charles d. 22 AUG 1952 in Lawrence, Douglas Co., Kan., bur. 25 AUG 1952 in a cemetery in the rural community of Beagle, Miami Co., Kan.
+ 126. MARY ANN "Molly" ALEXANDER, b. 29 JAN 1867 in Jamestown, Boone Co., Ind., m. 20 FEB 1889 in Linn Co., Kan. to Clem V. Guy. Mary Ann d. 10 NOV 1949 in Clare, Clare Co., Mich., bur. in a Cem. at

---

[1] Gravestone, Greeley Cemetery: ALEXANDER. / ABIGAIL A.E. / 1841-1887.
[2] Gravestone, Greeley Cemetery: ALEXANDER. / WILLIAM W. / 1836-1917.

Elk Rapids, Grand Co., Mich.

+ 127. SARAH ELIZABETH "Sadie" ALEXANDER, b. 27 JUL 1869 in Jamestown, Boone Co., Ind., m. 20 FEB 1889 in Linn Co., Kan. to Samuel Ramsey McCain. Sarah E. d. 16 (or 28th) JUL 1957 in Kansas City, Jackson Co., Mo., and bur. in Highland Park Cem. of Kansas City, Kan.

+ 128. GEORGE WASHINGTON ALEXANDER, b. 4 APR 1872 in Kan., m. c.APR 1900 in Paola, Miami Co., Kan. to Lena Mae Walthall. George d. 28 JUN 1936 in Lane, Franklin Co., Kan., and bur. 30 JUN 1936 in Beagle, Miami Co., Kan.

129. THOMAS JEFFERSON ALEXANDER, b. 29 MAR 1874 in Linn Co., Kan., m. 14 FEB 1899 in Parker, Kan.[1] to Ella Millard. Ella d. 8 JAN 1857 in Cherryvale, Montgomery Co., Kan. Thomas d. 12 OCT 1960 in Cherryvale, and bur. in Fairview Cem. there.

12(10). ROBERT ELMER ALEXANDER, b. 3 APR 1876 in Kan., m. 30 MAR 1904 in Paola, Miami Co. to Mary E. Prentice. Robert E. d. 9 JUL 1907 and bur. in the cemetery at Beagle, Kan. Mary Alexander m. (2) Mr. Stakley (or Stanley), and d. in Calif. Child:

12(10)1. WILLIAM NEWELL ALEXANDER, b. 1905, d. 1907, bur. in Beagle Cem.

12(11). SAMUEL PERRY ALEXANDER, b. 3 FEB 1878 in Kan., d. 26 OCT 1967 in Eureka, Greenwood Co., Kan., bur. near Howard, Elk Co., Kan., m. Mrs. Rachel (Arnold?) James. Child:

12(11)1a. Daisy James, daughter of Rachel, m. Mr. Cecil Wofford (according to Flossie (Alexander) Sullins).

12(12). VIRGINIA MAUDE "Maudie" ALEXANDER, b. 5 OCT 1880 in Kan., m. Nathan Leonard Trumbull. Maude d. 11 MAY 1909 at 1212 W. 17th St. in Pueblo, Pueblo Co., Colo., bur. 14 MAY 1909 in Mountain View Cem. there. From the cemetery records we find that Nathan L. Trumbull, who retired from the railroad, d. 3 NOV 1910 in LaJunta, Otero Co., Colo., age 40, and bur. 4 NOV 1910 in Mountain View Cem. Children:

12(12)1. WALTER LYNN TRUMBULL, lived in Fontana, Kan.

12(12)2. L.H. TRUMBULL, of LaJunta, Colo.

12(13). EDITH MYRTLE ALEXANDER, b. 1 JAN 1882/3 in Kan., d. 5 JAN 1907 of tuberculosis in Kansas City, Mo., bur. the next day in Union Cem. of Kansas City, m. in Kansas City to Dr. Romullus Ragan.

121. John Joseph Alexander
(1858-1929)

John Joseph Alexander was the eldest child of William W. Alexander and his first wife Abigail Ann Elizabeth Minger. He was born April 21, 1858 in Putnam County, Virginia (now West Virginia),[2] and was married twice. He was first married on August 1, 1883 to Fannie Eva Jones who died on July 16, 1889 at the age of 21 years, 1 month and 14 days, and was buried in the Quaker Cemetery at Spring Grove Friends Church east of Lane, Miami County, Kansas. John J. Alexander was remarried February 13, 1890 in Garnett, Anderson County, Kansas to Sarah Martha "Mattie" Reid. John was a farmer.

His family was enumerated on the 1900 Federal census for the city of Parker, Linn County, Kansas, and in Franklin Township in Linn County on the 1910 Federal census. John died September 20, 1929 of cancer of the bladder, in Parker, Kansas and was buried in Highland Cemetery there two days later. Sarah M. Alexander died at approximately 96 years of age in 1964 and was buried in the city cemetery at Lane, Franklin County, Kansas. Correspondants who assisted the compiler on this family included Flossie (Alexander) Sullins and Homer White.

Children of John Joseph Alexander:

1211. RETTA IRENE ALEXANDER, b. 17 NOV 1884 in Linn Co., Kan., d. 9 JAN 1903 in Linn Co., bur. in Spring Grove Quaker Cem. east of Lane, Kan.

1212. FLORA GRACE ALEXANDER, b. 7 JUN 1887 in Linn Co., d. 11 MAY 1926 in Parker and bur. in Highland Cem. there. Flora was m. 26 FEB 1908 in Parker, to Orian A. Sullivan. Children, order uncertain:

12121. THELMA LUCILLE SULLIVAN.

12122. ARLO ALEXANDER SULLIVAN.

12123. Stillborn child.

1213. ARNOLD ALEXANDER.[3] No further information.

1214. LOUIS CARL ALEXANDER, b. 25 FEB 1891, d. 2 DEC 1895, bur. Spring Grove Quaker Cem. east of Lane, Kan.

1215. INA FLORENCE ALEXANDER, b. 11 MAR 1893, d. 4 MAR 1894, bur. in Spring Grove Quaker Cem.

---

[1] Linn Co., Kan. Marriages, Bk. 7, p. 60.
[2] Place of birth listed on 1910 Federal census for Linn Co., Kan.
[3] Child placed here based on information received in person from Flossie (Alexander) Sullins.

1216.   ELSIE VIOLA ALEXANDER, b. 23 MAR 1896 in Parker, Linn Co., Kan., d. 1 FEB 1988 in Arkhaven Nursing Home of Garnett, Anderson Co., Kan., and bur. 4 FEB 1988 in Osawatomie Cem., m. 30 JUN 1926 in Lane to John Quincy Bledsoe, d. 13 AUG 1980. Elsie grew up in Parker, but after marriage she made her home in Ft. Scott, Kan. before moving to Osawatomie, Miami Co., Kan. in 1928. Children:
   12161. MARVIN E. BLEDSOE, b. 11 OCT 1931, d. 24 JUL 2001 in Oklahoma City, Okla.
   12162. THURMAN L. BLEDSOE, b. 24 JUL 1933, d. 2 SEP 2010 in Oklahoma City, Okla.
1217.   BERNICE LOUELLA ALEXANDER, b. 5 NOV 1898 in Kan., m. in Paola, Kan. to Jake Matile. Bernice d. 13 JUL 1982 in Americus, Lyon Co., Kan.
1218.   WILLIAM DAVID ALEXANDER, b. 11 MAR 1903 in Linn Co., Kan., m. 31 DEC 1938 to Mrs. Cecile (Shively) Chitwood. William d. 2 APR 1980 in Pueblo, Colo., and bur. in Imperial Gardens Cem. there. According to Flossie (Alexander) Sullins, William m. Cecil late in life, but was married to her 38 years before she died.
1219.   JOSEPH CLAYTON ALEXANDER, b. 26 FEB 1906 in Linn Co., Kan., d. 17 JAN 1907, bur. in Spring Grove Quaker Cem. east of Lane, Kan.
121(10).   RAYMOND GALEN ALEXANDER, m. three times: (1) first wife unknown; (2) Alma (   ); and m. (3) on 1 JUL 1965 in Anderson Co., Kan. to Grace Marie Geuy. He was bur. at Osawatomie, Kan.

Figure 8 - (l to r) Sarah E. Alexander McCain, Charles N. Alexander, John J. Alexander, George W. Alexander, Thomas J. Alexander, Samuel P. Alexander in 1929

125. Charles Newton Alexander
(1865-1952)

Charles Newton Alexander, a son of William W. Alexander and his first wife Abigail Ann Elizabeth Minger, was born January 2, 1865 in Gallipolis, Gallia County, Ohio. When he was a boy of 6 years old the family had moved from Ohio to Kansas. In 1980, May (Alexander) Amyx described that the family farm was located east of Greeley, Kansas:

The farm had a large running spring (never dry). Water ran through the barnyard and supplied the stock and chickens with plenty of water. The spring had a stone house built over it with huge flat stones on the floor where milk and butter cream were kept to cool. In a rainy season, the spring would flood and often things would float around, then the milk, cream and butter would be lost. The barn and other stock buildings were away from the house and a bridge was over the running spring where the cows milked and horses were fed.

Charles was married on January 1, 1894 at the home of the bride in Beagle, Miami County, Kansas to Emma Diehm, daughter of Fred and Mary Diehm. Emma was born March 5, 1870 in a log cabin on a farm near Beagle, and her parents were from Germany. Charles was a farmer.

The family of Charles Alexander was enumerated on the 1900 census for the city of Parker, Linn County, Kansas. On May 24, 1910 the family was enumerated in Liberty Township (sheet 133) of Linn County.

Emma Alexander died on September 30, 1939 in Lawrence, Douglas County, Kansas and was buried (Lot 79) in the cemetery at Beagle, Kansas. Charles died August 22, 1952 in Lawrence, Kansas and was buried (Lot 79) August

25, 1952 in the cemetery at Beagle, Kansas.[1] Correspondants who assisted the compiler on this family included Flossie (Alexander) Sullins and May (Alexander) Amyx.

Children of Charles Newton Alexander and Emma Diehm:

1251.   MILLIE MYRTLE "MAY" ALEXANDER, b. 25 MAY 1895 on a farm near Beagle, Miami Co., Kan., m. 13 OCT 1913 in Kansas City, Jackson Co., Mo. to Shouse Morton Amyx, b. 23 SEP 1888, d. in NOV 1969, bur. Memorial Park Cem., Lawrence, Kan. May Amyx resided at 415 Maple Street, #39, Eudora Rest Center, Eudora KS 66025, and died 12 SEP 1990, bur. Memorial Park Cem.
1252.   EDITH BLANCH ALEXANDER, b. 19 JUN 1897 in Beagle, m. c.1919 to Elba Clark Bowman, b. 31 DEC 1896, d. 20 JAN 1982, bur. Centerville Cem., Linn Co., Kan. Edith d. 1 MAR 1963 and bur. at Centerville Cem.
1253.   LEROY ALEXANDER, b. 2 NOV 1899 in Parker, m. 2 JAN 1926 in Leavenworth, Kan. to Geneva Leola Bateson, daughter of Jasper Newton Bateson and his wife Miss Cook, b. 15 JUL 1908. LeRoy, a retired foreman for the gas company, d. of cancer 13 JAN 1978 in Lawrence, Douglas Co., Kan. where he was bur. in Memorial Park Cem. Children:
   12531.   FRANCIS LEROY ALEXANDER, b. 13 AUG 1931 in Lawrence, m. there 2 JUL 1950 to Betty Lee Deplue, daughter of Adolph Deplue and Claudia Plumlee, b. 12 FEB 1931 in Frontenac, Kan. Francis worked for the police department, while Betty was a secretary and belonged to the Methodist church; res. 776 Elm Street, Lawrence, Kan. Children:
      125311.   LARRY JOE ALEXANDER, b. 26 MAR 1952 in Lawrence, m. and div. Children:
         1253111. LORI JO ALEXANDER.
         1253112. LARABE ALEXANDER.
         1253113. MEGAN ALEXANDER.
      125312.   RHONDA LYNN ALEXANDER, b. 2 JUL 1954, m. 27 MAY 1976 to Steven Busch. Children:
         1253121. JESSICA LEE BUSCH.
         1253122. STEVEN ALEXANDER BUSCH.
      125313.   DUANE FRANCIS ALEXANDER, b. 8 OCT 1958.
   12532.   BEVERLY ELAINE ALEXANDER, b. 16 SEP 1936 in Lawrence, m. there 16 OCT 1957 to James Allen Springer, son of Clarris Springer and Florence Anderson, b. 18 NOV 1934 in Lawrence. Their mailing address was Route 4, Box 150, Lawrence KS.
      125321.   JAMES ALEXANDER SPRINGER, b. 25 NOV 1959 in Lawrence, m. there 17 APR 1980 to Colleen D. Good. Children:
         1253211. BOBBIE JO SPRINGER.
         1253212. JAMES ALEXANDER SPRINGER, JR.
      125322.   GREGORY EUGENE SPRINGER, b. 18 JAN 1962 in Lawrence, m. there 25 OCT 1982 to Kimberly L. Farran. Children:
         1253221. LYNLY DAWN SPRINGER.
         1253222. MORGAN RENE SPRINGER.
1254.   RAY ELGIN ALEXANDER, b. 24 OCT 1903 in Parker, Kan., m. Annabelle Vansant, b. 5 FEB 1906, d. 29 JUN 2001 in Marietta, Okla., bur. Lakeview Cem. of Marietta, daughter of Lelan Vansant and Ida Mae Peterman. They moved to Marietta, Okla. He d. 28 OCT 1967. Child:
   12541.   DOROTHY ALEXANDER, m. _____ Fletcher, res. Lafayette, La. Child:
      125411.   TED FLETCHER, res. Knoxville, Tenn.
1255.   ARNOLD D. ALEXANDER, b. 8 MAY 1905 in Parker, rem. to Lawrence where he d. 16 MAR 1961, bur. Mt. Calvary Catholic Cem., Lawrence, Kan., m. Susan Monroe, b. OCT 1901, d. 26 MAR 1988, bur. Mt. Calvary Catholic Cem.

126. Mary Ann (Alexander) Guy
(1867-1949)

Mary Ann Alexander, daughter of William W. Alexander and his first wife Abigail Ann Elizabeth Minger, was born January 29, 1867 in Crawfordville, Boone County, Indiana. On February 20, 1889 she was married in Linn County, Kansas to Clemeth Valandingham Guy. Mr. Guy, a son of Dr. Samuel D. Guy and Phebe Ann Beymer, was born March 3, 1865 in Bryant, Jay County, Indiana.

---

[1] Information provided by Flossie (Alexander) Sullins, 15 JUN 1987; and May (Alexander) Amyx, 23 AUG 1987.

On May 29, 1946, Clem Guy died in Petoskey, Michigan, and was buried in Elk Rapids, Michigan. Mary Ann (Alexander) Guy died on November 10, 1949 in Clare, Clare County, Michigan and was also buried in Elk Rapids, Michigan.[1] Correspondants who assisted the compiler on this family included Barbara Underhill.

Children of Clemeth Valandingham Guy and Mary Ann Alexander:

1261. PEARL SADIE GUY, b. 3 APR 1890 in Bryant, Jay Co., Ind., m. 30 APR 1911 to Ernie Packer. Pearl d. 9 JAN 1940 in Petosky, Mich., and bur. in Elk Rapids, Mich. Ernie Packer, b. 31 MAR 1877, d. 5 MAR 1957 in Rapid City, Mich., bur. Elk Rapids, Minn.[2]
1262. SAMUEL EARL GUY, b. 5 OCT 1892 in Bryant, Ind., m. 26 JUL 1914 to Mildred Cleo Kinsey, daughter of Samuel A. Kinsey and Hattie J. Plank, b. 3 JUL 1899 in Curryville, Ind. He d. 1 JUL 1948 in Rapid City. Children:
    12621. EVELYN WINIFRED GUY, b. 4 MAY 1915 in Curryville, Ind., m. Gladwin Clifton.
    12622. Infant male, stillborn 27 MAY 1916.
    12623. ROBERT DALE GUY, b. 16 SEP 1917 in Rapid City, Mich., d. 18 NOV 1999 near Traverse City, Mich., m. Pauline McDonald.
    12624. MARY JANE GUY, b. March 24, 1919 in Rapid City, m. Darrell Clifton.
    12625. JACK KINSEY GUY, b. 24 JUL 1921 in Rapid City, d. 18 MAY 2003, m. Mabel Deater Barber.
    12626. CHARLES KENNETH GUY, b. 11 MAR 1921 in Rapid City, m. Dorothy Allen.
    12627. SAMUEL EARL GUY, JR., b. 17 MAY 1924 in Rapid City, m. Mary "Peggy" Jaenicki.
    12628. JOAN PEARL GUY, b. 30 MAR 1925 in Rapid City, m. Verle Zick.
    12629. BETTY LEE GUY, b. 25 AUG 1926 in Rapid City, m. William Zick, and d. 3 AUG 1955.
    1262(10). RICHARD CALVIN GUY, b. 20 MAY 1928 in Rapid City, m. Jean Zimmerman.
    1262(11). MAURICE LEROY GUY, b. 6 JUN 1932 in Rapid City, m. Carol Van Collie.
    1262(12). HARRIET JEAN GUY, b. 19 MAR 1945 in Rapid City, m. Kenneth Stoddard, and d. c.OCT 1965.
1263. RAY ALEXANDER GUY, b. 29 JUL 1895 in Seaman, Kan., m. 18 JUN 1924 in Rapid City, Mich. to Matilda Leone LaCure, daughter of Louis LaCure (an anglicized form of the French name Lucien Lecuyer) and Elizabeth Esther Sackett, b. in Rapid City, 22 MAY 1905. Ray, a retired employee of the C&O Railroad, d. in Traverse City, Mich., 13 JUN 1974, bur. Rapid City. Children:
    12631. MELBA ESTHER GUY, b. 6 NOV 1924 in Rapid City, m. 19 JUL 1941 to Richard Isham Jones.
    12632. DONALD EDWIN GUY, b. 19 NOV 1926 in Saginaw, Mich., m. 14 APR 1951 to Elain Joyce Love.
    12633. SHIRLEY JEAN GUY, b. 26 FEB 1928 in Saginaw, m. 21 JUL 1951 to Jack Dempsey Manwell.
    12634. PATSY LOU GUY, b. 18 JUN 1929 in Saginaw, m. (1) 28 JUN 1947 to Thomas Clark Schlotter, and m. (2) c.1977 to Milton Stockwell.
    12635. HELEN IRENE GUY, b. 11 OCT 1931 in Saginaw, m. 26 AUG 1950 to Walter Richard Younk.
    12636. IRMA BEVERLY GUY, b. 10 FEB 1933 in Saginaw, m. 28 JUL 1951 to George LeRoy Underhill.
    12637. SUE ANN GUY, b. 22 MAR 1935 in Saginaw, m. 23 JAN 1956 to Richard Oral Manchester.
1264. CLEMETH GALE GUY, b. 1 SEP 1898 in Bryant, Ind., m. (1) Mable (   ), and (2) on 17 JUL 1949 to Mary Green. Clem d. 17 JUL 1969 in Grand Rapids, Mich.
1265. MAURICE MANNING GUY, b. 20 MAY 1901 in Bryant, Ind., m. (1) 24 JUN 1926 to Dorothy Evelyn Hibner who b. 16 SEP 1900. After the death of Dorothy on 13 DEC 1965, Maurice m. (2) in FEB 1971 to Mrs. Alice Leonard. Children:
    12651. VIRGINIA ANN GUY, b. 16 APR 1927, m. 9 JUL 1948 to Melvin Sternhagen.
    12652. RUTH ELLEN GUY, stillborn 30 MAY 1930.
    12653. NANCY MARIE GUY, b. 6 JUN 1932, m. 17 JUN 1961 to Joe Malonis.
    12654. BARBARA JANE GUY, b. 2 DEC 1934, m. 9 JUN 1956 to Jack Hanson.
1266. WILLIAM KEITH GUY, b. 11 AUG 1903 in Bryant, Ind., d. there 30 NOV 1904.
1267. AUDREY VIRGINIA GUY, b. 6 JUL 1906 in Rapid City, m. 2 JUL 1927 to Roy Enos Kinsey, son of Samuel A. Kinsey and Hattie Plank. Children:
    12671. JAY KINSEY, b. 10 FEB 1933 in Clare, Mich., m. Shirley Shear.
    12672. CLARK ALLEN KINSEY, b. 13 SEP 1938 in Clare, m. Charlotte Gardner.
1268. LESTER GUY, b. 17 NOV 1911 in Bryant, Ind., m. 17 JUN 1932 to Marian Estella Barber b. 16 APR 1914 in Rapid City, Mich. Lester d. 13 MAR 1975 in Rapid City. Children:
    12681. GAY JANETTE GUY, b. 21 MAY 1933, m. Roger Mann.
    12682. GERALD WARNER GUY, b. 23 JUN 1936, m. Shirley May Rhody.
    12683. NADEAN LUCILLE GUY, b. 24 NOV 1938, m. Fred Elliott.
    12684. SANDRA LEE GUY, b. 27 MAY 1942, m. 10 SEP 1960 to Tracey Mariage.

---

[1] Information in part provided by Barbara Underhill, 125 Walnut #29, Danville KY 40422
[2] Letter, Barbara Underhill (Danville, Ky., 27 DEC 1988).

12685. RODNEY EARL GUY, b. 3 OCT 1948, m. Vanessa Yankee.
12686. KRISTY KAY GUY, b. 11 AUG 1952.

127. Sarah Elizabeth (Alexander) McCain
(1869-1957)

Sarah Elizabeth Alexander, daughter of William W. Alexander and his first wife Abigail Ann Elizabeth Minger, was born July 26, 1869 in Franklin County, Indiana.[1] On February 20, 1889, Sarah E. was married in Linn County, Kansas to Samuel Ramsey McCain.

Sam, a son of William McCain and Elizabeth Cook, was born in Illinois on January 26, 1868, and was known to be a painter and a wallpaper hanger. Sam died in Delphi, Carroll County, Indiana and was reportedly buried in a cemetery in Edna, Kansas.

Sarah died on July 16, 1957 in Kansas City, Jackson County, Missouri and was buried in Highland Park Cemetery of Kansas City, Wyandotte County, Kansas. Her residence at the time of death was 527 Everett St., Kansas City, Kansas. Correspondants who assisted the compiler on this family included James Franklin Monroe and Virginia McEntyre.

Children of Samuel Ramsey McCain and Sarah E. Alexander:

1271. ETHEL LILLIAN McCAIN, b. 25 MAR 1896 in Kansas City, Jackson Co., Mo., m. at Ft. Sill in Lawton, Okla. on 28 NOV 1917 to John Frederick Scott. John and Ethel were members of the First Christian Church. Ethel d. 3 JAN 1970 in Topeka, Shawnee Co., Kan., bur. in Mt. Hope Cem. there. John F., an ice cream

Figure 9 - Samuel R. McCain

manufacturer who served in World War I, was mayor of Topeka, Kan. between 1940 and 1942. John, son of Henry C. Scott and Alice Delana Teed, b. 26 JUN 1895 in Topeka, d. 5 FEB 1973 in Topeka, and was bur. in Mt. Hope Cem. Children:[2]
12711. JOHN FREDERICK SCOTT, JR., b. 2 APR 1920 in Topeka, m. there 25 OCT 1942 to Georgia Maxine Sherrill, daughter of George Hartley Sherrill and Caroline Fulton Ford, b. 18 AUG 1921 in Topeka. Children:
   127111. JOHN FREDERICK SCOTT, III, b. 10 SEP 1946 in Topeka, m. c.1968 there to Linda Sue Harper, daughter of Albert Goodrich Harper and Virginia Dean Garrett, b. July 10, 1947 in Topeka. Children:
      1271111. JOHN FREDERICK SCOTT, IV, b. 6 FEB 1969 in Topeka.
      1271112. JENNIFER REBECCA SCOTT, b. 25 MAY 1971 in Topeka.
   127112. ROBERT GREGORY SCOTT, SR., b. 6 SEP 1950 in Topeka, m. (1) Kathryn E. (   ) by whom he had two children, and m. (2) 22 MAY 1981 to Christal Laine Herrmann, daughter of George Herrmann and Peggy Lou Morris, b. January 10, 1957 in Topeka. Children, b.in Topeka:
      1271121. ROBERT GREGORY SCOTT, JR., b. 16 JAN 1971.
      1271122. HALEY NICOLE SCOTT, b. 15 OCT 1977.
12712. VIRGINIA ELIZABETH SCOTT, b. 26 DEC 1921 in Topeka, m. (1) there 25 JUN 1941 to Charles E. Fairman, Jr., son of Charles Edward Fairman, Sr. and Mary Marshall, b. 12 FEB 1919 in Manhattan, Kan. He d. 10 JUL 1943 in Sedalia, Pettis Co., Mo., bur. 5 days later in Sunset Cem. of Manhattan, Kan. Mr. Fairman served as a lieutenant in the Army and belonged to the Episcopal church. Virginia m. (2) in Topeka on 9 AUG 1948 to John Gerald McEntyre, son of John Guy McEntyre and Winifred Catherine Dwyer, b. 3 NOV 1920 in Topeka and served as a lieutenant colonel during World War II. Children:
   127121. CHARLES EDWARD FAIRMAN, III, b. 31 MAY 1943 in Topeka. Unmarried.
   127122. MARY DELANA McENTYRE, b. 3 JUL 1949 in Manhattan, Riley Co., Kan., m. 26 JUN 1971 in West Lafayette, Tippicanoe Co., Ind. to Paul David Prat, div. 23 JUL 1979.
   127123. GERALD SCOTT MCENTYRE, b. 3 FEB 1955 in Manhattan.

---

[1] Place of birth from Jim Monroe and Virginia McEntyre, September 1987, even though the Federal census and other records may indicate Jamestown, Boone Co., Ind.
[2] Information in part provided by Virginia McEntyre, 4 SEP 1987.

12713. SHIRLEY ANN SCOTT, b. 6 JUL 1932 in Topeka, m. there 7 JUN 1953 to Marvin Lee Samuelson,[1] son of Eben Samuelson and Mable Margaret Brown, b. in Home City, Kan., 25 JUL 1931. Marvin, a veterinarian, m. (2) Judith Mooney Ross, which caused the divorce of Shirley A. and Marvin, c.1972. Children:

    127131. VALORIE LEIGH SAMUELSON, b. 2 AUG 1954 in Manhattan, m. 4 APR 1981 in San Pedro, Calif. to John Mitchell Cameron, son of John Gordon Carmeron and Beatrice Rachel Haller, b. 26 SEP 1954 in San Pedro. Valorie works as a bilingual teacher while John is a sea navigator. Children:[2]

        1271311. JOHN SCOTT CAMERON, b. 14 APR 1984 in San Pedro, Calif.

        1271312. STEVEN LEE CAMERON, b. 23 DEC 1985 in San Pedro, Calif.

    127132. VONNA LYNN SAMUELSON, b. 13 OCT 1955 in San Pedro, Calif., m. 31 MAY 1980 to David Leonard Ault, a computer specialist, son of Leonard Fay Ault and Elizabeth Ethel Hathaway, b. 11 NOV 1950 in East Chicago, Lake Co., Ind. He has worked both as an air traffic controller and a computer technician.

    127133. SCOTT EBEN SAMUELSON, b. 3 AUG 1958 in San Pedro, Calif., d. (and possibly murdered) near Mt. Waterman, Calif., and bur. 30 MAY 1980 in San Pedro. Scott was a construction worker.

    127134. MELANIE SUE SAMUELSON, b. 11 FEB 1961 in San Pedro, works as a dental assistant.

1272. IRENE McCAIN, b. 9 DEC 1897 in Kansas City, Wyandotte Co., Kan., m. (1) there on 12 JUN 1918 to Charles Arden Monroe, Sr., son of George Monroe and Emma Catherine (Potts) Cleve was b. 25 OCT 1897 in Oceltree, Johnson Co., Kan. After being divorced c.NOV 1934, Irene m. (2) 5 AUG 1945 to Emmett Hibler Stambaugh. Irene d. 28 DEC 1985 in Belvue, Pottawatomie Co., Kan., and bur. 31 DEC 1985 in Greenwood Cem. there. Emmett, son of John Washington Stambaugh and Joanna VanSycle, was b. 15 OCT 1892 in Kaw Twp. of Wabaunsee Co., Kan. Emmett was first m. to Melva Olive Murphy, daughter of Mose Murphy and Adel Marchand, who was b. 15 NOV 1893 in Kaw Twp. of Waubausee Co., Kan.[3] Melva d. 5 FEB 1937 and was bur. two days later in Greenwood Cem. of Belvue, Kan. Emmet d. 24 DEC 1970 and was buried in Greewood Cem. Children, b. Kansas City, Kan.:[4]

12721. CHARLES ARDEN MONROE, JR., b. 18 APR 1919, d. 28 AUG 1930, bur. Highland Park Cem. of Kansas City, Kan.

12722. JAMES FRANKLIN MONROE, b. 21 SEP 1921 at Bethany Hospital, served in the U.S. Army for six years beginning in 1940, then graduated from Kansas University in 1951, d. 21 MAY 1989 of pneumonia in Tex.

12723. BETTY JEANNE MONROE, b. 10 AUG 1928, m. 10 AUG 1946 in St. Mary's Methodist Church to Edwin Emmett Stambaugh, son of Emmett Hibler Stambaugh and Melva Olive Murphy, b. 29 FEB 1924 in Kaw Twp. of Pottawatomie Co., Kan. Children:

    127231. JAMES STEVEN STAMBAUGH, b. 4 JUN 1947 in Wamego, Pottawatomie Co., Kan., m. 25 MAY 1969 in Corning, Nemaha Co., Kan. to Virginia Sue Cottrell, daughter of Arthur Cottrell and Esther E. Brenner, b. 4 JAN 1949 in Seneca, Nemaha Co., Kan. Children:

        1272311. PAUL JAMES STAMBAUGH, b. 24 JUL 1978 in Topeka, Kan.

        1272312. CHRISTOPHER MICHAEL STAMBAUGH, b. 3 APR 1982 in Salina, Kan.

    127232. JOHN CHARLES STAMBAUGH, b. 18 SEP 1948 in Topeka, m. 27 MAR 1981 there to Deanna Kay Delker, b. 29 MAR 1949 in Salina, Kan., daughter of Lester Delker and Dorothy Graves, who had prev. m. Don Johnson.

    127233. Infant STAMBAUGH, male, stillborn in Topeka, 18 NOV 1950, bur. Greenwood Cem.

    127234. ROBERT MARTIN STAMBAUGH, b. 18 OCT 1958 in Topeka, m. 26 AUG 1978 in Wichita, Kan. to Roberta Marie Smith, div. 1 NOV 1983, daughter of Billy D. Smith and Dungale Sophi Lankaitis, b. 14 MAY 1956 in Wichita, Kan.

    127235. JANET LOUISE STAMBAUGH, b. 28 NOV 1960 in Topeka, Kan.

1273. Infant McCAIN, stillborn 1903 in Kansas City, Kan.

1274. MARY McCAIN, b. 23 JUN 1901 in Kansas City, Kan., m. Terry Wesley Holmes who d. 5 APR 1955. Mary d. 10 OCT 1966 and bur. with her husband in Highland Park Cem. of Kansas City. Children:

12741. WILLIAM DALE HOLMES, b. 10 SEP 1927 in Topeka, d. 21 APR 1985, bur. Highland Park Cem.

---

[1] Information on the Samuelson family provided by Shirley Ann (Scott) Samuelson.

[2] Information in part provided by Valorie (Samuelson) Cameron.

[3] Two children by marriage of Emmett Hibler Stambaugh and Melva Olive Murphy were: Lois Melva Stambaugh, b. 6 JAN 1923 in Kaw Twp. of Wabaunsee Co., Kan., who m. 25 MAY 1947 in Maple Hill, Kan. to Howard Henry Hammarlund; and Edwin Emmett Stambaugh, b. 29 FEB 1924 (See 12723.). Howard Hammarlund, son of Oscar Hammarlund and Lillie Bell (   ), b. 13 MAY 1919 in Maple Hill, Kan., d. 25 SEP 1984 in Topeka, Kan. where bur. in Stone Church Cem. two days later. One son by marriage of Howard and Lois was Theodore Emmett Hammarlund, b. 6 NOV 1953 in Wamego, Kan., m. 26 JUL 1976 in Wichita, Kan. to Cheryl Ruth Freed, daughter of Ronald Freed and Kathy Kendall, b. 24 MAY 1956 in Wichita, Kan. Children of Theodore and Cheryl were: Daniel Charles Hammarlund, b. 4 JUL 1983 in McPherson, Kan., and Scott Robert Hammarlund, b. 24 OCT 1985 in McPherson, Kan.

[4] Information on this family compiled in part by James Franklin Monroe of Houston, Tex., received 7 DEC 1988.

12742. ROBERT KEITH HOLMES, stillborn 1 JAN 1932 in Kansas City, bur. Highland Park Cem.

12743. SARAH RUTH HOLMES, b. 23 AUG 1933 in Kansas City, d. 17 DEC 1986 in Lawrence, Kan.

12744. THOMAS RAY HOLMES, b. 10 JUN 1935 in Kansas City, Kan., m. 5 MAY 1955 to Joyce Marie DuBose, b. 24 SEP 1934 in Adel, Cooke Co., Ga.[1] Children, b. Kansas City, Mo.:

    127441. THERESA ANN HOLMES, b. 18 MAY 1957, m. 16 MAR 1985 to William Brian Finley, son of Robert Craig Finley and Gervaise Suzan White, b. 3 FEB 1959 in Peoria, Ill. Children, b. Kansas City, Mo.:[2]

        1274411. RYAN PATRICK FINLEY, b. 10 JUL 1986.

        1274412. DEVIN WILLIAM FINLEY (twin), b. 28 DEC 1987.

        1274413. DYLAN THOMAS FINLEY (twin), b. 28 DEC 1987.

    127442. SHERRI RAE HOLMES, b. 23 JAN 1961.

    127443. CYNTHIA MARIE HOLMES, b. 22 MAR 1962.

    127444. MICHELLE LYNN HOLMES, b. 9 OCT 1966, d. 5 JUN 1983, bur. Highland Park Cem., Kansas City, Kan.

12745. DOROTHY DELL HOLMES, b. 2 SEP 1939 in Kansas City, Kan., m. (1) to Donald Eugene Wellington, m. (2) to Richard Andrew Erecius, Sr., and m. (3) 7 NOV 1961 in Kansas City, Mo. to Lester Eugene Sanders, Jr., b. 22 JUN 1936 in Kansas City, Mo. Children:

    127451. VERONICA LYNN WELLINGTON, b. 13 AUG 1954 in Kansas City, Mo., m. 19 OCT 1968 there to Danny Eugene Falk, son of William Francis Falk and Louella Lee Lawbaugh, b. 4 SEP 1950 in Kansas City. He d. 19 JUN 1982 in Kansas City, bur. three days later in Floral Hills Cem. of Kansas City, Mo. Children, b. Kansas City, Mo.:[3]

        1274511. DANA LYNN FALK, b. 10 APR 1969.

        1274512. DANNY EUGENE FALK, JR., b. 28 JUL 1970.

    127452. RICHARD ANDREW ERECIUS, JR., b. 4 MAR 1958 in Kansas City, Mo., m. Linda (   ).

    127453. TRACY DAWN ERECIUS, b. 22 JUL 1959 in Kansas City, m. on her birthday in 1983 there to Harvey Joe Brown.

    127454. REX KEITH SANDERS, b. 7 DEC 1962 in Kansas City.

1275. MABEL FERN McCAIN, b. 5 MAY 1904 in Kansas City, Kan., m. (1) Carl Mosley, and m. (2) 15 APR 1931 to Carroll Kemper Carver, son of Virgile Bell and Cleora Myrtle S. Carver, b. 5 MAY 1903 and d. 24 APR 1953, bur. in Highland Park Cem. of Kansas City, Kan. Children:

12751. CAROL KAY CARVER, b. 13 OCT 1937 in Breckenridge, Mo., m. 10 NOV 1952 to Lawrence Robert Bayless, Sr., son of Lawrence Clarence Bayless and Orpha Ada Hammond, b. 15 OCT 1936 in Kansas City, Mo., worked for Ceco Steel Co. Children, b. in Kansas City, Jackson Co., Mo.:[4]

    127511. ROBIN CAROL BAYLESS, stillborn 31 JUL 1953.

    127512. LAWRENCE ROBERT BAYLESS, JR., b. 29 AUG 1954, m. (1) 4 AUG 1974 to Pamela Sue Garrett, and m. (2) 9 JUL 1985 to Joan (   ). Pamela, the daughter of James Garrett and Virginia Sands, b. 8 MAR 1958 in Kansas City, Kan., m. (2) Robert Graham. Children, b. Providence Hospital of Kansas City, Kan.:

        1275121. LAWRENCE ROBERT BAYLESS, III, b. 16 OCT 1975.

        1275122. KEVEN JAMES MARTIN BAYLESS, b. 3 JUN 1977.

        1275123. CATHY ELAINE BAYLESS, b. 10 AUG 1979.

    127513. CARLA JO BAYLESS, b. 13 APR 1957, m. 5 JUL 1976 to Michael Dean Cochran, div., son of Lark Cochran and Wanda Hill, b. 26 AUG 1946. Child:

        1275131. JULIAN MICHAEL COCHRAN, b. 29 JAN 1977 in Kansas City, Mo.

    127514. CLEORA ELAINE BAYLESS, b. 14 DEC 1962.

    127515. CATHY SUE BAYLESS, b. 29 JUN 1965, m. 11 OCT 1986 in the Berean Baptist Church of Kansas City, Kan. to Michael Jay Smith, son of Jackie Eugene Smith and Julia Mae Stancliff, b. 18 SEP 1968, res. Kansas City, Kan.

12752. FRANCES ELAINE CARVER, b. 1 JUL 1944 in Kansas City, Mo., m. (1) 5 JAN 1963 to John Martin, div. and m. (2) 28 AUG 1967 to Malcolm Kugler. Children:

    127521. ROBIN ELAINE MARTIN, b. 30 OCT 1963.

    127522. MICHAEL KUGLER, b. 17 APR 1969.

    127523. JASON KARL KUGLER, b. 21 FEB 1973.

---

[1] Information by Tom Holmes, 1012 Bennington, Kansas City MO 64126, on 16 AUG 1988, forwarded by James Franklin Monroe of Houston, Tex., December 1988.

[2] Information provided by Theresa Finley, 2000 E. 144th Terr., Kansas City MO 66062, on 19 AUG 1988, forwarded by James Franklin Monroe of Houston, Tex., December 1988.

[3] Information provided by Veronica L. Falk, 114 E. 147th St., Kansas City MO 64145, on 31 JAN 1988, forwarded by James Franklin Monroe of Houston, Tex., December 1988.

[4] Informaton forwarded by James F. Monroe of Houston, Tex., December 1988.

1276.   DOROTHY FAYE McCAIN, b. 12 JUN 1907 in Kansas City, Kan., m. George Lee Tarver, Sr., son of Ethelred Tarver and Augustine Bellier, b. 14 AUG 1899 in Hume, Bates Co., Mo., d. 20 FEB 1974 in Kansas City, Mo. and bur. two days later in Highland Park Cem. of Kansas City, Kan. Dorothy d. 8 JUN 1933 in Kansas City, Kan., and bur. two days later in Highland Park Cem. there. After her death, George m. Violet Norma Edwards, daughter of James Harvey Edwards and Eunice Ethel McNutt, b. 14 FEB 1914 in Kansas City, Kan. Children:
   12761.   GEORGE LEE TARVER, JR., b. 8 NOV 1926 in Kansas City, Kan., was shot down over Tokyo, Japan during World War II and d. 16 FEB 1945.
   12762.   DOROTHY JOANNE TARVER, b. 24 AUG 1930 in Bethany Hospital of Kansas City, Kan., m. (1) Mr. Moswell, m. (2) Mr. Irwin, and d. 6 MAR 1986, bur. in Floral Hills Cem. of Kansas City, Mo.
   12763.   BEVERLY ELAINE TARVER, b. 6 JUN 1933 in Kansas City, Kan., d. in July 1934, bur. Highland Park Cem.

128. George Washington Alexander
(1872-1936)

George Washington Alexander, a son of William W. Alexander and his first wife Abigail Ann Elizabeth Minger, was born April 4, 1872 in Greeley, Anderson County, Kansas. He was a farmer, and primarily grew corn crops.

On April 1, 1903 he was married in Paola, Miami County, Kansas to Lena Mae Walthall, daughter of Samuel White "Link" Walthall and Mary Elizabeth Diehm. Lena was born October 17, 1881 in Beagle, Miami County, Kansas. On May 24, 1910 this family was enumerated on the Federal census for Liberty Township (sheet 16B) in Linn County, Kansas.

On January 29, 1923, Lena died in Osawatomie, Miami County, Kansas, and was buried in Lot 45 of Beagle Cemetery. On Sunday, June 28, 1936, G.W. fell dead in his own yard in Lane, Franklin County, Kansas, and was buried on Tuesday, June 30, 1936 in the Beagle Cemetery of Beagle, Kansas. Correspondants who assisted the compiler on this family included Flossie (Alexander) Sullins.

Children of George Washington Alexander and Lena Mae Walthall:[1]

1281.   HAROLD JAY ALEXANDER, b. 21 MAY 1904 in Beagle, Miami Co., Kan., d. of inflamation of the bowels on 14 AUG 1905 and bur. in Beagle Cem., *Gone but not forgotten.*
1282.   HARRY JOSEPH ALEXANDER, b. 6 FEB 1906 in Beagle, m. 22 AUG 1935 in Pleasanton, Linn Co., Kan. to May Sanders. May, b. 22 MAY 1905 in Centerville, Kan., daughter of Lewis M. Sanders and Sybil Emma Cochran. Harry owns a dairy farm. Children:[2]
   12821.   GWENNETH LOU ALEXANDER, b. 15 MAR 1939, m. c.1959 to Roger Mickel.
   12822.   HARRY LOWELL ALEXANDER, b. 16 MAR 1942 in Garnett, Anderson Co., Kan., m. (1) 3 JUL 1964 in Milvane, Sumner Co., Kan. to Vicki Lockhart by whom he had no children. Harry L. m. (2) 22 JUL 1970 in Overland Park, Johnson Co., Kan. to Connie (Kimble) Hays from whom he div. in 1985. Harry m. (3) 28 MAR 1987 in Pittsburg, Crawford Co., Kan. to Lorna Martin, daughter of John Martin and Regina Margaret Ashbacker, b. 26 APR 1949 in LaCrosse, Wisc. Harry was a school administrator, and a director of special education in the Wyandotte Co. school system. Child:
      128221.   MIKE HAYS ALEXANDER, b. 15 OCT 1973 in Overland Park.
1283.   FLOSSIE ABIGAIL ALEXANDER, b. 15 DEC 1907 in Beagle, d. 8 OCT 1991, bur. Osawatomie Cem., Miami Co., Kan., m. 15 MAR 1930 in Olathe, Johnson Co., Kan. to Walter R. Sullins, b. 2 DEC 1902, d. 10 JAN 1980, bur. Osawatomie Cem. Children:
   12831.   VIOLET SULLINS, m. (1) Mr. Bastian, res. near Bonner Springs, Kan., d. 15 MAY 1989, bur. 18 MAY at Osawatomie, Kan.
   12832.   RITA SULLINS.
   12833.   WALTER LEON SULLINS, b. 19 APR 1939, d. 2 DEC 2000, bur. Osawatomie Cem.
   12834.   MAX SULLINS.
1284.   VELMA ELIZABETH ALEXANDER, b. 2 JUL 1910 in Beagle, Kan., d. 17 DEC 1996, bur. Osawatomie Cem., m. 19 JUN 1934 in Greeley, Anderson Co., Kan. to Marvin W. Cuddy, b. 1905, d. 1967, bur. Osawatomie Cem. Child:
   12841.   LEONARD CUDDY, res. in Alexandria, Va.
1285.   KENNETH WOODROW ALEXANDER, b. 27 MAR 1913 in Parker, Linn Co., Kan., m. 13 JUN 1938 in Greeley, Kan. to Agnes Sophia Katzer. Kenneth was a carpenter by trade, and Agnes was interested in

---

[1] Information in part provided by Flossie (Alexander) Sullins, 15 JUN 1987.
[2] Information provided by these individuals at the Alexander Family reunion in Parker, Kan., August 1987.

crafting quilted and fabric goods.

1286. OTTO LAVERNE ALEXANDER, b. 18 FEB 1915 in Parker, m. 8 MAY 1938 in Wellsville, Franklin Co., Kan. to Lorene Elizabeth Husted. They reside on one of the old Alexander farms in Liberty Twp. of Parker. Child:
12861. CLYDE WILBUR ALEXANDER, b. 28 SEP 1942, unmarried.

1287. ELMO WALTER ALEXANDER, b. 13 MAY 1918 in Parker, m. (1) 1 JUN 1942 in Stockton Field, Calif. to Lillian Jean Johnson, and (2) Edith Rugole Wilburn. Children:
12871. DEBORAH ALEXANDER.
12872. DENISE ALEXANDER.
12873. DEDRIE ALEXANDER.
12874. DAWN ALEXANDER.

1288. HELEN LAVESTA ALEXANDER, b. 17 JAN 1921 in Parker, m. (1) Bill O'Malley, div. She m. (2) James F. Henry, and resided in Waynesville, Mo.

1289. ALBERT CHARLES ALEXANDER, b. 2 JAN 1923 in Parker, was twice married, and d. 7 SEP 1983 in a motorcycle accident in Topeka, Kan., bur. in Rochester Cem. of Topeka. When a child, Albert was adopted by Ray Warbritton and Flossie Walthall, and was first married to Frances (   ).

129. Thomas Jefferson Alexander
(1874-1960)

Thomas Jefferson Alexander, son of William W. Alexander and Abigail Ann Elizabeth Minger, was born March 29, 1874 in Linn County, Kansas. On February 14, 1899,[1] Thomas was married in Parker, Linn County, Kansas to Ella May Millard. He was a farmer.

Ella, a daughter of Ransom H. Millard and Ann Smith, was born in Missouri on August 29, 1875, and died of respiratory failure, about ½ mile north of Cherryvale, Montgomery County, Kansas on January 8, 1957 and was buried in the Fairview Cemetery there on January 12, 1957.

Thomas died October 12, 1960 of heart failure in Sunset Retreat Nursing Home of Cherryvale, Kansas, and was buried in the Fairview Cemetery on October 15, 1960. Correspondants who assisted the compiler on this family included Mary Ruth Hirni.

Children of Thomas Jefferson Alexander and Ella May Millard:[2]

1291. HENRY THOMAS ALEXANDER, b. 17 MAY 1901, d. 29 MAY 1967, bur. Fairfiew Cem. of Cherryvale, m. Effie Corrine Bussert, b. 5 JUN 1901, d. 8 OCT 1991. Child:
12911. DONALD LEE ALEXANDER, engineer, b. 2 MAY 1931 in Morehead, Neosho Co., Kan., m. 3 JUL 1954 in Ashland, Clark Co., Kan. to Elaine Bowling, daughter of Ben Bowling and Iva Sawyers, b. 9 MAY 1934 in Ashland, Kan. Children:
129111. MARK DAVIS ALEXANDER, b. 7 DEC 1955 in Emporia, Lyon Co., Kan. Unmarried.
129112. TRENT LEE ALEXANDER, b. 20 FEB 1958 in Emporia, m. 2 OCT 1976 to Pamela Miller. Children:
1291121. DREW L. ALEXANDER.
1291122. VANESSA ALEXANDER.
129113. DARRELL JAY ALEXANDER, b. 8 SEP 1961 in Parsons, Labette Co., Kan.
129114. TODD WAYNE ALEXANDER, b. 10 JUL 1966 in Parsons.

1292. DELLA PEARL ALEXANDER, b. 12 OCT 1903.

1293. EDITH MAY ALEXANDER, b. 1 APR 1909, m. Dennis (   ).

1294. WILLIAM LOUIS ALEXANDER, a minister, b. 22 SEP 1913.

1295. MARY RUTH ALEXANDER, b. 14 DEC 1915, m. 12 MAR 1935 to Raymond Hadley Hirni, b. 13 OCT 1912. Children:
12951. PHYLLIS ANN HIRNI, b. 25 NOV 1935, m. in September 1953 to Forrest Lee Wheatley.
12952. WILLIAM ANTONE HIRNI, b. 4 JUN 1938, m. (1) 2 JUL 1960 to Linda Gayle Townsend, and m. (2) 10 JUN 1965 to Esperanza Gertrude Tafoya.
12953. CLIFFORD RAY HIRNI, b. 4 OCT 1946, m. 5 OCT 1968 to Gretchen Ann Mason.

---

[1] Linn Co., Kan. Marriages, Bk. 7, p. 60.
[2] Information in part provided by Mary Ruth Hirni, 1820 Meadowlark Drive, Flagstaff AZ 86001 (29 JUN 1987), and from death certificates.

13. Elizabeth Ann (Alexander) Davis Vint
(1842-1910)

Elizabeth Ann Alexander, daughter of John Bevans Alexander and his wife Ann W. Roberts, was born in January 1842 in Rockbridge County, Virginia. She was first married by Stuart Taylor, M.G., on November 22, 1860 at Walker's Creek, Rockbridge County, to Campbell Robert Davis, a millwright, who was killed during the Civil War. Mr. Davis, a son of Ellis and Sallie Davis, was born in Rockbridge County, c.1833, and died on April 7, 1865 while on retreat in Amelia Courthouse, Virginia.[1]

On August 5, 1869, Elizabeth was remarried in Lexington, Rockbridge County, to William Vint.[2] Mr. Vint, a son of John Vint and Delilah Bodkin, was born in 1809 in Pendleton County, Virginia (now West Virginia), had been previously married to Elizabeth McQuain.

William and Elizabeth (Alexander) Vint were enumerated on the 1880 Federal census for Makin County, Illinois where it is believed they buried two young children, Eli Vint and Lee Vint. By 1895, the couple was residing in the city of Lane, Franklin County, Kansas, and were enumerated there in Pottawatomie Township, Franklin County, Kansas in 1900. William Vint was a farmer.

Elizabeth died December 15, 1910 in Lane, Kansas and was buried in the city cemetery just east of town. Correspondants who assisted the compiler on this family included Homer White.

Figure 10 - Elizabeth Ann (Alexander) Davis Vint

Known children of Elizabeth Ann Alexander:

131.   VIRGINIA C. "Jenny" DAVIS, b. 5 JUL 1865 in Rockbridge Co., Va., d. 8 MAY 1940 in Harrisonville, Cass Co., Mo.,[3] m. 5 JUN 1884 in Decatur, Ill. to William Henry Williams.

132.   IDA MAY VINT, b. 7 SEP 1870, d. 10 JUL 1944 in Osawatomie, Kan., and bur. in Lane, Kan., m. (1) 15 MAY 1891 to Arthur Paul, son of Lewis Paul and Exira Gates, b. c.1867, div. Ida m. (2) 30 SEP 1897 in Miami Co., Kan. to John Platt Hopwood, son of Charles Hopwood and Ruth Ann Antill, b. 10 AUG 1866 in Leavenworth Co., Kan. John d. 24 SEP 1947 in Osawatomie, and bur. in Row 9, Lot 9 of Lane Cem. Children:[4]

    1321.   CLINTON AUGUSTUS PAUL, b. ca. 1891, m. Anna (   ), and d. in New Haven, Conn.

    1322.   WILLIAM CLYDE PAUL, b. 1895, m. Bessie Muncie, d. 16 JUL 1951 in Independence, Jackson Co., Mo. He was bur. by Ott & Mitchell Funeral Home, 18 JUL 1951 in Floral Hills Cem. of Kansas City, Mo.

    1323.   JUANITA ESTHER HOPWOOD, b. 8 JUL 1898 in Cass Co., Mo., d. 16 DEC 1966 in a hospital in Ottawa, Kan., bur. in Princeton, Franklin Co., Kan., m. 2 JUN 1926 in Independence to Stephen D. Needham.

    1324.   MEXA EVA HOPWOOD, b. 23 APR 1901 in Lane, Kan., m. 14 JAN 1920 in Independence to Harry Alvin White. She d. 18 JAN 1974 in Garnett, Kan., and bur. in Lane. Harry, an insurance and real estate man, son of James Franklin White and Electa May Davis, b. 17 MAY 1896 in Lane, d. 30 SEP 1977 in Kansas University Medical Center in Kansas City, Kan., bur. in Row 9 Lot 9 of Lane Cem. He served in Co. K of the 137th Infantry Division during World War I. Children:

        13241.   LEO ALVIN WHITE, b. 6 MAR 1921 in Lane, m. in June 1944 to Mary Ellen King.

        13242.   DONALD DEAN WHITE, b. 11 OCT 1923 in Greeley, Anderson Co., Kan., m. 14 NOV 1941 in Kahoka, Mo. to Bettie June Duncan. Don d. 26 JUL 1987 in Osawatomie, Kan., and bur. in Green Valley Cem. there.

        13243.   HOMER GEROLD WHITE, b. 27 OCT 1931 in Miami Co., Kan., m. 20 OCT 1967 in Anderson Co., Kan. to Bertha Alma Evans.

        13244.   ROYDEN LAVERNE WHITE, b. 26 JUL 1934 in Miami Co., m. 20 FEB 1954 in Anderson Co. to Janet Elaine Kimball.

    1325.   FLORA[5] MAY "Flossie" HOPWOOD, b. 23 DEC 1903 in Lane, Kan., m. 15 JUN 1922 in Paola, Miami Co., Kan. to John William Burkdoll, son of Francis Alonzo Burkdoll and Margaret Needham, b. 7 MAY 1892

---

[1] Rockbridge Co. Va. Death Register.

[2] In a letter from Susan Jane Alexander [later Dukes] of Moffat's Creek, Augusta Co., Va., to her uncle William B. Alexander of Waynesboro, Va., dated 26 FEB 1873, she quips that she has not heard from William for some time, he is now in Kansas; they "was all well;" we heard from them. Lizzie is married again. She married an old man by the name of Vint, they live in Highland County; we have one of her little girls with us. I have not seen Lizzie for more than three years; it was three years last August since she was married."

[3] Information provided by Homer White of Lane, Kan., 7 APR 1988.

[4] Information provided by Homer White of Lane, Kan., 7 APR 1988.

[5] Or Florence, as provided two different ways by Homer White.

in Princeton, Franklin Co., Kan. Flora d. 1 AUG 1985 in Mission Hospital of Ottawa, Kan., bur. in Princeton. Children:

13251. BETTY JEAN BURKDOLL, b. 12 FEB 1924 in Lane, Kan., m. 2 OCT 1944 in Miami, Fla. to Harold Dean Kimball.

13252. LLOYD FRANCIS BURKDOLL, b. 22 JAN 1928 in Lane, m. 21 MAR 1950 in Ottawa to Anna Faye Shofner.

13253. JOHN ELWIN BURKDOLL, b. 26 JAN 1930 in Lane, m. 29 JUL 1949 in Ozark, Ark. to Virginia Lee Vaughn.

133. IRA VINT, b. 18 JUN 1872 in Highland Co., Va., d. 8 DEC 1946 in Lane, Kan., m. 27 OCT 1906 in Ottawa, Franklin Co., Kan. to Mary Eva Loch. During the time of the 1910 Federal census, Ira was living with his mother in Lane, Kan., and was head of his own household by 1915. Mary Eva b. c.1888 in Kansas, reportedly d. in San Diego, Calif. Children:

1331. NAOMI ELLEN VINT, b. 31 JUL 1907 in Lane, m. (1) 2 APR 1927 by J. Omnsted in Ottawa, Kan. to James W. Lathrop, age 20, of Ottawa, Kan. Naomi m. (2) Ira Vaughn, and d. in DEC 1976 in San Diego Co., Calif.

1332. JOHN W. "Jack" VINT, b. 25 JUL 1909 in Lane, Kan., m. (1) Frieda ( ), and d. JAN 1979 in San Diego Co., Calif.

134. ASA VINT, b. 10 AUG 1875 in Highland Co., Va.,[1] m. 12 JUN 1904 by A.D. Lewis in Lane, Franklin Co., Kan., to Mary Etta McCord, daughter of Daniel McCord and Mary Elizabeth Day, b. 4 MAY 1882 in Fontana, Kan., and d. 17 NOV 1924 of para typhoid in Hatcher's Hospital of Wellington, Sumner Co., Kan., bur. in Lane, Kan. Asa d. 23 JAN 1959 of cerebral apoplexy at Hatcher's Hospital, and bur. in Lane Cem. Child:

1341. O'DELLA VINT, m. Donald Cardinal.

135. ELI VINT, b. c.1878 in Macon Co., Ill., d. after 6 JUN 1880 and bur. in Macon Co.

136. LEE VINT, b. c.FEB 1880 in Macon Co., d. and was buried there.

137. EVA VINT, b. c.1882 in Macon Co.

14. Susan Jane (Alexander) Dukes
(1845-1934)

Susan Jane Alexander, a daughter of John Bevans Alexander and his wife Ann W. Roberts, was born February 6, 1845 in Rockbridge County, Virginia. Before her marriage, she often wrote letters to her uncle William Benjamin Alexander of Waynesboro, and it was through these letters that we have learned much about the daily life of the Alexander Family. In 1873, she resided four miles from Newport, Virginia on Walker's Creek, on Mr. Jarvis' place, and asked correspondants to address letters to her to Moffat's Creek. She used to make great sorghum cookes, according to Flossie (Alexander) Sullins.

On February 11, 1875, Susan was married by J.M. Schreckhire in Walker's Creek, Rockbridge County, to William Henry Dukes, a son of Stephen and Susan Dukes, who was born in January 1815[2] in White County, Tennessee.

The couple was enumerated on the 1880 Federal census for Walker's Creek Township, Rockbridge County, and by 1900 was enumerated in Mound Township (page 8) of Miami County, Kansas. The Federal census reveals to us that William Dukes was illiterate, and was a farmer.

William H. Dukes died April 27, 1908 in Kansas City, Kansas and was buried in the Mt. Hope Cemetery there. In 1910, Susan was residing with her brother W.W. Alexander in Liberty Township of Linn County, Kansas. Susan died August 13, 1934 of chronic intestinal nephritis at 1445 South Hydraulic Street in Wichita, Sedgwick County, Kansas and was buried August 14, 1934 in Mt. Hope Cemetery of Kansas City, Kansas. Correspondants who assisted the compiler on this family included Anna (Dukes) Knight.

Children of William Henry Dukes and Susan Jane Alexander:[3]

141. HENRY SYLVESTER DUKES, b. 22 NOV 1875 in Rockbridge Co., Va., m. 18 MAR 1903 by C.E. Creager, M.G., in Osawatomie, Miami Co., Kan. to Viola Frances Hand, daughter of J.W. and Fidelia S. Hand, b. 4 FEB 1879 in Van Buren Co., Iowa.[4] According to her newspaper obituary, Viola d. 12 JUL 1946 at the home of her sister, Mrs. R.L. Mount in Everest, Kan. and was bur. in Memorial Park Cem. of Kansas City, Kan. Viola had a sister Ida B. Chase of Glendale, Calif. Henry S. Dukes, a stationary engineer for the Kansas City Quartermaster Depot, d. 16 AUG 1946 at Nora-Rae Restorium at 309 Garfield Street in Kansas City, Mo. and bur.

---

[1] His Kansas death certificate gives the state of birth as Illinois.
[2] Homer White of Lane, Kan. provided 1839 as the birth year.
[3] Information in part provided by Anna (Dukes) Knight of Topeka, Kan.
[4] Howard Dukes reported to me that his mother's birthday was 4 MAY 1879.

19 AUG 1946 in Memorial Park Cem. north of Kansas City, Wyandotte Co., Kan.[1] The residence at the time of death was 1435 State St., Kansas City KS. Children:[2]

1411.   FERN DUKES, b. 22 FEB 1904 in Osawatomie, Miami Co., Kan., m. 2 JUN 1933 by O.E. Allison,[3] in the Washington Avenue Methodist Church of Kansas City, Kan. to Dr. Wallace W. Peterson. Fern Peterson d. 16 OCT 1935 after a collapse of the circulatory system in Asbury Hospital of Salina, Saline Co., Kan., and bur. 18 OCT 1935 in Smoky Hill Cem. near Lindsborg, Kan. Wallace W. Peterson, son Carl Peterson and Rebecca North, b. 6 NOV 1904 in Bridge Port, Kan.,[4] d. 8 JUL 1967 in Wichita, Kan., bur. in Elmwood Cem. near Lindsborg, Kan. Carl and Rebecca Peterson were bur. in Smoky Hill Cem. Children:

14111.   WENDELL CHARLES PETERSON (twin), b. 4 OCT 1935 in Salina, Kan., m. Kay Lain.

14112.   WARREN HENRY PETERSON (twin), b. 4 OCT 1935, m. Sharlene Dee Savage.

1412.   EARL HAND DUKES, b. 16 MAR 1907 in Kansas City, Wyandotte Co., Kan., m. (1) 18 MAY 1930 in Hutchinson, Reno Co., Kan.[5] to Mary Bridget Ernest, div. JAN 1950.[6] Mary, daughter of T.E. O'Hara and wife Marguerite Jeffries, b. 26 JUN 1901 in Wellington, Kan., d. of heart disease 15 MAY 1964 in St. Francis Hospital of Wichita, Sedgwick Co., Kan., bur. 18 MAY 1964 in Calvary Cem. there. Her residence at the time of death was 2844 Wellington Place, Wichita KS. Earl d. 31 OCT 1967 in Wichita, and bur. in Kechi Cem. of Kechi, Kan. Adopted children:

14121a.   William "Billy" Dukes.

14122a.   Patrick Joseph Dukes.

1413.   HAROLD ELLIS DUKES, d.inf.

1414.   HOWARD HENRY DUKES, b. 29 MAY 1912 in Atchison, Atchison Co., Kan., d. 23 MAY 1995 in Johnson Co., Kan. At the time of his father's death in 1946, Howard resided at 205 Brush Creek Blvd., in Kansas City, Mo.

142.   JOHN WILLIAM DUKES, b. 20 DEC 1878[7] in Walker's Creek, Rockbridge Co., Va., was m. 19 FEB 1905 by J.W. Eldred in Sedgwick Co., Kan. to May Hume. The family was enumerated on the 1910 Federal census (E.D. 130, line 143) for Wichita, Kan. John d. 27 NOV 1963 at the age of 85 years and 26 days in Wichita County Hospital, and bur. 30 NOV 1963 in Hillside Cem. there. May, a daughter of William Angel Hume and Mary Winegar, b. 25 MAY 1882 in Chambersburg, Ill., d. 13 JAN 1964 at the age of 81 years, 7 months and 18 days at 2018 S. Washington St., Wichita, Kan., and bur. 16 JAN 1964 in Hillside Cem. there. Children:

1421.   WILLIAM BERNARD DUKES, b. 2 MAY 1906 in Kansas City, Wyandotte Co., Kan., m. 21 SEP 1929 by W.J. Shull in Newton, Harvey Co., Kan. to Mary Joy Killough, div. FEB 1947 while residing at 2303 South Mosley in Wichita, Kan. Mary, daughter of Aaron Bilderback Killough and wife Annie Elizabeth Miller, b. 28 AUG 1903 in Woodward Co., Okla.[8] On 29 NOV 1943 at Ft. Leavenworth, Kan., William was inducted into military service with the U.S. Army, and during such service, painted automobiles. He was honorably discharged 12 NOV 1945. William d. 4 AUG 1973 at Green Meadows Nursing Home in Haysville, Kan. and bur. in Maple Grove Cem. of Wichita, Kan. Mary J., a retired cook, d. of pneumonia 23 NOV 1987 in Hillhaven, 932 No. Topeka Street in Wichita, Kan. and bur. in Mt. Washington Cem. of Lenapah, Nowata Co., Okla. Children:

14211.   ANNA MAY DUKES, b. 30 APR 1930 in Wichita, Kan., m. 17 AUG 1946 by C.A. Lockhart, J.P., in Wichita to Fred Henry Knight,[9] son of John Jordan Knight and Zola Adaline Driver, b. 2 NOV 1927 in Claremore, Rogers Co., Okla.,[10] d. 8 JUN 1983 in Wichita, Kan. and bur. in Maple Grove Cem. there. Anna resided at 3120 South Richmond Street in Wichita, suffered from multiple sclerosis, d. 12 MAR 1992, bur. Maple Grove Cem. Children:

142111.   JOYCE ANN KNIGHT, b. 17 SEP 1947 in Wichita, Kan.

142112.   DONALD WAYNE KNIGHT, b. 17 FEB 1949 in Wichita, Kan.

142113.   JOHN WILLIAM KNIGHT, b. 7 DEC 1951 in Wichita, Kan.

---

[1] Information in part provided through a telephone conversation with Howard H. Dukes in August 1987, and Anna (Dukes) Knight.

[2] Information in part provided by Anna (Dukes) Knight, February 1988.

[3] Wyandotte Co., Kan. Marriages, Bk. 74, p. 548.

[4] According to information from Anna (Dukes) Knight, the father Carl Peterson b. 13 OCT 1872, and d. 13 MAY 1950 at Lindsborg, Kan. where bur. in Smoky Hill Cem. Rebecca North, to whom Carl was married c.1903, was b. c.1880 in Iowa, d. 7 OCT 1935 in Salina, Kan. and bur. in Smoky Hill Cem.

[5] Reno Co., Kan. Marriages, Bk. 20, p. 91.

[6] Divorce papers are on file in the District Court of Sedgwick Co., Kan., Case #A31554.

[7] Birthdate stated as 1 NOV 1878 in funeral home records provided by Anna (Dukes) Knight.

[8] From information provided by Anna (Dukes) Knight, we learn that Aaron B. Killough was born July 12, 1874 in Emporia, Kan. and died April 29, 1954 in Lenapah, Okla., bur. Mt. Washington Cem. there. Annie E. Miller, born September 7, 1877 in Welsey, Kan., died November 7, 1955 in Lenapah, Okla., bur. in Mt. Washington Cem.

[9] Sedgwick Co., Kan. Marriages, Bk. XX, p. 667.

[10] Anna (Dukes) Knight's information adds that John J. Knight, b. 18 DEC 1898 in Claremore, Okla., d. 4 MAR 1969 in Wichita, Kan., bur. in Resthaven Cem. there, m. there 19 FEB 1921 to Zola Adaline Driver, b. 15 MAY 1904 in Aurora, Ark., d. 28 OCT 1963 in Claremore, Okla., and bur. in Woodlawn Cem. there.

14212. DORIS ANN DUKES, b. 2 APR 1937 in Wichita, m. (1) Ernest L. Rutherford, and m. (2) Robert Henry Bash.

1422. MARVIN HARDIN DUKES, mechanic, b. 20 APR 1910 in Wichita, Sedgwick Co., Kan.,[1] lived in Las Vegas, Clark Co., Nev., d. 21 JUL 1976 of congestive heart failure in Sunrise Hospital of Las Vegas, bur. 23 JUL 1976 in Paradise Memorial Gardens there. Marvin m. 8 NOV 1933 by J. Henry Hornung, clergyman, in Wichita, Kan. to Alice Margaret Stringer,[2] daughter of Elmer Stringer and Lois Harris, b. 14 JAN 1919 in Oklahoma, d. of cancer in Sunrise Hospital of Las Vegas at 11:35 p.m. on 10 SEP 1972, bur. in Paradise Memorial Gardens. Alice was a sales auditor for department stores, and resided at 3208 E. Owens Avenue in Las Vegas. Children b. in Wichita, Kan.:

14221. KENNETH PAUL DUKES, b. 19 JUN 1934.
14222. WAYNE EDWARD DUKES, b. 21 JAN 1936, d. February 1936.
14223. BETTY JEAN DUKES, b. 8 JAN 1938.

1423. WALTER HENRY DUKES, b. 15 FEB 1913 in Sedgwick, Sedgwick Co., Kan., d. 4 MAY 1993 in Wichita, Kan., m. 11 APR 1937 by Samuel W. Keller, in Newton, Harvey Co., Kan. to Marjorie Lucille Locke, b. 18 DEC 1916, d. 30 AUG 2005 in Wichita. Child:

14231. LARRY EUGENE DUKES, b. 18 OCT 1942 in Wichita, Kan.

1424. MAYFRED ETHEL DUKES, b. 19 SEP 1915 in Sedgwick, m. (1) 7 NOV 1934 by C.V. Pearce, in Wichita to Wavil Dow McClurg,[3] div. MAY 1943.[4] Mr. McClurg, son of William Harvey McClurg and E. Pearl Hunter, b. 1 FEB 1896 in Scranton, Iowa, d. 12 NOV 1955 in Wichita, bur. in White Chapel Cem. there. Ethel m. (2) on 1 JUN 1943 in Kansas City, Mo. by Bernard W. Gnefken to Harold Simpson, b. 10 JAN 1922. She d. of bronchial pneumonia 14 FEB 1972 at Crawford Nursing Home in Wichita, and bur. in Hillside Cem. of Sedgwick, Kan. Children:

14241a. Barbara Jean McClurg, adopted, b. 18 AUG 1938 in Wichita, Kan.
14242. DENNIS HAROLD SIMPSON, b. 1 OCT 1947 in Wichita, d. 2 JAN 1981.
14243. RONALD PAUL SIMPSON, b. 23 JAN 1951 in Wichita.

1425. HAROLD PAUL DUKES, b. 1 JUL 1920 in Sedgwick, d. 3 NOV 1998 in Cedar Vale, Kan. He m. (1) 14 FEB 1938 in Wichita to Nellie Beaver, div. 1940, m. (2) 9 NOV 1943 in Wichita to Maxine Oliver. Children:

14251. BARBARA JEAN DUKES, b. 18 AUG 1938 in Wichita.
14252. GERALD DENNIS DUKES, b. 28 JUL 1946 in Kan.
14253. DONALD LEE DUKES, b. 12 OCT 1947 in Wichita.

1426. DOROTHY AILEEN DUKES, b. 23 JUL 1923 in Sedgwick, m. (1) 25 AUG 1938 in Wichita to Archie Monroe Ailshie, son of Asie Ailshie and Bessie Wampler, b. 20 JUN 1916 in Ford Co., Kan., d. 12 JUL 1977 of lung cancer in Wichita, bur. Hillside Cem. Dorothy m. (2) on 30 MAR 1978 in Wichita to J.L. Wadkins. Children:

14261. SHARON JANICE AILSHIE, b. 23 DEC 1940 in Wichita, m. Leroy L. Elliss.
14262. CAROLYN ELIZABETH AILSHIE, b. 2 FEB 1942 in Wichita, m. Mitch Ahlefeld.

143. GEORGE F. DUKES, b. in April 1881 in Va., was reportedly m. twice, first to Lena (   ). No further information.

144. GERTRUDE (or Gertie) DUKES, b. NOV 1883 in Va., and d. in Mt. Orab, Brown Co., Ohio,[5] m. Newton Ellis.

16. James Newton Alexander
(1851-1930)

James Newton Alexander, a son of John Bevans Alexander and Ann W. Roberts, was born June 23, 1851 in Rockbridge County, Virginia. He was most often referred to as Newton Alexander. On November 18, 1879, Newton was married in Lexington, Rockbridge County, to Martha Jane Patterson. Martha, a daughter of J. and C. Patterson, of Virginia, was born September 24, 1847 [or 9] in Rockbridge County. This couple was enumerated on the 1880 Federal census for Walker's Creek Township, Rockbridge County, and they are shown on the 1910 Federal census for Potawatomie Twp. of Franklin County, Kansas. He is listed on the 1915 enumeration for Franklin County, Kansas, as a farmer.

Martha died on Wednesday, January 23, 1901 in Lane, Franklin County, Kansas, and was buried January 24, 1901 in the city cemetery of Greeley, Anderson County, Kansas. James Newton Alexander died September 26, 1930 in

---

[1] Other information submitted by Anna (Dukes) Knight indicates Marvin was b. 20 APR 1910 in Wichita, Kan.
[2] Sedgwick Co., Kan. Marriages, Bk. JJ, p. 769.
[3] Sedgwick Co., Kan. Marriages, Bk. KK, p. 676.
[4] Divorce papers on file in the District Court of Sedgwick Co., Kan.
[5] Information from Homer White of Lane, Kan.

Lane, Kansas and was buried September 28 in Row 11 Lot 3 of Lane Cemetery.[1] He was a member of the United Brethren Church. Correspondants who assisted the compiler on this family included Barbara Underhill and Homer White.

Children of James Newton Alexander and Martha Jane Patterson:[2]

161.   JACOB ALEXANDER, d.inf. Rockbridge Co., Va.
162.   GERTRUDE ALEXANDER, b. 19 JUL 1885, d. 16 SEP 1889 and bur. in Greeley Cem., Anderson Co., Kan.
163.   JAMES WILLIAM "Bill" ALEXANDER, b. 4 APR 1886/7 in Rockbridge Baths, Rockbridge Co., m. 2 SEP 1917 in Lane, Franklin Co., Kan., to Susan R. Horn.[3] Bill d. 8 JUL 1959 in Ottawa, Franklin Co., Kan. and bur. in the Lane Cem. "Susie," daughter of George Washington Horn and Emma Caldwell, b. 26 JUL 1895 in Bakersfield, Ozark Co., Mo., d. 13 DEC 1979 in a nursing home in Ottawa, Kan. She was buried in Lane Cem. Children:
    1631.   GEORGE NEWTON ALEXANDER, b. 27 JUN 1918 in Lane, d. 27 DEC 2004 in Lane, m. 22 AUG 1962 in Mound City, Linn Co., Kan. to Mrs. Corina Belle Caylor McCollough.
    1632.   HELEN LOUISE ALEXANDER, b. 30 DEC 1919 in Lane, d. 19 JUL 2011 in Ottawa, m. 10 MAR in Ottawa to Harold Guy.
    1633.   JOSEPH D. (Donald or Donnel) ALEXANDER, b. 6 OCT 1925 in Lane, m. 6 OCT 1945 in Ottawa to Katherine E. LaFollette. Joe himself wasn't sure of his middle name, so prefered to use only an initial.
    1634.   JAMES WILLIAM ALEXANDER, JR., b. 24 AUG 1922 in Lane, missing in action from service in Korea, declared dead 31 DEC 1953.
164.   ANNA MAE ALEXANDER, b. 4 OCT 1888 in Lane, m. 27 FEB 1916 in Lane to Eli Brockus, son of Thomas B. Brockus and Mary Holloway, b. 14 JUN 1874 in Wisc. and d. 10 DEC 1954 in Rantoul, Kan. And bur. 3 days later in Lane Cem. "Mae" d. in the Crestview Nursing Home of Ottawa, Kan., 11 DEC 1963 and bur. 15 DEC 1963 in Lane Cem. The informant listed on her death certificate was Mrs. Ernest (Nellie) Miller of Rantoul, Kan. Children:[4]
    1641.   MARTHA EMILINE BROCKUS, b. 16 JAN 1918 near Lane, Miami Co., Kan., m. 27 MAR 1943 in Wichita to Perry W. Heckman. No issue.
    1642.   THOMAS NEWTON BROCKUS, truck driver, b. 11 DEC 1919 near Lane, d. 21 JUN 1997 at Wichita, bur. White Chapel Cem. there, m. (1) 8 MAR 1941 to Rose Finch Henry, div., and m. (2) before 1956 to Betty Jo Richey, d. 1986. Children:
      16421. ROGER NEWTON BROCKUS, b. 5 OCT 1941.
      16422. NORMAN JAMES BROCKUS, b. 28 SEP 1949.
      16423. THOMAS BROCKUS (twin), b. 22 OCT 1956.
      16424. TONYA BROCKUS (twin), b. 22 OCT 1956.
      16425. BRYAN BROCKUS, b. 1 MAY 1961.
      16426. JIM BROCKUS, b. 14 FEB 1963.
    1643.   CLIFFORD WAYNE BROCKUS, b. 23 SEP 1921 near Lane, d. 28 JAN 1993, bur. Princeton Cem. at Princeton, Kan., m. 27 APR 1942 to Eunice Finch, b. 9 JUL 1925, d. 21 JAN 2006, bur. Princeton Cem. Children:
      16431. DELORES JEAN BROCKUS, b. in DEC 1944, m. Mr. Evans, and d. 20 FEB 1976.
      16432. RONALD WAYNE BROCKUS, b. 30 AUG 1947, d. 5 SEP 1960, bur. Princeton Cem.
      16433. RICHARD DALE BROCKUS, b. 20 FEB 1958.
      16434. NANCY SUE BROCKUS, b. 21 JAN 1964, m. Mr. Collins.
    1644.   NELLIE MARIE BROCKUS, b. 31 DEC 1924 in Richmond, Franklin Co., Kan., d. 15 SEP 2002 in Rantoul, Kan., bur. Lane Cem., m. 27 MAR 1940 in Ottawa, Kan. to Ernest Alva Miller, b. 29 JAN 1917, d. 2 NOV 1994, bur. Lane Cem. Children:
      16441. DONALD EUGENE MILLER, b. 31 DEC 1941.
      16442. CAROLYN JEAN MILLER, b. 27 SEP 1943, m. Mr. Turley.
    1645.   ELDON EUGENE BROCKUS, b. 12 MAR 1927 near Princeton, Franklin Co., Kan., d. 16 MAR 1993 near Montgomery Co., Tex., m. Mrs. Della (Bickerstaff) Dancaster. Child:
      16451. ELDON RAY BROCKUS, b. 24 FEB 1954.

---

[1] Gravemarker, Lane Cemetery [note that dates are incorrect]: J. NEWTON ALEXANDER / 1849-1929.
[2] Information in part provided by Homer White, 16 AUG 1987; and Barbara Underhill, July 1987.
[3] Franklin Co., Kan. Marriages, Bk. G, p. 243.
[4] Letter, Nellie Miller (Ottawa, Kan., 4 AUG 1988).

2. ELEANOR TULL (ALEXANDER) THACKER
(1805-1885)

Eleanor Tull Alexander, eldest daughter of William Alexander and his wife Ann Bevans, was born in Virginia on December 26, 1805, presumably in Rockingham County. We know very little about her life, but know that she was mother to a dozen children. On October 20, 1823 in Port Republic, Rockingham County, William Alexander signed a statement as witnessed by Stephen Harnsberger, giving consent for William Thacker to marry his daughter Eleanor T. Alexander. William Thacker and Eleanor T. Alexander were married the same day. Mr. Thacker was born March 10, 1803, based on his grave marker that is found in Dayton Cemetery of Rockingham County, near Port Republic, Rockingham County, Virginia. He was a son of John and Frances[1] Thacker.

The family was enumerated on the 1850 (page 52) and 1860 (#2045/2003, p. 618) Federal census for Rockingham County. On July 25, 1870 the family was enumerated on the Federal census for Central Township (page 1) in Rockingham County. The Thacker Family has roots in Goochland County.[2]

William Thacker died of pneumonia at the age of 77 years, 4 months and 28 days on August 8, 1880 in Dayton, Rockingham County, and was buried in Row 13A of the cemetery there.[3] He was a farmer (1860 census) and a tanner. Eleanor Thacker died April 1, 1885, aged 79y 3m 5d, and was buried in the Dayton Cemetery.[4]

Children of William Thacker and Eleanor Tull Alexander:

21. MARY ANN THACKER, b. 31 MAR 1825,[5] in Clover Hill, Rockingham Co., Va., m. 23 APR 1846 in Rockingham Co. to Selah F. Denton. Selah d. 18 MAR 1895 of gangreen.[6] Mary Ann d. 13 OCT 1897 after being attacked by robbers[7] in Rockingham Co., and bur. in Arrey Family Cem.[8] in Rockingham Co., located at the top of a hill on Route 722 where it intersects Route 620 in Rockingham Co. Selah F. Denton, b. 15 JAN 1822, bur. in Arrey Family Cem. Child:
    211.   JAMES WILLIAM DENTON, b. 19 MAR 1847, d. 6 JUN 1883,[9] m. 3 APR 1870 to Elizabeth Josephine Kersh, b. 5 DEC 1849, d. 5 APR 1929,[10] both bur. at Friedens United Church of Christ Cem., Friedens, Va. Children:
        2111.   CHARLES LEE DENTON, b. 21 FEB 1871, d. 5 NOV 1934, m. 18 OCT 1898 to Emma Susan Huffman, b. 28 OCT 1871, d. 12 JUN 1943; both bur. St. Jacobs Spaders Lutheran Church Cem., Mt. Crawford, Rockingham Co., Va. Children:
            21111.   LUCY DENTON, b. 12 AUG 1900, d. 11 SEP 1988, m. Allen E. Claxton, b. 1 OCT 1901, d. 26 SEP 1966, both bur. at St. Jacobs Spaders Lutheran Church Cem.
            21112.   LILLIAN VIRGINIA DENTON, b. 21 MAY 1902, d. 16 JAN 1944, m. 16 AUG 1928 to Louis J. Keagy, b. 1907, d. 1998; both bur. at St. Jacobs Spaders Lutheran Church Cem. Son:
                211121.   WINFRED DENTON KEAGY, b. 9 JUL 1930, m. 27 APR 1951 to Margaret Elizabeth Skelton, b. 17 MAY 1932.
        2112.   ALICE F. DENTON, b. 22 NOV 1872, d. 18 FEB 1960, m. Robert E. Pirkey, b. 11 MAR 1873, d. 7 APR 1950; both bur. at Friedens United Church of Christ Cem.
        2113.   MARY J. DENTON, b. 21 JUN 1880, d. 5 FEB 1959, m. Edward J. Shaver, b. 22 NOV 1872, d. 15 APR 1950; both bur. at Friedens United Church of Christ Cem.
22. SARAH JANE THACKER, b. 8 JAN 1827 in Clover Hill, Va., d. 23 APR 1904 and bur. in Row 14 of Dayton Cem.
23. JAMES MORGAN THACKER, b. 22 OCT 1828 in Clover Hill, m. 13 APR 1852 in Rockingham Co. to Barbara Byrd. James d. 6 JUL 1896 and bur. in Ottobein Cem. of Rockingham Co.[11] Barbara, b. 4 MAY 1832, d. 7 DEC 1901 and bur. in Ottobein Cem. Children, order uncertain:

---

[1] May be the same Frances Thacker who is recorded in the coffin book of Mr. William B. Alexander of Waynesboro, Va., wherein it is stated "Frances Thacker died May 29, 1867."

[2] Charles Hughes Hamlin, The Thacker Genealogy, 1635-1870 (Richmond: By the Author, 1964), at the Library of Virginia in Richmond, Va.

[3] Gravestone, Dayton Cemetery: WILLIAM THACKER / Born / Mar. 10, 1803 / Died / Aug. 8, 1880 / Aged / 77 Yr. 4 Mo. & 28d.

[4] Gravestone, Dayton Cemetery: ELEANOR T. / THACKER, / Born / Dec. 26, 1805. / Died / Apr. 1, 1885. / Aged / 79 Yr. 3 Mo. & 5 ds.

[5] Date from tombstone, however a date of 18 FEB 1825 has been provided by Hillard J. Hayzlett, from a Bible record.

[6] In a letter from Fannie Grabill to her uncle William B. Alexander, dated 4 APR 1895, she notes that after the death of Selah Denton, widow Mary planned to live with her grandson Charley Denton and his mother.

[7] In a letter from Kate Moubray to her uncle William B. Alexander, dated 8 MAR 1898, she describes the death of Mary Ann Denton: She was a widow and lived all alone. One evening she went to the barn to milk and attend to her stock, when two masked men caught her, searched her pockets, put a pistol to her head and told her if she hollered they would kill her; they put a handkerchief in her mouth, threw a sack over her face; one of them held her while the other searched the house. They said money was what they were after. They got between 40-50 dollars and then left her; but the excitement was too much for her; she went into heart trouble and after a lingering spell she died; poor thing certainly did suffer.

[8] These grave markers are now found in the Friedens United Church of Christ Cem., at Friedens, Rockingham Co., Va.

[9] Death date inscribed on the cemetery stone, but information provided by Elizabeth (Denton) Keagy indicates death occurred 6 JUN 1883.

[10] Information from cemetery records, Elizabeth (Denton) Keagy has provided the death date as 6 APR 1928.

[11] Information in part provided by Russell Thacker of Woodstock, Va.

231.   MARY ANN THACKER, b. c.JUL 1856 in Rockingham Co.

232.   JOSEPH BYRD THACKER, b. c.JUN 1858 in North Mountain, Rockingham Co., m. 13 AUG 1879 in that county to Elizabeth Blain.

233.   LEVI J. THACKER, b. 12 MAR 1861, m. 25 DEC 1884 in Rockingham Co. to Virginia Walters. Levi d. 20 SEP 1938 and bur. in Ottobein Cem.

234.   MARY VIRGINIA THACKER, b. 15 FEB 1864 in Rockingham Co.

235.   HENRY THACKER, m. Virginia (   ).

236.   HESTER J. "Hetty" THACKER, b. 19 MAY 1869, d. 26 OCT 1922, m. 7 NOV 1895 in Rockingham Co. to Solomon C. Wenger, b. 8 DEC 1857, d. 10 OCT 1920, son of Daniel W. Wenger (1820-1889) and Sarah H. Coffman (1821-1897); both bur. in Pleasant View Mennonite Cem. at Routes 732 and 736 near Dayton, Va. Ten children, of whom:

    2361.   SARAH E. WENGER, b. 1905, d. 1905, bur. Pleasant View Mennonite Cem.

    2362.   Infant Wenger, b. 1914, d. 1914, bur. Pleasant View Mennonite Cem.

237.   JOHN THACKER.

    2371.   DELBERT R. THACKER, b. 1904, d. 1999, m. M. Gertrude Good, b. 1904, d. 1984, both bur. Weavers Mennonite Church Cem. of Harrisonburg, Va.

    23711. DONALD THACKER, of Harrisonburg.

238.   NEWTON S. THACKER, b. c.1872, m. Eliza J. Adams, and d. in 1945. Newton bur. in Beaver Creek Brethren Cem. on Road 752 in Rockingham Co. Eliza, b. 1871, d. 1960, bur. in Beaver Creek Cem. Children, order uncertain:

    2381.   GUY NEWTON THACKER, b. 1895, m. Katie Coffman, and bur. in 1962 in Beaver Creek Brethren Cem.

    2382.   Infant THACKER, d. 4 NOV 1898 and bur. in Beaver Creek Cem.

    2383.   CARL THACKER, b. 1 FEB 1900, d. 10 FEB 1910 and bur. in Ottobine Cem.

    2384.   RUSSELL JENNINGS THACKER, b. 22 SEP 1900, d. 24 SEP 1991, bur. East Lawn Memorial Gardens in Harrisonburg, Va., m. 27 OCT 1921 in Rockingham Co. to Ella Dorothy Evers.

    2385.   FLOYD HUBERT THACKER, m. 15 APR 1929 in Rockingham Co. to Goldie Raymond Caricofe.

    2386.   NORMAN ROBERT THACKER, b. 27 APR 1907, d. 29 JAN 1966, m. 1 JAN 1935 in Rockingham Co. to Catherine Susan Caricofe, b. 3 APR 1907, d. 11 SEP 1949, both bur. Oak Lawn Cem. of Bridgewater, Va. Children:

       23861. NORMA JANE THACKER, b. 2 DEC 1937, d. 29 FEB 2008 in Harrisonburg, Va., m. (1) Carl R. Dean, Sr., and m. (2) to Rome Benjamin Hensley, Jr., b. 1926, d. 1982. Norma and Rome were bur. in Mt. Olivet Cem. of McGaheysville, Rockingham Co., Va.

       23862. ELSIE THACKER, m. _____ Armentrout.

       23863. DAVID THACKER.

       23864. BARBARA THACKER, m. _____ Shoemaker.

       23865. PEGGY THACKER, m. _____ Heatwole.

24. FRANCES ELIZABETH "Fanny" THACKER, b. 25 JUN 1830 in Clover Hill, Va., m. 18 NOV 1855 in Rockingham Co. to John Henry Grabill. She d. 7 AUG 1898, bur. Dayton Cem.[1] Child:

    241.   MARY ELLEN GRABILL, b. 27 JUN 1857 at Mt. Clinton, Va., and d. on 18 APR 1923 of chronic nephritis, aged 65y 7m and 21d at Singers Glen, Rockingham Co. She lived with her aunt Kate, and bur. 19 APR 1923 in the Dayton Cem.

25. JOHN WESLEY THACKER, b. 10 JUN 1832 in Clover Hill, Va., d. 4 MAY 1880, bur. Pisgah Cem. of Perry Co., Ohio, m. 11 DEC 1862 to Catherine McCrary, b. 1864, d. 1884, bur. Pisgah Cem. We have a letter written by John in 1869 from Brownsville, Fayette Co., Pa. Child:

    251.   MARTHA GRUBB THACKER, b. 1863, d. 1888, bur. Pisgah Cem.

26. STEPHEN HANK THACKER, b. 8 JUN 1834 in Clover Hill, m. (1) 29 OCT 1857 in Rockingham Co. to Emma Applegate. Emma was a daughter of T. and H. Applegate, b. 11 MAY 1834, d. 28 SEP 1860 aged 26y 4m and 17d. She was bur. in Ottobein Cem. of Rockingham Co. Stephen d. 31 JAN 1914 near Franklin, W.Va. Children:

    261.   ROSA THACKER, b. 5 SEP 1858, d. 26 MAY 1878, aged 16y 8m and 21d and bur. in Ottobein Cem.

    262.   CHARLES S.H. THACKER, b. 15 SEP 1860, d. 2 FEB 1861, aged 4m and 17d and bur. in Ottobein Cem.

27. SAMUEL "HENNING" THACKER, b. 9 JUL 1836 in Clover Hill. A Henning Thacker was married to "the widow Green" and lived in Basic City, later incorporated as part of Waynesboro. He d. 2 JUL 1895.

28. MARTHA ELLEN THACKER, b. 12 MAY 1838 in Va., d. 10 FEB 1921, aged 82y 8m 28d, bur. Dayton Cem., m. 27 MAR 1877 in Rockingham Co. to Jefferson Fries, b. 10 SEP 1834, d. 28 MAY 1919, aged 84y 8m 18d, bur.

---

[1] In a letter dated 2 JUL 1894, Fannie Grabill writes here uncle William B. Alexander of the improvements in the little town of Dayton: "The Presbyterians are going to bild a church hear this summer, they have organised a class too weaks ago they have a good class; our little town is improving very fast. Mr. Briant has put up a larg[e] hotel on the corner strait across frome our house; Mr. Helms has a larg[e] carriag[e] house on the other side of the street and a drug store; there are five stores and will son hav[e] five churches."

Dayton Cem.
29. LYDIA CATHERINE "Kate" THACKER,[1] b. 18 APR 1841 in Singers Glen, m. 10 NOV 1863 in Rockingham Co. to Benjamin W. Moubray, d. 24 APR 1900, aged 61y 1m 21d, bur. Singers Glen Cem. In 1898 they lived in Singers Glen, Rockingham Co. "Kate" d. of heart trouble complicated by asthma, 24 NOV 1927 and bur. in St. John's Lutheran Cem. at Singers Glen in Rockingham Co., 26 NOV 1927. Children:
    291. WILLIAM OTTERBINE MOUBRAY, b. 14 NOV 1870, m. Lena Myers, and d. 20 SEP 1951. He is bur. in St. John's Lutheran Cem. Child:
        2911. Daughter MOUBRAY, m. Virgil Mathias, of Mathias, W.Va.
    292. MARY ALICE MOUBRAY, b. 30 NOV 1872 in Mt. Clinton, m. Aldine K. McMullen, son of Stephen McMullen and Mary Ann Daugherty, b. 25 MAR 1865, d. 25 APR 1943. "Alice" was bedridden for 14 years, d. 11 JUL 1935 of chronic arthritis, and was marked with multiple bed sores and secondary infection. Both bur. in Singers Glen Cem. Child:
        2921. LEOLA D. McMULLEN, b. 24 APR 1909, d. 10 NOV 1997, bur. Singers Glen Cem.
2(10). WILLIAM HOUCK THACKER, b. 23 APR 1843 in Va., d. 14 NOV 1865.
2(11). REBECCA CAROLINE THACKER, b. 14 MAY 1845 in Va., d. 9 AUG 1910, bur. Dayton Cem., m. (1) 26 DEC 1875 in Rockingham Co. as the second wife of St. Clair Detamore, town sergeant of Dayton, b. 24 JAN 1825, d. 15 JAN 1906, bur. Dayton Cem. Rebecca m. (2) 11 NOV 1908 to William Berry. The 1900 Federal census for Dayton shows that Rebecca was the mother of no children.
2(12). MARGARET "Maggie" ADALINE THACKER, b. 15 JUL 1847 in Ottobein, Rockingham Co., d. 16 OCT 1934, bur. Dayton Cem., m. 9 JAN 1898 in Rockingham Co., to Abraham Whitmer, b. 22 MAY 1832, d. 26 MAR 1912, bur. Dayton Cem.

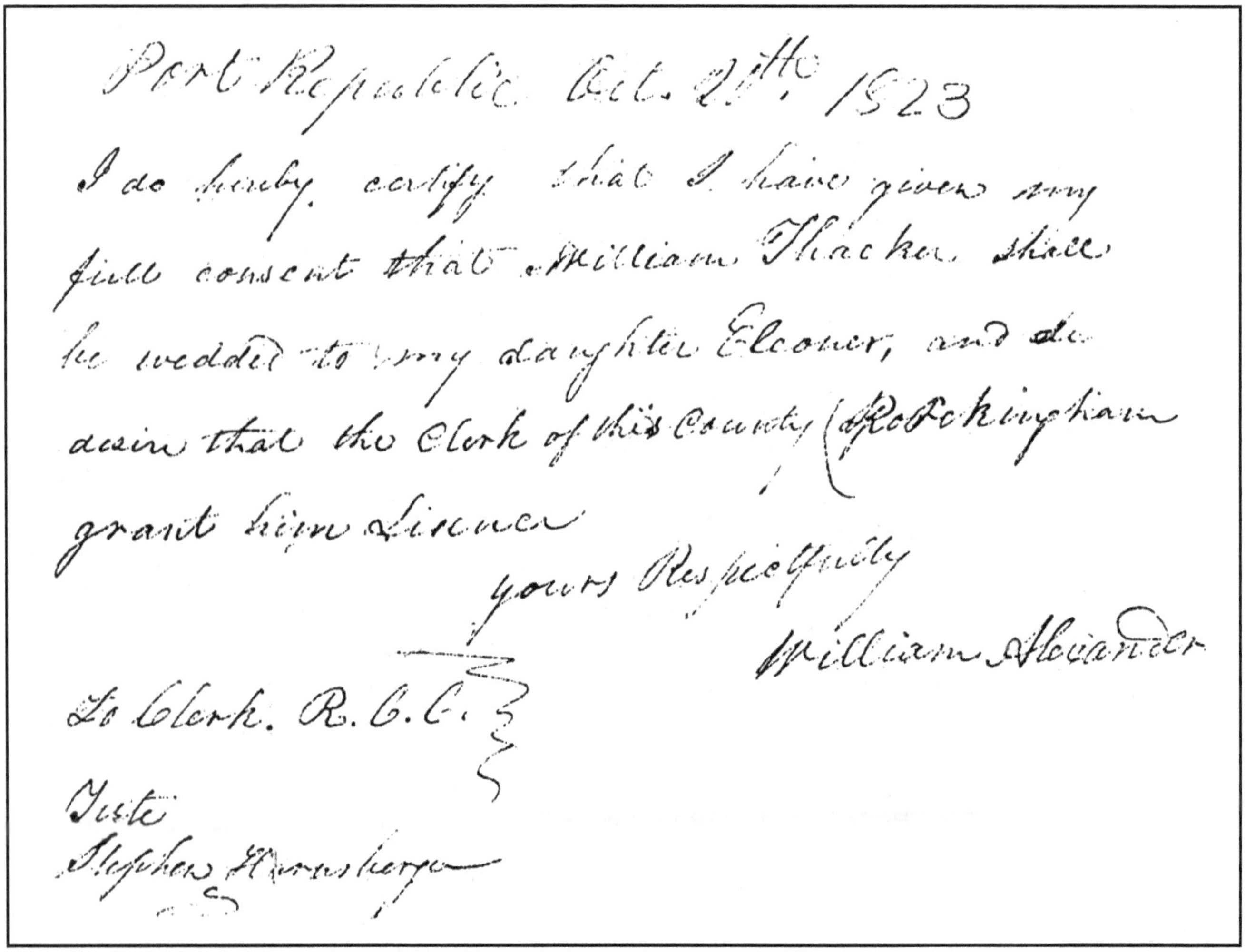

Figure 11 - Parental consent for marriage of William Thacker to Eleanor Tull Alexander, 1823

[1] It is "Kate L. Moubray" on her cemetery stone.

6. MOSES LISTON ALEXANDER
(1815-1902)

Moses Liston[1] Alexander was born in Virginia on April 4, 1815, a son of William Alexander and wife Ann Bevans. Not much is known of this part of the family, but from probate records it appears that Moses had a rough time keeping property and staying afloat. He was described as a bankrupt between 1873 and 1888 in Augusta County, Virginia.[2]

Family history records kept by various individuals have documented that he was married to a Liney Golliday, but a Rockingham County marriage record[3] for June 25, 1835 gives the wife as Nancy F. Hamilton. Property deeds on file in Augusta County are for *Moses L. and wife Nancy*.

It seems that Moses moved from Rockingham County to Waynesboro in Augusta County, and purchased property from President Wilson's grandfather—the land upon which they had a female school. The school had burned and he bought the place from Reverend Wilson who had moved to Staunton.[4] He did cabinet making and in 1828 started a furniture making business, and also an undertaking business. By 1838, the business was known as the Alexander Casket and Furniture Company. His brother William Benjamin Alexander, later took charge of the businesses, and Moses moved to a place on Back Creek near Lyndhurst.

Nancy, a daughter of John Hamilton, was born in Virginia on December 18, 1810. Moses was a farmer, and was enumerated on the 1850 and 1860 (Staunton, page 548) Federal census for Augusta County.

On the 1900 Federal census, Moses was boarding with his nephew Edwin Andrew Jackson in Augusta County. Moses L. Alexander, of Back Creek, left a will which was dated October 26, 1900 (codicil March 2, 1901) and was recorded in Augusta County.[5] By his initial will he left 63 acres of land to his granddaughter Lina Lee Moses (and revoked this by codicil), and it mentions Charles Moses, who we know was Lina's husband.

Moses died October 30, 1902,[6] and his wife died September 24, 1889. Moses and Nancy were both buried in the old Presbyterian Cemetery off Broad Street in Waynesboro, but the graves mysteriously were not moved along with those of other family to Riverview Cemetery.

In 2007, an account was found to be up for auction. It was created by Moses L. Alexander between the years 1837 and 1840. It included entries for the manufacture of secretaries, china presses, bureaus, safes, bedsteads, a variety of tables, work stands, benches, coffins, etc. The sale was from a McKenney Family of Mint Spring, Virginia. The final whereabouts of this record is unknown.

Children of Moses Liston Alexander and Nancy F. Hamilton:

61. MARY ELIZABETH ALEXANDER, b. c.1836 in Va., m. 31 MAR 1855 in Augusta Co. to John Wine, b. c.1824 in Va. The 1860 Federal census lists this family in Staunton, living next to Moses L. Alexander. The 1870 Federal census lists John Wines [sic], age 45. On the 1880 Federal census this family lived in the South River Twp. of Augusta Co., next to the household of M.L. Alexander. Children:
611. MARY FRANCES WINE, b. 7 AUG 1856 in Augusta Co., Va.,[7] not listed on the 1870 Federal census.
612. SARAH MARGARET "Maggie" WINE, b. 24 JUL 1859 in Augusta Co.
613. JOHN ALEXANDER WINE, b. 9 JUN 1863 in Augusta Co., d. 29 MAY 1916 in Augusta Co., bur. Springdale Cem. of Waynesboro.
614. POLENA LEE "Lina" WINE, b. 6 JUN 1866 in Augusta Co.,[8] d. 29 DEC 1942 at home in Lyndhurst, bur.

---

[1] The middle name of Liston is found in the writings of Emma Jane (Alexander) Whitlock as provided by her granddaughter Mary Jane (Chambers) Bird of Wilmington, Del. I believe it is a significant point in connecting the Alexander ancestry to Somerset and Worcester Counties in Maryland where we have found both Moses and Liston Alexander to be sons of a William Alexander, Jr.

[2] Augusta Co. Chancery Causes, 1874-055, *George W. Hensley v. Moses L. Alexander*, and 1888-076, *Jane Switzer v. Moses L. Alexander*.

[3] Rockingham Co. Marriages, Bk. 3, p. 1045.

[4] Deed of 1 OCT 1842, between Hetty S. Wilson [or Willson], widow and relict of James C. Wilson, late of Augusta Co., Thomas W. Shelton and wife Mary Rachel, late Mary Rachel Wilson, Elizabeth F. Wilson, Otho Gapen, executor of James W. Wilson, dec., and Elishbe Wilson, widow and relict of James W. Wilson, all heirs and representatives of James C. Wilson, to Moses L. Alexander ... a lot on the hill adjoining the town of Waynesboro, being part of a lot purchased by James C. Wilson of Jacob Larew containing 1 acre, 1 rood and 12 poles. Also, by deed of 17 SEP 1857, William B. Alexander purchased another adjacent parcel that was once owned by the heirs of James C. Wilson [Augusta Co. Deeds, Bk. 77, p. 445].

[5] Augusta Co., Va. Wills, Bk. 58, pp. 303-5, wit. by John A. Stuart and Charles N. Moses. An executor bond was issued to E.A. Jackson and John A. Wine on 24 NOV 1912 [Augusta Co. Executor and Administrator Bonds, Vol. 14, p. 448]. Also see Augusta Wills, Bk. 59, p. 589 for estate account; Bk. 58, p. 438 for appraisal and sale.

[6] Old Presbyterian Cemetery, Waynesboro, Va., grave marker, fallen: M.L. ALEXANDER / Born / April 4, 1815 / Died / Oct. 30, 1902. / Aged / 87 yrs. 6 mos. & 26 ds. / *At Rest*.

[7] Augusta Co., Va. Register of Births, 1853-1874, entry #2663.

[8] Ibid., entry #7263, gives birth year 1866, but grave marker gives year 1865. Also there is variance in the spelling of her first name, from Pollina, Paulina, or Polena.

Riverview Cem., Waynesboro, Va., m. 5 AUG 1886 by Rev. A.L. Crouse in Waynesboro[1] to Charles N. Moses, farmer, son of Samuel M. Moses, b. JAN 1865 in Alleghany Co., Va., d. 1949, bur. Riverview Cem. Children:

> 6141. LEONARD HOUSTON MOSES, b. 20 JUL 1890, d. 30 JUL 1965, m. Lena Virginia Breedlove, b. 7 MAR 1884, d. 20 AUG 1974; both bur. Augusta Memorial Park Cem., Waynesboro.
>
> 6142. ELWOOD LESTER MOSES, b. 1894, d. 1954, res. Luray, Page Co., m. Mamie E. (   ), b. 1897, d. 1958; both bur. Thornrose Cem., Staunton, Va.
>
> 6143. Infant MOSES.
>
> 6143. WILLIE FRANKLIN MOSES, b. 26 AUG 1906, d. 13 NOV 1992, m. in 1924 in Augusta Co. to Emma Jane Sweet, b. 12 JAN 1907, d. FEB 1982; both bur. Augusta Memorial Park Cem.

62. JOHN WILL ALEXANDER, b. 27 JUN 1837 in Waynesboro, Va., farmer, m. (1) on 16 FEB 1858 in South River Twp. of Augusta Co. to Dorothy A. "Dolly" George. He served in Company B of the 52nd Virginia Infantry, C.S.A., 1862-1864. After his first wife died, John was m. (2) on 5 MAR 1885 in Staunton to Susan Burton, daughter of John and Martha Burton. They lived near Lyndhurst. John d. of heart disease 16 MAR 1920 in South River Dist. at the age of 82y 8m and 17d, and bur. by the Alexander Funeral Home the next day in Bethlehem Church Cem. of Waynesboro. Susan (Burton) Alexander d. 20 NOV 1920 in Western State Hospital of Staunton, of lobar pneumonia and bur. by Alexander Funeral Home in Augusta Co., 21 NOV 1920 in Bethlehem Church Cem. of Waynesboro.

63. HARRIET A. "Hetty" ALEXANDER, b. c.1844, m. 5 AUG 1862 by J.A. Latané in Staunton to George William Stanton, a shoemaker, b. c.1844 in Rockingham Co., son of M.C. Stanton and Nancy Kice. The couple is residing with her father Moses L. Alexander on the 1870 Federal census for Fishersville post office. In 1897, George W. Stanton filed for divorce from Harriet because she had abandoned him some time about 1892.[2] She was mentioned as Hetty A. Stanton in her father's will in 1900. Children:

> 631. MARTHA E. "Mattie" STANTON, b. c.1864 in Va., m. 18 FEB 1879 in Sherando, Augusta Co. to Joseph Patterson, farmer, son of John Patterson and Phebe Painter. Mattie Patterson, weaver, heads a household in Basic City on the 1900 Federal census. Child:
>
> > 6311. PERCY A. PATTERSON, b. DEC 1899 in Va. He heads a household, with his mother, in Waynesboro on the 1910 Federal census.
>
> 632. Daughter STANTON, m. Mr. Cook. Child:
>
> > 6321. EDGAR G. COOK, b. MAY 1890 in Va.

[1] Augusta Co., Va. Register of Marriages, 1883-1935, p. 33.
[2] Augusta Co., Va. Chancery Causes, 1897-126, *George W. Stanton v. Harriet A. Stanton.*

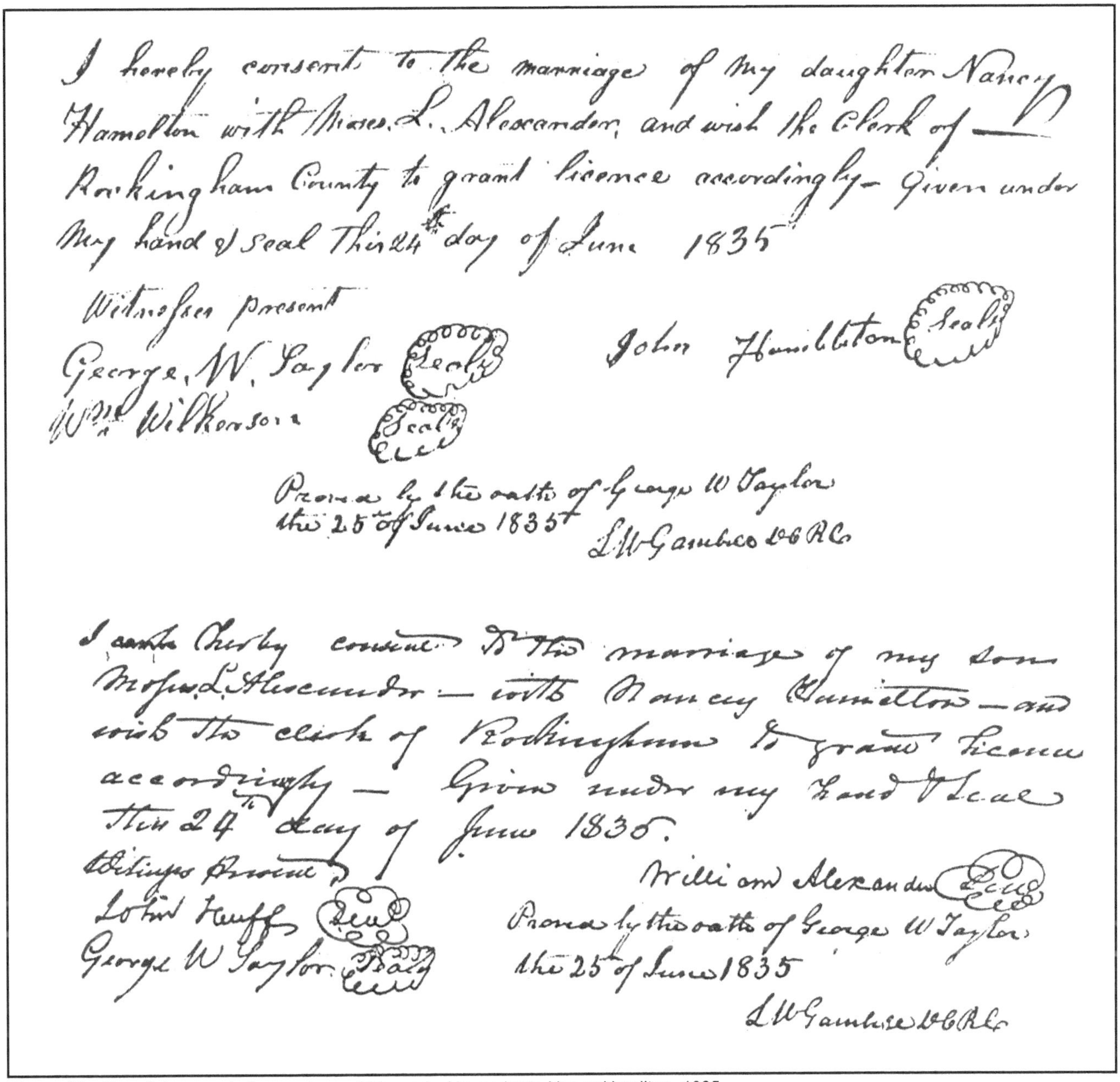

I hereby consent to the marriage of my daughter Nancy Hamilton with Moses L. Alexander, and wish the Clerk of Rockingham County to grant licence accordingly. Given under my hand & seal this 24th day of June 1835

Witnesses present

George W. Taylor {Seal}   John Hamilton {Seal}

Wm Wilkerson {Seal}

Proved by the oaths of George W Taylor
the 25 of June 1835   L W Gambill D C R C

I hereby consent to the marriage of my son Moses L. Alexander — with Nancy Hamilton — and wish the clerk of Rockingham to grant licence accordingly — Given under my hand & seal this 24th day of June 1835.

Witnesses present,

John Huff {Seal}   William Alexander {Seal}

George W Taylor {Seal}   Proved by the oaths of George W Taylor
                                 the 25 of June 1835

                                 L W Gambill D C R C

Figure 12 - Parental consents for marriage of Moses L. Alexander to Nancy Hamilton, 1835

7. ELIZABETH ANN (ALEXANDER) JACKSON
(1818-1873)

Elizabeth Ann Alexander, daughter of William Alexander and Ann Bevans, was born April 4, 1818 in Virginia, probably Rockingham County, and was married January 2, 1849 by George W. Israel in Rockingham County to Willis Jackson, a shoemaker, born c.1800 in Virginia.

Willis Jackson was a member of the Port Republic Lodge of Sons of Temperance from 1853 to 1856.[1] He was a shoemaker with an estimated $50 in real property, was head of household #1897 on the Federal census taken August 17, 1860 in District No. 1 of Rockingham County (post office Harrisonburg), page 602. He was head of household #653 on the Federal census taken 25 JUL 1870 in the 2nd District of Augusta County (post office Mt. Sidney), p. 299. Willis Jackson died January 7, 1876 at the age of 80, as noted in the Augusta County death register. His grave site has not been located.

According to the record of Edith (Whitlock) Chambers, Elizabeth died June 5, 1873. She was buried in the old Presbyterian Cemetery off Broad Street in Waynesboro.

Known children of Willis Jackson and Elizabeth Ann Alexander:

71. MARY ELLEN MARGARET ANN JANE FRANCES JACKSON, b. c.1850 in Va. (age 10 in 1860)
72. EDWIN ANDREW THOMAS HERRON JACKSON, millwright and dairy farmer, b. 29 JAN 1857 in New Hope, Augusta Co. He m. 8 JUN 1895 in Waynesboro to Mary Gertrude Diddle, b. 19 APR 1878 in Grayville, Ill., d. 18 DEC 1947, daughter of F. Diddle and E. Charles.[2] In 1900, the couple lived next to Moses L. Alexander and Charles N. Moses. The couple resided in Cabin Creek of Kanawha Co., W.Va. on the 1910 Federal census. He d. 9 MAY 1943 of chronic nephritis at his home in South River Dist. near Lyndhurst in Augusta Co., and bur. by Etter Funeral Home of Waynesboro, 11 MAY 1943 in Block 95, Lot 4B of Riverview Cem. in Waynesboro. Funeral expenses were billed to Mr. D.E. Diddle of Johnson City, Tenn. Child:
    721. BESSIE JACKSON, b. 1901 in Kanawha Co., W.Va.
73. GEORGE KEMPER JACKSON, b. JAN 1861 in Augusta Co., Va. (age 8 in 1870). On the 1880 Federal census for South River District of Augusta Co., Va., "Kemper" Jackson is shown as a farm laborer and living with his cousin (62.) JOHN WILL ALEXANDER and wife Dorothy A. George.

---

[1] George Elliott May, Port Republic: The History of a Shenandoah Valley River Town (Staunton: Lot's Wife Publishing, 2001), p. 170.
[2] Augusta Co., Va. Marriage Register 1, 1854-1900, entry #8061.

8. WILLIAM BENJAMIN ALEXANDER
(1820-1901)

It has been through much of the surviving paperwork kept by William Benjamin Alexander that we have been able to progress in research on the surname as a whole. He was a businessman who resided nearly his entire life in Waynesboro, Augusta County, Virginia.

William Benjamin[1] Alexander, born July 20, 1820 in Port Republic, Rockingham County, Virginia, was a son of William Alexander and Ann Bevans. At an early age he moved from Rockingham County to Waynesboro to live with his brother Moses Liston Alexander, who had built his home on the foundation of the old Wilson Family property on Main Street. This move was so that William could be an apprentice to his brother's business of making household furniture, church furniture, coffins, and in undertaking. He later was at the head of the business that Moses had begun and was known as the Alexander Casket and Furniture Company. It formerly stood where was later found the General Wayne Motor Inn parking lot.

On November 4, 1844, William Benjamin Alexander was married in Albemarle County to Sarah Ann Maxwell. Sarah Ann, a daughter of Moses Maxwell and Mary Ann McCue, was born December 23, 1824 in Albemarle County. The couple each claimed they were christened in the Presbyterian Church in 1834.

From tax receipts, we find that by 1842, William B. Alexander paid a levy for a gold watch, and in subsequent years for a horse and a metal clock. By 1851, he was levied in Augusta County, and among the usual horse, watch and metal clock, he had more than one slave.

Because of county deeds found in Saline County, Missouri[2] and personal records kept by William B. Alexander, we know that he was responsible for disposing of bounty land awarded his father William Alexander, which was situated in Saline County, Missouri. The property was finally sold by deed dated March 14, 1860.[3]

On August 19, 1850, the family of William B. Alexander, a cabinet maker, was enumerated on the Federal census (page 374) in District 2½ in Augusta County.

Figure 13 - William Benjamin Alexander and granddaughter Edith Whitlock

On October 18, 1864 at New Market, William B. Alexander was mustered into Company H of the Fifth Virginia Infantry as a private under Captain Gibson. He was released as a prisoner of war on May 15, 1865 at Staunton, and on that date he was recorded as being aged 45 years, only 59½" tall, dark complexion, dark hair, and blue eyes. He was further declared too old for service, had 9 children, and discharged. William B. Alexander was enumerated as head of family number 883 on the 1870 Federal census for Augusta County, and number 66 in the city of Waynesboro on the 1880 Federal census for Augusta County. Records of this branch of the family are documented in a family Bible, which was last found to be with Mary Jane (Chambers) Bird in Wilmington, Delaware.

During the time of the Civil War, Mrs. Sarah Alexander died of a heart attack at 7:00 p.m. on May 5, 1864, and was buried in the old Presbyterian Cemetery off Broad Street in Waynesboro. Her grave, as well as others of the immediate family, was later moved by Edith (Whitlock) Chambers to the more modern Riverview Cemetery.

Sarah Maxwell's parents were married March 13, 1821 in Nelson County. Moses Maxwell, who was a son of James Maxwell and Jane Boyd, and a grandson of Bezaleel Maxwell and Rebecca Boyd, was born May 22, 1797, and

---

[1] His middle name is not found recorded on any old family documents, but passed down through writings from family members. It appears in error as William Benton Alexander in a biographical sketch on his son Moses Harvey Alexander, in the History of St. Louis, Missouri.

[2] Saline Co., Mo. Deeds, Bk. 3, p. 122.

[3] Augusta Co., Va. Deeds, Bk. 122, p. 3. Effected by and sold to his attorney, George W. Allen, the parcels of land situate in the County of Saline in the State of Missouri; that is to say the east half of the north east quarter of Section Seven (7) and the east half of the north east quarter of Section (17) Seventeen and all in Township Fifty (50) of Range (21) Twenty one containing in all 160 acres more or less agreeable to Government Survey.

died June 18, 1880 in Covesville, Albemarle County, Virginia.[1]

Mary "Polly" McCue, a daughter of Charles McCue and Anna Maxwell, with paternal grandparents John McCue and wife Eleanor Mathews, and maternal grandparents of Bezaleel Maxwell and wife Rebecca Boyd, was born March 22, 1795 in Nelson County, Virginia. Polly died June 7, 1865 in Covesville in Albemarle County.[2] Moses Maxwell of Albemarle county, signed his last will and testament on March 23, 1872, as witnessed by D.E. Watson, A.S. Watson and William H. Harris, and it was entered into probate on October 4, 1880.

From clues found in the funeral records of John W. Wagner of Kansas City, Missouri, it is believed that William B. Alexander traveled to Kansas City, Missouri when his brother James Washington Alexander died in 1893.[3] However, family tradition is that it was Moses Harvey Alexander who came from Marshall, Missouri to arrange for the funeral.[4] William B. Alexander died shortly after reading his afternoon mail at his home on 703 West Main Street[5] in Waynesboro on September 12, 1901, without leaving a will. He is buried in Riverview Cemetery of Waynesboro.[6]

By 1919, the Alexander Family owned Lots 47 and 49, called "Spring Valley," and Lots 46 and 48, on South Mulberry Street.[7] In 1929, the heirs of William B. Alexander petitioned the court to sell to Elmo Gibson Alexander, Executor, their interest in a ½-acre parcel of land on Main Street owned by the estate and for which the deed and plat had been lost.[8]

Children of William Benjamin Alexander and Sarah Ann Maxwell:

+ 81. THOMAS WOODWARD ALEXANDER, b. 13 OCT 1845, m. Emma Jane Bateman.
+ 82. MARY ANN ALEXANDER, b. 13 SEP 1847, m. William Franklin Fauber.
+ 83. EMMA JANE ALEXANDER, b. 6 SEP 1849, m. C. Augustus Whitlock.

Figure 14 - James Franklin Alexander

+ 84. SARAH MARGARET ALEXANDER, b. 4 APR 1851, m. John Cassius Whitlock.
+ 85. CHARLES WILLIAM ALEXANDER, b. 4 JUL 1853, m. Elizabeth B. Jesser.
+ 86. ALICE CORNELIA ALEXANDER, b. 3 JUN 1855, m. William H. McCormick.
+ 87. MOSES HARVEY ALEXANDER, SR., b. 9 JUL 1857, m. Eliza H. Guthrey.
  88. JAMES FRANKLIN "Jimmy" ALEXANDER, b. 1 JUN 1859 in Waynesboro, Augusta Co., unmarried, d. 4 APR 1886 of the flu in Waynesboro, aged 26y 10m and 3d, bur. in Riverview Cem.[9]
+ 89. BETTY LEE ALEXANDER, b. 4 SEP 1862, m. Horatio T. McCormick.

---

[1] Birth and death dates for Moses Maxwell and his wife Mary McCue are found in the Bible record of the Charles William Alexander Family.
[2] For further information consult John Nolley McCue's The McCues of the Old Dominion (Mexico, Mo., 1912).
[3] John W. Wagner Funeral Home records, Kansas City, Mo.
[4] Letter, Mildred Warren (Harrisonville, Mo.), 15 JUL 1989.
[5] The Alexander Family owned property on Main Street in Waynesboro up to 1956 when descendant Mary Jane (Chambers) Bird initiated a chancery cause against the estate of Homer Jesser Alexander, insolvent, to distribute the proceeds of the sale of a parcel of 3.29 acres among heirs.
[6] Riverview Cemetery, Waynesboro, grave marker: [relief] / Mother-Father. / SARAH ALEXANDER / Born / Dec. 23, 1824 / Died / May 5, 1864. / Wm. B. ALEXANDER / Born / July 20, 1820 / Died / Sep. 12, 1901. / Parents dear how we miss you, / Miss you more than tongue can tell, / But in heaven will try to meet you, / Never there to say farewell! / ALEXANDER.
[7] Augusta Co., Va. Deeds, Bk. 194, p. 331.
[8] Augusta Co., Va. Deeds, Bk. 242, pp. 287-91. In 1931, Elmo and wife Lula put this and other property in trust with his aunt Emma J. (Bateman) Alexander for 7 years.
[9] Riverview Cemetery, Waynesboro, grave marker: JAMES F. / Son of / W.B. & S.A. Alexander / Died / April 4, 1886. / Aged / 26 Yr. 10 Mo. & 3ds. / Rest in peace.

Figure 15 - Furniture store operated by the William B. Alexander family, located in Waynesboro, Va., about where Maple Avenue ends at Main Street, c.1890's. (left to right) Charles W. Alexander, Thomas W. Alexander, William B. Alexander

Figure 16 - Alexander Family homestead in Waynesboro, Va. The structure had a canon ball embedded in the right chimney during the Civil War.

Figure 17 - William Benjamin Alexander

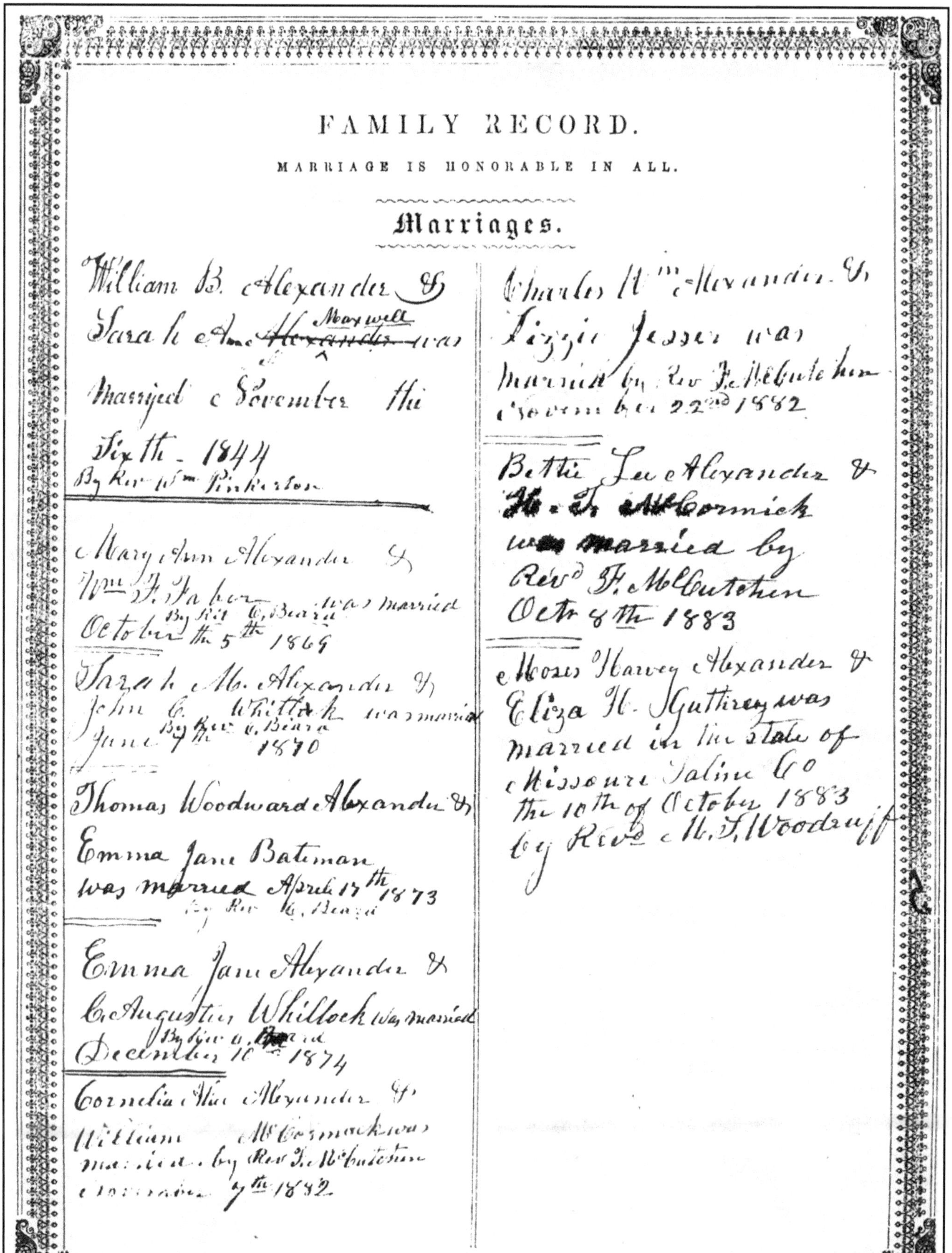

FAMILY RECORD.

MARRIAGE IS HONORABLE IN ALL.

Marriages.

William B. Alexander & Sarah Ann Maxwell was Married November the Sixth - 1844 By Rev Wm Pinkerton

Mary Ann Alexander & Wm F. Faber was married October the 5th 1869 By Rev C. Beard

Sarah M. Alexander & John C. Whitlock was married June 9th 1870 By Rev C. Beard

Thomas Woodward Alexander & Emma Jane Bateman was married April 17th 1873 By Rev C. Beard

Emma Jane Alexander & C. Augustus Whitlock was married December 10th 1874 By Rev C. Beard

Cornelia Alice Alexander & William McCormack was married by Rev F. McCutchen November 9th 1882

Charles Wm Alexander & Lizzie Jesse was married by Rev F. McCutchen November 22nd 1882

Bettie Lee Alexander & H. T. McCormick was married by Revd F. McCutchen Octr 8th 1883

Moses Harvey Alexander & Eliza H. Guthrey was married in the state of Missouri Saline Co the 10th of October 1883 by Revd M. T. Woodruff

Figure 18 - Bible record, William B. Alexander Family, Marriages

50

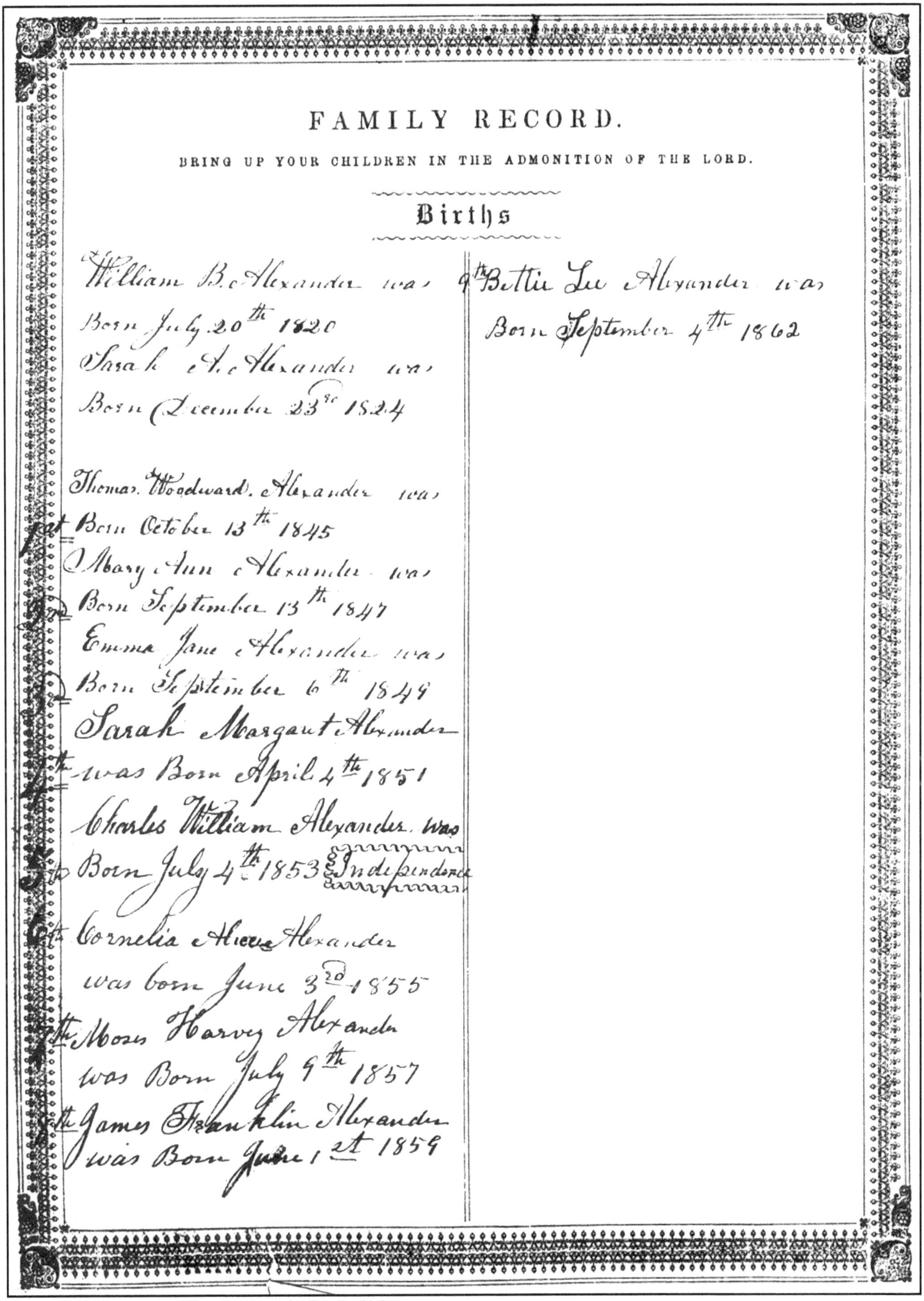

FAMILY RECORD.

BRING UP YOUR CHILDREN IN THE ADMONITION OF THE LORD.

Births

William B. Alexander was
Born July 20th 1820
Sarah A. Alexander was
Born December 23rd 1824

Thomas Woodward Alexander was
1st Born October 13th 1845
Mary Ann Alexander was
2nd Born September 13th 1847
Emma Jane Alexander was
3rd Born September 6th 1849
Sarah Margaret Alexander
4th was Born April 4th 1851
Charles William Alexander was
5th Born July 4th 1853 Independence
6th Cornelia Alice Alexander
was born June 3rd 1855
7th Moses Harvey Alexander
was Born July 9th 1857
8th James Franklin Alexander
was Born June 1st 1859

9th Bettie Lee Alexander was
Born September 4th 1862

Figure 19 - Bible record, William B. Alexander Family, Births

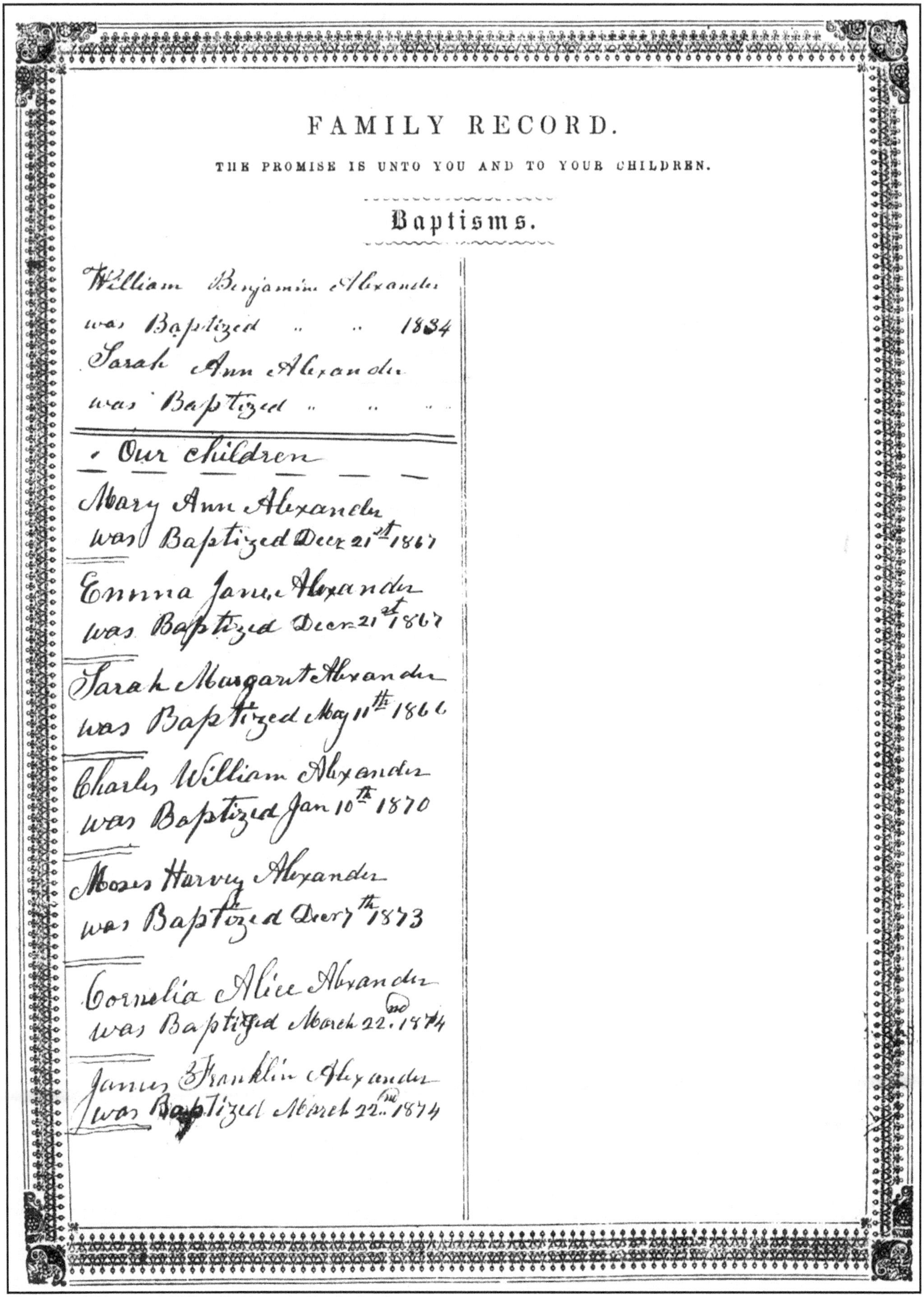

FAMILY RECORD.

THE PROMISE IS UNTO YOU AND TO YOUR CHILDREN.

Baptisms.

William Benjamin Alexander
was Baptized 1854

Sarah Ann Alexander
was Baptized .. .. ..

—— Our children ——

Mary Ann Alexander
was Baptized Decr 21st 1867

Emma Jane Alexander
was Baptized Decr 21st 1867

Sarah Margaret Alexander
was Baptized May 11th 1866

Charles William Alexander
was Baptized Jan 10th 1870

Moses Harvey Alexander
was Baptized Decr 7th 1873

Cornelia Alice Alexander
was Baptized March 22nd 1874

James Franklin Alexander
was Baptized March 22nd 1874

Figure 20 - Bible record, William B. Alexander Family, Baptisms

52

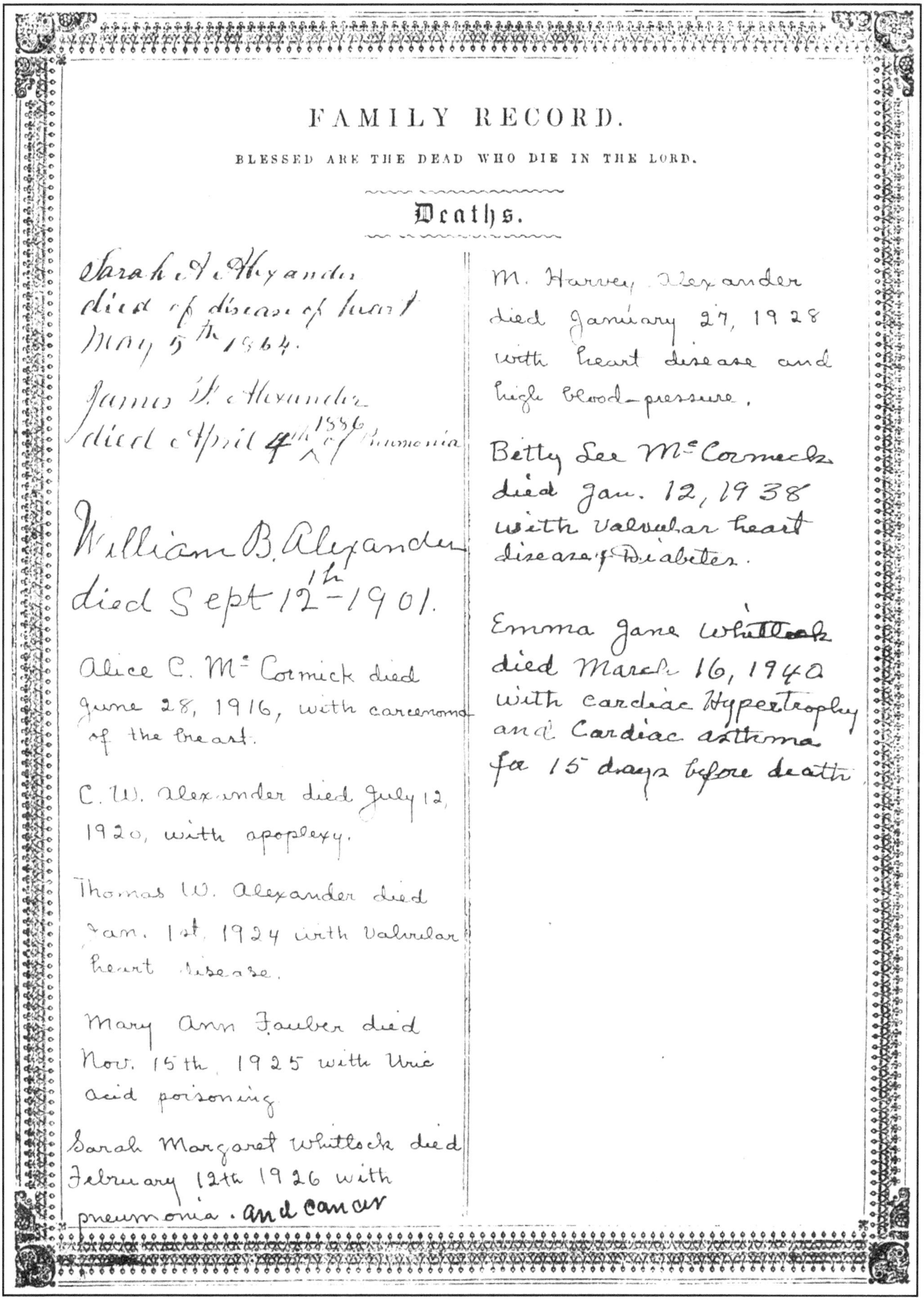

FAMILY RECORD.

BLESSED ARE THE DEAD WHO DIE IN THE LORD.

Deaths.

Sarah A. Alexander died of disease of heart May 5th 1964.

James P. Alexander died April 4th 1886 of pneumonia

William B. Alexander died Sept 12th - 1901.

Alice C. McCormick died June 28, 1916, with carcenoma of the breast.

C. W. Alexander died July 12, 1920, with apoplexy.

Thomas W. Alexander died Jan. 1st 1924 with Valvelar heart disease.

Mary Ann Faubex died Nov. 15th 1925 with Uric acid poisoning.

Sarah Margaret Whitlock died February 12th 1926 with pneumonia. and cancer

M. Harvey Alexander died January 27, 1928 with heart disease and high blood-pressure.

Betty Lee McCormick died Jan. 12, 1938 with Valvular heart disease & Diabetes.

Emma Jane Whitlock died March 16, 1940 with cardiac Hypertrophy and Cardiac asthma for 15 days before death

Figure 21 - Bible record, William B. Alexander Family, Deaths

The Alexander Family Reunion [1892]

A most delightful family reunion took place at the residence of Mr. Wm. B. Alexander on last Saturday. Mr. Wm. B. Alexander the immediate progenitor of the Alexander family in this community is a hale hearty old gentleman of 72 years, and has been an honored, upright citizen of this place for over 56 years. On last Saturday was gathered under the ancestral roof tree all the children and grandchildren now living, and a day of profit and pleasure was enjoyed that will be marked with a white stone in the calendar of time by all who participated in the occasion.

There were present three sons and five daughters and twenty grandchildren. Our popular artist, Mr. Jos. Clem, grouped the grandfather and twenty grandchildren together and took a large sized photograph of the group. Rev. A.R. Cocke next christened the infant son of Mr. and Mrs. McCormick, "Freddie Alexander," the youngest grandchild present. After these ceremonies were over, the company were invited to the well spread dinner table, which was prepared under the drooping shade of trees and literally groaned under its burden of good things. Covers were laid for thirty-eight, and it is needless to say that ample justice was done to the tempting viands. Ye editor had the good fortune to be placed opposite Rev. A.R. Cocke, and after the sumptuous repast was over we felt convinced that while the cloth may be earnestly striving for the good things that are promised above, they are yet duly sensible and properly appreciative of those that belong to this sublunary sphere.

The members of the family present were: Mr. M.H. Alexander and wife and four children from Marshall, Saline County, Mo.; C.W. and T.W. Alexander, wives and children; Mrs. J.C. Whitlock, of Staunton; Mrs. C.A. Whitlock; Mrs. Mollie Fauber, of Waynesboro; Mr. H.T. McCormick and wife, of Waynesboro; Mr. W.H. McCormick and wife of Radford, Va.; in addition were the twenty grandchildren. The invited guests were Rev. A.R. Cocke, wife and daughter; Mr. Clarke, of Delaware, Ohio; and Mrs. E.V. McCormick, Old Providence, Va.

The Alexanders are among our best, most reliable, and substantial citizens and belong to that class of old Virginia people whose word is as good as their bond. The SENTINEL extends its best wishes, and hope they may have many happy returns of the pleasant occasion.

Staunton Spectator and Vindicator, Friday, September 13, 1901.[1] After a protracted illness and at the ripe old age of 81 years, Mr. W.B. Alexander died at his home in Waynesboro yesterday afternoon at 2 o'clock. His trouble was a complication of causes and death came after a lingering and failing illness. He enjoyed the distinction of being the oldest citizen in his community and is survived by a large family. The sons are T.W. and C.W. Alexander of Waynesboro, and M.H. Alexander of St. Louis, the daughters are Mrs. M.A. Fauber, Mrs. Emma Whitlock, Mrs. W.H. McCormick and Miss Bettie Alexander of Waynesboro, and Mrs. J.C. Whitlock of this city. The funeral services will take place from the late residence Saturday afternoon at 3 o'clock.

Mary Jane (Chambers) Bird described the house to the compiler in November 1987: The old Alexander home place in Waynesboro, Virginia, had six bedrooms: three in back and three upstairs. The house had an apple orchard in back and many small buildings on the property, one of which was between the house and the orchard and was used to store and keep food cold. A small building called the "bean house" was on the left. The house was located at 703 Main St. in town, and when telephones were installed, its number was 88R. Betty and Emma lived in the house until they died. During the Civil War the Alexanders hid Confederate soldiers in the rafters and kept horses in the dining room. A cannon ball was lodged in the chimney on the right end of the house.

---

[1] It may be interesting to note that President McKinley had been shot on Friday, 6 SEP 1901.

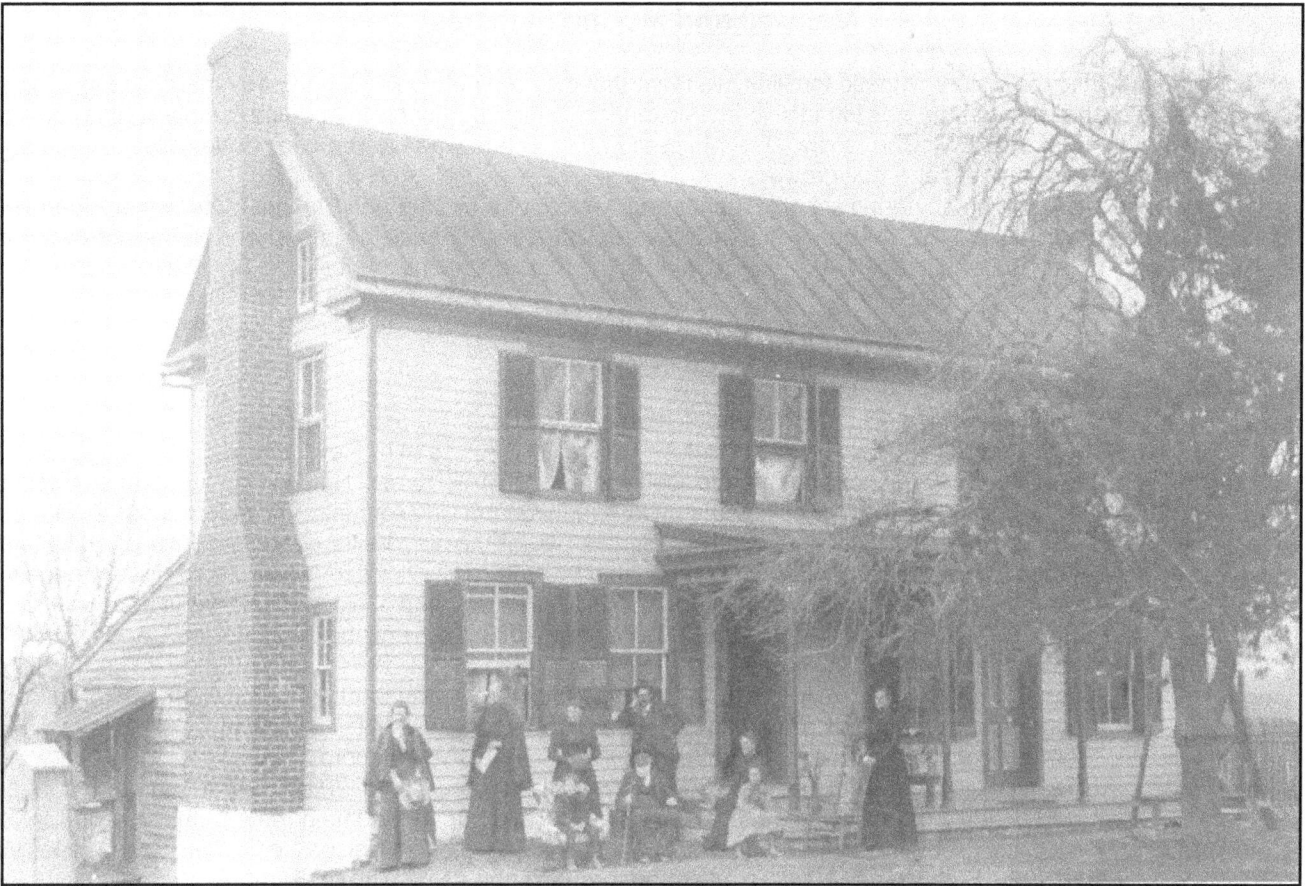

Figure 22 - William B. Alexander Family Home, at 703 W. Main St., Waynesboro, Va.

Know all men by these presents, That we Wm B. Alexander and Moses Maxwell are held and firmly bound unto the Commonwealth of Virginia in the just and full sum of one hundred and fifty dollars, current money, to which payment well and truly to be made, we bind ourselves, jointly and severally, and each of our joint and several heirs, executors and administrators, firmly by these presents. Sealed with our seals, and dated this 4th day of March 1844

The condition of the above obligation is such, that whereas there is a marriage shortly to be had and solemnized between the above bound Wm B Alexander and Sarah Ann Maxwell of Albemarle County. If, therefore, there shall be no lawful cause to obstruct said marriage—then the above obligation to be void, otherwise to remain in full force and virtue.

Witness:

William B Alexander [SEAL]

Moses Maxwell [SEAL]

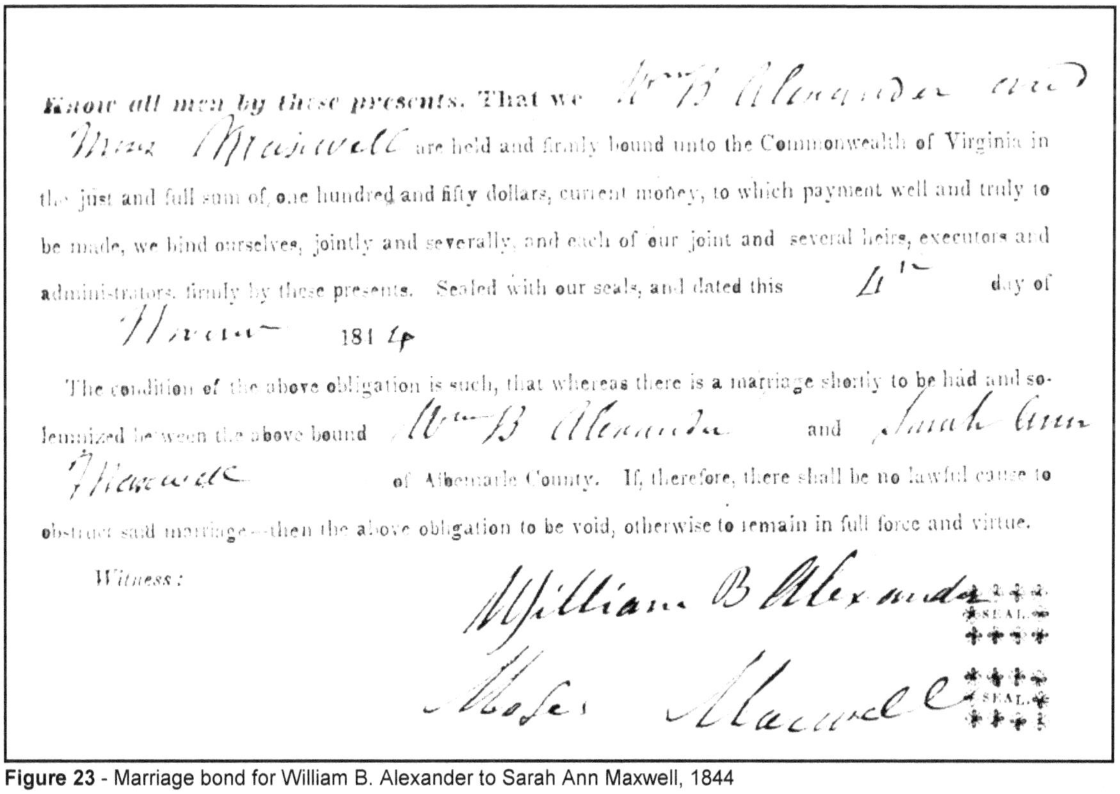

Figure 23 - Marriage bond for William B. Alexander to Sarah Ann Maxwell, 1844

Maxwell and McCue Families

With study into the history of these families, we learn that they are networked together by marriages in several generations. Many surnames found on early Alexander Family documents in Augusta County can be tied into either the Maxwell or McCue family. The Maxwell Family estate was located near Covesville in Albemarle County, and they were farmers and fruit growers.

Charles McCue, a presbyterian school teacher and son of John McCue and Eleanor Mathews of Albemarle County, was born February 7, 1762, and married Anna Maxwell, daughter of Bezaleel Maxwell and Rebecca Boyd from Nelson County.[1]

Children of Charles McCue and Anna Maxwell, order uncertain:

M1.   Robert McCue of Nelson Co.
M2.   John McCue of Nelson Co., is thought to have married Simson (   ) and moved to Tennessee.
M3.   Elizabeth "Betsy" McCue, b. 8 JUL 1793 in Nelson Co., m. 24 MAR 1814 by Rev. John McCue in Augusta Co. to Thomas Catling. They obtained a marriage license dated 18 MAR 1814 in Nelson Co. "Aunt Betsy Catling" d. 19 JUL 1886, aged 93y and 11d in Augusta Co., and was bur. in Mountain View Cem. near Piedmont, Augusta Co. Mr. Catling served in William C. Scott's Co. of the Va. Militia during the War of 1812, and because of the service was granted bounty land which was sold previous to 1855. From military pension records we found Betsy's residences of 1851 to 1855 in Nelson Co., and at New Hope, Augusta Co. in 1871.[2] In that record, she signed her name *Elizabeth Catlin*. Mr. Catling d. at his home in Nelson Co. on 12 MAR 1850. Children:
  M31.   Amanda J. Catling, b. 28 JAN 1816, d. 26 JUL 1910, bur. Liberty Baptist Church Cem. of Stony Point, Albemarle Co., obtained a marriage license dated 15 NOV 1841 from Nelson Co.[3] to marry Mr. Thomas D. Herring. Surety was William B. Alexander of Waynesboro.
  M32.   Julia A. Catling, "Cousin Julia," b. 29 MAR 1817 in Augusta Co., d. 20 MAR 1889, unmarried, aged 71y 11m and 21d at Coyner's Store, Augusta Co., and bur. in Mountain View Cem. of Augusta Co.
  M33.   Eliza Catling, obtained a marriage license dated 14 MAY 1838 in Nelson Co. to marry Mr. Charles W. Mathews. Surety was Mr. William Lobban, probably the same who m. Sarah A. McCue.
M4.   Mary "Polly" McCue, b. 22 MAR 1795 in Nelson Co., m. 13 MAR 1821 by William H. Foote in Nelson Co. to Moses Maxwell.[4] Mr. Maxwell, b. 22 MAY 1797, d. of cancer on 18 JUN 1880 in Covesville, Albemarle Co., son of James Maxwell and Jane Boyd. Mary d. 7 JUN 1865 of breast cancer in Covesville. Children:
  M41.   Sarah Ann Maxwell, b. 23 DEC 1824 in Albemarle Co., m. 4 NOV 1844 there to (8.) WILLIAM BENJAMIN ALEXANDER. She d. 5 MAY 1864 in Waynesboro, *q.v.*
  M42.   Elizabeth "Betsy" Maxwell, b. 19 NOV 1826, d. 15 FEB 1858, unmarried.
  M43.   Ella (or Eliza) Maxwell.
  M44.   James Maxwell, b. 24 SEP 1831 in Va., m. 11 NOV 1852 to Mary (Speece?) Jennings. He d. 8 AUG 1855 of small pox and his widow Mary remarried Mr. Robinson.
  M45.   John Harvey Maxwell, b. 20 NOV 1836, m. 19 DEC 1865 in Nelson Co. to Sally Page. "Harvey" d. 14 JAN 1910 in Albemarle Co. Is it believed that Sally had a half-sister named Mollie who married Hunter Hogshead.
M5.   James Wakefield McCue, b. 10 AUG 1799 in Nelson Co., m. 7 FEB 1828 there to Martha Jane Lobban. He d. November 27, 1858 in Afton, Va.
M6.   Bazaleel "Bazel" McCue, b. Nelson Co., m. 1 APR 1830 there to Elizabeth W. Machet.
M7.   William Boyd McCue, b. Nelson Co., m. Frances Winebarger and d. near Stone Coal Creek.
M8.   Sarah A. "Sallie" McCue, b. 18 FEB 1808 in Nelson Co., d. 21 DEC 1892, bur. Rock Spring Cem. of Faber, Nelson Co., m. 17 MAY 1831 there by Rev. Cleveland to William Lobban. In 1855, this couple resided in Nelson Co. and were witnesses for Elizabeth Catling (above) when she applied for a widow's pension based on military service of Thomas Catling.
M9.   Jane McCue, b. Nelson Co., m. 24 FEB 1825 there by Rev. Hammersly to David Gentry.
M10.   Cyrus McCue, b. c.1810 in Nelson Co., m. 29 APR 1850 there to Frances Jane Glenn. He d. 6 OCT 1882 in Nelson Co.

---

[1] Also see Florence A.W. Houston, Maxwell History and Genealogy (Indianapolis, Ind.: Press of C.E. Pauley, Indianapolis Engraving Co., 1916), and John Nolley McCue, The McCues of the Old Dominion (Mexico, Mo.: Missouri Printing and Publishing Co., 1912).
[2] National Archives, War of 1812, widows pensions, Betsy Catling, file #96,520.
[3] Nelson Co., Va. Marriage Register 1 and 2, p. 42.
[4] Augusta Co., Va. Deeds, Bk. 75, pp. 190-1. In 1855, Moses Maxwell and wife Mary, of Albemarle Co., sold to William B. Alexander, of Augusta Co., a lot of ground on the hill adjoining the town of Waynesboro, it being the same lot that Maxwell got from Moses Liston Alexander and wife by deed in 1846.

Catling Family

Mr. Joshua Catling, the bondsman for the marriage of William Alexander and Ann Bevans in Albemarle County in 1803, was married possibly three times, and was related to the Alexander Family. First, a bit of historical background. John Alexander of Somerset County, Maryland, removed to Northumberland County, Virginia, where he died testate in 1767. His son John Sheldon Alexander moved to Albemarle County, Virginia, then on to Augusta County where he died. John Sheldon Alexander's son William Alexander was married in 1803 in Albemarle County of Ann Bevans, daughter of John Bevans, of the *Warwick* tract in Worcester County, Maryland. John Bevans was married to Eleanor "Nelly" Tull, born c.1751 in Somerset County, who after his death married second to Joshua Merrill Catling. Eleanor removed c.1797 to Albemarle County, Virginia where it is presumed she died. Eleanor was a daughter of Jonathan Tull (c.1719-1787) and Mary Fountaine of Somerset County, Maryland.

On November 21, 1809, Joshua Catling was married, probably for the second time, by Rev. Douglas in Rockingham County, to Elizabeth, widow of Thomas Williams.[1] Mr. Catling is listed on the 1810 Federal census for Rockingham County (page 7). On March 8, 1813, Joshua Catling was married by Rev. John Gill Watt in Rockingham County, to Miss Tracey Tressco.[2] As a side, Joshua's daughter Mary Catling was married in Albemarle County on December 6, 1808 to Zachariah Mills.[3]

In 1820, Joshua Catling was enumerated in Port Republic (page 177A), the same area as the family of William Alexander and Ann Bevans. In 1825, Joshua Catling with wife Tenisha conveyed to Rice W. Wood in trust a lot in the town of Port Republic.[4] Joshua Catling heads a household in Rockingham County in both the 1830 Federal census (page 205) and the 1840 Federal census (page 37).

81. Thomas Woodward Alexander
(1845-1924)

The first child and eldest son of William Benjamin Alexander and wife Sarah Ann Maxwell, was Thomas Woodward Alexander who was born October 13, 1845 in Augusta County, Virginia.

On April 17, 1873, he was married by Rev. Beard in Fishersville, Augusta County, to Emma Jane Bateman. Emma Jane, daughter of Elijah Bateman and Isabella M. Hamilton, was born December 8, 1850 in Augusta County.[5]

On March 10, 1862 in New Market, Thomas joined Company H, Fifth Regiment of the Virginia Infantry, as a private under the service of Captain Antrim. In February 1863 he was found "in arrest," later absent for the period December 31, 1863 through August 31, 1864, and possibly court martialed by General Order 33, dated March 6, 1863. His military attendance record revealed that on May 12, 1864, Thomas was taken prisoner, and captured at Spotsylvania, Pennsylvania after which he was released under General Order 109 on June 12, 1865. The soldier's complexion was light, with brown hair.

On the 1880 Federal census the family was enumerated in the town of Waynesboro. On November 1, 1887, Thomas Alexander was a member of Zion-St. James Evangelical Lutheran Church of Waynesboro.

Figure 24 - Thomas Woodward Alexander

---

[1] Rockingham Co. Marriage Bonds and Licenses, Bk. 2, p. 434, bond of Joshua Catling to marry Elizabeth Williams, widow of Thomas Williams, also signed by John Clark, wit. by William Taylor.

[2] Rockingham Co. Marriage Bonds and Licenses, Bk. 6, p. 854.

[3] The signature of Joshua Catling as future groom in 1813 and bondman in 1808 are identical. Also, Zachariah Mills did not live long, as we find his will dated 21 FEB 1818 in Albemarle Co., which names wife Mary Mills and daughter Lucy Wyatt Mills [Albemarle Co. Wills, Bk. 7, pp. 242-3].

[4] Albemarle Co. Deeds, Bk. 27, p. 40, filed 1 FEB 1828, wit. by John B. Watts, A.H. Jameson and John C. Wells.

[5] Riverview Cemetery, Waynesboro, grave marker is also found for Emma's sister: Sister. / ISABELLE M. BATEMAN / Born / Sept. 22, 1858 / Died June 21, 1916. / *Gone but not forgotten.*

Thomas continued the family business of making church furniture, as T.W. Alexander & Son,[1] while his brother Charles handled the undertaking activities. The furniture business passed to son Elmo Gibson Alexander then grandson William Woodward Alexander. W.W. Alexander continued up until World War II when the National Casket Company forced the small family business out of the market. At that time William W. sold the old Alexander Family shop on Alexander Lane.

On January 1, 1924, Thomas died suddenly at 8:30 a.m. of a heart attack, and was buried in Riverview Cemetery of Waynesboro, block 77, plot 8A.[2] Emma died November 21, 1933,[3] and was also buried in Riverview Cemetery of Waynesboro. She had a sister Maggie B. Bateman (age 41 on 1900 Federal census).

Children of Thomas Woodward Alexander and Emma Jane Bateman:

811. LULA B. ALEXANDER, b. in 1873, d. 11 JUN 1963, bur. Cedar Hill Cem. of Covington, Alleghany Co., Va., m. by A.R. Cocke[4] on 17 OCT 1892 in Waynesboro to Fred C. Jesser. Fred, a confectioner, was a son of Jacob F. Jesser and Emma Hay, was b. c.1867 in Philadelphia, Pa., and d. 30 MAY 1938. Fred C. Jesser moved his family in February 1900 to Covington where he opened the Covington Bakery and Confectionery Company. He was well known for launching the local volunteer fire department. We have photographs of John Jesser and Rosa Kohler of Germany. Children, order uncertain:

Figure 25 - Elmo Gibson Alexander

  8111. EMMA L. JESSER, b. 6 JAN 1896 in Va., d. 2 OCT 1913, bur. Riverview Cem., m. _____ Kunkle.
  8112. FRED JESSER, b. 1895 in Va.
  8113. MARGARET JESSER, b. 1898 in Va.
  8114. ELSIE JESSER, b. 1900 in Va.

812. ELMO GIBSON ALEXANDER, cabinet maker, b. 20 AUG 1875 in Augusta Co., was m. by Charles R. Stribling, 24 NOV 1902 in Waynesboro to Lula Ann Michael. Lula Ann, daughter of William Henry Michael and Mary Frances Pence, b. 11 AUG 1880 in Good's Mill, Rockingham Co. The family resided at 909 West Main St. in Waynesboro. Elmo, d. 17 FEB 1939 in Waynesboro and bur. in Riverview Cem. there (Block 77, plot 7).[5] His wife, Lula, d. Friday, 6 MAY 1966 in Oak Hill Nursing Home of Staunton, and bur. 8 MAY 1966 in Riverview Cem. of Waynesboro. Only child:

  8121. WILLIAM WOODWARD ALEXANDER, b. 20 AUG 1903 in Waynesboro, Augusta Co., m. at the Fourth Street Methodist Church in Louisville, Ky., 13 MAY 1944 to Elizabeth Dunavant. "Bill" d. 31 JAN 1979 after an accident at his home at 324 Crompton Rd. in Waynesboro, and bur. in Riverview Cem. there.[6] Mr. and Mrs. Alexander were members of the Presbyterian Church, and Bill was a building contractor before he

---

[1] A brochure about the operations of T.W. Alexander & Son of Waynesboro was published c.1928, and states "one hundred years ago T.W. Alexander and Son turned out its first piece of furniture." It is thought that the first year would be when Moses Liston Alexander began making furniture. The company specialized in making baptismal fonts, alter rails and furniture, pulpits and pulpit furniture, bulletin boards, and pews. Locations that included works by this company included the Presbyterian Church of Waynesboro, Old Stone Church of Fort Defiance, St. Paul's Memorial Church of Charlottesville, Emory M.E. Church of Washington, D.C., Tacoma Park Presbyterian Church of Washington, D.C., Trinity Lutheran Church of Homer City, Pa., Grace Episcopal Church of Ocala, Fla., Our Lady of the Nazareth Catholic Church of Roanoke, Va., Catholic Churches in Staunton, Norfolk and Harrisonburg, Raleigh Court Presbyterian Church of Roanoke, West End M.E. Church of Richmond, Woodland Heights M.E. Church of Richmond, Pulaski Baptist Church of Pulaski, Va., Main Street Baptist Church of Luray, Highland Park Christian Church of Richmond, First Presbyterian Church of Covington, and Jewish Synagogues in Roanoke, Martinsville, Harrisonburg, and Staunton, Va. The walnut used for St. Paul's Memorial Church in Charlottesville came from an old abandoned distillery in Augusta County, and some of the church members were uncomfortable with the provenance of the lumber.

[2] Riverview Cemetery, Waynesboro, grave marker: THOMAS W. / ALEXANDER / Oct. 13, 1845 / Jan. 1, 1924.

[3] Riverview Cemetery, Waynesboro, grave marker: EMMA J. / ALEXANDER / Dec. 8, 1850 / Nov. 21, 1933.

[4] The Bible record of the Charles William Alexander Family notes Dr. A.R. Cocke died 23 AUG 1901. Also see Augusta Co. Marriage Register 1, 1854-1900, entry #6524.

[5] Riverview Cemetery, Waynesboro, grave marker: ALEXANDER. / ELMO G. / Aug. 20, 1875 / Feb. 17, 1939. / LULA A. / Aug. 11, 1880 / May 6, 1966.

[6] Riverview Cemetery, Waynesboro, grave marker: ALEXANDER. / WILLIAM W. / Aug. 20, 1903 / Jan. 31, 1979. / ELIZABETH D. / Sept. 1, 1906 / June 25, 2001.

retired. Elizabeth, daughter of Ollie Brown Dunavant (s/o Joseph Samuel Dunavant and Elizabeth Jenkins) and his wife Melissa Lamar (d/o James Larkin Lamar and Elizabeth Foust), *a preacher's daughter*, b. in Pulaski, Giles Co., Tenn., 14 SEP 1906, d. 25 JUN 2001. Elizabeth was very helpful to the compiler by loaning family papers for copying and giving key documents.

    81211. WILLIAM WOODWARD ALEXANDER, JR., b. 17 AUG 1946 in the Univ. of Va. Hosp. of Charlottesville, Albemarle Co., m. (1) 19 AUG 1970 in Johnson City, Tenn. to Nancy Goodman. Nancy initiated div. proceedings which were filed in El Paso, Tex. W.W. m. (2) in 1896 in West Berlin, Ger. to Mrs. Hannelore Brigitte "Annie" Keller.

    81212. RICHARD BROWN ALEXANDER, b. 20 APR 1949 in University of Va. Hosp., bapt. 28 JAN 1951 in First Presby. Church of Waynesboro, was employed by Interarms of Alexandria, Va.

813.   CLARENCE B. ALEXANDER, b. 11 JAN 1895 in Va., d. 16 JUL 1907 and bur. in Riverview Cem.[1]

82. Mary Ann (Alexander) Fauber
(1847-1925)

    Mary Ann Alexander, a daughter of William Benjamin Alexander and wife Sarah Ann Maxwell, was born September 13, 1847 in Augusta County. On October 2, 1869,[2] Mary Ann was married in Waynesboro to William Franklin Fauber. Mr. Fauber, a son of Joseph Fauber and Elizabeth Harnes, was born at Doom's Station, Augusta County, on April 1, 1846. Mary Ann was christened December 21, 1867.

    Mr. Fauber, a farmer, served in the military during the Civil War and belonged to the Lutheran church. On October 3, 1884, Mr. Fauber died at Doom's Station, and was buried in Riverview Cemetery of Waynesboro.

    Mary Ann died November 15, 1925 of uric acid poisoning at 11:50 p.m. in Waynesboro, and was buried November 17, 1925 in Riverview Cemetery there.[3]

Children of William Franklin Fauber and Mary Ann Alexander:

821.   CHARLES MAXWELL FAUBER [later FABER], b. 31 JUL 1870 in Augusta Co., d. 1935, m. Ada McCormick, b. 1873, d. 8 DEC 1950. The husband and wife are bur. in Riverview Cem. of Waynesboro (Block 58, lot 2).[4] Children, order uncertain:

    8211. SARA FABER, b. 1899 in Va.

    8212. WILLIAM F. FABER, b. 1902 in Va., res. Huntingdon, W.Va.

    8213. MARY LUCILLE FABER, b. 1902 in Va., m. Vastine Coiner, res. Waynesboro, Va.

    8214. CHARLES MAXWELL FABER, JR., b. 1905 in Va., res. Blacksburg, Va.

    8215. EDWIN McFADDIN FABER, b. 6 OCT 1906, d. 7 AUG 1907, bur. Riverview Cem.

    8216. HAROLD HAMILTON FABER, aviator, b. 12 MAY 1910, d. 4 SEP 1961, bur. Augusta Memorial Park Cem. of Waynesboro, m. Dorothy Winn.

822.   LOTTIE HILDRETH FAUBER, b. 7 OCT 1876[5] in Augusta Co., never married. She d. Friday 23 DEC 1966 in Guggenheim Nursing Home of Lynchburg, and bur. 24 DEC 1966 in Riverview Cem. of Waynesboro. She might best be remembered for her efforts in documenting the history of our part of the Alexander Family.

823.   JOSEPH EVERETT FAUBER, b. 4 AUG 1879 in Augusta Co., m. 27 NOV 1907 in Charlottesville to Alma Carter. J.E. Fauber was a funeral director in Lynchburg. He d. 22 FEB 1959 of multiple causes (including a fractured hip received at home on February 13th and broncho pneumonia) in Virginia Baptist Hospital of Lynchburg, and bur. 23 FEB 1959 in Spring Hill Cem. of Lynchburg. Alma, daughter of Charles D. Carter and Lucy Dufner, was b. 17 NOV 1884 in Charlottesville. She d. Saturday, 14 MAR 1959 at 1917 Rivermont Avenue in Lynchburg, and bur. two days later in Spring Hill Cem. there. Lucy was a member of many social organizations, one of which was the United Daughters of the Confederacy. Child:

    8231. JOSEPH EVERETTE FAUBER, JR., architect, b. 15 AUG 1908 in Va., m. Ella Williams, and resided at 501 V.E.S. Road in Lynchburg. "Everette" d. 1 APR 1987 in Lynchburg General Hospital and bur. two days later in Spring Hill Cem. there. Children, order uncertain:

    82311. RODGER W. FAUBER, of 4629 Locksview Road in Lynchburg.

    82312. STUART FAUBER, of Lynchburg.

    82313. JOSEPH EVERETTE FAUBER, III.

---

[1] Riverview Cemetery, Waynesboro, grave marker visited in 2011 appears nearly illegible.
[2] County record, but marriage date is listed as October 5 in family Bible.
[3] Riverview Cemetery, Waynesboro, grave marker: FAUBER. / WILLIAM F. / April 1, 1846 / October 3, 1884. / MARY A., his wife / September 13, 1847 / November 15, 1925. / LOTTIE H. / Their Daughter / Died Dec. 23, 1966.
[4] Riverview Cemetery, Waynesboro, grave marker: FABER. / CHARLES MAXWELL / 1870-1935. / ADA McCORMICK / 1873-1950.
[5] County record gives birth month as November.

83. Emma Jane (Alexander) Whitlock
(1849-1940)

Emma Jane Alexander, daughter of William Benjamin Alexander and Sarah Ann Maxwell, was born in Augusta County on September 6, 1849, and baptized December 21, 1867. In the family Bible, we find that she was married December 8, 1874[1] in Waynesboro in Augusta County, to C. Augustus Whitlock.

"Gus" Whitlock, a son of Robert T. and Margaret D. Whitlock, was born August 9, 1846 in Augusta County, and was a plasterer. Gus died March 11, 1890 in Waynesboro and is buried in Riverview Cemetery there.[2]

Emma died of old age on March 16, 1940 at 6:30 a.m. Saturday, at the Alexander home at 703 West Main Street, Waynesboro, and was buried March 18, 1940 in Riverview Cemetery.[3] Emma was a member of the Wayne Avenue Presbyterian Church in Waynesboro.

Children of C. Augustus Whitlock and Emma Jane Alexander:

831.   LEOLA RICHARDSON WHITLOCK, b. c.1875 in Va., d. on 21 JUN 1894 in Waynesboro, when being engaged to be married, aged 18y 7m and 22d, and was bur. in Riverview Cem.

832.   EDITH RICE WHITLOCK, b. 25 OCT 1889 in Waynesboro, was m. 12 AUG 1919 there by W.A. Lynch to Claude Caesar Chambers, a soap manufacturer. Mr. Chambers was editor and owner of the *Augusta County Independent* newspaper in Staunton, and Edith served as the Augusta County Registrar. According to the Augusta County marriage records, Claude, a son of Robert G. Chambers and Eliza J. Roberts, was b. c.1882 in Bowman, Elbert Co., Ga. The couple was separated, and we know little about the fate of Mr. Chambers after 1930. Edith died at 6:00 p.m. on Sunday, 9 AUG 1953 in a hospital in Waynesboro, and was bur. 11 AUG 1953 in Riverview Cem. there.[4] Child:

8321.   MARY JANE CHAMBERS, b. 12 MAY 1920 at 703 West Main St. in Waynesboro, d. 12 SEP 1999 in Wilmington, Del., bur. Memorial Gardens at Christ Church, Greenville, Del., m. 23 JUN 1941 at the Wayne Avenue Presbyterian Church there to Robert Montgomery Bird, an employee of the DuPont Corporation. Mr. Bird, a son of Robert M. Bird, Sr. and Jacqueline Snow, was b. in 1917 in Bethlehem, Pa. He and his wife Mary Jane reside in Wilmington, Del. Children:

83211.   ROBERT M. BIRD, III, res. Stamford, Conn.
83212.   PEYTON BIRD, m. _____ Sise.
83213.   JOHN WOODBRIDGE BIRD, b. c.1947.

Figure 26 - Emma Jane (Alexander) Whitlock

84. Sarah Margaret (Alexander) Whitlock
(1851-1926)

Sarah "Margaret" Alexander, daughter of William Benjamin Alexander and Sarah Ann Maxwell, was born in Waynesboro on April 4, 1851, and baptized on May 11, 1866. On June 7, 1870, Margaret was married in Waynesboro to John Cassius Whitlock, a miller. John was born c.1847 in Augusta County, and a son of John A. Whitlock and Mary Depriest. John Cassius Whitlock died November 7, 1919 and was buried in Thornrose Cemetery of Staunton, Virginia.

---

[1] Augusta Co., Va. Death Register, gives date 10 DEC 1874.
[2] Riverview Cemetery, Waynesboro, grave marker: [relief] / C.A. WHITLOCK. / Died / March 11, 1890. / in the / 44. Year of his age. / *A devoted Husband / and Father.*
[3] Riverview Cemetery, Waynesboro, grave marker: [relief] / EMMA J. ALEXANDER / Wife of / C.A. WHITLOCK. / Born Sept. 6, 1849, / Died Mar. 16, 1940. / Aged 90 yrs. 6 mo. 10 da. / *She hath done what she could.*
[4] Riverview Cemetery, Waynesboro, grave marker: [relief] / EDITH WHITLOCK / CHAMBERS / Oct. 25, 1889 / Aug. 9, 1953.

Margaret died of cancer on Friday, February 12, 1926, at 337 North Lewis Street in Staunton, and was buried February 14, 1926 in Thornrose Cemetery of Staunton.[1]

Children of John Cassius Whitlock and Sarah Margaret Alexander:

841.   EMMA LOTTIE WHITLOCK, b. 1 MAR 1871, d. 18 JUL 1871 at the age of 7 years, 6 months and 19 days in Mt. Sidney.
842.   MARY BESSIE WHITLOCK, b. 26 FEB 1873, m. Charles Gates Clinedinst. Bessie bur. 26 AUG 1957 in Thornrose Cem., and followed her husband who bur. there 22 JUN 1937. No issue.
843.   WILLIE BRUCE WHITLOCK, b. 27 AUG 1875, d. 14 SEP 1915, m. Margaret Laing, b. 13 MAR 1879, d. 29 MAR 1929, bur. Thornrose Cem. Children:
    8431.   (Dr.) JOHN WILLIAM WHITLOCK.
    8432.   ELIZABETH WHITLOCK, b. 17 SEP 1912 in Va., d. 30 JUL 1973, bur. in Thornrose Cem., m. _____ Downs.
    8433.   MAXWELL BRUCE WHITLOCK, b. 1 APR 1915 in W.Va., d. 7 JUN 1971, bur. in Thornrose Cem.
    8434.   JAMES A. WHITLOCK, b. 1915 in Va.
844.   NINA BELLE WHITLOCK, b. 21 JUL 1879, d. unmarried 22 SEP 1952, bur. in Thornrose Cem.
845.   LYDIA AUGUSTA WHITLOCK, b. 7 JUL 1884, d. unmarried 24 JAN 1906 and bur. in Thornrose Cem.
846.   ETHEL LOUISE WHITLOCK, b. 20 APR 1887, d. unmarried, and bur. 4 MAY 1965 in Thornrose Cem.

---

[1] Her death certificate is recorded under the name Marguritte Whitlock.

85. Charles William Alexander
(1853-1920)

Charles William Alexander, a son of William Benjamin Alexander and wife Sarah Ann Maxwell, was born in Waynesboro on July 4, 1853. According to the family Bible record, he was baptized on June 10, 1870. On November 22, 1882, he was married in Staunton to Elizabeth "Lizzie" B. Jesser. Miss Jesser, a daughter of John Jesser and Rosa Kohler of Germany, was born October 1, 1861 in Pennsylvania.[1]

By 1886, Charles mostly maintained the family funeral home business, as C.W. Alexander & Company Furniture & Undertaking, and two years later his brother Thomas handled the manufacturing of church furniture as T.W. Alexander & Son. Charles was appointed by Gov. Davis as one of five members of the Virginia State Embalming Board.

A retail furniture store was located on the east side of the family casket and furniture building, and a residence was maintained at 723 W. Main St., where Homer would live. The Alexander planing mill was located at 920 Alexander Lane, was purchased in 1938 by Fred A. McCormick and was made part of the McCormick Lumber Company. The building was destroyed by fire in April 1953 and was rebuilt.

Charles died Monday, July 12, 1920 in Waynesboro, and was buried July 15, 1920 in Riverview Cemetery there. Elizabeth, died December 28, 1934 in Waynesboro and was buried in Riverview Cemetery. His death notice read: "On Monday evening, Mr. C.W. Alexander, accompanied by his young nephew Master Richard Jesser, drove over to the Basic Manufacturing Company in a light one-horse wagon for a log of lumber. On the return trip they were driving slowly over the hill, about 4:00, when the little boy observed the reins drop from Mr. Alexander's hands, and he settled back in his seat, dying almost instantly."[2]

Figure 27 - Charles William Alexander

After Charles' death in 1920, his son Homer Jesser Alexander continued the family business, using the name C.W. Alexander and Company.

Children of Charles Wesley Alexander and Elizabeth B. Jesser:

851. HOMER JESSER ALEXANDER, b. 6 SEP 1883 in Va., m. Nettie Calvert. Homer was a graduate of the Philadelphia Training School for Embalming, and in 1921 built a more modern funeral home at 811 W. Main St. in Waynesboro. From here in 1935, Homer operated two ambulances and two hearses. In Augusta Co. deed records, we find that Homer was declared incompetent in 1955. Suffering from alcoholism and ill health for years, Homer d. Monday, 27 FEB 1956 in a hospital in Waynesboro, and bur. in Lot 1A Block 201 of Riverview Cem. on Wednesday, 1 MAR 1956. Nettie, daughter of James Calvert and Mary Croft, b. in Staunton, d. 27 MAY 1976 at 8:10 p.m. just outside Waynesboro, and bur. by McDow Funeral Home in Riverview Cem. Her last residence was 1601 Mulberry St., and the informant on her death certificate was Mrs. Arron Pannell. Child:

   8511. CHARLES HOMER ALEXANDER, b. 31 DEC 1911 in Waynesboro, m. (1) 29 JUL 1934 in Richmond, Henrico Co.[3] to Aleath V. Leonard, div.; m. (2) Ruth Sheets who resided in Fishersville. One of his last occupations was an operator at an Amoco Service Station. "Homer" d. of immediate "myocardial infarction" at 1:35 a.m. 5 MAR 1961 in Waynesboro Community Hospital, and bur. two days later by McDow-Tyree Funeral Home in Riverview Cem. of Waynesboro.

852. ROSA LEE ALEXANDER, b. 4 DEC 1887 in Augusta Co., Va., m. 22 OCT 1913 in Staunton to Vincent David Bacigalupo, a merchant. Mr. Bacigalupo was a son of James Bacigalupo and Mary L. Boro, b. 30 AUG 1869

---

[1] Riverview Cemetery records and the Bible record of the Charles William Alexander Family show: Rosa Kohler Jesser, b. 4 FEB 1837, died 9 JUL 1886; and John Jesser, b. 13 DEC 1833, d. 24 SEP 1887.
[2] *Valley Virginian Newspaper*, Waynesboro, Friday, 16 JUL 1920.
[3] Marriage license on file at Staunton, Va., indicates place of marriage was Richmond, Va.

Figure 28 - Charles William Alexander in 1882

in Borzonosca, Italy.[1] Vince d. 6 FEB 1934 in Richmond, bur. there 8 FEB 1934. Children:

8521. WILLIAM VINCENT "Billy Vince" BACIGALUPO, SR., b. 5 NOV 1916, d. 25 FEB 2002, m. to Maybelle E. ( ). Mrs. Bacigalupo b. 31 AUG 1914, d. 2 SEP 1987; both bur. in Riverview Cem. Children:

85211. BETTY BACIGALUPO, m. Rob Cooley, res. Waynesboro.

85212. Daughter.

85213. WILLIAM VINCENT BACIGALUPO, JR.

8522. JAMES ALEXANDER BACIGALUPO, b. 15 JUL 1921, d.inf. 19 DEC 1922, bur. Riverview Cem.

853. CAROLINE VIRGINIA ALEXANDER, b. 28 JUL 1889 in Waynesboro, Va., m. in 1918 to Clarence Elijah Wine. "Carrie" d. of heart failure on 16 FEB 1985 at the Liberty House Nursing Home of Waynesboro. Carrie last resided in a large white house at 812 W. Main St. in Waynesboro, which had been built in 1887 by her father. Carrie bur. by McDow Funeral Home in Riverview Cem. of Waynesboro. No children.

854. PEYTON ALEXANDER, b. 10 MAY 1892, d.inf. 14 JUL 1892 and bur. in Riverview Cem.

86. Alice Cornelia (Alexander) McCormick
(1855-1916)

Alice Cornelia Alexander, daughter of William Benjamin Alexander and wife Sarah Ann Maxwell, was born in Waynesboro, Augusta County, on June 3, 1855. According to a family Bible, she was baptized on March 2, 1874.

On November 4, 1882[2], Alice was married in Waynesboro to William Holcome McCormick, a blacksmith and contractor from Radford, Virginia. Mr. McCormick, a son of William Steel McCormick and Virginia Organ, was born September 9, 1856 in Augusta County. The father was born January 19, 1825 and was killed in the Civil War. Wm. H. belonged to the Old Providence Church, and worked for the C&O Railroad. His brother Horatio Thompson McCormick was married to Alice Alexander's sister Betty Lee Alexander. Another brother, Steele S. McCormick, resided in Johnson City, Tennessee.

Alice died of breast cancer on June 28, 1916 in Waynesboro, and was buried in Riverview Cemetery there. Wm. H. remarried on July 27, 1927 to Mrs. Maud M. Landers, believed to be the same as Willie Maude Landers McCormick who died October 5, 1943 and buried in Lot 15C, Block 59 of Riverview Cemetery.[3] Wm. H. McCormick died January 4, 1933 in Waynesboro, and was buried Friday, January 6, 1933 in Riverview Cemetery there.[4] No issue.

Figure 29 - Alice Cornelia (Alexander) McCormick

---

[1] Information from the Augusta Co., Va. Marriage Records at Staunton, Va.

[2] Date from the family Bible, however the county record is 7 NOV 1882.

[3] Riverview Cemetery, Waynesboro, grave marker: MAUDE M. McCORMICK / June 25, 1878 / October 5, 1943.

[4] Riverview Cemetery, Waynesboro, grave marker: [relief] / WILLIAM H. McCORMICK, / Born Sept. 9, 1856, / Died Jan. 4, 1933. / ALICE C. ALEXANDER, / Beloved wife of / W.H. McCormick. / Born June 3, 1855, / Died June 28, 1916. / McCORMICK.

Figure 30 - Stables of Moses Harvey Alexander, situated on the corner of Lafayette Avenue, Marshall, Mo.

Figure 31 - New House of Moses Harvey Alexander, Marshall, Mo., before 1893

87. Moses Harvey Alexander, Sr.
(1857-1928)

We have found an interesting biographical sketch on this person while he was residing in the city of Marshall, Saline County, Missouri, which appeared in a biographical history book.[1] I will take the liberty here to use this sketch as the framework to document what information we have learned through research.

In olden days the office of embalmer was considered as sacred as that of the priest, and no unsanctified hand might touch the body in which the spirit should be re-incarnated. Today only science enters into the profession, and he who has best mastered the art is most regarded. Mr. Alexander certainly acquired a high reputation in this respect, and in the sad but necessary capacity of a funeral director he showed himself to have great tact and all regard for the proprieties. Aside from this, he is the owner of large sale stables at the corner of LaFayette and Morgan Streets. His business connections in this city began ten years ago.

The original of this sketch was born in Waynesboro, Augusta County, Virginia, July 9, 1857. According to the family Bible, he was baptized on December 7, 1873. He was a son of William Benjamin Alexander and Sarah Ann Maxwell, the former being by calling a manufacturer of furniture and an undertaker. M.H. received his education at his home town, Waynesboro, and after that he learned the trade with his father, who still remained in his native place, although retired from active business affairs, having sold out to two of his sons who carried on the business in Waynesboro. He was a native Virginian, and for many years has been a member of the City Council. His wife died in

Figure 32 - Moses Harvey Alexander, Sr.

1864, leaving a family of nine children, who had been brought up in the teachings of the Presbyterian Church.

Our subject remained with his father for some time, finally going on the road as a commercial traveler for a Richmond firm. He then entered the mercantile business, which he conducted for a year, when he decided to come West, and after prospecting through the various cities determined to locate here. He first established the undertaking business, later adding the livery to it. He is an expert embalmer, having been graduated in the art under Prof. J. Clark of Kansas City. As he was the only one in Saline County who is familiar with the business, he was naturally kept constantly employed. He began his livery business in 1885, and kept a full line of vehicles, ranking from the ordinary cart to the finest coupe and bus. He also had fine riding and driving horses. Aside from these interests Mr. Alexander was the owner of the County Agricultural Fair Grounds, upon which was a very fine track. He used this for training his own horses, and has some thoroughbred animals in his stables whose blood is of the best, while in this section he was a well-known breeder, and had a number of fine trotting horses. He had a farm of two hundred and forty acres on section 21, township 52.

Mr. Alexander possessed a beautiful home, which was built to his own order and design at No. 544 North Jefferson Street. We have a photograph of one large home of Mr. Alexander after it was newly built. This was presided over very graciously by his wife, who was Miss Eliza Guthrey and to whom he was married in Marshall on October 10, 1883. She was a daughter of John Garnett Guthrey,[2] a hotel keeper (and his wife Elizabeth Hawkins[3]) of Miami, which was her former home, although she was a native of Yonkers, New York. It was possibly at the Guthrey Hotel that James Washington Alexander met his last wife Mary Rice.[4] The appearance of the Guthrey home in Miami, Missouri was changed and in 1971 was an antique shop.

---

[1] Portrait and Biographical Record of Lafayette and Saline Counties, Missouri (Chicago: Chapman Brothers, 1893), pp. 377-378.

[2] John Garnett Guthrey, son of John Guthrey and Elizabeth Palmer, b. 2 MAY 1810 in Cumberland Co., Va. He married Elizabeth Hawkins in Brooklyn, N.Y. on 5 NOV 1862 and d. 13 JUN 1886 in Miami, Mo. They were the parents of seven children, Eliza being the eldest. Information in part from History of Saline County, Missouri (1881), p. 826.

[3] Elizabeth Seymour Hawkins, daughter of Joseph Sexton Hawkins and wife Eliza Myrick Hayden, b. 21 FEB 1841 in Yonkers, N.Y. Information from Mrs. John Guthrey of Maquoketa IA 52060.

[4] Letter, from Jessie (Brown) Bruce of Mound City, Kan.

Both Mr. and Mrs. Alexander were members of the Episcopal Church. Harvey had a thriving business[1] in Marshall until 1893, when he was burned out; so he collected his affairs and moved to St. Louis, Missouri. From an article in a St. Louis biography,[2] we note that M.H. was involved in the following: president of Modern Realty Co.; vice-president of Olive Street Bank; director of Beredith Realty Company Democrat; was on the State Board of Embalming four years; city undertaker of St. Louis four years and four months; President State, and vice-president National Funeral Directors associations; a Mason (Occidental Lodge, St. Louis Chapter; St. Aldemar Commandery, K.T. Missouri Consistory); Odd Fellow; Maccabee Club. Between 1896 and 1898, M.H. resided at 2939 Olive, then in 1910 at 2835 Olive, and one of the later residences of M.H. Alexander in St. Louis was at 5603 Clemens Avenue.

Eliza died December 5, 1902 at the age of 41 years, 11 months and 21 days, and was buried in Lot 2817 of Bellefontaine Cemetery of St. Louis two days later.

Harvey died on January 27, 1928, of high blood pressure and heart disease, at his residence on Clemens Avenue in St. Louis at 2:30 p.m. and was buried two days later by Alexander & Sons undertakers in Bellefontaine Cemetery there.

Children of Moses Harvey Alexander and Eliza Guthrey:

871. WILLIAM GUTHREY ALEXANDER, known as "Guthrey," b. 5 MAY 1885 in Marshall, Saline Co., Mo., d. 28 JAN 1939 in St. Louis, bur. Valhalla Cem. there, m. Therese F. Schleper. No issue.

872. SARAH SEYMOUR ALEXANDER, b. 23 AUG 1887 in Marshall, Mo., m. 10 OCT 1915 in St. Louis, Mo. to George Ernest Wilucki. Mr. Wilucki preceded Sarah in death in 1934. Sarah had a clear mind and was very much interested in family history. She d. Saturday, 17 MAY 1986 in St. Louis' Bethesda Dilworth Hospital and bur. 20 MAY 1986 in Bellefontaine Cem. of St. Louis. No issue.

873. MARY GIBSON ALEXANDER, b. 31 OCT 1889 in Marshall, Mo., m. Edwin Hunt, Jr., div. Mary d. 16 JUL 1980 and bur. two days later in Bellefontaine Cem. They had an adopted daughter:

Figure 33 - Moses Harvey Alexander, Jr.

   8731a. Mary Frances Hunt, m. Ernest Shapiro.
      8731a1. Terri Shapiro, m. 2 APR 1966 to Bruce Machaffie. Child:
        8731a11. Samuel Oliver Machaffie, b. 14 APR 1984.
      8731a2. Michael Guthrey Shapiro, b. 24 DEC 1944, m. December 2, 1965 to Sandra Wise. Child:
        8731a21. Sonam Shapiro, b. 10 OCT 1969.
      8731a3. Nicholas Gleyre Shapiro, b. 23 JUL 1949, m. Mary Crowley. Children:
        8731a31. Justin Shapiro, b. 7 JUN 1974.
        8731a32. Bryan Shapiro, b. 28 MAY 1975.
      8731a4. Jesse Maxwell Shapiro, b. 28 MAR 1951, m. Joan ( ). Children:
        8731a41. Nicolas Joseph Shapiro, b. 30 NOV 1971.
        8731a42. Kevin Shapiro.

874. MOSES HARVEY ALEXANDER, JR., b. 31 JAN 1892 in Marshall, Mo., m. 6 OCT 1913 to Ruth Ernestine Stansbury. He gave up his stock in the funeral home business on 14 SEP 1939. "Harvey" d. 29 APR 1959 in Clayton, Vernon Co., Mo. and bur. in Lot 2817 of Bellefontaine Cem. in St. Louis on 1 MAY 1959. Children, order uncertain:

   8741. RUTH VIRGINIA ALEXANDER, b. 10 APR 1916, m. 18 MAR 1939 to Harrison Bailey Stubbs. Children:
      87411. HARRISON ALEXANDER STUBBS, b. 8 JAN 1945.
      87412. SUSAN BAILEY STUBBS, b. 22 OCT 1948, m. 14 AUG 1971 to Mark White. Children:
        874121. ETHAN JAMES WHITE, b. 20 DEC 1975.
        874122. AMANDA WHITE, b. 8 SEP 1978.
        874123. ALEXANDER WHITE.

---

[1] Letterhead from the company reads "B.A. Fray–M.H. Alexander. Office of Fray & Alexander, Eclipse Livery, Feed & Sale. Stables. Marshall, Mo."
[2] John W. Leonard, The Book of St. Louisans (St Louis: The St. Louis Republic, 1906), p. 18.

8742. SARAH JEAN "Sally" ALEXANDER, b. 5 AUG 1919, m. 5 DEC 1942 to Bruce Sala Higginbotham. Children:

87421. ELIZABETH BRUCE HIGGINBOTHAM, b. 4 DEC 1947.

87422. ANN CAMERON HIGGINBOTHAM, b. 15 MAR 1950, m. 23 OCT 1976 to Dr. Jerry Niederman. Children:

874221. EMILY NIEDERMAN, b. 5 OCT 1978.

874222. SARAH NIEDERMAN, b. 31 JUL 1981.

874223. MATTHEW NIEDERMAN, b. 3 MAY 1984.

874224. TOBIAS NIEDERMAN, b. 17 JUN 1986.

87423. KENT RICHARD HIGGINBOTHAM, SR., b. 13 DEC 1953, m. Melody (   ). Children:

874231. KENT RICHARD HIGGINBOTHAM, JR., b. 30 SEP 1985.

874232. ERIN HIGGINBOTHAM, b. 20 MAY 1986.

8743. JAMES HARVEY ALEXANDER, b. 2 MAY 1922, m. 28 JUN 1946 to Lois Dixon. Children:

87431. JAMES DIXON ALEXANDER, b. 28 JUL 1948, m. Maria (   ). Children:

874311. CHRISTINE MARIE ALEXANDER, b. 25 JUL 1974.

874312. REBECCA STACY ALEXANDER, b. 9 SEP 1978.

874313. PATRICIA ANN ALEXANDER, b. 15 OCT 1981.

87432. SARAH LYNN ALEXANDER, b. 14 OCT 1950, m. David Henderson. Child:

874321. ERIN HENDERSON.

87433. ANITA RUTH ALEXANDER, b. 1 OCT 1952, m. Clint Reeves.

87434. MARY ALEXANDER, b. 26 AUG 1962.

8744. WILLIAM GUTHREY ALEXANDER, b. 16 APR 1927, m. (1) Marie Luker, then m. (2) Jean Dekker. Children:

87441. WILLIAM GUTHREY ALEXANDER, b. 28 FEB 1954, m. 3 SEP 1977 to Sally Streiber. Child:

874411. NICOLE MICHELLE ALEXANDER, b. 2 OCT 1978.

87442. KIMBERLY ALEXANDER, b. 30 JUL 1958.

87443. DANA ALEXANDER, b. 31 MAR 1965, m. George Meyer.

8745. INFANT ALEXANDER, d. at birth.

875. ELIZABETH GARNET ALEXANDER, b. 3 OCT 1894 in St. Louis, d. 5 JUN 1895.

876. VIRGINIA AMELIA ALEXANDER, b. 10 AUG 1896 in St. Louis, d. 1 OCT 1896.

877. ELIZABETH LEE ALEXANDER, b. 10 OCT 1897 in St. Louis, m. there 3 APR 1918 to Harry Seaver George Theis. Mr. Theis, b. 22 AUG 1897, d. in 1959. On July 12, 1982, Elizabeth suffered a stroke of paralysis which left her unable to read or write. Children:

8771. ALEXANDER ALBERT THEIS, b. 26 APR 1919, m. 27 APR 1940 to Gertrude Elizabeth Bakewell. In 1943, changed his name to JOHN SEAVER ALEXANDER. Children:

87711. JUDY ALEXANDER, b. 3 MAR 1942, m. Tom Dull. Children:

877111. BETSY DULL, b. 4 DEC 1964.

877112. JOHN SCOTT DULL, b. 14 NOV 1966.

87712. KATHLEEN ALEXANDER, b. 11 DEC 1943, m. 20 AUG 1978 to Charles Cepeda.

87713. NANCY ALEXANDER, b. 18 NOV 1945, m. 5 MAY 1967 to Ronald Zucker. Children:

877131. JENNIFER MARIE ZUCKER, b. 8 APR 1969.

877132. CINDY GAIL ZUCKER, b. 30 NOV 1970.

877133. JULIE ANN ZUCKER, 8 MAY 1973.

877134. ZACHARY ZUCKER, b. 14 OCT 1977.

87714. JOHN WHITLOCK ALEXANDER, b. 21 OCT 1947, m. 19 AUG 1972 to Theresa Pietropouli. Children:

877141. RICHARD JOHN ALEXANDER, b. 20 FEB 1978.

877142. CATHARINE ALEXANDER, b. 5 MAR 1984.

8772. BETTY LEE THEIS, m. (1) 21 DEC 1942 to Garth Delmar Salisbury, and div. in 1955. Betty m. (2) on 24 APR 1965 to Wallace H. Williams, Jr. Children:

87721. FAITH ELIZABETH SALISBURY, b. 15 AUG 1944, m. 2 APR 1966 to Wallace H. Williams, Jr. Children:

877211. ADAM SCOTT WILLIAMS, b. 8 FEB 1968, m. 10 OCT 1985 to Rena Smedley. Child:

Figure 34 - Moses Harvey Alexander, Jr. and Elizabeth Lee Alexander c.1900

8772111.   DANIEL SCOTT WILLIAMS, b. 13 SEP 1985.
    877212.   PETER CHRISTOPHER WILLIAMS, b. 10 FEB 1972.
    87722. GARTH DAVID SALISBURY, b. 9 APR 1947.
    87723. JOHN THEIS SALISBURY, b. 2 SEP 1953.
  8773. VIRGINIA DEAN THEIS, b. 19 APR 1928 to m. 11 AUG 1950 to Hal Berrien Coleman, and div. in 1969. Children:
    87731. CRAIG BERRIEN COLEMAN, b. 2 MAY 1953, m. 1 OCT 1977 to Vicki Shaw. Children:
      877311.   CALEB BERRIEN COLEMAN, b. 6 OCT 1980.
      877312.   LAUREN NICOLE COLEMAN, b. 25 FEB 1982.
      877313.   ZACHARY COLEMAN, b. 20 MAY 1987.
    87732. TIMOTHY DEAN COLEMAN, b. 15 APR 1957, m. 9 OCT 1987 to Barbara Fath. Child:
      877321.   CODY RAY COLEMAN, b. 8 OCT 1988.
    87733. TRACY LEE COLEMAN, b. 29 SEP 1959.
878.   MARCELINE EMMA ALEXANDER, b. 8 AUG 1899 in St. Louis, m. (1) 3 JUN 1923 there to Eugene Long Crutcher. Marceline m. (2) 5 SEP 1936 to Ralph H. Dumbell and d. 25 APR 1985 in New Melle, Mo. Burial in Oak Grove Cem. of St. Louis. Children:
  8781. EUGENE LONG CRUTCHER, b. 23 APR 1925, m. 29 AUG 1952 to Bettie Davis. Children:
    87811. ANNIE CRUTCHER, b. 5 JUN 1953.
    87812. ELIZABETH HARRIS CRUTCHER, b. 15 APR 1955, m. Ron Wasson. Child:
      878121.   ERIC LEE WASSON, b. 31 JUL 1986.
    87813. KATHERINE CRUTCHER, b. 27 APR 1957.
    87814. SARA CRUTCHER, b. 5 APR 1959, m. Keith Barnes, Sr. Child:
      878141.   KEITH BARNES, Jr., b. 7 DEC 1980.
    87815. RALPH CRUTCHER, twin, b. 30 MAY 1960.
    87816. DAVID CRUTCHER, twin, b. 30 MAY 1960.
  8782. JAMES ALEXANDER CRUTCHER, SR., b. 20 JUN 1928, m. 7 JAN 1950 to Doris Sullivan. Children:
    87821. JAMES ALEXANDER CRUTCHER, JR., b. 22 AUG 1950, m. Diane Cearlock. Children:
      878211.   PAUL ANTHONY CRUTCHER, b. 16 JUL 1978.
      878212.   KARI NICOLE CRUTCHER, b. 15 DEC 1979.
      878213.   BENJAMIN JAMES CRUTCHER, b. 18 NOV 1981.
    87822. SUSAN MARGARET CRUTCHER, b. 17 JUL 1951.
    87823. ROBERT PAUL CRUTCHER, b. 12 DEC 1953, m. Ruth (   ). Children:
      878231.   RACHEL CRUTCHER, b. 1984.
      878232.   REBECCA CRUTCHER.
      878233.   ROBERT DONALD CRUTCHER, b. 23 SEP 1988.
    87824. DONALD EUGENE CRUTCHER, b. 24 MAY 1955, d. 12 AUG 1978.
    87825. ROY CRUTCHER, b. 29 OCT 1957.
    87826. JANET DALE CRUTCHER, 7 NOV 1959.
    87827. PATRICK JOSEPH CRUTCHER, b. 19 OCT 1963.
879.   JAMES ALEXANDER, stillborn.

89. Bettie Lee (Alexander) McCormick
(1862-1938)

    Bettie Lee Alexander, daughter and youngest child of William Benjamin Alexander and Sarah Ann Maxwell, was born September 4, 1862 in Waynesboro, Augusta County. She was married by Reverend Frank McCutchan in Waynesboro on October 6, 1883[1] to Horatio Thompson McCormick.

    "Thompson" McCormick, as his wife would call him, was a son of William Steele McCormick and Eliza Virginia Organ, who were married November 13, 1850 in Virginia, and had a family of six children. He was born in Locust Springs of Augusta County, on March 17, 1858. He was a younger brother of William Holcome McCormick whose first wife was Alice Cornelia Alexander, sister of Bettie Lee Alexander.

    H.T. McCormick had served in Company H. of the 2nd Virginia Infantry during the Civil War and had a leg shot off by a shell in the Battle of Winchester on May 25, 1862. In the family Bible in the possession of Frederick Campbell McCormick of Earlysville, Virginia, we note that it is described that Wm. S. McCormick had an initial amputation of part of his leg, but died May 28, 1862 in Winchester after a second amputation.

---

[1] The county record is 6 OCT 1883, however Bible record date is 8 OCT 1883.

Dr. William Steele McCormick was born January 17/8, 1825 near Greenville, Augusta County, and was one of eight children of Robert McCormick and Sarah "Sally" Steele who were married March 4, 1824 in Virginia. Robert died December 4, 1879, and his wife Sally, the daughter of Nathaniel Steele, Jr. and Jean McCulland, died September 4, 1881.[1] Robert McCormick was a son of William McCormick and Mary Steele, and grandson of Robert McCormick, born c.1738 who was married in 1770 to Martha Sanderson. According to published records of the family of James McCormick of Londonderry, Ireland, this Robert was a son of Thomas McCormick, born c.1702, m. 1728 to Elizabeth Carruth, and d. c.1762. Thomas McCormick was son of their family emigrant, James McCormick.

Thompson and Bettie lived for a short time in Saline County, Missouri, and by November 1894 in Greenhorne, Colorado, where Thompson worked for The Southern Colorado Coal Company. They were then by January 1895 in Apache, Colorado. He died August 15, 1895 and was buried in Riverview Cemetery of Waynesboro.[2] On census records we note that he was a blacksmith. Betty Lee (Alexander) McCormick was easily recognizable in old photographs as having somewhat of a mustache. In late life, she suffered from diabetes, and due to gangrene had a leg removed above the knee after which she was confined to a wheel chair. Bettie died of valvular heart trouble and diabetes at the old Alexander home place at 703 Main Street in Waynesboro, at 5:00 p.m. on January 12, 1938. She was buried in Riverview Cemetery there.

Only Child of Horatio Thompson McCormick and Bettie Lee Alexander:

891.   FREDERICK ALEXANDER McCORMICK, owner of McCormick Lumber Co., b. 22 FEB 1892 in Waynesboro, Augusta Co., m. 9 JUN 1920 near Shadwell, Albemarle Co. to Nellie Riley Campbell. Nellie, daughter of William Campbell and Katherine Riley, b. 27 NOV 1891 in Shadwell (near Charlottesville). The couple resided in Waynesboro. Fred d. suddenly on his way to work on 22 OCT 1962, and bur. in Riverview Cem. Block 165, Lot 1A. "Nell" d. 19 FEB 1972 in Waynesboro and bur. in Riverview Cem. Children:
8911.   WILLIAM THOMPSON McCORMICK, b. 13 JUN 1921 in Charlottesville, Albemarle Co., m. c.1947 in Waynesboro to Hazel Patrick, of Leicester, England. They were div. early in the marriage. He d. 29 DEC 1983 in University of Virginia Hospital in Charlottesville, and bur. in Riverview Cem. of Waynesboro. Child:
89111. PATRICIA McCORMICK, m. Robert McLean, res. in N.Y.
8912.   FREDERICK CAMPBELL McCORMICK, b. 18 JAN 1926 in Waynesboro, m. 3 APR 1954 at William and Mary Chapel of Williamsburg to Anne Edwards Benthall, daughter of Henen Christian Benthall and Ada Cornelia Edwards of Hurtford Co., N.C. They reside in Earlysville. Child:
89121. REBECCA ANNE McCORMICK, b. 25 MAY 1960 in Charlottesville, m. 29 JUN 1985 at Meadows Presbyterian Church of Charlottesville, to John Justice Disosway from Newburn, N.C. No Children, res. Cary, N.C.
8913.   KATHERINE ELIZABETH McCORMICK, b. 13 FEB 1929 in Waynesboro, m. (1) c.MAY 1952 in Washington, D.C. to Joseph Piplico, and m. (2) circa October 1971 in Waynesboro to George Carson Lennox. Katherine manages a realty company of Waynesboro where she resides.
8914.   KEITH STEELE McCORMICK, b. 6 SEP 1930 in Waynesboro, d. 6 DEC 1952 in an automobile accident near Ruckersville, Greene Co., Va., bur. in Riverview Cem. of Waynesboro, Block 165, Lot 1C.

---

[1] Mildred Searson Goeller, The Steeles of Steeles Tavern, Virginia (Ripplemead, Va., 1974).
[2] Riverview Cemetery, Waynesboro, grave marker: McCORMICK. / In Loving Memory of / H.T. McCORMICK / March 17, 1858 / August 15, 1895. / His Wife / BETTIE LEE / September 4, 1862 / January 12, 1938.

Figure 35 - Horatio Thompson McCormick

Figure 36 - Bettie Lee Alexander

Figure 37 - Emma Whitlock with Caroline Alexander and Betty Whitlock

9. JAMES WASHINGTON ALEXANDER
(1821-1893)

James Washington Alexander, my ancestor and a child of William Alexander and Ann Bevans of whom we probably know the least, was born March 23, 1821/3 in Rockingham County, Virginia.[1] He was known as a carpenter, but may have branched to other lines of work later in life. In nearly every public record found about him he is styled as "J.W. Alexander."

J.W. was reportedly married five times; from research we can prove three marriages, and others may not be surprising. My great aunt, Mildred I. (Pippenger) Warren, submitted that J.W. Alexander's first wife and mother to his eldest daughter Sarah Catherine Alexander, was a woman named Samantha (   ). Further support of this connection has not been located.[2]

On June 19, 1844, J.W. wrote a letter from Kanawha Salines,[3] Kanawha County, West Virginia to his brother William B. Alexander of Waynesboro. Though he talked primarily about his health and prospects for work, the letter is valuable in placing J.W.'s location during the time. On August 12, 1849, J.W. Alexander was married to Louisa Forqueran in Kanawha County, West Virginia.[4] The couple was enumerated on the 1850 Federal census for the 46th district of Putnam County, [West] Virginia, on 22 JUL 1850, residing with John Forqueran, innkeeper, and his mother Sarah Miller (dwelling 417, family 431).[5] On April 23, 1851, Louisa Alexander died at the age of 22 years, 7 months and 22 days and was buried in the Alexander-Amos Cemetery of Putnam County, West Virginia.[6]

By August 1860, J.W. Alexander and his daughter Sarah were enumerated on the Federal census in Salt Pond Township (near Marshall[7]) of Saline County, Missouri (page 510, family 1006), without a wife.

Figure 38 - Pair of photographs believed to be James Washington Alexander (by Hutchings) and wife Mary (Rice) Gover (by D.P. Thompson).

According to my aunt Marjorie Jeanne Pippenger, late of Kansas City, Mo., her grandmother Nina Lee (Alexander) Pippenger said that her dad J.W. was a soldier in the Civil War, and after being captured and held a prisoner, carved

---

[1] Taken from his age in birth record of daughter Mary Alice Alexander as found in Saline Co., Mo. probate records. Another old family record in the possession of Jared Craun Alexander, of Weyers Cave, Va., indicates J.W. was born in 1832, but we know this is absolutely incorrect for two reasons: his daughter Sarah Catherine was born in 1841, and he was proprietor of his own small business in Kanawha Co., W.Va. in 1844—all events that could not have taken if 1832 were to be his birth year.

[2] A genealogical chart in the possession of Mrs. (Elizabeth D.) William Woodward Alexander of Waynesboro, Va. gives a marriage of this J.W. Alexander to Emily Woodson on 16 FEB 1843 in Augusta Co., Va. This has not been proven by me to be for our ancestor.

[3] In 1845, Kanawha Salines was described by author Henry Howe as a flourishing town about 6 miles above Charleston, containing 4 dry-goods and 2 grocery stores, an extensive iron-foundry, 1 Episcopal, 1 Presbyterian, and 1 Methodist church, and a population of about 800. [Henry Howe, Historical Collections of Virginia (1845), pp. 343-7]

[4] Kanawha County Marriages, Record Bk. 1816-1843, p. 167.

[5] The census notes the couple had been married within the year, but have living with them his daughter Sarah Alexander, age 4, from a previous marriage.

[6] The cemetery is located in Winfield, W.Va., between Route 35 and the river, and about 6 streets north of the bridge. Her tombstone notes she was the wife of James W. Alexander.

[7] An early advertisement for Marshall notes: Marshall was situated upon the Chicago and Alton Railroad, with two other railroads projected and surveyed, which will be constructed in the near future. Has water and gas works, one of the finest fair grounds and race tracks, three fine public school buildings, and the best system of graded schools of any town in the state, besides a flourishing Catholic Academy, a $75,000 courthouse, an opera house costing $35,000, with five churches, four banks, two building and loan associations, one daily and three weekly papers, two roller-process flouring mills, two elevators, one creamery, one nursery, one cigar factory, one wagon factory, one carriage factory, one tile factory, one fruit evaporator, one planing mill, and three large lumber yards. It is the largest and best horse and mule market in central Missouri. Marshall wants a starch factory, broom factory, canning factory, and a sugar factory. Saline County wants men of means and enterprise to divide up her large farms, practice skillful extensive farming and intelligent stock-breeding.

combs from tortoise shell for women. We have been unable to confirm his military service. We have found a service record for a James W. Alexander of Shenandoah County,[1] who also is listed there on the 1860 Federal census—but our J.W. Alexander was enumerated in Missouri during that time, so it seems the record may not be for our ancestor.

On August 17, 1870, J.W. Alexander and [his third wife] Mary (   ) (age 54 in 1870, born in Virginia) were enumerated in Miami Township of Saline County, Missouri (page 217A, family 177). This Mary Alexander is not the correct age to be his last wife Mrs. Mary (Rice) Gover, and we are uncertain of the identity of this person. The age for her on the census is clearly recorded as 54, born in Virginia.

On August 10, 1873, J.W. Alexander was married by E.W. Hoone, M.G. in Saline County, Missouri to Nannie Ashley, his fourth wife. This marriage is coincidentally confirmed by family records of Lottie Hildreth Fauber of Waynesboro. Miss Fauber claimed J.W. had five wives, and that

he went west and settled in Marshall, Missouri. He married [Nannie Ashley] and had a child named Nannie by this last wife [Ed. He had another wife, Mary Rice], *who died at the birth of this baby. This baby was adopted by her mother's best friend Mrs. Guinn. After Nannie's father's death (1893) the Guinn family moved to Palo Alto, California and Nannie married James W. McCurdy, a native of Lexington, Virginia.*

About 1875, J.W. Alexander was married to Mrs. Mary (Rice) Gover, his fifth wife. The spelling of the name comes from notes of my father's aunt Madeline Clarke who stated her grandmother told her the name was spelled *Rice*, but pronounced *Reese*. I have checked county records for a 100-mile radius of Marshall, Missouri, and a record of marriage has not been located.[2] Mary was perhaps previously married to Walter Gover, and had a child Martha Mae "Mattie" who later assumed the surname Alexander. A marriage record for or further information about Walter Gover has not been located. Madeline Clarke recalled that her grandmother Mary said "*I lived with this one family and took their name. It was Reese. As a child one family treated her badly, cutting her heals with a hoe. So she got up in the night, crawled out a window, and left.*" Considering this clue, we have no idea as to the actual maiden name of Mary.

The name of J.W. Alexander appears on the 1876 Tax Roll for Saline County, Missouri. On the 1880 census for Miami Township, Saline County, Missouri, J.W. was listed on page 18 as a carpenter, and not living within the city limits of Miami, but nearby. He is listed as a carpenter in the birth records of his daughter Mary Alice in 1883 and daughter Emma Leola in 1885 in Saline County. In 1888 we find J.W. listed in the city directory of Kansas City, Missouri, residing at 1717 Chestnut Avenue, and the next year the directory showed his residence as 2539 Gladstone.

On June 17, 1893, James W. Alexander died of a heart condition at his home at 2507 Monroe Street in Kansas City, Missouri. Even though a newspaper obituary said he was a dentist, he was always known by family as a carpenter. Mr. Alexander was buried by John W. Wagner Funeral Home[3] in Elmwood Cemetery of Kansas City, Missouri (Block L, plot 54) on June 19, 1893.

In 1897, Mary Alexander, widow, was listed in the city directory for Kansas City, as residing at 2408 Holmes Street, with her son Louis Fry Alexander, and the following year she was listed at 2321 Holmes Street. On the 1900 Federal census, Mary was residing with son Louis Fry Alexander at 43 McClure Place in Kansas City, Missouri. In 1906, Mary was residing at 32 McClure Place, the same address as my great-grandfather's uncle Daniel C. Pippenger—interesting!

Mary Alexander died of cerebral hemorrhage February 8, 1907 at 32 McClure Place in Kansas City, and was buried 11 FEB 1907 in Block G of Elmwood Cemetery. Her daughter Emma Leola was with her in the last days.[4]

Children of James Washington Alexander:

+   91.   SARAH CATHERINE ALEXANDER, b. 16 SEP 1841/6 in Waynesboro, Augusta Co., Va., m. (1) Daniel R. King, m. (2) John Eynon, and m. (3) Samuel T. Barker.
    92.   NANNIE ALEXANDER GWINN, b. 10 JAN 1875 in Miami, Saline Co., Mo., m. James W. McCurdy. Nannie was reportedly taken and raised by in-laws of her father J.W. Alexander (per Lottie Hildreth Fauber). We know Nannie was raised by Thomas Wilhite Gwinn and Lydia E. Neff in Jefferson twp. of Saline Co., Mo. Nannie, a former resident of Gilliam and Slater in Saline Co., Mo., d. of brain cancer, 13 NOV 1944 in Willow Brae

---

[1] James W. Alexander, private in the 33rd Reg. of Va. Vols., Shenandoah Co. K, enlisted 15 JUL 1861 in Winchester, Va. for one year, discharged 25 AUG 1862 from service in the C.S.A. A James W. Alexander appears on a roll of Prisoners of War who were forwarded from Wheeling, W.Va. to Camp Chase, Ohio on 30 JUN 1862. Date of capture 13 JUN 1862.
[2] Conversation with Madeline Clarke, 12 JUL 1987, who thought Mary Rice was from Hackensack, Minn. I note the Rice Family is numerous in Cass Co., Minn., but cannot make a connection to Mary.
[3] Records now maintained by McGilley Memorial Chapels, Linwood & Main Streets, Kansas City MO 64111. McGilley's told me over the telephone that J.W. Alexander's funeral expenses were paid by William B. Alexander of Marshall, Mo. [Note: W.B. Alexander must have been visiting Missouri, as he resided in Waynesboro, Va. where he conducted an active business.] When I wrote for a copy of that reference, it could not be located again.
[4] In a letter to Madeline Clarke (post marked January 1966, Chula Vista, Calif.), Mary Louise (Gilliam) Baggett wrote that after her grandfather J.W. Alexander died, grandmother Mary had been living with some girls and working in a laundry. She did not feel well one morning and stayed home. The others went to work as usual. Emma decided to go to see her mother that day and when she got there she found that she had had a stroke and fallen unconscious. She was not dead but died soon thereafter. Mary died in 1907.

Sanitarium of rural San Jose, Santa Clara Co., Calif., aged 69y 10m and 3d, bur. two days later in Alta Mesa Cem. Nannie's death certificate, which gives the Gwinns as her parents, indicates she lived in California for 40 years, and resided at 351 Channing Avenue in Palo Alto.[1] I attempted to follow leads from both in the Roller & Hapgood Funeral Home records and an informant S.H. Grimes, but made no progress locating descendants of Nannie in order that we might learn more about her ancestry. James W. McCurdy d. of arterial sclerosis when aged 69y 6m and 7d, 19 SEP 1930, and bur. 22 SEP in Alta Mesa Cem. (SE ½ Lot 131 Section B).

+   93a.   MARTHA MAE "Mattie" GOVER ALEXANDER, daughter of Mary Rice and Walter Gover, was raised by J.W. Alexander. Mattie m. Edward Marshall Gilliam.

+   94.   LOUIS FRY ALEXANDER, b. 29 APR 1876 in Miami, Saline Co., Mo., m. (1) Rosa E. Davis, and m. (2) Mrs. Inez Ellen (Barker) King.

+   95.   ANNIE AMELIA ALEXANDER, b. 6 SEP 1879 in Miami, Mo., m. Charles Peake McLaughlin.

+   96.   NINA LEE ALEXANDER, b. 22 AUG 1881 in Miami, Mo., m. John Wesley Pippenger.

    97.   MARY ALICE ALEXANDER, b. 2 OCT 1883 in Miami Twp., Saline Co., Mo.,[2] d. there 27 JUL 1884 of cholera infantum. Her grave has not been located.

+   98.   EMMA LEOLA ALEXANDER, b. 7 SEP 1885 in Miami, Mo., m. Clyde Delose Teft.

+   99.   HENRIETTE CATHERINE "Retta" ALEXANDER, b. 5 OCT 1886 in Kansas City, Jackson Co., Mo., m. John J. Barrett.

+   9(10).   BERTHA IRENE ALEXANDER, b. 18 JAN 1890 in Kansas City, Mo., m. James Emmet O'Neill.

---

[1] Next of kin in funeral records include: Marian Thomas Gwinn and Wilbur Gwinn of San Mateo, Calif.; Mrs. S.H. Grimes of Palo Alto, Calif.; her brother Dr. William Madison Gwinn of Atherton, Calif. who d. 26 NOV 1951 and had a son Dr. C.D. Gwinn of 1250 Jones Street in San Francisco, Calif.; and W.E. McCurdy of Berkeley, Calif.
[2] Saline Co., Mo. Births, LDS microfilm reel #946944, p. 1.7

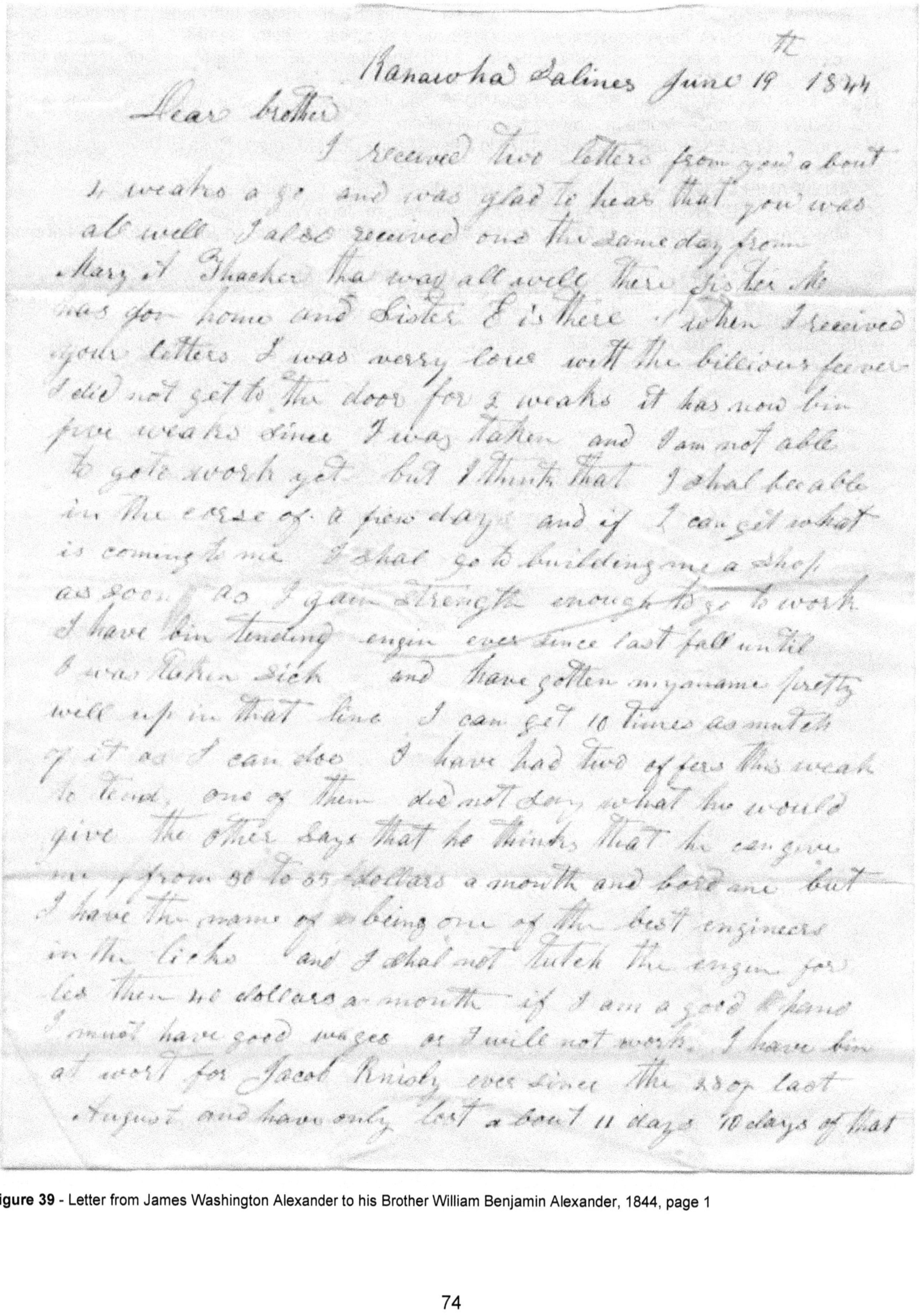

Kanawha Salines June 19 1844

Dear brother

I received two letters from you about 4 weaks a go and was glad to hear that you was all well I also received one the same day from Mary & Thacker tha was all well there Sister M was gor home and Sister E is there when I received your letters I was verry low with the billious feaver I did not get to the door for 2 weaks it has now bin five weaks since I was taken and I am not able to gote work yet but I think that I shal be able in the corse of a few days and if I can get what is coming to me I shal go to building me a shop as soon as I gain strength enough to go to work I have bin tending engin ever since last fall until I was taken sick and have gotten my name pretty well up in that line I can get 10 times as mutch of it as I can doe I have had two offers this weak to tend, one of them did not say what he would give the other says that he thinks that he can give me from 30 to 35 dollars a month and bord me but I have the name of being one of the best engineers in the licks and I shal not tutch the engin for les then 40 dollars a month if I am a good hand I must have good wages or I wile not work. I have bin at wort for Jacob Knisly ever since the 2dof last August and have only lost about 11 days 10 days of that

Figure 39 - Letter from James Washington Alexander to his Brother William Benjamin Alexander, 1844, page 1

74

was for my Christmas frollick I quit J P R one week before I was taken sick and commenced working for one ... Mr porter he was to give me $300 a day it was at his ... house that I was taken sick. I never was better treated at enny place in my life it appeared that tha did not know how to treat me as well as tha wished.

Mr porter is a salt maker and a fine man and I am sorry to say that he has had verry bad luck his salt water failed and he had to have one of his wells bored deeper I helped to doe the booring it was four hundred and forty seven feet deep, we made it 800 feet and his water is not good yet, he sent for Knob yesterday, to come and boor 200 feet more, tha get 18 bushels of salt for each foot that we bored but he says that he will not boor eny more for salt. the deepest well in the licks is now in the 16 hundred and tha are still a booring in it and in les then 5 years tha will have to go 2000 feet some of the salt makers makes salt with out burning one stick of wood or one lump of coal tha have struck a viane of gas in some of the wells that will blow the water 150 feet in the air it saves the trouble of pumping the water it blows the water in to the sisterns through pipe fogs and the ... lead the gas from there to the furnace and there tha set fire to it and it answers in the place of coal only it is better it is nothing more then air at one of these furnace tha will make from 80 to 100 barrels of salt every day a barrel holds 7 bushels of salt if I ever should

Figure 40 - Letter from James Washington Alexander to his Brother William Benjamin Alexander, 1844, page 2

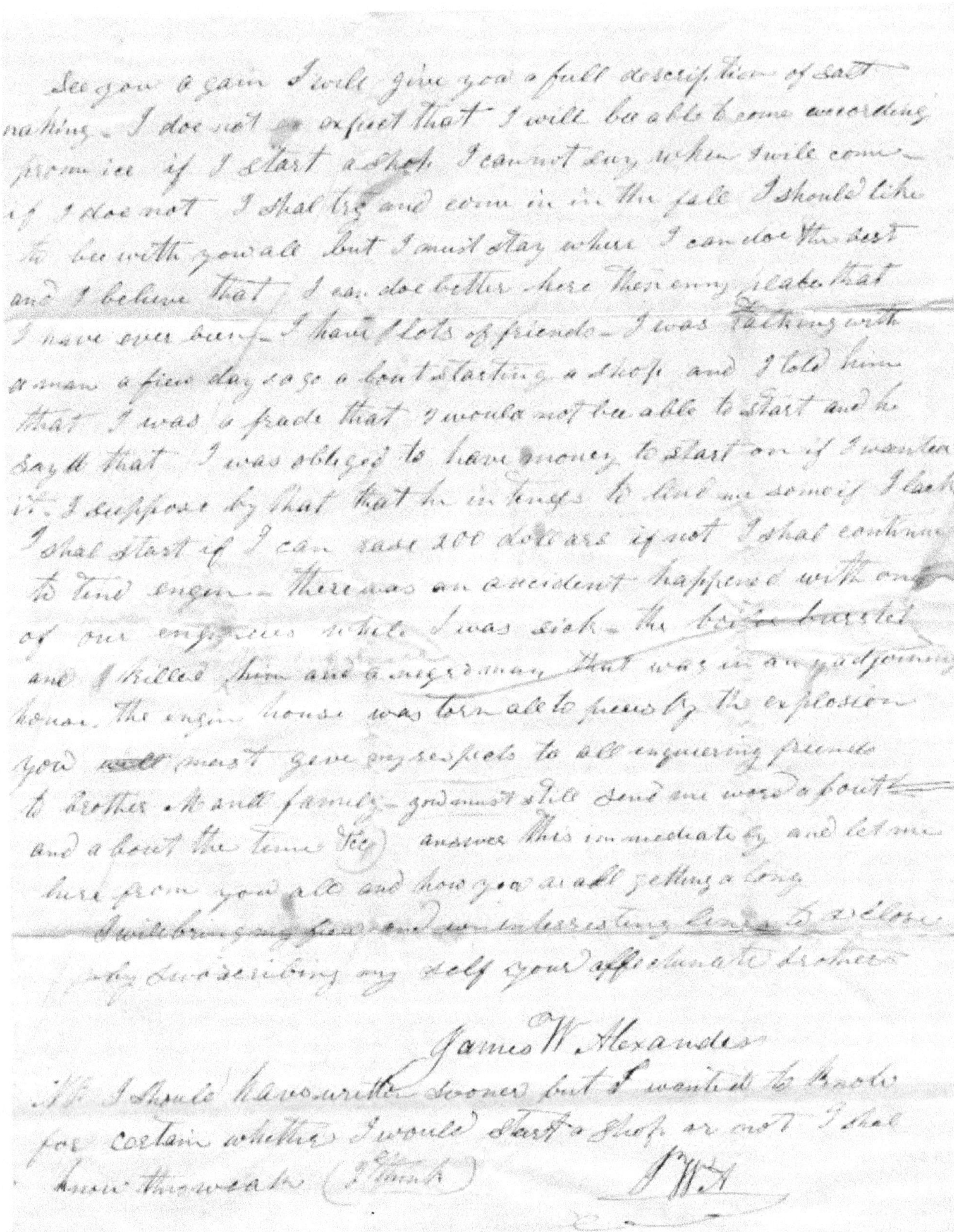

see you again I will give you a full description of salt
making — I doe not expect that I will be able to come according
promice if I start a shop I cannot say when I will come
if I doe not I shall try and come in in the fall I should like
to bee with you all but I must stay where I can doe the best
and I believe that I can doe better here then enny place that
I have ever been — I have flots of friends — I was talking with
a man a few days ago a bout starting a shop and I told him
that I was a fraid that I would not be able to start and he
sayd that I was obliged to have money to start on if I wanted
it — I suppose by that that he intends to lend me some if I lack
I shal start if I can rase 200 dollars if not I shal continue
to tend engin — there was an accident happened with one
of our engines while I was sick — the boiler bursted
and I killed him and a negro man that was in an adjoining
house the engin house was torn all to pieces by the explosion
you must give my respects to all enquiring friends
to brother M and family — you must still send me word about
and a bout the time (&c) answer this immediately and let me
here from you all and how you ar all getting a long
I will bring my few and uninterresting lines to a close
by discribing my self your affectionate brother

James W Alexander

N.B. I should have written sooner but I wanted to know
for cartain whether I would start a shop or not I shal
know this week (I think)

JWA

Figure 41 - Letter from James Washington Alexander to his Brother William Benjamin Alexander, 1844, page 3

Figure 42 - Letter from James Washington Alexander to his Brother William Benjamin Alexander, 1844, mailing cover

91. Sarah Catherine (Alexander) King Eynon Barker
(1841/6-1914)

Sarah Catherine Alexander, the eldest daughter of James Washington Alexander, was born September 16, 1841/6[1] in Waynesboro, Augusta County, Virginia. It has been said that her mother's name was Samantha, but official record of this information has not been located.

On Sunday, March 26, 1865, Sarah C. Alexander was married by Jesse J. Ferril, Justice of the Peace in the Saline County Court at his residence in Miami, Missouri to Daniel R. King.[2] Mr. King, a laborer who was born about 1841 in Missouri, died January 29, 1884 in a mine accident.

After the death of Daniel R. King, Sarah was remarried May 17, 1886 in Marshall, Missouri by Rev. M.C. Sandidge[3] to her second husband John Eynon. Mr. Eynon was born 1835 in Wales, served in Co. B of the 179th New York Infantry during the Civil War. He had children by a previous marriage, and died in Marshall, Missouri about 1892.[4] His body was buried in Pleasanton, Linn County, Kansas.[5]

Figure 43 - John Eynon and wife Sarah Catherine Alexander, with baby Esther Maude Eynon (Taken by R.W. Harris of Pleasanton, Kansas)

On the 1900 Federal census for Potosi Township, Linn County, Kansas, Sarah was enumerated with her third husband Mr. Samuel T. Barker, son of Joseph V. Barker.[6] Samuel T. Barker, whom Sarah married February 11, 1900, had been previously married to Martha Mary Jane Bell who died near Pleasanton, Kansas on June 3, 1899.

Samuel, born June 5, 1833 in Ohio. He died of general debility brought on by a cold on the lungs on August 31, 1914, and was buried September 2, 1914 with his former wife Martha Mary Jane (Bell) Barker (d. 1899) in Lettel Cemetery, located east of Pleasanton in Linn County, Kansas.

In 1908, the house in which Sarah and her family were living burned to the ground, and nothing was saved.

Sarah died August 8, 1914 of mitral regurgitation in Pleasanton, Linn Co., Kansas, and was buried August 9, 1914 in Pleasanton Cemetery. On her death certificate, informant Omer Brown gave West Virginia as Sarah's place of birth.

Figure 44 - (left to right) Samuel T. Barker, a neighbor, Omer Brown, Jr., Sarah Catherine (Alexander) Eynon Barker, two neighbors, Jessie (Brown) Bruce

---

[1] She is age 4 on the 1850 Federal Census for Putnam Co., W.Va., with father J.W. Alexander and step-mother Louisa Forqueran.

[2] Saline Co., Mo. Marriages, Bk. B, p. 224.

[3] Saline Co., Mo. Marriages, Bk. 2, p. 277.

[4] Notes of Betty Schultz show Mr. Eynon died in 1891 in a coal mine accident.

[5] Grave marker, Pleasanton Cem.: EYNON. / SARAH K. / 1841-1914. / JOHN / 1835-1892.

[6] Sarah was married to Mr. Barker c.1909. *The Pleasanton Observer* (7 MAY 1881), announced the death of Mr. Joseph V. Barker at his home in Bates Co., Mo., 8 miles east of Pleasanton, on Sat. April 30th, age 50 years. He was buried in the Salem Cem. of Foster, Mo. Mr. Barker was born in Manchester, Eng. in 1828. He came to this country in 1855 and settled in Kalamazoo, Mich., later removing to Kansas City in 1857, and successively resided in Linn, Labette and Bourbon Counties. He finally settled in Bates Co. about a year since. He leaves a wife and nine children.

Figure 45 - Lorene Estelle King

Figure 46 - Ernest Carlee Brown

Figure 47 - Jessie Brown Bruce

Figure 48 - Gay Lee Brown and Barbara Dell Brown

Children of Sarah Catherine Alexander and Daniel R. King:[1]

911.	FRANCIS MARION KING, carpenter, b. 4 NOV 1866 in Montgomery City, Montgomery Co., Mo., m. 21 SEP 1900 to Margaret "Maggie" Reed. About 1902 the couple moved to Ludlow, Livingston Co., Mo. Frank dropped dead at his home in Ludlow on 29 JAN 1934 aged 67y 2m and 25d, and bur. 30 JAN 1934 in Monroe Cem. of Ludlow, Mo. He was a member of the Christian church. Children:

Figure 49 - (l to r) Lester King, Ernest King, and Frank King

  9111.	JESSE D. KING, b. 1902 in Mo., res. Kansas City, Mo.
  9112.	FLOYD ARTHUR KING, b. 1904 in Mo., res. Ludlow, Mo.
  9113.	EVA G. KING, b. 1908 in Mo., res. Ludlow, Mo.

912.	CHARLES R. KING, railroad conductor, b. c.1868, m. Alma Ishmael, res. Los Angeles, Calif. Children:
  9121.	VIRGINIA KING.
  9122.	ROBERT KING.

913.	LESTER GLEN KING, b. 1875, m. Inez Ellen Barker, daughter of James Franklin Barker and his first wife Martha Tryphena Molden, q.v. He died 15 NOV 1917, and was buried in Lot 303 of the city Cem. in Pleasanton, Linn Co., Kan.[2] After Lester died, Inez remarried (2) to (94.) LOUIS FRY ALEXANDER, q.v., on 9 SEP 1918, and d. 27 APR 1942 in Independence, Mo. Children:

  9131.	LESTER LEE KING, b. 29 DEC 1905 in Rosedale Community, Wyandotte Co., Kan., m. Lucille Georgia Milling, b. Topeka KS, d. 21 JAN 1973 in Research Hospital in Kansas City, Mo. after injuries from being struck by a car while crossing Gregory Blvd., bur. Mt. Moriah Cem. Lester d. 9 JUN 1957. No children.

  9132.	LORENE ESTELLA KING, b. 19 OCT 1907 in Pleasanton, Linn Co., Kan., m. 19 NOV 1926 in Independence, Mo. to Randall Robert Nazer. Lorene d. 3 SEP 1986 at Baptist Medical Center in Kansas City, Mo. and bur. 6 SEP 1986 in Mt. Washington Cem. of Independence, Mo. Mr. Nazer, a native of Utah, b. 19 NOV 1902 in Utah, worked for the U.S. Postal Service. He d. Tuesday, 9 AUG 1983 at Independence Sanitarium, and bur. Friday, 12 AUG 1983 at Mt. Washington Cem. Child:

    91321.	BETTY LOUISE NAZER, m. 23 DEC 1950 in Independence, Mo. to Clifford Glen Schultz. Children:
      913211.	SUSAN EILEEN SCHULTZ, stillborn in N.M.
      913212.	SCOTT ANDRES SCHULTZ.
      913213.	MELORA ANN SCHULTZ.
      913214.	LORANELLE LOUISE SCHULTZ, b. Evansville, Ind., m. Ralph Lockyear.

  9133.	ERNEST JAMES "Vernie" KING, carpenter, b. 17 DEC 1910 in Pleasanton, Linn Co., Kan., m. (2) to Evelyn Pearl Lask. He d. Saturday, 16 DEC 1978 at the University of Kansas Medical Center in Kansas City, Kan. He was a carpenter for the R.L. Faubion Company for 15 years, a Mason, and a member of the Fraternal Order of Eagles. Children:
    91331.	ERNEST D. KING, SR., m. Patricia Pow, res. 927 Norton, Kansas City (1978). Children:
      913311.	ERNEST D. KING, Jr.
      913312.	DAVID KING.
    91332.	ROBERT E. KING, m. Barbara Marie Allen, res. Excelsior Springs, Mo.

914.	ERNEST CLINTON KING, b. 2 OCT 1877 in Saline Co., Mo., m. Jessie Ellis, daughter of William Ellis and Mollie Ham, b. 17 FEB 1884 in Mo., who was quite a large woman.[3] Jessie d. 14 MAR 1955 and bur. by Marcy Funeral Home on 17 MAR 1955 in Mount Moriah/Hill Crest Memorial Park of Omaha, Nebr., MMB Lot 82 grave 12. Ernest was crippled with arthritis, and walked with two canes. He d. 8 OCT 1966 in Elmwood, Nebr. and bur. 11 OCT 1966 in Mount Moriah/Hill Crest Memorial Park. Child:
  9141.	JACK KING, was a policeman, m. Harlien [or Peggy], res. Omaha, Nebr. Jack preceded his parents in death. Child:
    91411.	JAMES KING.

Child of Sarah Catherine Alexander and John Eynon:

915.	ESTHER MAUD EYNON, b. 20 MAY 1887 in Miami, Saline Co., Mo., m. 28 MAY 1905 at the home of Frank

---

[1] Information in part provided by Jessie (Brown) Bruce of Mound City, Kan.
[2] Gravestone, Pleasanton Cem.: LESTER KING / 1875-1917.
[3] Letter, Mildred I. (Pippenger) Warren (Harrisonville, Mo.), 15 JUL 1989, further stating that Mary L. (Pippenger) Abbas thought Jessie was about 5'10" tall and weighed over 200 pounds. Ernest and Jessie often drove their Model T car from Omaha, Nebr. to Kansas City, Mo. for visits.

Campbell by Probate Judge Newman in Fulton, Bourbon Co., Kan., to Omer Franklin Brown, Sr., a lived in Pleasanton, Kan. Esther d. 28 MAY 1966 in Mercy Hospital of Ft. Scott, Bourbon Co., Kan., and bur. in Woodland Cem. at Mound City, Kan. Omer, a blacksmith, was a son of William Thomas Brown and Anna Alice Morrow,[1] b. 2 JUN 1886 in LaDue, Mo. He d. at 9035 Newton Drive in Overland Park, Kan., on 20 AUG 1966 and was bur. 23 AUG 1966 in Woodland Cem. of Mound City, Kan. A sister of Omer Brown, Julia Ann (Brown) Cox, was born 1890, d. 1965 and bur. in Woodland Cem. Children:

9151. Infant Brown, b. Fulton, Kan.

9152. Infant son Brown, no dates, bur. Woodland Cem.[2]

9153. JESSIE BERNICE BROWN, b. 4 FEB 1908 in Pleasanton, Linn Co., Kan., d. 26 JUL 1990 at her home in Mound City, Kan., bur. 28 JUL 1990 in Woodland Cem. of Mound City, Kan., m. 18 MAY 1928 by Rev. Woods, in Mound City, Kan. to "E." Delbert Bruce. Mr. Bruce, b. 13 JUL 1907 in Las Animas, Colo., d. 8 SEP 1987 in Ft. Scott, Kan. and bur. in Woodland Cem. of Mound City, Kan. Delbert was a truck driver, a Mason, and left a brother Donald Bruce of Victoria TX and sisters Ruth Mings and Margaret Boots of Mound City, Kan. Children:

91531. ROBERT FRANKLIN BRUCE, b. 9 FEB 1932 in Mound City, Kan., m. 27 DEC 1955 there to Helen Murray. Res. at 14801 Endicott Drive in Austin, Tex., then Santa Clara, Calif. (1990). Bob, with previous service in the U.S. Air Force, worked as a civil engineer and belonged to the Assembly of God Church. Helen, daughter of Charles Murray and Suzie West, b. 16 AUG 1930 in Versailles, Morgan Co., Mo. Children:

915311. JACK ALLEN BRUCE, b. 20 JUL 1956 in Elk City, Beckham Co., Okla., m. 20 MAR 1982 at Baton Rouge, La. to Stephanie Gautreau. Child:

9153111. KIMBERLY BRUCE.

915312. CHARLES DELBERT BRUCE, b. 15 OCT 1957 in Elk City, Okla., m. Mikaela Mitchell. Children:

9153121. REBECKA JEAN BRUCE, b. 23 AUG 1981.

9153122. ROBERT BRUCE.

9153123. ANN BRUCE.

915313. JULIA ANN BRUCE, b. 1 MAR 1960 in Kansas City, Mo.

91532. MARY ANN BRUCE, b. 15 OCT 1933 in Mound City, Kan., m. 14 APR 1955 to Eugene Jamison, res. Ft. Scott, Kan. (1990). Children:

915321. SHARON KAY JAMISON, b. 28 AUG 1963 at Ft. Scott, Kan.

915322. KAREN ANN JAMISON, b. 14 JUN 1965 at Ft. Scott, Kan.

915323. JENNIFER LOUISE JAMISON, b. 4 JUL 1974.

9154. OMER FRANKLIN BROWN, JR., b. 22 JAN 1910 in Pleasanton, Kan., m. 16 MAY 1929 at the home of Rev. Woods, in Mound City to Nellie Victoria Paddock. Nellie, daughter of George Henry Paddock and Amanda Shields, b. 5 JUN 1908 in Blue Mound, Linn Co., Kan., and bapt. c.1920 in the Methodist Church of Osawatomie, Kan. Mr. Brown retired in 1977 as vice president of Lift and Clark Construction Company, was a Navy Veteran of World War II, and a member of the Hewitt New Post of the American Legion, the Oscar Dewey Chapter of the Order of the Eastern Star, and the Masonic Lodge of Mound City, Kan. Omer suffered a heart attack while mowing the lawn at his home on Tuesday, 7 JUN 1983, declared dead at Shawnee Mission Medical Center in Overland Park, Kan., and bur. 10 JUN 1983 in Woodland Cem. of Mound City, Kan. Children:

91541. GAY LEE BROWN, b. 5 JUL 1933 in Mound City, Kan., m. 27 AUG 1963 there to Larry Daniel Douglas. Children:

915411. RONALD DOUGLAS, b. 12 OCT 1956.

915412. GREGORY DOUGLAS, b. 5 SEP 195_.

915413. AMY JANELLE DOUGLAS, b. 27 FEB 1965.

91542. BARBARA DELL BROWN, b. 6 OCT 1935 in Mound City, m. 10 JUL 1955 there to James Richard Queen. Children:

915421. JAYME QUEEN, b. 3 FEB 1961, m. SEP 1981 to Tommie Morris.

915422. BARRY QUEEN, b. 8 MAR 1964.

9155. ERNEST CARLEE BROWN, b. 19 FEB 1912 in Pleasanton, Kan., d. 21 AUG 1999 in Albuquerque, N.M., m. 22 OCT 1933 in Mound City to Imogene Mills. Child:

91551. DAVID BROWN, b. 8 MAR 1941, m. Frances Louise McCleron. Children:

915511. LESLIE JEAN BROWN, b. 9 SEP 1962.

915512. JENNIFER BROWN, b. 25 JAN 1967.

---

[1] William Thomas Brown, b. 10 JUL 1857, d. 7 JAN 1929, m. Anna Alice Morrow, b. 13 MAR 1862, d. 1952, both are bur. in Pleasanton Cem.
[2] Gravestone, Woodland Cem.: INFANT SON / of / O.F. & E.M. Brown.

93a. Martha Mae (Gover) Alexander Gilliam
(1871-1947)

Martha Mae "Mattie" (Gover) Alexander, was born April 2, 1871 in Miami, Saline County, Missouri, and was said to be the daughter of Walter Gover and Mary Rice. About 1883, when Mattie was nearly age 13, she was taken from her mother, Mary, by Mrs. William Good and sent to live with the Gilliam Family where she lived about a year. About this time her mother Mary had a child, Mary Alice Alexander (b. 1883, d. 1884), who did not live long, after which time Mattie stayed with her mother for a year, then returned to the Gilliam Family.[1] She was raised, and presumably adopted, by J.W. Alexander and Mary Rice. She used the surname Alexander.

On September 17, 1892, Mattie was married by S.P. Ewing, Justice of the Peace, in Keytesville, Chariton County, Missouri to Edward Marshall Gilliam. Mr. Gilliam, a son of James Sanders Gilliam and Martha Martin, was born in Keytesville on November 27, 1853.[2] He was a farmer. In 1898 he bought a farm and later went broke, and in 1905 he moved his family to Love County, Oklahoma. In route they stopped in at Kansas City to visit Mary (Rice) Alexander.

Mr. Gilliam died in Marietta on December 14, 1921. Eulalia McClintock writes: "When I was 2 [in about 1905], my father mortgaged the home and bought cattle. The price went down and he lost the home," causing the family move to Indian Territory, which later became Oklahoma.

E.M. Gilliam was buried December 16, 1921 in Lakeview Cemetery of Marietta. Mattie died October 27, 1947 at McCurdy Clinic of Purcell, McClain County, Oklahoma and was buried in Lakeview Cemetery near Marietta, Oklahoma on October 29, 1947.

Children of Edward Marshall Gilliam and Martha Mae (Gover) Alexander:[3]

93a1. Walter Harvey Gilliam, b. 27 JUL 1893 in Keytesville, Chariton Co., Mo., m. 29 SEP 1917 in Marietta, Love Co., Okla. to Harriett "Hattie" Odessa Bellows, b. 23 NOV 1894 in Tex., d. 5 AUG 1974 in Marietta, Okla., bur. Rose Hill Cem. of Ardmore, Okla. Walter d. 3 JUN 1968 in Ardmore Memorial Hospital of Ardmore, bur. at Rose Hill Cem. of Ardmore. No children.

93a2. Mary Louise Gilliam, b. 12 AUG 1895 in Keytesville, Mo., d. 5 MAY 1975 in Chula Vista, San Diego Co., Calif., bur. Glen Abbey Memorial Park of Bonita, Calif., m. 14 MAY 1917 in Marietta, Okla. to Denver Enos Baggett, b. 21 JUL 1892, d. in August 1962. Children:

Figure 50 - Gilliam Family, children Emma, Mary and Walter with their father Edward Marshall Gilliam (taken in Marceline, Mo.)

 93a21. Franchelle Baggett.
 93a22. Lynn Richard Baggett.
93a3. Ralph Edward Gilliam, b. 26 JUL 1897 in Keytesville, Mo., d. 21 MAR 1972 in Ardmore Memorial Hospital of Ardmore, Okla., bur. in Lakeview Cem. of Marietta, Okla., m. 9 FEB 1920 in Marietta to Ella Mae Enoch, b. 10 NOV 1893, d. 22 JUL 1973, bur. Lakeview Cem. Adopted child:
 93a31a. Charles Edward Gilliam.
93a4. Emma Pauline Gilliam, b. 1 NOV 1901 in Greenville, Indian Territory, Okla., m. (1) in July 1918 to Harry Hammond, and m. (2) in June 1934 to Ted G. Morris. She d. 10 SEP 1976 in San Diego, Calif. and bur. in El Camino Cem. of San Diego. Child:
 93a41. Elizabeth Pauline Hammond.
93a5. Sallie Eulalia Gilliam, b. 13 DEC 1907 in Greenville, Okla., m. 28 FEB 1932 in Alex, Grady Co., Okla. to Rex Wilford McClintock, b. 27 NOV 1906 in Henderson, Tenn., son of James Walter McClintock and Mary Leota Coppedge, res. Chula Vista, Calif. Child:

---

[1] Conversation with Madeline Clarke, 12 JUL 1987.
[2] From information provided by Shirley Haynes, Route 1, Box 16, Gilliam MO, we learned that James Sanders Gilliam, b. 1819 and d. 23 AUG 1903 near Keytesville, Mo., was one of 10 children of William Richardson Gilliam (1775-1837) and Judith Ann Woodson (1782-1844) from Prince Edward Co., Va.
[3] Information in part provided by Sallie Eulalia McClintock of Chula Vista, Calif., 1978.

93a51. Willa Claire McClintock, b. 28 NOV 1934 in Chickasha, Grady Co., Okla., m. 30 JUN 1960 at Warehouse Point, Conn. to Edward Raymond Krause, b. 1 AUG 1929 in Milwaukee, Wisc., son of Edward Herman Krause and Margaret Brown, d. 4 JUN 1954 at Rochester, Minn. Three children.

Figure 51 - Sisters (l to r) Nina Lee (Alexander) Pippenger, Emma Leola (Alexander) Teft, Annie Amelia (Alexander) McLaughlin, and their sister-in-law Inez Ellen (Barker) King Alexander

Figure 52 - (l to r) Ralph E., Mary L., and Walter H. Gilliam

Figure 53 - (l to r) Mary L., Edward M., Emma P., Ralph E., Sallie E., Martha Mae, and Walter H. Gilliam in 1908

Figure 54 - (l to r) Martha Mae "Mattie" Gilliam (step-daughter of J.W. Alexander), Ralph Edward Gilliam, Emma Pauline Gilliam, Eulalia Gilliam [McClintock], Walter Harvey Gilliam, Edward Marshall Gilliam, Mr. Duncan (a farm worker).

Figure 55 - Rex Wilford McClintock and Sallie Eulalia Gilliam in 1982

Figure 56 - Mary Louise Gilliam Baggett in 1944

94. Louis Fry Alexander
(1876-1934)

Louis Fry Alexander, son of James Washington Alexander and wife Mary (Rice) Gover, was born in Miami, Saline County, Missouri on April 28, 1876. His curious middle name has not been connected to any allied family of the Alexander's, yet Fry was a common surname in Waynesboro, Augusta County, Virginia.[1]

It was not common knowledge that he was first married on October 12, 1901 in Kansas City, Wyandotte County, Kansas to Rosa E. Davis who became ill with the measles before a child was born. Both the mother and child soon died.[2]

On September 9, 1918, Louis was married in Mound City, Linn County, Kansas to Mrs. Inez Ellen (Barker) King. Inez, born March 3, 1883 in Pleasanton, Linn County, Kansas, was the daughter of Dr. James Franklin Barker and Martha Tryphena Molden,[3] and had been previously married to Lester Glen King. Inez Alexander, a resident of Fairmount, Missouri, died April 27, 1942 in Independence Sanitarium and was buried the following Wednesday at Pleasanton, Kansas.

Louis was a private in Company B of the 19th Regiment, First Engineering Corps during the Spanish American War, and from the service applied under application #1626154 on October 17, 1928 for pension. Lacking the exact period of service, his application for pension from the U.S. Government was denied. Louis F. Alexander, a boiler maker for the C.M. & St. Paul Railroad who resided at 801 Fairview, died two days after a cystotomy operation at 9:30 a.m. on February 5, 1934 in the Independence Sanitarium of Independence, Jackson County, Missouri and was buried February 7, 1934 in Pleasanton Cemetery of Pleasanton, Kansas.[4]

Only child of Louis Fry Alexander:

941.   INA MAE ALEXANDER, b. 16 AUG 1921 at 7th and Kensington Streets in Kansas City, Jackson Co., Mo., d. JAN 1996, m. 19 JUL in Independence, Mo. to Carl Christy Maness (pronounced "main-ess"), res. Independence, Mo. Children:
   9411.   CARLA DIANNE MANESS, b. 16 OCT 1942 in Independence, m. to Kassim Zainie from whom she div. in Kuching, Malaysia. Carla resides in Antonio, Tex.
   9412.   MARYLA ANN MANESS, b. 13 NOV 1947 in Independence, m. 26 AUG 1972 in Grandview, Mo. to John George Miller, III.

95. Annie Amelia (Alexander) McLaughlin
(1879-1960)

Annie Amelia Alexander, daughter of James Washington Alexander and last wife Mary Rice, was born September 6, 1879 in Miami, Saline County, Missouri. She was baptized in the Budd Park Christian Church of Kansas City, Missouri on November 10, 1912.

On September 18, 1895, Annie was married in Kansas City, Missouri to Charles Peake McLaughlin, a street car operator. Mr. McLaughlin, son of John Henry McLaughlin and Susan Jewett Bradshaw, was born February 24, 1873 in Kansas City, Missouri. He too was baptized in the Budd Park Christian Church, on January 22, 1913. Louis F. Alexander lived with his sister Annie for a while, and after that she went to work as a pie baker for Montgomery Wards of Kansas City.

The family was enumerated on the 1900 Federal census for Kaw Township in Kansas City (E.D. 100), and later lived at 342 North Topping Street in Kansas City. Charles P. died October 12, 1913 at his residence at 342

Figure 57 - Charles Peake McLaughlin and wife Annie Amelia Alexander, 1895

---

[1] I tried to link him to a Lewis Rees who was an early settler in Saline Co., Mo., without success. Also, I did not find a Rees Family household on any Federal census that had a child named Mary who would be the age of Mary Rice.
[2] Letter, Mildred I. (Pippenger) Warren (Harrisonville, Mo.), 15 JUL 1989.
[3] Dr. James Franklin Barker, b. 18 SEP 1859 in Olathe, Johnson Co., Kan., d. 7 DEC 1938 in Memorial Park Hospital of Caldwell, Idaho, and wife Martha Tryphena Molden, d. 11 FEB 1892, were bur. in Littell Cem. of Pleasanton, Kan.
[4] Gravestone, Pleasanton Cem.: † / LOUIS F. / ALEXANDER / Missouri / Pvt. Fcl. / [illegible] / February 5, 1934.

N. Topping St. in Kansas City, Missouri and was buried in Woodlawn Cemetery of Independence, Missouri.

Annie died November 6, 1960 of respiratory failure at the Elms Nursing Home in Kansas City, Missouri and was buried by Blackman Guardian Funeral Home on November 8, 1960 in Mt. Moriah Cemetery of Kansas City, Missouri.

Children of Charles Peake McLaughlin and Annie Amelia Alexander:[1]

951.   MILDRED AMY McLAUGHLIN, b. 24 AUG 1896 in Kansas City, Mo., bapt. 1922 at Bethany Baptist Church in Kansas City, m. 15 AUG 1915 in Topeka, Kan. to Robert [Henry] Searcy. Robert, a telegrapher, a Mason, was a son of Wakefield Paul Searcy and Sarah Wallace,[2] b. 17 FEB 1895 in Kansas City, Mo. and bapt. in 1927 at Bethany Baptist Church. He d. 7 JUL 1980 of a stroke in Shawnee, Okla. and was bur. 10 JUL 1980 in Mt. Moriah Cem. of Kansas City, Mo. Mildred worked as a recording clerk for the Board of Education administrative offices in Kansas City, Mo. She died 7 SEP 1991 of kidney failure, and was bur. at Mt. Moriah Cem. Children:[3]

9511.   ROBERT EUGENE SEARCY, department store manager, b. 1 JUN 1916 in Kansas City, Mo., m. 1 JUN 1935 there to Ada Carolyn Jones, res. Raytown, Mo., d. 18 MAR 1998 of brain cancer, bur. Mt. Moriah Cem. Ada, daughter of Robert Lee Jones and Maude Ethel Dannatt, b. 8 FEB 1915 in Calhoun, Henry Co., Mo. and bapt. in the Baptist Church there. Ada worked for Pioneer Insurance Co. of Kansas City, and was a teacher. Ada d. 29 AUG 1983 of cancer at her home in Raytown, and bur. 2 SEP 1983 in Mt. Moriah Cem. in Kansas City. Children:

95111.   ROBERT GAYLE SEARCY, b. 1 MAY 1939 in Kansas City, Mo., stillborn, bur. in Mt. Moriah Cem. of Kansas City.

95112.   KAREN KAY SEARCY, b. 24 JUN 1941 in Kansas City, m. 23 NOV 1961 in Topeka, Crawford Co., Kan. to David Edgar Fox, son of Charles Fox and Frances Miller, div. in 1970, res. Raytown, Mo. Children:

951121.   KIMBERLY KAY FOX, b. 14 MAR 1963 in Topeka, Kan., m. 25 JUN 1983 in Jacksonville, N.C. to George Gilbert Schumacher, div. in 1987, res. Raytown, Mo.

951122.   KELLI KRISTEN FOX, b. 16 NOV 1965 in Kansas City, m. 26 JUL 1986 in Kansas City to Robert Dean Jordan, res. Aurora, Colo.

95113.   ROBERT KEITH SEARCY, b. 19 MAY 1945 in Kansas City, Mo., m. 14 JUL 1973 in Chicago, Ill. to Marce Lynn Platt, daughter of Raymond and Bernice Platt, res. Scottsdale, Ariz. Child:

951131.   ALANNA KIERSTEN SEARCY, b. 13 OCT 1976, res. Calif.

9512.   MILTON NORMAN SEARCY, b. 29 APR 1920 in Kansas City, Mo. He was a pilot and served with Chenault's Flying Tigers in the Air Force, and was injured in a plane crash in India. He was a professor and asst. school superintendent. Milton m. 8 DEC 1943 in the First Baptist Church of Shawnee, Okla. to Claire Lee Ward, b. 8 NOV 1922 in Poplar Bluff, Butler Co., Mo., daughter of Raymond Lee Ward and Sarah Vitura Somers, d. of a heart condition. Children, b. Shawnee, Okla.:[4]

95121.   MICHAEL "Mike" WARD SEARCY, b. 5 MAY 1956.

95122.   SARAH ANN SEARCY, b. 14 MAR 1958.

95123.   TIMOTHY LEE SEARCY, b. 11 NOV 1964.

952.   NORMAN ALEXANDER McLAUGHLIN, b. 30 AUG 1899 in Kansas City, Mo., bapt. 25 NOV 1912 in Budd Park Christian Church in Kansas City, m. 5 MAR 1927[5] there to Dorothy Hollen Day. Norman owned a school supply business, and d. 19 JUL 1970 of natural causes, pronounced dead upon arrival at the Independence Sanitarium of Independence, Mo., bur. 22 JUL 1970 in Mt. Moriah Cem. of Kansas City. Dorothy d. Tuesday, 4 AUG 1987 and was bur. on Thursday, 6 AUG 1987 at Mt. Moriah Cem. Children:

9521.   NORMAN EUGENE McLAUGHLIN, m. 3 JUL 1964 to his cousin, Jeannine Lee Bell, daughter of Berwin Irving Bell and Mildred Irene Pippenger, who was b. 5 NOV 1940 in St. Joseph Hospital of Kansas City, Mo., res. Blue Springs, Mo., q.v.

9522.   DOROTHY ELEANOR McLAUGHLIN, b. 25 AUG 1929 in Kansas City, m. 2 NOV 1951 at Linwood Methodist Church there to Kenneth Charles Edscorn, b. 25 JUL 1925 in St. John's, Mo., retired from Missouri Pacific Railroad in 1983, res. Kirkwood, Mo. Children:

95221.   CHRISTOPHER MARK EDSCORN, b. 20 SEP 1954 in Jackson Co., Mo., m. 11 SEP 1982 in St. Louis Co., Mo. to Carol Ann Sordillo. Carol, daughter of Vincent Frank and Claire Ann Sordillo, b. 24 MAR 1954 in Southington, Conn. The couple res. Jaffrey, N.H. Children:

---

[1] Information in part provided by Jeannine L. (Bell) McLaughlin, 17 OCT 1984.
[2] Sarah (Wallace) Searcy, b. 28 JUN 1866, daughter of Robert Wallace of Scotland and Margaret Connelly of Ireland, d. 28 DEC 1914 in Kansas City, Mo.
[3] Information in part provided by Bob Searcy, August 1987.
[4] Letter, Mildred I. (Pippenger) Warren (Harrisonville, Mo.), 15 JUL 1989.
[5] Jackson Co., Mo. Marriages, Bk. 110, p. 78.

952211. LUKE VINCENT EDSCORN, b. 5 APR 1986 at home in Shrewsbury, St. Louis Co., Mo.
952212. MARIELLE EDSCORN.
952213. DAVID ALEXANDER EDSCORN.
952214. JOSEPH EDSCORN.
952215. CHRISTOPHER EDSCORN.
95222. JULIE ANN EDSCORN, b. 2 SEP 1958 in Kansas City, Mo., m. 6 SEP 1980 in St. Louis, Mo. to Robert Leo Noelle. Mr. Noelle, son of Leo J. Noelle and Donna Frost, b. 22 NOV 1956 in Omaha, Douglas Co., Nebr. and bapt. in a Catholic church there in May 1964. Children:
952221. JASON TYLER NOELLE, b. 19 FEB 1984 in Sioux City, Iowa, res. Lincoln, Nebr.
952222. BRYCE ALEXANDER NOELLE.
953. WILLIAM JEWEL McLAUGHLIN, b. 14 OCT 1902 in Kansas City, Mo., d. 6 FEB 1994 at Blue Hills, Mo., bur. Mt. Moriah Cem., (1) c.1918 to Jeanette Sheets,[1] and m. (2) 7 JUN 1926 in California, Moniteau Co., Mo. to Lela Mae Hammond who had been raised by her mother, Margaret Funkhauser [McCoy], and was married previously. Bill was bapt. 17 MAR 1914 in the Budd Park Christian Church of Kansas City, Mo. Lela, b. 24 JUL 1895 in Paris, Ill., d. 6 NOV 1981 in Research Medical Center of Kansas City, Mo. and was bur. by Mt. Moriah Funeral Home on Monday, 9 NOV 1981 at Mt. Moriah Cem. of Kansas City. Adopted child:
9531a. Margye Ann "Jan" McLaughlin, b. 28 DEC 1935 in Kansas City, m. 3 MAY 1956 at Linwood Methodist Church there to Roy Lee Thornton, b. 26 JUL 1932 in Kansas City, son of James Roy Thornton and Ida Bowles. Children:
9531a1. Thomas Lee Thornton, b. 1 JAN 1960 in Dallas, Tex., m. Sherri Tribble, div. Children:
9531a11. Nathaniel Thornton, b. 4 AUG 1993.
9531a12. Malory Thornton, b. 28 DEC 1991.
9531a2. Terry Ann Thornton, b. 3 FEB 1961 in Dallas, Tex.
954. CHARLES LOUIS McLAUGHLIN, an iron worker, b. 11 JUL 1906 in Kansas City, m. 2 JUL 1927 in Leavenworth, Jackson Co., Kan., to Dorothy Alice McGinnis, d. 18 DEC 1992 in Kansas City. Charles d. 2 FEB 1971 in Independence, Mo.; both bur. in Woodlawn Cem. there. Children:
9541. CHARLES WILLIAM McLAUGHLIN, school principal, b. 1931, m. 5 DEC 1952 in Kansas City to Doris Ferguson, daughter of Walter Edwin Ferguson and Evelyn Walker, b. 9 APR 1934 in Kansas City, Kan. Children:
95411. EVELYN DENICE McLAUGHLIN, b. 20 OCT 1955 in Columbia, Mo., m. (1) 3 AUG 1974 to Richard Earl Minnich, div., m. (2) to Ronald Fredman, div., res. Seattle, Wash. Children:
954111. ALLISON MINNICH.
954112. RACHEL FREDMAN.
95412. SARAH ANN McLAUGHLIN, b. 16 DEC 1962 in St. Paul, Minn., m. George McMillen, res. Overland Park, Kan. Children:
954121. MARGARET ANN McMILLEN, b. 1988.
954122. MADELINE ROSE McMILLEN, b. 1993.
95413. GEORGIA SUE McLAUGHLIN, b. 1 MAY 1965 in West Salem, Wisc., m. (1) Michael Feagans, div., m. (2) Timothy Siebenmorgen, res. Tampa, Fla. Children:
954131. NICHOLAS JACOB FEAGANS, b. 1985.
954132. ANTHONY CHARLES SIEBENMORGEN, b. 9 NOV 1998.
95414a. Wanda Kay McLaughlin, b. 5 MAY 1966 in Wisc., m. Kiplin Dobbs, res. Atlanta, Ga. Children:
95414a1. Ashley Lynn Dobbs.
95414a2. Dillon Dobbs.
95415. KELLY MARIE McLAUGHLIN, b. 31 OCT 1969 in Tenn., d. 16 MAY 2007 in Virginia Beach, Va., m. (1) James Shaults, div., m. (2) Lee A. Wilkinson. Children:
954151. DREW A. SHAULTS, b. 1988.
954152. KYLE R. SHAULTS, b. 1998.
9542. DAVID LEE McLAUGHLIN, m. Carol Sue Peggs, div., d. suicide. He suffered a massive stroke, res. John Knox Village of Lee's Summit, Mo. Child:
95421. MICHAEL DAVID McLAUGHLIN, m. Jennifer ( ), res. Lee's Summit.
955. MARGUERITE EVELYN McLAUGHLIN, b. 12 AUG 1909 in Kansas City, Mo., d. 14 MAR 1996 at Virginia Beach, Va., m. 23 AUG 1937 in Sayre, Beckham Co., Okla. to Van Dulare Sebastian, b. 3 JUL 1906, d. JUL 1955. Children:
9551. BARBARA ANN SEBASTIAN, b. 1938, m. Robert George Baumgarten. Children:
95511. MICHAEL DUAYNE BAUMGARTEN.
95512. DEBORAH LYNN BAUMGARTEN.

---

[1] Her parents had the marriage annulled.

9552. JERRY VAN SEBASTIAN, b. 1945, m. Gail Tatum, res. Norfolk, Va. Child:

  95521. LOREN LEE SEBASTIAN.

956. MADELINE LOUISE McLAUGHLIN, b. 7 NOV 1913 in Kansas City, Mo., d. 29 MAY 2007, m. there 7 JAN 1929[1] to James Granville Clarke, Sr., b. 6 NOV 1909 in Kansas City, d. 4 JUN 2002 in Blue Springs, Mo.; both bur. Mt. Moriah Cem. of Kansas City. Children:

9561. JAMES GRANVILLE CLARKE, JR., of Mulberry Hill Farms, m. Patricia Ann Abston, daughter of Howard T. and Alta Abston. "Pat," a decorative painter, b. 26 FEB 1935 in Kansas City, d. 26 MAY 2001 at her home in Pleasant Hill, Mo., bur. Mt. Moriah Cem. of Kansas City. Children:

  95611. JAMES STEVEN "Steve" CLARKE.

  95612. JANE LEIGH CLARKE.

  95613. BRETT THOMAS CLARKE, m. Marilyn (   ).

  94514. JOHN KEVIN CLARKE.

9562. JUDITH ALTA CLARKE, b. 27 APR 1938 in St. Joseph's Hospital of Kansas City, Mo., unmarried, physical education instructor, retired 1996, res. Boone, N.C.

---

[1] Jackson Co., Mo. Marriages, Bk. 116, p. 511.

Figure 58 - Charles Peake McLaughlin

Figure 59 - Annie Amelia Alexander McLaughlin

Figure 60 - Robert Henry Searcy

Figure 61 - Norman Eugene McLaughlin

89

Figure 62 - Alexander and Pippenger Family Reunion, Kansas City, Mo., 1936

Front row (l to r, sitting): Marjorie Pippenger, Mary Ann Abbas, Norman McLaughlin, Jimmy Clarke in overalls, Mary Ann Bruce, Billy McLaughlin, Charles "Buddy" Pippenger, Dorothy McLaughlin, Helen O'Neill, Jim Abbas, Gay Lea Brown, Bob Bruce, Barbara Dell Brown, Betty Nazer. **Second row** (l to r, kneeling): Norman McLaughlin, Bob Searcy, Omer Brown, Jr., Roy Abbas, Chuck Pippenger, Bobby Searcy, Ada Searcy, Alberta O'Neill, Peggy Pippenger, Dorothy Cockel, Nelly Brown, Lorene Nazer, Hallie Palmer, Robert Olan Cockel. **Third row** (l to r, standing): Louis McLaughlin, Dorothy McLaughlin, Dorothy McLaughlin, Mildred Searcy, Ina Mae Maness, Mildred Bell, Inez King, Bertha O'Neill, Annie Alexander McLaughlin, Emma Alexander Teft, Lucy Pippenger Cockel, Esther Brown, Margaret O'Neill, Ward Becksted, Jimmy O'Neill. **Back row** (l to r, standing), Mary Pippenger Abbas, Margaret "Pete" Funkhauser, Lela McLaughlin, Madeline Clarke, William "Pearl" Pippenger, John Pippenger, Berwyn Bell, Jim O'Neill, Nina Alexander Pippenger, Omer Brown, Sr., Jim Clarke, Judy Clarke, Gene Hagberg, Jessie Brown Bruce. Bill McLaughlin took the picture in the yard of John W. and Nina L. (Alexander) Pippenger, so he is not shown.

96. Nina Lee (Alexander) Pippenger
(1880-1963)

Note: See this compiler's Pippenger and Pittenger Families, 'A Genealogical History of the Descendants of William Pippenger of New Jersey and Allied Families' (Baltimore: Gateway Press, 1988), for additional information on the descendants of Nina Lee Alexander and husband John Wesley Pippenger.

Nina Lee Alexander, daughter of James Washington Alexander and Mary Rice was born August 22, 1880 in Miami, Saline County, Missouri. Nina only went to school up to the third grade, as she was left-handed and the teachers could not teach her to write.[1] She was married February 25, 1907 in Kansas City, Wyandotte County, Kansas[2] to John Wesley Pippenger, born March 29, 1884 in Barton County, Missouri, son of Simon Peter Pippenger and Malissa Malvina Pippinger.

John and Nina set up house in the flats where their son Charley Wesley Pippenger was born December 13, 1907. John was a coal miner, hunter and a fisherman, and during his early years of marriage, worked at Peltzman Bottle Company where he drove a team of mules and picked up empty bottles. He became a laborer in construction work and was among the founders of the A.F. & L. in Kansas City, Missouri.

The last home to John and Nina Pippenger was out in the country at 12903 East 87th Street, Raytown, Missouri, on property which he purchased from Charles D. and Clara T. Burton on October 22, 1934.[3] This tract originally contained 4½ acres and was later, in part, distributed among their children.[4]

Nina Lee Pippenger died February 27, 1963 at the age of 82 years, of a cerebral vascular accident and was buried on Friday, March 1, 1963 in grave 3-5 lot 118 block 19 (heading west) of the Mt. Moriah Cemetery of Kansas City, Missouri. John was so saddened by being without his wife that he committed suicide. He was found dead on May 5, 1963 by his granddaughter Nina Sue Pippenger in the garage where he had died from a self-inflicted gunshot wound to the abdomen. John was buried May 8, 1963 in grave 1-3 lot 118 block 19 (heading west) of Mt. Moriah Cemetery of Kansas City, Missouri.

Figure 63 - Nina Lee Alexander

Children of John Wesley Pippenger and Nina Lee Alexander:

961.   CHARLEY "Chuck" WESLEY PIPPENGER, b. 13 DEC 1907 in Kansas City, Mo., m. 15 MAY 1929 in Kansas City to Marguerite Pearl "Peggy" Palmer, daughter of Charles Henry Palmer and Harriett Elsaba Bennett, b. 30 MAY 1912 in Kansas City. Chuck d. 26 SEP 1981 at his home at 12021 Brickyard Road, and was buried three days later in Space 12, Lot 229, Block 24 of Mt. Moriah Cem. in Kansas City. Marguerite d. 25 JUN 1997 at her apartment at 6140 Raytown Rd., in Raytown, Mo., and was bur. in Mt. Moriah Cem. Children:
9611.   MARJORIE JEANNE PIPPENGER, electronics assembler and circuit board designer, b. 15 FEB 1930 in Kansas City, d. 5 SEP 2003 in Lee's Summit Hospital in Lee's Summit, Mo., unmarried.
9612.   CHARLES WESLEY PIPPENGER, (Jr.), b. 30 SEP 1931 in Kansas City, m. 7 JUN 1953 in Kansas City to Zora Eileene Davison, daughter of Chester Leland Davison and Velma Pearl Allen, b. 5 MAR 1932 in Kansas City. Eileene is a direct descendant of the Davison Family of County Armagh, Ire., as well as of Philip Ridgeway who fought in the Revolutionary War. Res. in Littleton, Colo. Children:
96121.   WESLEY EUGENE PIPPENGER, b. 22 JUN 1956 in Kansas City, retired from NASA Headquarters in Washington DC, res. Tappahannock, Va.
96122.   PATRICE PIPPENGER, b. 15 DEC 1957 in Kansas City, d. 16 JUL 1959 in Kansas City.
96123.   RACHEL PIPPENGER, b. 31 JAN 1959 in Kansas City, m. (1) 21 MAY 1982 at St. James Presbyterian Church in Littleton, Colo. to Alan Garfield Swanson, div., m. (2) 1 MAR 1985 in Denver, Colo. to Logan James Lucas. Res. in Littleton, Colo. Child:
961231.   CHRISTOPHER WESLEY LUCAS,[5] b. 12 OCT 1982 in Denver, Colo., d. 12 DEC 2009 in Englewood, Colo.
9613.   NINA SUE PIPPENGER, librarian, b. 23 OCT 1947 in Kansas City, m. 9 JUN 1966 in Kansas City to Jon David McCormick Faye, son of John Daniel Heavner Faye and Irene Lavelle McCormick, b. 15 AUG 1944 in Philadelphia, Pa. Res. Hyattsville, Md. Child:

---

[1] Conversation with Madeline Clarke, 12 JUL 1987.
[2] Wyandotte Co., Kan. Marriages, Bk. 21, p. 123.
[3] Jackson Co., Mo. Deeds, Bk. 634, p. 631.
[4] Tract known as the White Oak Addition of Section 22, Twp. 48 (Brooking), Range 32.
[5] When adopted by his step-father, Logan James Lucas, Christopher's name was changed from Christopher William Swanson.

96131. WENDY SUE FAYE, information architect, b. 25 JAN 1967 in Evanston, Ill., m. 25 JAN 1987 to Grant Newsham, b. 9 JUN 1965 in Colne, Lancashire, Eng., son of Roy Newsham and Beatrice Mona Hardin of Nelson, Eng., div., res. Silver Spring, Md. Children:

    961311. DAVID GRANT NEWSHAM, b. 10 NOV 1991 in Dayton, Ohio.

    961312. MICHAEL ANTHONY NEWSHAM, b. 31 JUL 1993, in Kettering, Ohio.

962. MARY LEE PIPPENGER, b. 15 APR 1910 in Kansas City, Mo., m. 6 OCT 1928 in Kansas City to LeRoy Edward Abbas, son of James Shultz Abbas and Ella Brinston, b. 27 SEP 1907 in Kansas City, res. Raymore, Mo. Mary d. 12 MAR 2001 in Raymore, bur. Floral Hills Cem. of Kansas City, Mo. Children:

9621. JAMES LEROY ABBAS, pilot, owner of Abbas Aviation, Inc., manager of Sedalia Airport, b. Saturday 28 MAR 1931 in Kansas City, d. 8 NOV 2000 while a resident of Raymore, m. 17 JUL 1954 Kansas City to Barbara Jean Severin, b. 9 NOV 1936. Children:

96211. PAMELA SUZANNE ABBAS, b. 11 FEB 1958 in Kansas City, m. 6 JUN 1987 in Raymore to Lawrence Holder, res. in Peculiar, Mo. Children:

    962111. MELISSA HOLDER.

    962112. MATTHEW HOLDER.

96212. JAMES CRAIG ABBAS, b. 15 SEP 1959, res. Newton, Kan.

9622. MARY ANN ABBAS, b. 19 MAY 1934, m. (1) "Corky" Shea, and m. (2) after 1953 in Kansas City to Harold "Hal" Leslie Day, b. 23 SEP 1934 in Raytown, son of Elijah Day and Beulah Wagner, d. 10 JUL 2011 at Raymore, bur. Floral Hills Cem. Children:

96221. JANICE LEANN DAY, b. 13 OCT 1951, m. 22 JUN 1974 in Pleasant Hill, Mo. to Derias Wayne Bowers, b. 16 JUL 1953. Child:

    962211. KRISTINA DEE BOWERS, b. 23 MAR 1978 in Mt. Ayr, Iowa.

96222. JOAN LOUISE DAY, b. 26 MAY 1953, m. 23 MAR 1974 to Randall David Barnett, b. 27 SEP.

96223. HAROLD LESLIE "Hal" DAY, JR., b. 23 NOV 1956 in Kansas City, Mo., res. San Francisco, Calif., unmarried.

963. MILDRED IRENE PIPPENGER, "Toots," b. 18 JUL 1914 in Kansas City, m. (1) on 16 JAN 1938 to Berwyn Irving Bell, son of Irving Bell and Amy Markwell, d. 24 JUL 1959 by suicide by jumping from the St. James Street bridge into the Kaw River, bur. 27 JUL 1959 at Memorial Park Cem. in Kansas City, m. (2) 25 DEC 1961 to Tas "Ted" Manley Warren, b. 25 JAN 1904 in Ponotoc, Miss., d. 12 MAR 1995 in Harrisonville, Mo., bur. Mt. Moriah Cem. of Kansas City, Mo. "Toots" d. 10 DEC 2009 in Harrisonville, Mo., bur. Mt. Moriah Cem. Children:

9631. TERRY LYNN BELL, b. 19 NOV 1938 in Kansas City, m. 24 APR 1964 to Corrine Kay Muir, daughter of Albert and Frances Muir. Children:

96311. BERWYN WARREN BELL, b. 8 MAR 1968, m. 3 JAN 1987 to Cynthia Gail Plattner, daughter of Charles W. Plattner.

96312. AMY FRANCES BELL, b. 4 APR 1969.

96313. THOMAS LYNN BELL, b. 10 MAY 1971.

9632. JEANNINE LEE BELL, b. 5 NOV 1940 in Kansas City, d. 11 SEP 2011,[1] m. 3 JUL 1964 to her 3rd cousin, (9521.) NORMAN EUGENE McLAUGHLIN, son of Norman Alexander McLaughlin and Dorothy Hollen Day, *q.v.* Child:

96321. LESLIE CAROL McLAUGHLIN, b. 21 MAY 1965 in Kansas City, unmarried.

9633. JOHN IRVING BELL, b. 15 NOV 1944 in Kansas City, m. (1) in NOV 1968 to Diana Lynn Giffin, daughter of Everett and Dorothy Giffin, m. (2) in NOV 1975 to Deborah Patricia Perkins, div. the next year. Children:

96331. MICK AARON BELL, b. 30 SEP 1971, m. Kim (   ). Child:

    963311. HARLEE BELL, b. 30 MAY 1994.

96332. JEFF ALAN BELL, b. 28 NOV 1972.

---

[1] See Wesley E. Pippenger, Pippenger and Pittenger Families (Baltimore: Gateway Press, 1988).

Figure 64 - Nina and John Pippenger

Figure 65 - Nina and John Pippenger in 1960

93

98. Emma Leola (Alexander) Teft
(1885-1970)

Emma Leola Alexander, daughter of James Washington Alexander and his fifth wife, the former Mrs. Mary (Rice) Gover, was born on September 7, 1885 in Miami, Saline County, Missouri.[1] When young she worked as a maid for the Bowen Family, and through her experiences with them she learned the habits of the home: how to set a pretty table, eating etiquette, etc.

Figure 66 - Clyde Delose Teft

On May 21, 1905, Emma was married by W.L. Winship, Justice of the Peace, in Kansas City, Wyandotte County, Kansas to Clyde Delose Teft.[2] Mr. Teft, a son of Wayne Teft and Ida Brova, was born in Sawyer, Berrien County, Michigan on August 24, 1883.[3] The couple were members of Bethany Baptist church, and Clyde worked as a guard for the water department. Emma worked in a garment factory. The 1920 Federal census shows the couple living in Ward 16 of Kansas City, Missouri.

Figure 67 - Emma Leola Alexander, wife of Clyde Delose Teft

Clyde D. Teft died March 12, 1943 at 9:15 a.m. of immediate cerebral thrombosis due to angina at 137 N. Oakley Street in Kansas City, Missouri and was buried three days later by D.W. Newcomer and Sons in Mt. Washington Cemetery of Kansas City, Missouri.

Emma died on September 2, 1970 at 6:00 a.m. of congestive heart failure in Kansas City General Hospital and Medical Center and was buried three days later by funeral director R. Blackman, Sr. in Mt. Washington Cemetery.

Child of Clyde Delose Teft and Emma Leola Alexander:

981.   RAY DELOSE TEFT, b. 16 JUL 1912 on North Topping Street in Kansas City, Mo., m. 28 JUN 1932 in Kansas City to Bessie Marie Shelley, sister of Sam Shelley of Deepwater, Mo. Ray d. 28 JUL 1969 and was bur. by Blackman Guardian Funeral Home, 30 JUL 1969 in Mt. Washington Cem. Bessie, b. 28 JUN 1913 in Birch Tree, Mo., was a cosmetics packer for Luzier Personalized Cosmetics for 30 years, retiring in 1976[4], d. 14 FEB 1991 at a hospital in Clinton, Mo., bur. Deepwater, Mo. Bessie m. (2) to Clarence Thomas. They res. for some time at 315 N. Lawndale in Kansas City, Mo. In early 1989, Bessie suffered a stroke of paralysis and was diagnosed as having a brain tumor, while Clarence was moved from their residence to a nursing home. He d. 28 MAY 1989 in Clinton. Child:

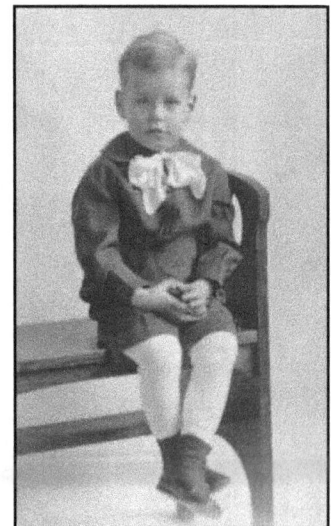
Figure 68 - Ray Teft, age 4

9811.   SHIRLEY MARIE TEFT, b. 8 FEB 1935 in St. Mary's Hospital of Kansas City, Mo., d. 3 NOV 2005, m. 28 NOV 1957 in Kansas City, to Mr. Ermel Ernest "Pete" Miller. Mr. Miller b. 14 JAN 1927 in Independence, Mo., res. Clinton. Child:

98111.   RICK ALLEN MILLER, b. 15 NOV 1958 at Clinton, res. Clinton.

[1]   Saline Co., Mo. Births, LDS reel #94699, p. 2.
[2]   Wyandotte Co., Kan. Marriages, Bk. 19, p. 121.
[3]   His draft registration card for World War I has his birth year as 1879, making him 4 years older.
[4]   Obituary, Kansas City Star (Kansas City, Mo., no date available).

99. Henriette Catherine (Alexander) Barrett
(1886-1925)

Henriette Catherine Alexander, known to family as "Retta", was born October 5, 1886 in Kansas City, Jackson County, Missouri, and was a daughter of James Washington Alexander and Mary (Rice) Gover.[1] For a time Retta was a maid in the hotel owned by the Malloy Family, somewhere around 10th and Troost in Kansas City.

On June 1, 1904, Retta was married by Winfield Freeman, Probate Judge, in Kansas City, Wyandotte County, Kansas to John Joseph Barrett, of Kansas City, Missouri.[2] At some point in his life Mr. Barrett was paralyzed on one side.

While residing at 5037 14th St., "Retta" died March 11, 1925 of cancer of the cervix in Grace Hospital of Detroit, Wayne Co., Michigan and was buried March 12, 1925 in an unmarked grave in the Barrett Family plot in St. Mary's Catholic Cemetery at 22nd and Cleveland Streets in Kansas City, Missouri.

John J. Barrett, residing at 1333 Grand Ave., died April 5, 1942 of a ruptured gall bladder in Kansas City General Hospital and was buried 3 days later in St. Mary's Catholic Cemetery (Lot M264).

The couple had no children.

Figure 69 - Henriette Catherine Alexander Barrett

Figure 70 - John Barrett and "Retta" Alexander in 1924

Figure 71 - Henriette Catherine Alexander Barrett

---

[1] Information provided on Henriette's death certificate by widower John J. Barrett notes she was the daughter of Mary Reed [sic] of Quincy, Ill.

[2] John Barrett's sister Mae Barrett was married to Fritz Malloy, a hit man for the Kansas City mafia massacre at Union Station.

9(10). Bertha Irene (Alexander) O'Neill
(1890-1962)

Figure 72 - Bertha Irene Alexander

Bertha Irene Alexander, the youngest child of James Washington Alexander and wife Mary (Rice) Gover, was born January 18, 1890 in Kansas City, Jackson County, Missouri.

On March 7, 1910 she was married in Leavenworth, Leavenworth County, Kansas to James Emmet O'Neill. Mr. O'Neill, a son of Thomas O'Neill and Katherine Brown, was born September 29, 1887 in Hot Springs, Arkansas, but had roots in County Cork, Ireland. For a while the couple resided at 7927 Montgall in Kansas City, Missouri and moved to 908 Dewey in Grandview, Missouri.

Mr. O'Neill died June 8, 1962 in Kansas City, Missouri and was buried in Mt. Moriah Cemetery there. Bertha died June 2, 1962 in Grandview, Missouri and was buried in Mt. Moriah Cemetery.

Children of James Emmet O'Neill and Bertha Irene Alexander, all born in Kansas City, Missouri:[1]

9(10)1. EMMET CLAIBORN O'NEILL, b. in November 1910/1, d. of convulsions and bur. 14 NOV 1912 in Elmwood Cem. of Kansas City, Mo.[2]

9(10)2. JOHN EDWARD O'NEILL, b. 28 OCT 1912 in Kansas City, m. 11 MAY 1933 in Independence, Mo. to Margaret Kate Messmer, b. 16 NOV 1912 in Kansas City, Mo., daughter of Charles E. Messmer and Anna Kencht. Children:

9(10)21. HELEN MARIE O'NEILL, b. 7 SEP 1935 in Kansas City, m. 15 FEB 1953 in Belton, Cass Co., Mo. to George Edward Thornton, son of George Thornton and Alice (   ), b. 8 NOV 1935 in Nevada, Mo. Children:[3]

9(10)211. THOMAS PATRICK THORNTON, b. 18 DEC 1957 in Belton, Mo., m. Brenda Kay Hendrickson. Child:

9(10)2111. GARETT EVAN THORNTON, b. 17 JUN 1987.

9(10)212. BRETT EDWARD THORNTON, b. 14 JAN 1963, Belton.

9(10)22. RUTH ANN O'NEILL, b. 30 DEC 1938 in Kansas City, Mo., m. 29 JUN 1956 in Belton, Cass Co., Mo. to Larry Lynn Bowes, son of Karl Bowes and Stelline (   ). Children:[4]

9(10)221. LORI DIANE BOWES, b. 25 JUL 1959 in Kansas City, Mo., m. 31 MAY 1980 in Urich, Mo. to Keith Vogt. Children:

9(10)2211. TRACY ANN VOGT, b. 1 OCT 198?.

9(10)2212. BYRON KEITH VOGT, b. 21 DEC 198?.

9(10)222. LARRY JOE "Jody" BOWES, b. 25 NOV 1961, m. 12 OCT 1985 to Terri Bowes. Children:

9(10)2221. JUSTIN JOE BOWES, b. 7 AUG 1986.

9(10)2222. HANNAH NICOLE BOWES, b. 18 MAY 198?.

9(10)223. JANET LYNN BOWES, b. 9 JUL 1964, m. 21 JAN 1984 to Kenneth Chancellor.

9(10)3. JAMES PATRICK O'NEILL, b. 24 DEC 1914, m. 10 SEP 1949 in Hickman Mills, Mo. to Mariam Harper. He d. 16 JUL 1983 in St. Luke's Hospital of Kansas City, Mo., and was bur. three days later in Mt. Moriah Cem. there. The cause of death was Lupus Erythematosis.[5] Child:

9(10)31. NANCY LOU O'NEILL, b. 25 MAY 1953, m. Mr. Everson.

9(10)4. BARNEY CLAYTON O'NEILL, b. August 1920, d. in July 1924 in Kansas City, Mo., bur. in Forest Hill Cem. of Kansas City.

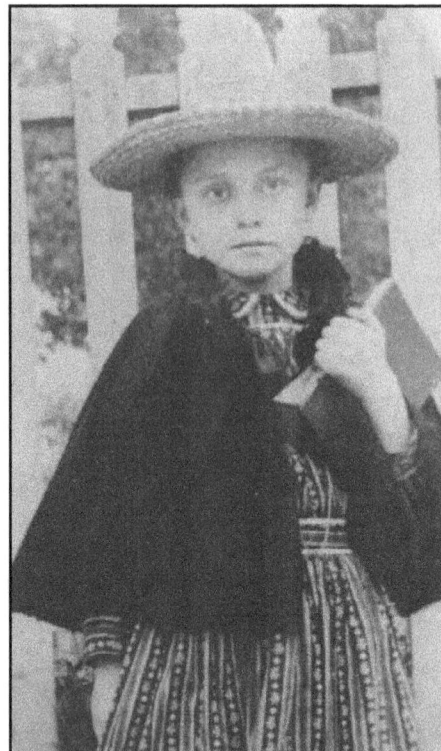

Figure 73 - Bertha and Jim O'Neill

[1] Information provided by Alberta Corteville, 12 FEB 1978.

[2] Cemetery records indicate the infant's age was 2 years and was buried by J.C. Duffy Funeral Home in the single grave section, Block V North, Row 43, grave 7.

[3] Letter, Mildred I. (Pippenger) Warren (Harrisonville, Mo.), 15 JUL 1989.

[4] Ibid.

[5] Ibid.

9(10)5. ALBERTA IRENE O'NEILL, b. 18 JUL 1921 in Kansas City, d. 9 APR 2001 at Research Medical Center near Kansas City, bur. at Calvary Cem. of Kansas City, m. 5 NOV 1941 in St. Catherine's Church of Hickman Mills, Mo. to William Joseph Corteville. "Bill", son of Victor Corteville and Leonie Van Dew, a postal mail carrier, was b. 22 APR 1917 in Raytown, Mo., and d. 1 DEC 2000 at home, bur. Calvary Cem. Children:

Figure 74 - Alberta O'Neill and Bill Corteville

9(10)51.   WILLIAM PATRICK CORTEVILLE, b. 22 FEB 1944 in Kansas City, m. 7 NOV 1964 to Drucilla Matiecawiez, res. Independence. Children:

9(10)511.   WILLIAM DONALD CORTEVILLE.

9(10)512.   PAMELA MICHELLE CORTEVILLE.

9(10)513.   THOMAS MICHAEL CORTEVILLE, a welder, d. 10 JAN 2011 of a heart attack, m. Jacque McDonald, a paramedic. Children:

9(10)5131.   OLIVIA CORTEVILLE, b. c.1994.

9(10)5132.   ELIZABETH CORTEVILLE, b. c.1997.

9(10)52.   COLLEEN PATRICIA CORTEVILLE, b. 8 OCT 1946 in Kansas City, m. 21 DEC 1966 there to Joseph Theodore Welch, res. Raymore. Child:

9(10)521.   JOSEPH MICHAEL WELCH.

9(10)53.   JOSEPH MICHAEL CORTEVILLE, b. 9 DEC 1950 in Kansas City, d. at birth, bur. Calvary/Forest Hill Cem.

9(10)54a.   Brian Kenneth Corteville, b. 6 JAN 1953 in Dublin, Ireland, m. 2 APR 1976 in Kansas City to Carole Clark, res. Belton.

9(10)55a.   Rita Maureen Corteville, b. 14 JAN 1959, m. 20 JUL 1984 at Christ the King Catholic Church in Kansas City to Richard E. Allen, res. Raymond, Mo. Child:

9(10)55a1. Brittany Allen.

9(10)56a.   Kathleen Teresa Corteville, b. 30 MAY 1961 in Kansas City, m. 13 APR 1985 there to Michael Edward Hegarty.

9(10)57a.   Timothy John Corteville, b. 20 JUL 1963 in Kansas City, m. 25 JUL 1987 in Independence to Lianne Curtis, res. Ellisville, Mo.

9(10)58.   JAMES THOMAS CORTEVILLE, d. as an infant.

Figure 75 - McLaughlin Family

Front row (l to r): William J. McLaughlin, Dorothy (McGinnis) McLaughlin, Annie (Alexander) McLaughlin, Dorothy (Day) McLaughlin, and Norman McLaughlin. Back row (l to r): Marguerite (McLaughlin) Sebastian, James G. Clarke, Sr., Madeline (McLaughlin) Clarke, Charles L. McLaughlin, Mildred (McLaughlin) Searcy, and Robert Searcy

A11412. SARAH (ALEXANDER) WALTON
(c.1783-ante 1834)

Sarah Alexander, a daughter of John Sheldon Alexander and Leah Fleming, was born previous to 1783, as reflected on the 1783 tax list for Pocomoke Hundred of Worcester County, Maryland, and the 1790 Federal census for Worcester County.

Sarah was married January 27, 1807 by bond in Albemarle County, Virginia to Richmond Terril Walton,[1] as witnessed by Alexander Garrett, and signed by Curtis Roberts. On January 27, 1807, John Alexander gave consent for Richmond Walton to marry his daughter Sarah Alexander, and the consent was signed by the bride's parents John Alexander and Sarah Alexander. Richmond T. Walton, a farmer, was born c.1784 in Albemarle County.[2]

The 1820 Federal census shows a Richmond Walton as a head of household in Albemarle County, with no other white males, four white females. The 1830 Federal census for Albemarle County shows a Richmond Walton as a head of household with five other white males with him, and four white females. This entry suggests his father, Richmond Walton, is residing in the household. The family moved to Bath County where they are listed on the personal property tax list of March 5, 1842. The same year Richmond T. Walton and wife Nancy acquired 160 acres in Falling Spring Valley of Bath County from the heirs of James Armstrong, late of Lancaster County, Pennsylvania.[3]

It is presumed Sarah died by 1834 when Richmond T. Walton was married (2) on July 20, 1834 in Bath County to Nancy Armstrong, formerly the widow of William Ball and then the widow of James Armstrong who had died in 1831 in Lancaster County, Pennsylvania.[4] Nancy died by 1855, as Richmond T. Walton, widower, was married (3) on February 15, 1855 in Bath County to Catharine A. Tyree, age 44, daughter of John and Elizabeth Tyree.

Richmond T. Walton died September 23, 1862 in Warm Springs, Bath County. He left a will that was proved in January 1863 in Bath County.[5] His third wife Catharine (Tyree) Walton died in 1870.

Children of Richmond Terril Walton and Sarah Alexander:

A114121.   MARY "Polly" WALTON, b. 1807 in Albemarle Co.[6], m. William Kesterson,[7] b. 1807 in Augusta Co., Va.,
           d. 1860 near Green Valley, Bath Co. Children:
   A1141211.   FRANCIS M. KESTERSON, carpenter, b. 1834 in Augusta Co., m. 31 JAN 1856 in Bath Co. to Jane
               Fry, b. 1821 in Augusta Co., daughter of John and Mary F. Fry.
   A1141212.   ELIZABETH KESTERSON, b. 1835 in Augusta Co.
   A1141213.   JOHN KESTERSON, b. 1837 in Augusta Co.
   A1141213.   SARAH E. KESTERSON, b. c.1837.
A114122.   JANE WALTON, b. c.1811-1820 (under age 10 in 1820).
A114123.   SAMUEL WALTON, b. c.1811-1814 (of age 10 but under 16 years on the 1830 Federal census).
A114124.   ELI WALTON, b. 1811-1814 (of age 16 but under 20 years on the 1830 Federal census).
A114125.   NANCY WALTON, b. c.1814 (under age 10 in 1820).
A114126.   JOHN NICHOLAS WALTON, farmer, b. DEC 1822 in Augusta Co., served in Co. A of the 57th Va. Inf. In
           the C.S.A., d. APR 1912 in Bath Co., bur. in the Walton-Campbell Family Cem. (Highway 606), Healing
           Springs, Bath Co. Nicholas Walton m. 6 OCT 1840 in Bath Co. to [Mary] Ann Smith, daughter of Thomas
           Smith. Children:
   A1141261.   THOMAS WALTON, b. 1843 in Va.
   A1141262.   WILLIAM WALTON, b. 1845 in Va.
   A1141263.   JOHN SAMUEL WALTON, b. APR 1847 in Bath Co., d. 27 JUL 1922 in Montrose, W.Va., m. Rebecca
               Ann Moore; both bur. in Mt. Pleasant Cem. of Clover Dist., Tucker, W.Va.
A114127.   Son Walton, b. c.1821-1825 (of age 5 but under 10 years on the 1830 Federal census).

---

[1] Richmond Terril Walton is a son of Richmond Walton of Fredericksville Parish of Albemarle Co. who left a will in Augusta Co. [Augusta Co., Va. Wills, Bk. 10, p. 312], proved 7 NOV 1831, mentions wife Elizabeth [Thompson]. In 1786, Richmond Walton signed a deed of gift for personal and real property to his children [Albemarle Co., Va. Deeds, Bk. 7, p. 514, dated 12 JAN 1786], and the document is important for genealogy of that family because it lists middle names for the children.
[2] 1850 Federal census for Bath Co., Va., taken in July, p. 115 (typed).
[3] Bath Co. Deeds, Bk. 9, p. 397, dated 9 AUG 1842.
[4] Also see Bath Co. Chancery, *Arthur Armstrong et al v. Richmond T. Walton et al.* Nancy, wife of Richmond T. Walton, was administratrix of the estate of James Armstrong.
[5] Bath Co., Va. Wills, Bk. 6, p. 348, will of Richmond T. Walton, dated 13 SEP 1862, proved January Court 1863, mentions wife Catherine. The 1862 will mentions children, Samuel Walton, Polly Walton [who married William Kesterson], Nancy Walton, John N. Walton, Jane Walton, and Eli Walton. The Executor of R.T. Walton was Anthony Mustoe.
[6] County of birth is taken from the 1850 Federal census for Bath Co., Va., p. 130 (typewritten), with household #295 headed by William Kesterson.
[7] The 1860 Federal census lists the couple in Bath Co., Va., p. 40 (handwritten), in Green Valley.

A11413. REUBEN ALEXANDER
(c.1784/94-ante 1830)

Reuben Alexander was a son of John Sheldon Alexander and his wife Leah [or Sarah] (Fleming?), and is known to have been born c.1784 in Maryland. He had a brother William Alexander, of Rockingham County, who stated that Reuben Alexander served with him in the War of 1812.[1] Reuben Alexander was discharged from his term in the War of 1812 on February 8, 1815 by General John H. Cocke.

Reuben Alexander was married by bond dated July 23, 1810 in Albemarle County to Sarah "Sally" Smith (born c.1784/94), daughter of John M. Smith who is known to have deceased by 1818.[2] The marriage bond was witnessed and signed by William Beddow who also signed a statement that the groom was at least 21 years of age.

This couple and their family is found on the 1810 Federal census for Fredericksville Parish, Albemarle County, page 184, and also on the 1820 Federal census for Augusta County, Greenville District, page 3A.

On June 23, 1824, Reuben Alexander and his wife Sally, along with her brother John Smith, sold for $73 a 100-acre parcel of land in Albemarle County which had been purchased by Sally's father, John M. Smith, from David Wood, deceased, to Thomas Smith of Albemarle County.[3] Subsequent Federal census records for Virginia and surrounding states do not place Reuben Alexander, and, unless other records can be located, he is then presumed to have either died by 1830, or left Virginia.

Children of Reuben Alexander and Sarah "Sally" Smith:

	A114131.	(Possibly) HENRY ALEXANDER, b. 1810/1820 in Va. (under 10 in 1820).[4]
+	A114132.	DAVID ALEXANDER, b. 29 DEC 1813 in Va., m. 21 MAR 1839 in Augusta Co. to Margaret Stickley.
	A114133.	Daughter, b. 1810/1820 in Va. (under 10 in 1820).
	A114134.	Daughter, b. 1810/1820 in Va. (under 10 in 1820).

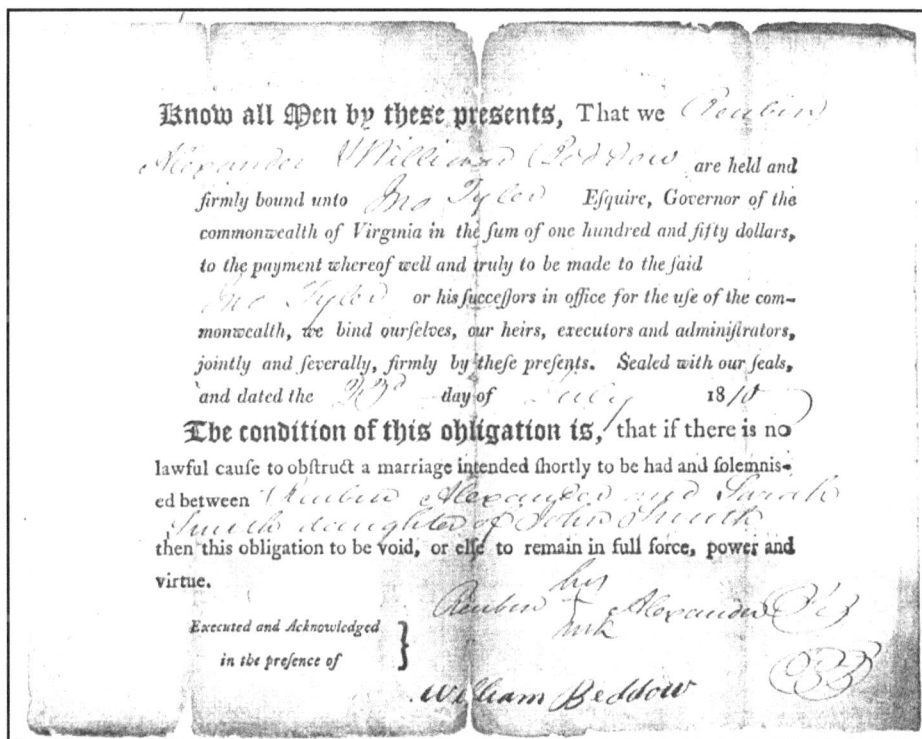

Figure 76 - Bond for Reuben Alexander to marry Sarah Smith in 1810

---

[1] National Archives, War of 1812 Pension Records, file #W.O. 1208, W.C. 1030 for Ann (Bevans) Alexander, widow of soldier William Alexander. Also see Virginia Militia in the War of 1812, Vol. 1, p. 343; the pay roll shows private Reuben Alexander served for 5 months and 14 days (2 weeks shorter than his brothers Samuel Alexander, William Alexander and Asa Alexander.

[2] Lyman Chalkley, Chronicles of the Scotch-Irish Settlement in Virginia ... (Baltimore, Genealogical Publishing Co., 1965), Vol. II, p. 236. *Smith vs. Wood - O.S. 320; N.S. 115 - Bill, 1818, by children and heirs of John M. Smith of Albemarle who disappeared 15 years ago and has since died, intestate, viz: William, John, Thomas Smith, Sally, wife of Reuben Alexander; Nancy, Polly, Betsey, James, and Willis Smith (infant). In 1794, John bought land from David Wood. Wood is dead, intestate, leaving widow _____ and children, viz: Thomas, Nicholas L., Maria, wife of James Clarkson; John W., Wm. L., Robt. W., Margaret L., and David I. Margaret L. married James Rogers.*

[3] Albemarle Co. Deeds, Bk. 24, p. 334.

[4] Letter received from Marion Harold Alexander contained a note that his great grandfather David Alexander had a brother Henry Alexander.

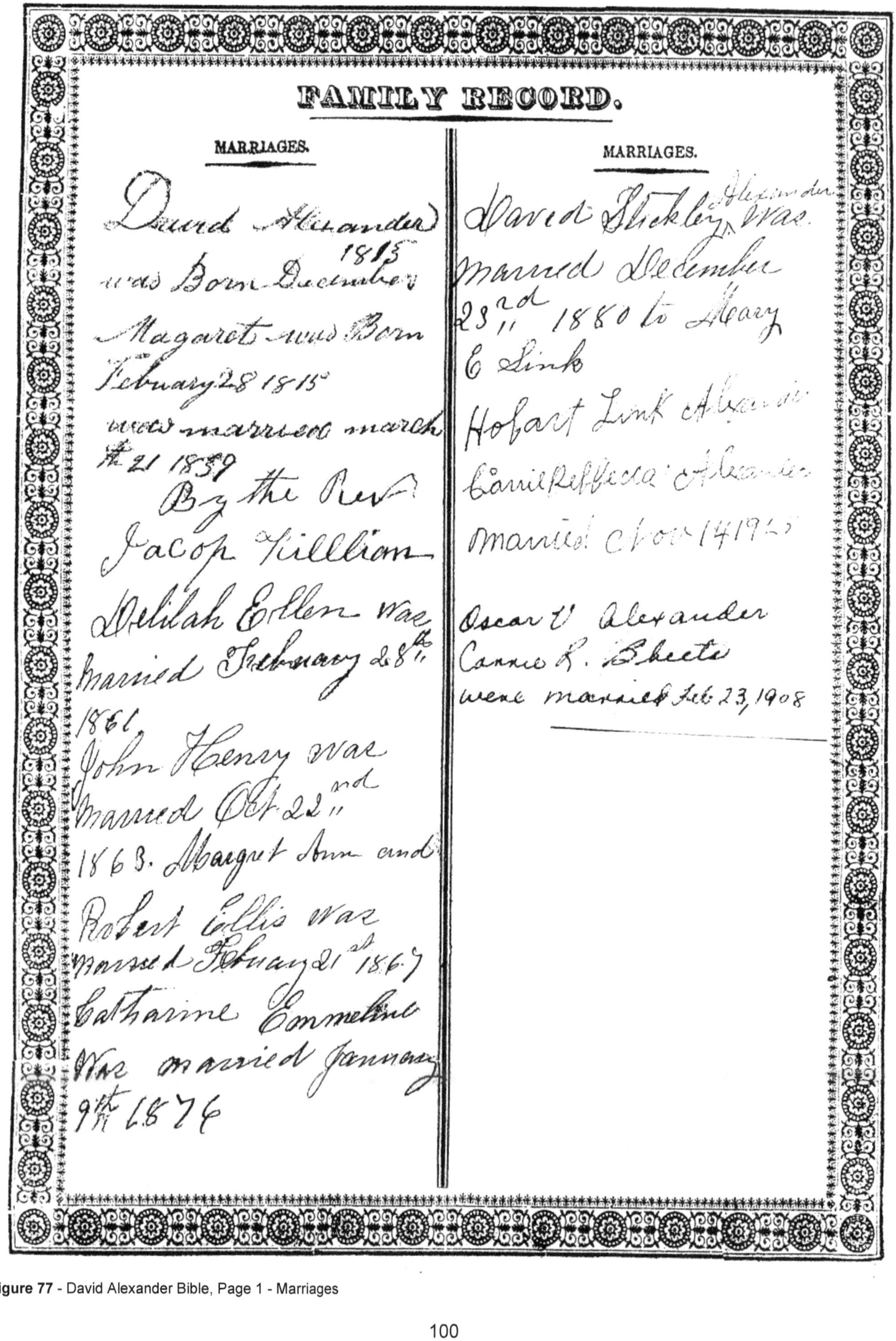

FAMILY RECORD.

MARRIAGES.

David Alexander was Born December 1815

Magaret was Born Febuary 28 1815

was married march th 21 1859

By the Rev Jacob Killian

Delilah Ellen Was Married Febuary 28th 1861,

John Henry was Married Oct. 22nd 1863. Marget Ann and

Robert Ellis Was Married Febuary 21st 1867

Catharine Emmeline Was married January 9th 1876

MARRIAGES.

David Stickley Alexander Was Married December 23rd 1880 to Mary C Link

Hobart Link Alexander

Carrie Rebecca Alexander Married Nov 14 1942

Oscar V Alexander Carrie L. Sheets were married Feb 23, 1908

Figure 77 - David Alexander Bible, Page 1 - Marriages

100

FAMILY RECORD.

BIRTHS.

John henry Alexander
was Born March 26 1840
was Babtise october 11 1840
Robert Giles Alexander
was Born August 3 1841
was Babtise May 8 1842
Deliah Ellen Alexander
was Born march 26 1843
was Babtise June 4 1843
Rebecca Frances Alexander
was Born March 8 1845
was Babtise August 31 1845
Margaret Ann Alexander
was Born December 18 1846
was Babtise

Sarah Agness Alexander
was Born June 5 1849
was Babtise november 13 1853

Mary Elisabeth Alexander
was Born July 9 1852
was Babtise November 13 th
1853
Katharine Emmaline
Alexander was Born
Jannary 27 1856 Was Babtise
David S. Alexander
Was Born October 28 - 1859

BIRTHS.

D. S. Alexander 1853
was Born October 28
Mary E. Alexander
was Born April 30 1854
Abner A. Alexander
Born March 9 1882
Gabriel L. Alexander
was Born july 17 1884
Oscar R. Alexander
was Born October 19. 1885
James B. Alexander
was Born february 8 1887
John R. Alexander
was Born November 24 1888
William C. Alexander
was Born November 11 1891
David S. Alexander
was Born October 8. 1893
Hobart S. Alexander
was Born december 14. 1894
Flossie E. Alexander
was Born August 20. 1898

Figure 78 - David Alexander Bible, Page 2 - Births

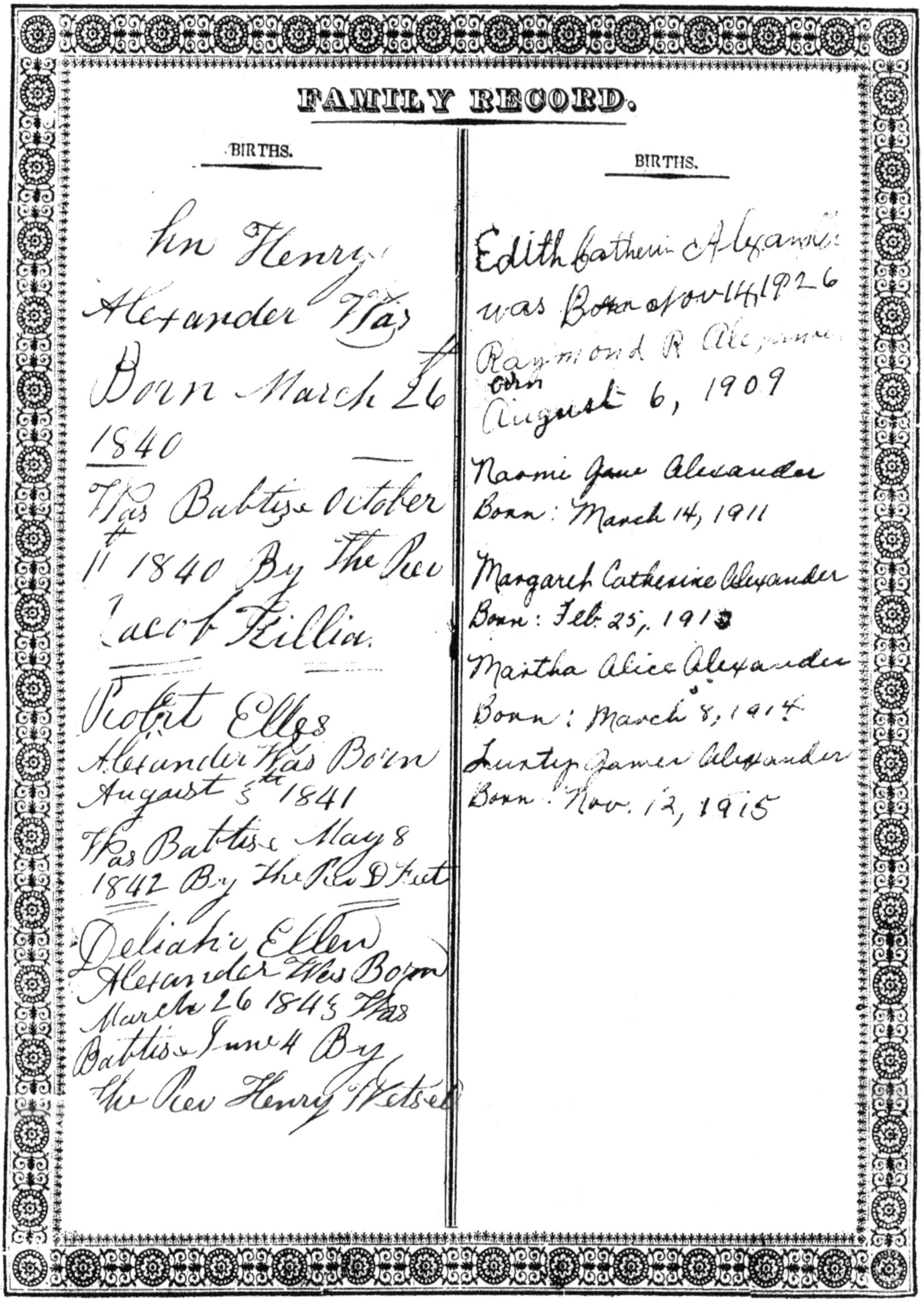

FAMILY RECORD.

BIRTHS.

Im Henry Alexander Was Born March 26th 1840

Was Babtize October 11th 1840 By The Rev Jacob Killia.

Robert Elles Alexander Was Born August 5th 1841

Was Babtise May 8 1842 By The Rev D Fiet

Deliah Ellen Alexander Was Born March 26 1843 Was Babtise June 4 By the Rev Henry Wetsel

BIRTHS.

Edith Catherin Alexander was Born Nov 14 1926

Raymond R Alexander Born August 6, 1909

Naomi Jane Alexander Born: March 14, 1911

Margaret Catherine Alexander Born: Feb. 25, 1913

Martha Alice Alexander Born: March 8, 1914

Luster James Alexander Born: Nov. 12, 1915

Figure 79 - David Alexander Bible, Page 3 - Births

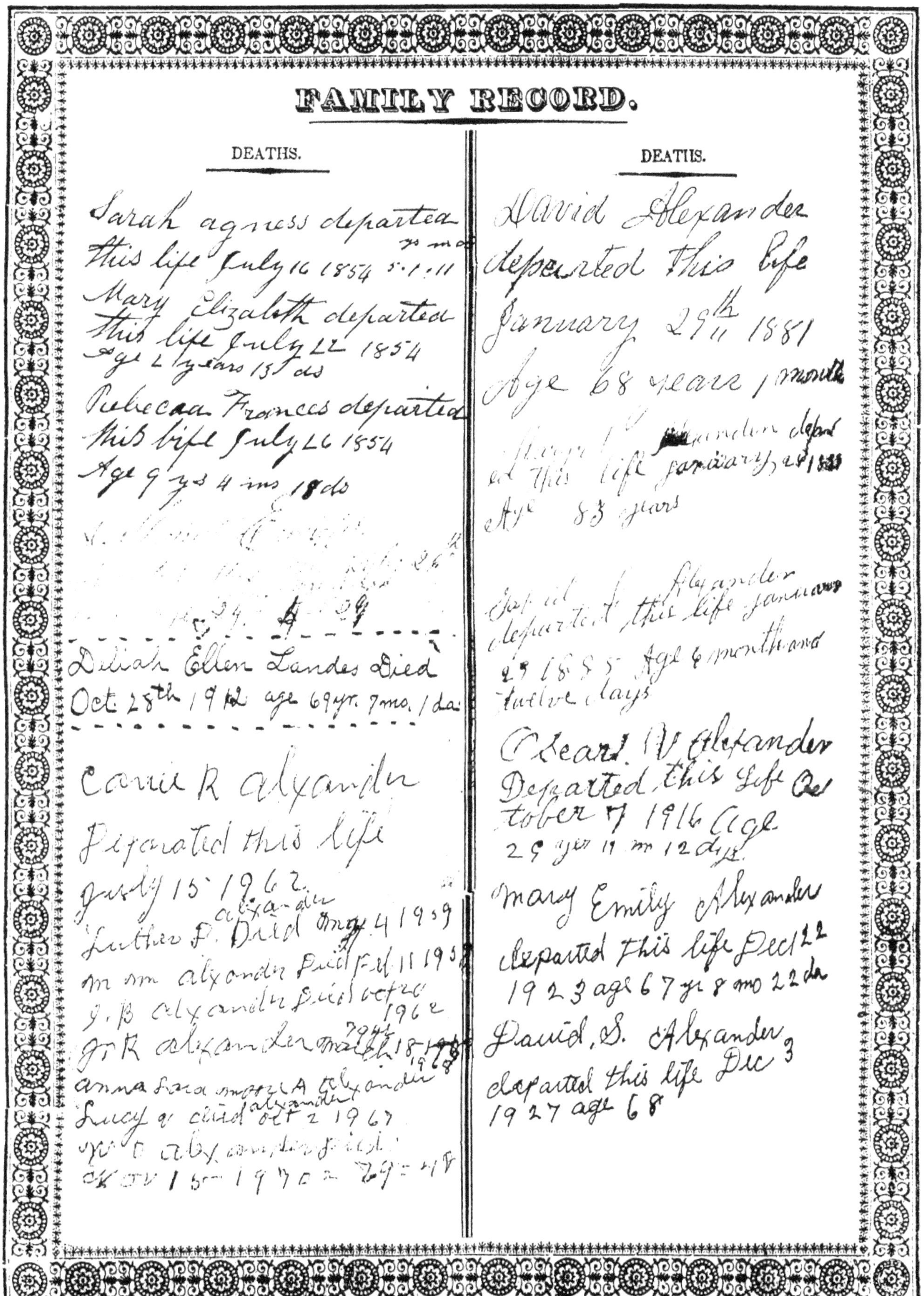

FAMILY RECORD.

DEATHS.

Sarah agness departed this life July 16 1854 5-1-11

Mary Elizabeth departed this life July 22 1854 age 2 years 13 ds

Rebecca Frances departed this life July 26 1854 age 9 ys 4 ms 18 ds

illegible line

Diliah Ellen Landes Died Oct 28th 19 _illegible_ age 69 yr. 7 mo. 1 da

Carrie R Alexander Departed this life July 15 1962 Luther D. Alexander Died May 4 1959 m m alexander Died Feb 11 195_ J B Alexander Died oct _ 1962 Jr R alexander march 18 19_ Anna Sara _illegible_ A alexander Lucy g _illegible_ alexander oct 2 1967 _illegible_ alexander died _illegible_

DEATHS.

David Alexander departed this life January 29th 1881 Age 68 years 1 month

illegible Alexander departed this life January 29 18_ Age 83 years

illegible Alexander departed this life January 29 1855 Age 6 month and twelve days

O Sear. W Alexander Departed this Life October 7 1916 age 29 yr 11 m 12 dys

Mary Emily Alexander departed this life Dec 22 1923 age 67 yr 8 mo 22 da

David S. Alexander departed this life Dec 3 1927 age 68

Figure 80 - David Alexander Bible, Page 4 - Deaths

103

A114132. David Alexander
(1813-1881)

David Alexander, son of Reuben Alexander and Sarah "Sally" Smith,[1] was born December 29, 1813 in Virginia, possibly near Cook Creek, Rockingham County,[2] but also possibly in Albemarle County.

Marriages of Augusta County reveal that David was married March 21, 1839 in Waynesboro, Virginia to Margaret Stickley, daughter of Gabriel Stickley and Rebecca Keller, born February 28, 1815 in Virginia. An entry in the Bible of David Alexander reveals that the couple was married by the Rev. Jacob Killiam.

Burials of Trinity Lutheran Cemetery, located near Crimora, Virginia, established in 1772, reflect that Gabriel Stickley was born November 13, 1791, died September 16,[3] 1856,

Figure 81 - Residence of David Alexander, south of Harrisonburg, Va. on Route 11 (Roller House)

and his wife Rebecca Keller was born November 2, 1792, and died April 3, 1873.

Margaret Stickley had a sister Elizabeth Stickley, born January 23, 1823, who died May 27, 1909, and was buried in Mt. Pisgah Cemetery. Elizabeth was married March 25, 1847 by minister George H. Martin in Augusta County to Peter Kennedy, born January 26, 1823, and died January 10, 1860.[4]

Ordinance records of Augusta County, indicate that David Alexander was licensed in the August 1843 Court term to *keep a house of private entertainment* until the May 1844 Court term, to be located in the town of Port Republic.[5] David and Margaret Alexander purchased 150 acres in Augusta County on April 4, 1847.[6]

The graves of both David and Margaret Alexander are to be found in Salem Lutheran Church Cemetery near Mt. Sidney, revealing that David died January 29, 1881,[7] and his wife died on January 26, 1899, aged 83 years 10 months 28 days.[8] According to a family record, David died *from injuries rec'd. in runaway*, aged 68 years and 1 month.

A Bible which belonged to David Alexander and lately in the possession of Lurty James Alexander, is reproduced here.[9]

Children of David Alexander and Margaret Stickley:

+ A1141321. JOHN HENRY ALEXANDER, b. 26 MAR 1840, d. 9 JAN 1915, m. 22 OCT 1863 to Sarah Elizabeth Craun.
+ A1141322. ROBERT ELLIS "Buzz" ALEXANDER, b. 3 AUG 1841, d. 12 DEC 1918, m. 21 FEB 1867 to Mary Susan Jordan.
  A1141323. ELLEN DELILAH[10] ALEXANDER, b. 26 MAR 1844 in Va., bapt. 4 JUN 1843 by Rev. Henry Wetzel,[11] d. 28 OCT 1912, age 69y, m. 28 FEB 1861 in Augusta Co. to William Austin Landes, b. 20 DEC 1833, d. 27 OCT 1907, both bur. Salem Lutheran Church Cem. Children:
  A11413231. LAURA FRANCES LANDES, b. 31 JAN 1861, d. 8 JUL 1941, m. 23 DEC 1880 in Mt. Sidney to Martin Luther Link, b. 17 MAR 1858, d. 7 OCT 1937, son of Daniel W. Link and Catharine Craun.
  A11413232. NANCY MARGARET LANDES, b. 14 FEB 1864 in Mt. Sidney, d. 1930, m. 24 NOV 1890 in Mt. Sidney to John P. Simmons.

[1] Philip Alexander Bruce, <u>History of Virginia</u> (Chicago and New York: The American Historical Society, 1924).
[2] <u>Letter</u>, Marion Harold Alexander, no date.
[3] Augusta Co. Death Register, #1106, gives Gabriel Stickley d. 17 SEP 1856 aged 66y.
[4] Augusta Co. Death Register, entry #2020, aged 37y 10m 22d.
[5] Rockingham Co. Ordinances.
[6] Augusta Co. Deed Bk. 67, p. 164.
[7] Gravestone: Salem Lutheran Church Cemetery: DAVID ALEXANDER / [hand pointing upward] / Died / June 29, 1881, / Aged / 68 Yrs. & 1 Mo. / *At peace*.
[8] Gravestone: Salem Lutheran Church Cemetery: In Loving Remembrance of / Our Mother / MARGARET / Wife of / David Alexander / Died / Jan. 26, 1899 / Aged / 83 yrs. 10 mos. & 28 ds. / *We miss you ...*
[9] Bible title page: <u>The New Testament of Our Lord and Savior Jesus Christ, Translated out of the Original Greek, and with The Former Translations Diligently Compared and Revised</u> (Philadelphia: Kimber and Sharpless, no date).
[10] Delilah Landes on her tombstone; however as Ellen D. on the Federal census for 1870, 1880 and 1900.
[11] Bible of the David Alexander Family.

A11413233. SARAH JANE LANDES, b. 1865, d. 27 SEP 1889 in Mt. Sidney, bur. Salem Lutheran Church Cem., m. 20 OCT 1887 in Stonewall, Augusta Co. to William M. Simmons. Child:

 A114132331. BESSIE C. SIMMONS, b. AUG 1888 in Augusta Co.

A11413234. JOHN ALEXANDER LANDES, farmer, b. 27 NOV 1868, d. 21 FEB 1948, m. 17 NOV 1889 in Augusta Co. to Luella M. Moore, b. 27 MAY 1868, d. 25 FEB 1950; both bur. Salem Lutheran Church Cem. Child:

 A114132341. EMMA PEARL LANDES, b. 14 AUG 1895, d. 20 OCT 1897.

A11413235. Infant Landes.

A11413236. MARTHA FLORENCE LANDES, b. 30 JUL 1872, m. 22 JAN 1891 near Mt. Sidney to Luther Hamilton Reed, son of Andrew Reed and Julia Smith.

A11413237. REBECCA ELLEN LANDES, b. FEB 1875, m. David Baylor. Child:

 A114132371. HELEN SANDS BAYLOR [or Bayler], m. 2 MAR 1929 in Staunton to Wale Guy Henderson.

A11413238. WILLIAM K. LANDES, b. 19 OCT 1878, d. 23 AUG 1880.

A11413239. Infant Landes.

A1141323(10.) CHARLES STUART LANDES, b. 10 JAN 1882, d. 6 JUL 1952, m. Nora Rimel.

A1141323(11). WALLACE VALENTINE [or Peyton] LANDES, b. 3 DEC 1884 at Naked Creek, Augusta Co., d. 15 JUN 1872, m. Sadie Byers.

A1141324. REBECCA FRANCES ALEXANDER, b. 8 MAR 1845 in Va., bapt. 31 AUG 1845, d. 26 JUL 1854 of flux in Augusta Co., aged 9y 4m 18d.

A1141325. MARGARET ANN "Mag" ALEXANDER, b. 18 DEC 1846 in Va., d. 3 JUL 1920 at her home nr. Mt. Sidney, m. 21 FEB 1867 in Rockingham Co. to David Samuel Wine,[1] b. 29 SEP 1847 in Rockingham Co., d. 19 MAY 1926 at his home nr. Mt. Sidney, son of George Wine and Catharine Good. Both bur. in Salem Lutheran Church Cem., 3 miles west of Mt. Sidney. Children:[2]

 A11413251. SAMUEL WALTER WINE, b. 25 OCT 1867, d. 10 JUN 1950, bur. Salem Lutheran Church Cem., m. 11 JUN 1893 in Augusta Co. to Dora Lula Hulvey, daughter of B. Hulvey and Elizabeth M. Houff, b. 7 JUN 1875, d. 6 MAR 1949, bur. Salem Lutheran Church Cem.

 A11413252. JOHN WENDELL WINE, b. 22 MAR 1869, d. 6 DEC 1944, bur. Salem Lutheran Church Cem., m. 29 MAR 1891 at Mt. Sidney to Julia Frances Link, daughter of Daniel W. Link and Catharine Craun, b. 2 JUL 1868, d. 18 MAY 1959, bur. Salem Lutheran Church Cem. Children:

  A114132521. SADIE C. WINE, b. 14 OCT 1891, d. 15 JUN 1966, m. Harrison M. Whitesell, b. 31 AUG 1888, d. 21 MAR 1956; both bur. Salem Lutheran Church Cem.

  A114132522. MARGARET WINE, b. 15 NOV 1895, d. 16 JUL 1981, m. 12 MAR 1914 in Washington, D.C. to Jesse L. Harshbarger, b. 15 NOV 1895, d. 29 AUG 1975; both bur. Salem Lutheran Church Cem. Child:

   A1141325221. DALLAS WILLIAM HARSHBARGER, b. 1925, d. 1987, bur. Salem Lutheran Church Cem.

  A114132523. NELSON P. WINE, b. 28 AUG 1901, d. 22 MAR 1979, m. 10 MAY 1924 in Washington, D.C. to Virginia C. Hudson, b. 22 AUG 1906, d. 3 MAY 1990; both bur. Salem Lutheran Church Cem.

  A114132524. RICHARD H. WINE, b. 26 DEC 1906, d. 25 OCT 1981, m. Beatrice Price, b. 2 FEB 1923, d. 6 JAN 2008; both bur. Mt. Pisgah Cem. of Mt. Sidney, Va. Child:

   A1141325241. BETTY LOUISE WINE, b. 24 AUG 1959, d. 1 MAR 1986, bur. Mt. Pisgah Cem.

 A11413253. SARAH ELLEN WINE, b. c.1870, d. c.1940, m. 1 MAR 1888 near Mt. Sidney to Luther H. Reed, farmer, son of John Reed and Julia A. Grandstaff, b. 1869, d. 5 DEC 1937; both bur. Salem Lutheran Church Cem.

 A11413254. GEORGE DAVID WINE, b. 1872, d. 1956, bur. Salem Lutheran Church Cem., m. (1) Catherine Hemp, and m. (2) 14 OCT 1897 in Augusta Co. to Roberta "Bertie" Hoover, daughter of R.D. Hoover and E.J. Shuey, b. 26 DEC 1867, d. 28 FEB 1933, bur. Salem Lutheran Church Cem.

 A11413255. LUCY ANNE WINE, b. 20 MAY 1876, d. 16 FEB 1949 in Fauquier Co., bur. Salem Lutheran Church Cem., m. (1) Gabriel Dewitt Coiner, b. 1853, d. 1925, bur. Mountain View Cem. of Crimora, Va., she m. (2) George Jackson, m. (3) as the 3rd wife of James William Croushorn, b. 1871, d. 1956, bur. Salem Lutheran Church Cem.

 A11413256. CHARLES GABRIEL WINE, b. 26 SEP 1878, d. 8 SEP 1953, bur. Salem Lutheran Church Cem., m. Stella Catherine Byers, b. 7 NOV 1881, d. 4 JAN 1961, bur. Salem Lutheran

---

[1] Letter, Dennis H. Wine.
[2] Ibid.

Church Cem.

A11413257.   JAMES HARVEY WINE, b. 14 SEP 1881, d. 4 MAR 1970, bur. Salem Lutheran Church Cem., m. Daisey Pearl Landes, b. 20 FEB 1888, d. 31 JUL 1986, bur. Salem Lutheran Church Cem.

A11413258.   MARY KATHERINE "Katie" WINE, b. 23 FEB 1884, d. 9 AUG 1943, bur. Salem Lutheran Church Cem., m. George Emory Sheets, b. 13 AUG 1882, d. 16 DEC 1952, bur. Salem Lutheran Church Cem.

A11413259.   ARCHIBALD EARL WINE, b. 9 OCT 1888, d. 28 SEP 1964, bur. Salem Lutheran Church Cem., m. (1) Ora Landes, m. (2) Cora Gladdy.

A1141325(10).   IDA ELLEN WINE, unmarried.

A1141326.   SARAH AGNES ALEXANDER, b. 5 JUN 1849 in Va., bapt. 13 NOV 1853, d. of flux on 16 JUL 1854 in Augusta Co., aged 5y 1m 11d, bur. Mt. Pisgah Cem., 8 m. north of Staunton at Routes 620 and 742.

A1141327.   MARY ELIZABETH ALEXANDER, b. 9 JUL 1852[1] in Va., bapt. 13 NOV 1853, d. of flux on 22 JUL 1854 in Augusta Co., aged 2y 13d, bur. in Mt. Pisgah Cem.

A1141328.   Infant son, bur. Mt. Pisgah Cem., 8 miles north of Staunton at Routes 620 and 742.

A1141329.   CATHERINE EMALINE ALEXANDER, b. 27 JAN 1856 in Va., d. 26 JUL 1880, aged 24y 5m 27d,[2] m. 3 JAN 1876[3] in Augusta Co. to Daniel Melanchton Link, b. 3 OCT 1852, d. 22 JAN 1926, son of Daniel W. Link and Catherine Craun. Both bur. in Salem Lutheran Church Cem. Daniel m. (2) 26 JAN 1882 to Elizabeth Harriet Fry, b. 18 JUL 1857, d. 5 JAN 1914, bur. Salem Lutheran Church Cem. Children:[4]

A11413291.   LAURA AGNES "Addie" LINK, b. 8 JUN 1878, d. 14 AUG 1942, m. Paul C. Hudson, b. 23 JUL 1875, d. 17 JAN 1945, bur. Salem Lutheran Church Cem.

A11413292.   DAVID DANIEL LINK, b. 25 JUL 1880, d. 18 NOV 1945, m. (1) Bertie Houff, m. (2) Annie Van Lear.

+   A114132(10).   DAVID STICKLEY ALEXANDER, b. 28 OCT 1859, d. 3 DEC 1927, m. 23 DEC 1880 to Mary Emily Link.

A1141321. John Henry Alexander
(1840-1915)

John Henry Alexander, son of David Alexander and Margaret Stickley, was a farmer, and was born March 26, 1840 in Rockingham County. From the David Alexander Family Bible and other family records it is known he was baptized October 11, 1840 by Rev. Jacob Killiam.[5] John Henry Alexander was married on October 22, 1863 in Augusta County to Sarah Elizabeth Craun.[6] Sarah, born January 1, 1843, was a daughter of Daniel Harvy Craun (b. January 10, 1818, d. May 7, 1879, aged 61y 3m 27d) and Lucinda Wise (b. March 25, 1823, d. March 4, 1894, aged 70y 11m 9d) who were married February 11, 1840.

John Henry Alexander died January 9, 1915 in Augusta County, and was buried in St. Michaels Reformed Church Cemetery south of

Figure 82 - Residence of David Craun Alexander, Highway 42

Bridgewater, in Rockingham County. Sarah died July 5, 1922 in Weyers Cave, and was buried in St. Michaels Reformed Church Cemetery.

---

[1] David Alexander Family Bible, gives date of birth as 9 JUL 1852.
[2] David Alexander Family Bible.
[3] David Alexander Family Bible, gives date of marriage as 9 JAN 1876.
[4] Letter, Karl R. Alexander, Jr. (Westminster, Md.).
[5] Family Record in possession of Jared Craun Alexander of Weyers Cave, Va.
[6] Bible Record.

Children of John Henry Alexander and Sarah Elizabeth Craun (birth dates from the family Bible):

A11413211.   JOHN ADAM ALEXANDER, an attorney, b. 25 NOV 1864 in Augusta Co., Va., d. c.1950 poss. in Enid, Okla., m. 28 JUN 1889[1] to Miss James Ella Selman, daughter of Capt. James Wilson Selman, of Ga., div. John was a member of the Staunton Bar Association, Masonic Order, Knights Templar, and a Shriner. Among his other interests were orcharding, forestry and the study of history. His home "Stirling" sat on N. Augusta St. in Staunton; he became involved in a land scandal and left the area.

A11413212.   MARY FRANCES "Fannie" ALEXANDER, b. 31 OCT 1866, d. 9 OCT 1938, aged 71y 11m 22d [Bible], bur. St. Michaels Reformed Church Cem., unmarried.

A11413213.   LUCINDA MARGARET ALEXANDER, b. 17 AUG 1868 in Va., d. 8 MAY 1948, aged 79y 8m 21d, bur. St. Michaels Reformed Church Cem., unmarried.

A11413214.   DAVID CRAUN ALEXANDER, b. 6 DEC 1871 in Weyers Cave, Augusta Co., d. 5/6[2] MAR 1930 in Mt. Solon, bur. St. Michaels Reformed Church Cem., m. 27 OCT 1897[3] there by Rev. Welfinger to Sarah Rebecca Huffman, b. 7 APR 1877 in Bridgewater, Rockingham Co., d. 11 MAR 1969 in Rockingham Memorial Hospital, bur. St. Michaels Reformed Church Cem., daughter of Brown Marion Huffman (b. 22 MAR 1849, d. 22 NOV 1915) and Mary Margaret Landes (b. 4 MAR 1850, d. 10 APR 1906), bur. St. Michaels Reformed Church Cem., granddaughter of Benjamin Hoffman (b. 12 FEB 1803, d. 17 MAY 1887), also bur. St. Michaels Reformed Church Cem. Children:[4]

Figure 83 - David Craun Alexander

A114132141.   HUGH LEE ALEXANDER, b. 14 JUN 1898 in Augusta Co., d. 3 APR 1969, bur. St. Michaels Reformed Church Cem., m. 17 JUN 1941 to Thelma Dorothy Kelley, b. 23 JUN 1917 in Deerfield, Augusta Co., d. 9 MAY 1986, bur. St. Michaels Reformed Church Cem., res. at Dayton, Va.

A114132142.   JOHN BROWN ALEXANDER, b. 30 AUG 1900 in Augusta Co., d. 14 FEB 1984, bur. St. Michaels Reformed Church Cem., m. 16 DEC 1925 to Kathryn Racer, b. 4 JUN 1904 in Luray, Page Co., d. 26 APR 1981, bur. St. Michaels Reformed Church Cem. Children[5]:

A1141321421.   JARED CRAUN ALEXANDER, b. 26 JAN 1927 in Weyers Cave, m. 18 JUL 1947 to Margaret Ellen Shufflebarger, b. 11 FEB 1929 in Bastian, Bland Co., res. Weyers Cave. Jared has the oldest Alexander Bible record of this family. Child:

A11413214211.   GLEN BROWN ALEXANDER, b. 15 JUN 1950 in Harrisonburg, m. 17 JUN 1972 to Donna Stuart Coffman, b. 15 JAN 1950 in Staunton, Augusta Co. Children:

A114132142112.   SARAH BETH ALEXANDER, b. 29 APR 1978 in Alconbury, England, d. 28 JAN 1983 in Wales, bur. Salem Lutheran Church Cem. of Mt. Sidney.

A114132142113.   WENDY DENISE ALEXANDER, b. 22 OCT 1981 in Bangor, Wales.

A1141321422.   NORMA GENE ALEXANDER, b. 6 JUN 1930 in Weyers Cave, m. 17 MAR 1950 to Lawrence Ervin Terry, b. 12 MAR 1929 in Mt. Crawford, Rockingham Co., res. Weyers Cave. Children:

A11413214221.   CAROLYN FAYE TERRY, b. 27 JAN 1951 in Harrisonburg, Va.

A11413214222.   THOMAS NELSON TERRY, b. 17 AUG 1955, m. Janet Catherine Gibson, b. 20 JUL 1955 in Augusta Co. Child:

A114132142221.   RANDALL THOMAS TERRY, b. 23 AUG 1983 in Augusta Co.

A1141321423.   MERVIN RACER ALEXANDER, b. 20 OCT 1933 in Augusta Co., d. 30 MAR 1934, bur. St. Michaels Reformed Church Cem.

A1141321424.   BROWNIE BELLE ALEXANDER, b. 9 JUL 1936 in Augusta Co., m. 4 NOV 1955 to Lerty Leon Moats, b. 27 AUG 1935 in Augusta Co., res. Weyers Cave. Children:

---

[1] Philip Alexander Bruce, History of Virginia (Chicago and New York: The American Historical Society, 1924), Vol. V, p. 317.
[2] Bible record gives date of death as 5 MAR 1930, yet tombstone in St. Michaels Reformed Church Cem. gives 6 MAR 1930.
[3] Rockingham Co., Va. Marriages, Bk. 2, p. 2.
[4] Letter, Rudolph B. Alexander.
[5] Victor S. Craun, Craun Family in America (1950), p. 56; Betty Jane (Alexander) Swecker.

A11413214241. KATHRYN ARLENE MOATS, b. 2 JAN 1957, m. (1) 27 FEB 1976 to Douglas Page Fry, b. 26 DEC 1951, she m. (2) 5 AUG 1983 to James Edward Crissman, b. 24 NOV 1953 in Clarksville, Tenn. Children:

A114132142411. AMY MICHELE FRY, b. 7 JUL 1979 in Staunton.

A114132142412. ERIN RENEE CRISSMAN, b. 23 APR 1987 in Staunton.

A11413214242. JOHN LEON MOATS, b. 8 OCT 1961 in Harrisonburg, m. 31 JUL 1982 to Sarah Patricia Michael, b. 20 JUL 1964 in Winston-Salem, N.C., res. Mt. Solon. Child:

A114132142421. KARISSA DAWN MOATS, b. 21 APR 1985 in Harrisonburg, Va.

A1141321425. ROBERT WAYNE ALEXANDER, b. 22 NOV 1942 in Harrisonburg, m. 14 DEC 1962 to Peggy Yvonne Long, b. 17 FEB 1942 in Harrisonburg, res. Mt. Crawford, Va. Children, all b. in Harrisonburg:

A11413214251. LISA RENEE ALEXANDER, b. 21 JAN 1964.

A11413214252. JILL LYNN ALEXANDER, b. 5 DEC 1967.

A11413214253. MATTHEW ROBERT ALEXANDER, b. 31 JAN 1973, d. 4 APR 1973, bur. Mill Creek Church of the Brethren Cem., Port Republic, Va.

A11413214254. BRETT HUNTER ALEXANDER, b. 10 MAY 1974.

A114132143. WILLIAM DUDLEY ALEXANDER, b. 7 OCT 1902 in Augusta Co., d. 16 SEP 1975 in Waynesboro, m. 12 JUL 1926 in Verona, Augusta Co. to Reba Virginia Sandy, b. 22 FEB 1906, d. 1 APR 1984, bur. Waynesboro, res. Covington. Children:[1]

A1141321431. CHARLOTTE ELLEN ALEXANDER, b. 27 FEB 1928 in Bridgewater, Rockingham Co., m. 16 MAY 1953 to Herbert Winston French, b. 26 AUG 1928 in Shenandoah Co., res. Harrisonburg. Children:

A11413214311. SCOTT WINSTON FRENCH, b. 28 DEC 1955, m. 9 JUN 1984 to Linda Michelle Peay, b. 15 JUN 1961 in Tappahannock, Essex Co., Va., div., res. Harrisonburg.

A11413214312. KIRK LEE FRENCH, b. 21 NOV 1957 in Harrisonburg, res. Harrisonburg.

A11413214313. DAWN GAY FRENCH, b. 20 JAN 1961 in Harrisonburg, m. 14 JUL 1984 to Danny Edward Jones, b. 22 MAY 1958 in New London CT, res. Dumfries, Prince William Co., Va.

A11413214314. KELLY JOE FRENCH, b. 9 APR 1965 in Harrisonburg.

A1141321432. BETTY JANE ALEXANDER, b. 29 OCT 1930 in Mt. Jackson, Shenandoah Co., m. 14 JUN 1952 to Charles Emmett Swecker, b. 20 FEB 1925 in Salem, res. Roanoke. Children:

A11413214321. CHARLES EMMETT SWECKER, JR., b. 18 JUN 1953, m. 13 FEB 1984 to Gail Marcene Stuart Arnold, b. 20 MAY 1955 in Bristol, Tenn. Child:

A114132143211. CARA STUART SWECKER, b. 9 MAR 1985 in Newport News.

A11413214322. SUZANNE SWECKER, b. 25 AUG 1955 in Wise, Va.

A11413214323. MELANIE SWECKER, b. 30 JUL 1957 in Wise.

A11413214324. STEPHANIE SWECKER, b. 27 JAN 1959 in Wise, m. 13 JUN 1981 to Joseph Paul Hedrick, b. 18 JUL 1958. Child:

A114132143241. REBECCA GRACE HEDRICK, b. 5 FEB 1987 in Salt Lake City, Utah.

A1141321433. ROBERT DONALD ALEXANDER, b. 29 SEP 1933 in Warm Springs, Bath Co., d. 13 OCT 1980 in Harrisonburg, bur. Eastlawn Memorial Gardens, m. (1) 13 OCT 1953 to Marie Laughtin, div., m. (2) 17 APR 1959 to Janet Louise Myers, b. 2 NOV 1934 in Mt. Jackson, Shenandoah Co. Children:

A11413214331. KEITH MICHAEL ALEXANDER, b. 11 NOV 1956 in Woodstock, Shenandoah Co.

A11413214332. ERIC ALAN ALEXANDER, b. 28 APR 1956 in Timberville, Rockingham Co., m. 14 MAY 1978 to Deborah Susan Bowman, b. 17 JAN 1956 in Staunton. Children:

A114132143321. HEATHER ADELE ALEXANDER, b. 5 OCT 1978 in Harrisonburg.

A114132143322. MICHAEL GORDON ALEXANDER, b. 3 SEP 1985 in Staunton.

A11413214333. TODD WILLIAM ALEXANDER, b. 23 MAY 1959 in Mt. Jackson, m. 20 JUN 1981 to Mary Graham Hedrick, b. 28 MAY 1960 in Harrisonburg, res. Mt. Crawford.

A11413214334. NEIL WADE ALEXANDER, b. 5 DEC 1963 in Harrisonburg, m. 24 DEC 1981 to Lisa Dawn Miller, b. 11 DEC 1965 in Harrisonburg, div. Child:

A114132143341. JENNIFER MARIE ALEXANDER, b. 24 NOV 1981 in Richmond.

A114132144. Infant Alexander, d. 13 NOV 1904, bur. St. Michaels Reformed Church Cem.

---

[1] Craun, p. 53.

Figure 84 - Eva Blanch Craun and Rudolph Bell Alexander

Figure 85 - Marshall Huffman Alexander

A114132145. RUDOLPH BELL ALEXANDER, b. 27 APR 1906 in Weyers Cave, Augusta Co., m. 3 AUG 1937 there to Eva Blanch Craun, b. 18 APR 1905 in Weyers Cave, d. 8 OCT 1981 in Harrisonburg, bur. Eastlawn Memorial Gardens, daughter of Samuel Henry Craun and Null,[1] d. 8 OCT 1981. Child:

A1141321451. MARY ANN ALEXANDER, b. 14 FEB 1945 in Harrisonburg, m. 16 JUL 1983 to Alvin Delmas Secrist, b. 14 DEC 1945 in Fulks Run, Rockingham Co., res. Grottoes. Children of Alvin by former marriage:

A11413214511a. Aaron Daniel Secrist, b. 1 DEC 1971 in Falls Church, Va.

A11413214512a. Derek Anthony Secrist, b. 3 AUG 1973 in Falls Church.

A11413214513a. Erica Michelle Secrist, b. 25 AUG 1975 in Warwick, N.Y.

A114132146. MARSHALL HUFFMAN ALEXANDER, b. 24 JUL 1908 in Augusta Co., d. 14 NOV 2004, m. 15 MAY 1937 to Doris G. Allen, b. 23 AUG 1913 in Roanoke, daughter of Roscoe Miller Allen and Mary E. Brown, b. 23 AUG 1913, d. 4 NOV 1994; both bur. Evergreen Burial Park of Roanoke, Va. Children:

A1141321461. DANIEL GARY ALEXANDER, b. 16 AUG 1946 in Roanoke.

A1141321462. (Dr.) GREGG ALLEN ALEXANDER, b. 27 JAN 1950 in Roanoke, m. 19 JUL 1980 to Sandra Lynn Stroberg, b. 21 MAY 1954 in Waterbury, Conn., res. Tallahassee, Fla.

A114132147. LESLIE CRAUN ALEXANDER, b. 4 MAR 1911 in Weyers Cave, d. 26 JUL 2006, m. 31 MAY 1934 to Elva F. Simmons, b. 17 FEB 1913 in Sugar Grove, W.Va., d. 27 JAN 1997 in Indian Harbour Beach, Fla. Children:[2]

A1141321471. WILLIAM NOEL ALEXANDER, b. 9 DEC 1934 in Winchester, Va., m. 1 FEB 1966 to Helen L. Fitzpatrick, b. 13 DEC 1940 in North Platte, Nebr., res. Indian Harbor Beach, Fla. Children:

A11413214711. JOHN LESLIE ALEXANDER, b. 25 DEC 1966 in Sasebo, Japan.

A11413214712. BRIGID ROSE ALEXANDER, b. 27 MAR 1969 in Quantico, Prince William Co., Va.

A1141321472. DOUGLAS WADE ALEXANDER, b. 10 FEB 1944 in Harrisonburg, m. (1) Anadel Vines, m. (2) 7 MAR 1976 to June Victoria Merrell, b. 1 JUN 1949 in Huntsville, Ala., res. Albertville, Ala. Children, b. Huntsville, Ala.:

A11413214721. CONNIE LEVADA ALEXANDER, b. 2 OCT 1971.

A11413214721. TAMMY LAVONNA ALEXANDER, b. 18 JAN 1977.

A114132148. NEVA VIRGINIA ALEXANDER, b. 11 JAN 1916 in Augusta Co., m. 19 OCT 1940 to John Paul Michael, b. 28 SEP 1908 in Sangerville, Augusta Co., res. Waynesboro. Child:[3]

A1141321481. DEANNA LYNN MICHAEL, b. 18 JUL 1946 in Waynesboro, m. 15 JUN 1968 to Eugene Paul Moser, II, b. 8 OCT 1943 in Alexandria, Va., res. Hampton, Va. Children:

A11413214811. EUGENE PAUL MOSER III, b. 1 AUG 1970 in Newport News.

A11413214812. SARAH ELIZABETH MOSER, b. 10 SEP 1974 in Hampton.

A1141321482. SALLIE DALE MICHAEL, b. 8 JUN 1950 in Waynesboro.

A1141321483. JEANNIE SUE MICHAEL, b. 1 SEP 1952 in Waynesboro.

A114132149. DAVID BEYDLER ALEXANDER, b. 6 MAY 1920 in Augusta Co., m. (1) 31 MAY 1947 to Marie Theresa Desoulets, b. 18 OCT 1922 in Winooski, Vt., div., m. (2) 31 DEC 1981 to Doris Ann Huffman Spiggle Sibert, b. 1 APR 1935 in Woodstock, Shenandoah Co., res. Edinburg.

---

[1] Craun, p. 53.
[2] Ibid., p. 56.
[3] Ibid.

Children:[1]

A1141321491. GAIL CHARLENE ALEXANDER, b. 20 MAR 1948 in Sioux City, Iowa, m. 11 AUG 1973 to James Gale Simmons, b. 25 JUN 1947 in New Albana, Miss., res. Columbia, Md. Child:

A11413214911. GEOFFREY SCOTT SIMMONS, b. 10 SEP 1983 in Cheverly, Md.

A1141321492. SCOTT BARRY ALEXANDER, b. 10 JUN 1951 in Seattle, Wash., m. 23 AUG 1975 to Nancy Elizabeth Chaney, b. 12 JUN 1954 in Baltimore, Md., res. Midlothian, Va. Children:

A11413214921. MATTHEW DAVID ALEXANDER, b. 26 JUL 1978 in Blacksburg, Va.

A11413214922. ANDREW CHARLES ALEXANDER, b. 9 JUN 1981 in Richmond, Va.

A1141321493. DAVID THOMAS ALEXANDER, b. 3 MAR 1955 in Ft. Meade, Md., m. 5 APR 1986 to Judy Fischer, b. 18 DEC 1954 in Fresno, Calif., res. Foster City, Calif.

A11413214(10). MARGARET C. ALEXANDER, b. 25 FEB 1913, d. 29 JUL 1913, bur. Salem Lutheran Church Cem. near Mt. Sidney.

A11413215. ADA AGNES ALEXANDER, b. 5 JAN 1874 [Bible], d. 5 JUL 1935, aged 61y 6m [Bible], bur. St. Michaels Reformed Church Cem.

A11413216. REBERTHA VIRGINIA ALEXANDER, b. 14 JAN 1876 [Bible], d. 10 NOV 1887 of diphtheria at Naked Creek, Augusta Co., age 11y 9m 26d,[2] bur. St. Michaels Reformed Church Cem., age on tombstone 11y 11m 10d.

A11413217. LEE ANN[3] ALEXANDER, b. 11 FEB 1878 [Bible], d. 15 FEB 1956, aged 78y 6d [Bible], m. 19 MAR 1904 [Bible] to Charles Homer Craun, b. 12 OCT 1879, d. 6 NOV 1946; both bur. Salem Lutheran Church Cem. Children:[4]

A114132171. C. RANDOLPH CRAUN, b. 4 JUL 1904, d. 19 FEB 1973, m. Naomi Rimel [tombstone], daughter of Charles Rimel, b. 2 OCT 1905, d. 17 AUG 1984; both bur. Salem Lutheran Church Cem.

A114132172. RICHARD F. CRAUN, b. 28 JUN 1904, m. Lutie Wineberg, res. Charlottesville, Va.

A114132173. EVA CRAUN, b. 6 FEB 1906, m. John Pumphry, res. Middlebrook, Augusta Co.

A114132174. JAMES W. CRAUN, b. 15 APR 1907, m. Ida Bell.

A114132175. RUBY E. CRAUN, b. 25 APR 1910, d. 3 JUL 1994, bur. Salem Lutheran Church Cem., unmarried.

A114132176. GRANVILLE CRAUN, b. 14 JUN 1913, unmarried.

A114132177. JOHN CRAUN, b. 1 SEP 1918, m. Margaret Brown.

A11413218. LYDA ELIZABETH ALEXANDER, b. 27 AUG 1880 [Bible], d. 20 APR 1966, bur. Otterbine Cem. in Harrisonburg, m. 24 DEC 1901 [Bible] to Horace Greely Simmons, son of Christian Simmons, b. 22 AUG 1872 in Highland Co., d. 17 JUN 1953 in Dayton, bur. St. Michael's Reformed Church Cem. Children[5]:

A114132181. RAYMOND ALEXANDER SIMMONS, b. 2 NOV 1904, d. 16 JAN 1973, m. Hazel Thompson, b. 26 FEB 1911, d. 22 APR 1998; both bur. St. Michael's Reformed Church Cem.

A114132182. HELEN SIMMONS, b. 5 NOV 1911, m. Stacel Kincaid.

A11413219. NETTIE BELLE ALEXANDER, b. 12 JUN 1883 [Bible], d. 5 JUL 1921, aged 38y 23d, m. 3 JAN 1917 [Bible] in Weyers Cave to Arthur Wayne Young, b. 3 OCT 1884, d. 26 MAY 1959; both bur. Salem Lutheran Church Cem.

A1141321(10). IRENE MAY ALEXANDER, b. 16 APR 1885 [Bible], d. 29 APR 1954, aged 69y 13d [bible], bur. St. Michaels Lutheran Church Cem.

A1141321(11). FRANKLIN R. ALEXANDER, b. 13 MAY 1887 [Bible], d. 20 JUN 1890, bur. St. Michaels Lutheran Church Cem., age 3y 1m 7d.

---

[1] Ibid., p. 57; Letter from Betty Jane (Alexander) Swecker.
[2] Augusta Co., Va. Death Register.
[3] Bible record gives name as Leanah Alexander.
[4] Craun, p. 57.
[5] Ibid., p. 57.

A1141322. Robert Ellis Alexander
(1841-1918)

Figure 86 - Residence of Robert E. Alexander, Grottoes, Va.

Robert Ellis "Buzz" Alexander, a son of David Alexander and Margaret Stickley, was born August 3, 1841 in a home on what is now Route 11, just south of Harrisonburg in Rockingham County,[1] in Grottoes. He was baptized May 8, 1842 by Rev. D. Feet, and died December 12, 1918, aged 77y 4m 9d, with burial in Salem Lutheran Church Cemetery.

Robert E. Alexander was married February 21, 1867 in Augusta County, to Mary Susan Jordan, born October 6, 1844, who died February 28, 1900, aged 55y 9m 9d, with burial in Salem Lutheran Church Cemetery.

Child of Robert Ellis Alexander and Mary Susan Jordan:

A11413221. JAMES DAVID ALEXANDER, a grocer, b. 5 DEC 1867 in Augusta Co., d. 28 OCT 1953 in Harrisonburg, m. (1) 22 DEC 1898 in Rockingham Co. to Myrtilla Susan Berry, age 24y, daughter of James and Naomi Berry.[2] Myrtie d. 10 SEP 1927 at High Point, N.C.,[3] and James m. (2) Hattie Virginia Hook, daughter of John Calvin Hook and Emma Van Lear, b. OCT 1882, d. JUL 1946. Children:

A114132211. KARL RUSSELL ALEXANDER, SR., b. 4 JUL 1900 at Grottoes, Rockingham Co., d. 3 NOV 1976 in Bridgewater, m. 28 OCT 1924 in Port Republic to Willie Odessa Garrett, b. 23 SEP 1901 at Wheatfield, Shenandoah Co., daughter of William H. Garrett, b. 11 SEP 1856 in Frederick Co. and wife Phylenna Hawkins, b. 30 AUG 1867 in Hampshire Co. WV and d. 14 JUL 1915. Children:

A1141322111. BETTY BERRY ALEXANDER, b. 12 AUG 1926 at Grottoes, m. Henry K. Williams, b. DEC 1922. Children:

A11413221111. STEVE WILLIAMS, b. OCT 1950.

A11413221112. MICHAEL WILLIAMS, b. DEC 1953.

A11413221113. MARK WILLIAMS, b. OCT 1956.

A1141322112. KARL RUSSELL ALEXANDER, JR., b. 1 SEP 1928 at Harrisonburg, Rockingham Co., m. Barbara Spaulding, b. NOV 1930. Children:

A11413221121. KARL RUSSELL ALEXANDER III, b. FEB 1954, m. Mary Dupree.

A11413221122. RICHARD BRIAN ALEXANDER, b. APR 1956, m. Marguerite Dougherty, b. MAR 1958. Child:

A114132211221. CLAYTON PHILLIP ALEXANDER.

A11413221123. DAVID WILLIAM ALEXANDER, b. SEP 1957, m. Patricia Nevius. Children:

A114132211231. ERIN VICTORIA ALEXANDER, b. APR 198?.

A114132211232. TANYA MARIE ALEXANDER, b. JUN 1986.

A114132211233. BAILEY LYNN ALEXANDER, b. JUN 1989.

A11413221124. JOHN EDWARD ALEXANDER, b. JAN 1961.

A1141322113. JAMES WILLIAM ALEXANDER, b. 15 NOV 1933 at Harrisonburg, d. 8 OCT 1973 at Harrisonburg.

A114132212. JAMES ROBERT ALEXANDER, b. 28 OCT 1903 at Grottoes, d. 27 JAN 1960 in Winchester, m. 3 DEC 1937 in Winchester to Elsie P. Crim, d/o of William and Anna Crim, res. Winchester.

A114132213. HALLAH FRANKLIN ALEXANDER, b. 30 OCT 1908, d. 2 MAR 1969 in Baltimore, Md.

A114132214. HARRY WILSON ALEXANDER, b. 7 NOV 1912, d. 22 NOV 1993 at Grottoes, Va., m. MaDora Jordan, b. JUL 1920.

A114132215. HELEN VIRGINIA ALEXANDER, b. 6 APR 1917 in Grottoes, d. AUG 2005 in Springfield, Va., m. William Preston Armentrout.

A11413222. EMMA CORA ALICE ALEXANDER, b. 30 NOV 1872, d. 18 OCT 1961 in Harrisonburg, unmarried.

---

[1] Interview, Karl R. Alexander, Jr.

[2] Rockingham Co., Va. Marriages, Bk. 2, p. 2.

[3] William Couper, History of the Shenandoah Valley (New York: Lewis Publishing Co., 1952), Vol. III, p. 247.

A11413223.   (Rev.) HOMER BIRELY ALEXANDER, SR., b. 11 AUG 1877, d. 2 AUG 1957, bur. Port Republic
            Cem., m. (1) c.1899 to Jenny Null, m. (2) c.1910 to Mary Laura Maupin, b. 24 OCT 1881, d. 25 DEC
            1919, bur. Port Republic Cem., m. (3) 15 NOV 1923 at Harrisonburg, by Rev. W.D. Eye to Minnie B.
            Bowman, b. 29 FEB 1896 at Harrisonburg, daughter of Hannah R. Beery and Samuel R. Bowman,
            son of Benjamin and Catherine Bowman,[1] res. 145 Valley St. in Harrisonburg. Children:
A114132231.   PAULINE ALEXANDER, b. 14 FEB 1908 in Port Republic, d. 28 OCT 1974, m. 15 MAY 1931
            there to Edward Blair Melton, Sr. Children:
A1141322311.   MARY LEE MELTON.
A1141322312.   EDWARD BLAIR MELTON, JR.
A1141322313.   JAMES ALLEN MELTON.
A114132232.   GORDON WEINBURG ALEXANDER, b. 16 JUN 1910, d. 13 MAY 1975, m. Margie Hensley.
A114132233.   MADGE MAUPIN ALEXANDER, b. 23 JAN 1918, d. 23 NOV 1918 at Syranic Lake, N.Y.
A114132234.   REBECCA JORDAN ALEXANDER, b. 11 FEB 1925 at Port Republic, medical secretary, m. 6
            OCT 1956 at Port Republic by her father Rev. Homer B. Alexander to John Leigh Wood, b. 16
            JUN 1926 at Roanoke, mechanical engineer, son of Carroll Wood and Jennie Shaw, res. 434
            High St., Salem (1991). Children:
A1141322341.   REBECCA LEIGH WOOD, b. 13 NOV 1957.
A1141322342.   JOHN ALEXANDER WOOD, b. 7 JUN 1959.
A114132235.   (Dr.) HOMER BIRELY ALEXANDER, JR., child of third marriage, b. 2 AUG 1927 at Port Republic,
            dentist, m. 29 SEP 1949 at Port Republic by his father Rev. Homer B. Alexander to Doris Lucinda
            Pearl, b. 28 AUG 1929 at Port Republic, daughter of Joseph Pearl and Ann Groah, res. *Carter
            Hall*, Stephens City, Frederick Co. Children:
A1141322351.   LUCINDA ANN ALEXANDER, b. 1 SEP 1940, m. John Simms Toney, b. NOV 1930.
A114132236.   (Dr.) ROBERT BOWMAN ALEXANDER, b. 3 NOV 1930 at Port Republic, dentist, d. 7 FEB 1991
            at Rockingham Memorial Hospital in Harrisonburg,[2] m. 25 APR 1959 at Alexandria City, Ala. by
            Rev. Painter to Mary Hodnett, b. 29 APR 1936 at Alexandria City, daughter of Gaines Hodnett,
            res. Rte. 1, Harrisonburg. Robert was graduated from Roanoke College and the Medical College
            of Va. School of Dentistry in 1957, and served in the Air Force. Children:
A1141322361.   ROBERT STEPHEN ALEXANDER, b. 13 SEP 1960, m. Lisa Faith Townsen, res. Vienna,
            Fairfax Co.
A1141322362.   ROBERTA STEPHANIE ALEXANDER, b. 7 MAR 1964, m. _____ Berry, res.
            Stanardsville, Greene Co.
A114132237.   (Dr.) JOSEPH MOORE ALEXANDER, SR., b. 29 APR 1936 at Port Republic, dentist, m. 29 MAY
            1960 at Petersburg, W.Va. by Rev. Young to Paige Snell, b. 28 APR 1938, daughter of Ralph
            Snell and Dorothy Northup, res. Petersburg, W.Va. (1991). Children:
A1141322371.   JOSEPH MOORE ALEXANDER, JR., b. 4 SEP 1961, m. Linda Carlson.
A1141322372.   AARON BOWMAN ALEXANDER, b. 11 MAR 1963, m. Patricia Loving.
A1141322373.   MOLLY SNELL ALEXANDER, b. 20 DEC 1965, m. Jeffrey P. Herrick.

A114132(10). David Stickley Alexander
(1859-1927)

David Stickley Alexander, son of David Alexander and Margaret Stickley, was born October 28, 1859 in Mt. Sidney,
Augusta County, Virginia. He was married December 23, 1880, by license issued three days prior in Augusta County,
to Mary Emily Link.

David died December 3, 1927 after falling down steps at his barn in Mt. Sidney, and was buried in Salem Lutheran
Church Cemetery.

Mary Emily was born April 30, 1856 in Mt. Sidney, and a daughter of Daniel W. Link (b. April 21, 1822, d. testate
on March 18, 1875) and Catherine Craun (d. May 7, 1897, age 72y 4m 26d), and she died December 22, 1923 at the
age of 67y 8m 22d, in Mt. Sidney, and was buried in Salem Lutheran Church Cemetery, located at Routes 804 and
852 near Mt. Sidney, Virginia.

Children of David Stickley Alexander and Mary Emily Link:[3]

A114132(10)1. MINOR MERVIN ALEXANDER, b. 9 MAR 1882 in Augusta Co., d. 11 FEB 1957, bur. Salem Lutheran

---

[1] Paul G. Holsinger, Descendants of David Holsinger of Virginia (Ann Arbor, Mich.: Edward Brothers, 1969), p. 306.
[2] The News-Virginian (Waynesboro, Va., 8 FEB 1991), p. 6.
[3] Letter, Minor H. Alexander (February 1986); David Alexander Family Bible.

Church Cem., m. 3 DEC 1908 in Washington, D.C. to Anna Laura Moore, d. 1 APR 1967. Children:[1]

A114132(10)11.   MARY ALICE SHANKLIN ALEXANDER, b. 13 SEP 1909, d. 26 DEC 1991, m. Elwood Link.

A114132(10)12.   WILBER DAVID ALEXANDER, b. 27 JAN 1912, d. 5 DEC 1990, m. Viola Graham.

A114132(10)13.   GLADYS ALBERTA ALEXANDER, b. 28 FEB 1914.

A114132(10)14.   RICHARD F. ALEXANDER, b. 9 SEP 1916, d. 27 MAY 1984.

A114132(10)15.   CLARENCE M. ALEXANDER, b. 5 MAR 1920, d. 1944, m. Gunivere Arey.

A114132(10)16.   HOWARD OSCAR ROLLER ALEXANDER, b. 5 JUN 1922.

A114132(10)17.   EVELYN MAE ALEXANDER, b. 14 MAY 1925.

A114132(10)18.   PHYLLIS PAULINE ALEXANDER, b. 14 DEC 1927, m. Don Martin Argenbright.

A114132(10)2.   GABRIEL DEAN ALEXANDER, b. 17 JUL 1884, d. 29 JAN 1885, age 6m 12d, bur. Salem Lutheran Church Cem.

A114132(10)3.   OSCAR VASTINE ALEXANDER, b. 28 OCT 1885 in Augusta Co., d. 7 OCT 1916[2] in Bridgewater, Rockingham Co., age 29y 11m 12d, bur. Salem Lutheran Church Cem., m. 23 FEB 1908[3] [or 28 OCT] in Mt. Sidney to Carrie Rebecca Sheets, b. 11/26 JUL 1888 in Augusta Co.,[4] d. 15 JUL 1962,[5] daughter of Charles Sheets and Sarah Wine. Children:[6]

A114132(10)31.   RAYMOND ROBERT ALEXANDER, b. 6 AUG 1909, d. 23 MAR 1992, m. Mary Croushorn. Child:

A114132(10)311.   VIRGINIA JOYCE ALEXANDER, b. 8 JUL 1933, m. Mr. McDonald.

A114132(10)32.   NAOMI JANE ALEXANDER, b. 14 MAR 1911.

A114132(10)33.   MARGARET CATHERINE ALEXANDER, b. 25 FEB 1913, d. 21 JUL 1913.

A114132(10)34.   MARTHA ALICE ALEXANDER, b. 8 MAR 1914, m. Martin Luther Good, Sr. Children:

A114132(10)341.   DONALD ALFRED GOOD, b. 2 OCT 1937, m. Eva Louisa Wonderly.

A114132(10)342.   NORMAN EUGENE GOOD, b. 1 AUG 1940, m. Daima Melinda Dalby.

A114132(10)343.   MARTIN LUTHER GOOD, m. Mary Jane Sheets.

A114132(10)344.   SAMUEL DAVID GOOD, m. Doris (   ).

A114132(10)345.   BETTY GAIL GOOD, m. Richard Baber.

A114132(10)346.   GARY ALEXANDER GOOD, m. Debbie Huffer.

A114132(10)35.   LURTY JAMES ALEXANDER, b. 12 NOV 1915.

A114132(10)4.   IRENUS BEDFORD ALEXANDER, farmer, b. 2 FEB 1887 in Mt. Sidney, Augusta Co., d. 20 OCT 1962 in King's Daughters Hospital of Staunton, bur. Salem Lutheran Church Cem., m. 15 JAN 1911 at Mt. Sidney to Mary Bettie Reed, daughter of John W. Reed and Sarah J. Cochran, b. 24 APR 1892 in Mt. Sidney, d. 23 NOV 1979 in Waynesboro, bur. Salem Lutheran Church Cem. Children:[7]

A114132(10)41.   ELVIN GARDELL ALEXANDER, SR., b. 31 MAR 1911 at Mt. Sidney, d. 28 SEP 1993 in Waynesboro, m. (1) MAY 1931 to Reba Frances Cash, b. MAY 1907 in Montebello, d. 27 DEC 1974 in Waynesboro Community Hospital, bur. Augusta Memorial Park of Fishersville, m. (2) Mattie B. Troyer, b. MAR 1938. Children:

A114132(10)411.   ELVIN GARDELL ALEXANDER, JR., b. 15 MAR 1932 in Mt. Sidney, m. 25 SEP 1954 in Spottswood, Augusta Co. to Mary Frances Sorrells, b. 6 JAN 1932 in Fairfield, Rockbridge Co. Child:

A111432(10)4111.   DOUGLAS WAYNE ALEXANDER, b. 15 JUN 1955 in King's Daughter Hosp. of Staunton, m. 30 APR 1977 in Goshen Paths to Shelby Jean Jones.

A114132(10)412.   HILDA LEE ALEXANDER, b. JUL 1934, m. Ernest Greenberry Baber, b. SEP 1928. Children:

A111432(10)4121.   STEPHEN GREENBERRY BABER, b. MAY 1956, m. Carolyn L. Blackwell, b. JAN 1959.

A111432(10)4122.   VICKI LEE BABER, b. NOV 1958.

A111432(10)4123.   ERNEST NEIL BABER, b. MAY 1963.

A114132(10)413.   HAROLD PHILLIP ALEXANDER, b. APR 1937, m. Madeline Miller, b. MAY 1943. Children:

A114132(10)4131.   DARRELL SCOTT ALEXANDER, b. SEP 1965.

A114132(10)4132.   JENNIFER LYNN ALEXANDER, b. JUN 1969.

A114132(10)42.   CATHERINE L. ALEXANDER, b. 15 JUL 1914, m. 29 AUG 1933 in Verona to Clyde Jorid Stockdale, b. SEP 1910.

---

[1] Craun, p. 265.

[2] David Alexander Family Bible.

[3] Ibid., gives marriage date of 23 FEB 1908.

[4] Paxson Rude Link, The Link Family ... (Paris, Ill.: By the Author, 1951), p. 518.

[5] David Alexander Family Bible.

[6] Craun, p. 265; David Alexander Family Bible.

[7] Craun, p. 266.

A114132(10)43.   WILLIAM DAVID ALEXANDER, b. 2 MAR 1916 in Augusta Co., d. NOV 1988, m. 20 JUL 1940 in Staunton to Maybeth Lyle Ramsey, b. 12 JUN 1920 in Nelson Co. Children:
    A114132(10)431.   CAROLYN MAY ALEXANDER, b. SEP 1942, m. Roy Erskin Hevener, b. JAN 1940.
    A114132(10)432.   JOAN DALE ALEXANDER, b. DEC 1945, m. James O. Perdue, b. APR 1947.
    A114132(10)433.   SHELBY JEAN ALEXANDER, b. MAR 1947, d. SEP 1953.
    A114132(10)434.   DAVID DEAN ALEXANDER, b. 30 JAN 1955 in King's Daughters Hospital of Staunton, m. 24 JUN 1979 in Swansboro, N.C. to Barbara Ann Huff, b. OCT 1956.[1]
    A114132(10)435.   DONALD LEE ALEXANDER, b. JAN 1955, m. Gail Altenburg, b. SEP 1955.
A114132(10)44.   CHARLES EDWARD ALEXANDER, b. 18 AUG 1918, d. JUN 1973.
A114132(10)45.   DOROTHY ROBERTA ALEXANDER, b. 21 AUG 1921 in Augusta Co., d. FEB 1981, m. 15 AUG 1943 in Staunton to John Joseph Barille.[2]
A114132(10)46.   JOHANNA LUCILLE "Janie" ALEXANDER, b. 11 FEB 1927, m. William Lee Ramsey, b. NOV 1926. Child:
    A114132(10)461.   SANDRA LEE RAMSEY, b. APR 1949, m. Clarence Ernest Hutchens, b. MAY 1945.
A114132(10)47.   BONNIE LOU ALEXANDER, b. 2 SEP 1933, m. Howard Parrish.
A114132(10)5.   JOHN ROBERT ALEXANDER, architect, b. 24 NOV 1888 in Mt. Sidney, d. 18 MAR 1968 in Harrisonburg, Rockingham Co., bur. Salem Lutheran Church Cem., m. 7 JAN 1914 by Rev. Asa Richard in Mt. Sidney to Lena Edna Elizabeth Young, daughter of H.W. Young and Martha R. Ocheltree. Lena b. 25 SEP 1891 in Weyers Cave, d. 20 DEC 1971 in Harrisonburg, bur. Salem Lutheran Church Cem. Children:[3]
    A114132(10)51.   MARION RICHARD ALEXANDER, b. 5 DEC 1914, d. 5 DEC 1914.
    A114132(10)52.   REDA FRANCES ALEXANDER, b. 28 MAY 1916, d. 13 MAY 1999 in Waynesboro, m. Hugh A. Christian. Children:
        A114132(10)521.   LOLA LEE CHRISTIAN, b. 21 JAN 1942.
        A114132(10)522.   HUGH A. CHRISTIAN, b. 27 NOV 1945.
    A114132(10)53.   STANLEY ROLLER ALEXANDER, b. 3 JUL 1918, d. 18 NOV 2004, bur. Salem Lutheran Church Cem., m. Kathaleen Borden. Child:
        A114132(10)531.   ROSA LINDA ALEXANDER, b. 14 FEB 1948.
    A114132(10)54.   JOSEPH ALFRED ALEXANDER, b. 17 SEP 1920, d. 29 JAN 1999 in Harrisonburg, m. Vada Delane Gochenour.
    A114132(10)55.   PAUL GARDNER ALEXANDER, b. 23 OCT 1921, m. Julia Lee Dunsmore.
    A114132(10)56.   EDWIN GLENN ALEXANDER, b. 28 FEB 1924, d. 2 MAR 1996 in Stuart, Fla., m. Adelina Sarah Black.
    A114132(10)57.   NELSON JOHN ROBERT ALEXANDER, b. 24 NOV 1925, m. Lois M. Wine, res. Rte. 8, Box 61 of Harrisonburg, Va. (1986).
    A114132(10)58.   ROSCOE VERNON ALEXANDER, b. 23 OCT 1926 in Weyers Cave, Augusta Co., m. 17 NOV 1962 in Timberville, Rockingham Co. to Phyllis Ruth Lambert. Child:
        A114132(10)581.   RUTH ANN ALEXANDER.
    A114132(10)59.   LINDBERG CRAWFORD ALEXANDER, b. 22 MAY 1928, m. Sharon Barney Wine.
A114132(10)6.   WILLIAM ONEY ALEXANDER, farmer, b. 11 NOV 1891 in Mt. Sidney, d. 15 NOV 1970, bur. 18 NOV 1970 in Salem Lutheran Church Cem., m. 23 OCT 1920 in Staunton, Augusta Co. to Lucy Virginia Meyerhoeffer, b. 26 APR 1900 at Ft. Defiance, d. 2 OCT 1967, bur. 5 OCT 1967 in Salem Lutheran Church Cem. Child:
    A114132(10)61.   MELVIN HARRY ALEXANDER, b. 4 JUL 1921, d. 25 MAR 1989, bur. Salem Lutheran Church Cem.
A114132(10)7.   LUTHER[4] DAVID ALEXANDER, farmer, b. 8 OCT 1893 in Mt. Sidney, d. 4 MAY 1959 in Weyers Cave, bur. Salem Lutheran Church Cem., m. 6 SEP 1916 in Springhill, Augusta Co. to Grace Pearl Cook, b. 25 MAR 1896 in Mt. Sidney, d. 3 APR 1982 in Weyers Cave, bur. Salem Lutheran Church Cem. Children:[5]
    A114132(10)71.   ROBERT DAVID ALEXANDER, b. 14 FEB 1918, d. 14 MAR 1976, bur. Salem Lutheran Church Cem., m. (1) Madeline Roach, div., m. (2) Peggy Eutsler.
    A114132(10)72.   MARY LOUIS ALEXANDER, b. 8 SEP 1920 in Augusta Co., d. 18 FEB 2011 in Mt. Crawford, Rockingham Co., m. 15 DEC 1947 to Ralph V. Puffenbarger, d. 4 AR 1982. Children:
        A114132(10)721.   BONNIE PUFFENBARGER, m. Phillip Driver.

---

[1] Letter, David D. Alexander.
[2] City of Staunton Marriage Register, p. 59.
[3] Craun, p. 266.
[4] David Alexander Family Bible gives the name of this child as David L. Alexander.
[5] Craun, p. 267.

A114132(10)722.   DAVID PUFFENBARGER.

A114132(10)73.   CLEO ALEXANDER, b. 17 AUG 1923, d. 12 MAY 1989, bur. Salem Lutheran Church Cem., m. Howard J. Hollaway.

A114132(10)74.   MARION HAROLD ALEXANDER, b. 16 DEC 1925 in Mt. Sidney, m. 28 FEB 1948 there to Mary Shull.

A114132(10)75.   EMALINE ALEXANDER, b. 16 MAY 1928, d. 13 FEB 2010, m. Mr. Landes, div.

A114132(10)76.   JAMES WALLACE ALEXANDER, b. 4 AUG 1930, d. 15 JAN 1984, bur. Salem Lutheran Church Cem.

A114132(10)77.   MARIE DELAINO ALEXANDER, m. Arlon Hottinger, res. Weyers Cave.

A114132(10)8. HOBART LINK ALEXANDER, b. 14 DEC 1896 in Mt. Sidney, d. 8 OCT 1971, bur. Salem Lutheran Church Cem., m. 14 NOV 1925 to Carrie Rebecca (Sheets) Alexander. Child:

A114132(10)81.   EDITH REBECCA ALEXANDER, b. 26 NOV 1926, d. 11 SEP 1975, bur. Augusta Stone Presbyterian Church Cem. at Ft. Defiance, Va., m. (1) Clyde Stogdale, m. (2) Ray Christian Brubeck, b. 18 FEB 1924, d. 1 MAR 1986, bur. Augusta Stone Presbyterian Church Cem.

A114132(10)9. FLOSSIE CATHERINE ALEXANDER, b. 20 AUG 1899 in Mt. Sidney, d. 11 JUN 1974, bur. Salem Lutheran Church Cem., m. 8 JUN 1923 in Staunton, Augusta Co. to Rollie Omega Moore, b. 10 JUL 1900 at Staunton, d. 23 MAY 1976, bur. Salem Lutheran Church Cem., son of Robert L. and Josephine (Landes) Moore. Child:

A114132(10)91.   MAHRLIN ALEXANDER MOORE, b. 4 NOV 1924.

B. ANDREW ALEXANDER
(c. 1648-between 1700-1702)

Andrew Alexander was born c.1648 in Ireland, and is thought to have been a son of William Alexander of Eredy, County Donegal, Ireland. It is believed he was married to Ann Taylor, daughter of George Taylor and Comfort Anderson,[1] though others have thought his wife was Jane McKnitt, daughter of John McKnitt and Elizabeth Wallace.

Andrew is thought to have lived and died in Cecil County, Maryland. He is recorded in Somerset County on September 15, 1677 for the birth of his first child Abigail Alexander. Andrew Alexander is mentioned in the 1692 will of William Anderson in Accomack County, as having lived on land adjoining his.[2]

Known children of Andrew Alexander [and Ann (Taylor)?]:

B1. ABIGAIL ALEXANDER, b. 15 SEP 1677 in Somerset Co., Md.[3]
+ B2. ELIAS ALEXANDER, planter, b. 26 FEB 1679 in Somerset Co., Md.,[4] d. c.1747 in York Co., Pa., known to m. (1) to his cousin SOPHIA ALEXANDER, daughter of Joseph Alexander and Jane McKnitt, and thought by some to m. (2) Ann Taylor.
B3. ARTHUR ALEXANDER, a farmer and planter, b. c.1682, d. before 1771 in Cecil Co., Md., m. his paternal first cousin (C(13.)) ANN WALLACE, daughter of Matthew Wallace and Elizabeth Alexander. Children:
    B31. MATTHEW ALEXANDER, b. 1700 in Cecil Co., Md., d. testate before 12 JUN 1754 [5] in Cecil Co., Md., m. Rosanna McCracken. Children:
        B311. ARTHUR ALEXANDER, b. 1730 in Cecil Co., Md.
        B312. MATTHEW ALEXANDER, b. 1732 in Cecil Co., Md.
    B32. ARTHUR ALEXANDER, JR., b. 1720 in Cecil Co., Md.

B2. Elias Alexander
(1679-c.1747)

Elias Alexander, son of Andrew Alexander of Somerset County, Maryland, was born there February 26, 1679. He may have been married twice: (1) c.1705 in Cecil County to his cousin (G1.) SOPHIA ALEXANDER, daughter of Joseph Alexander (the tanner) and Jane McKnitt of Cecil County, Maryland, q.v.[6] In 1718 he is called a planter.[7] Sophia Alexander died after December 13, 1726 in Slate Hill, Cecil County, Maryland, which is now part of Lancaster County, Pennsylvania. It is thought Elias Alexander remarried to Ann Taylor.[8]

It is thought Elias died c.1747 in Frederick County, Maryland, as he left a will there dated in December 1726. Letters of administration were granted to wife Ann Alexander in Frederick County, Maryland by her bond dated May 17, 1751.[9] An inventory of his estate was made June 11, 1751 in Frederick County, Maryland[10] by appraisers John Jones and Elisha Lawrence who mentioned next of kin John Flenniken and Arthur Alexander, and creditors Nathaniel Alexander and Adam Alexander.

Known children of Elias Alexander:

B21. JEDEDIAH ALEXANDER, "of Slate Hill," b. 1702, m. Ann (   ),[11] rem. to Slate Hill, York Co., Pa. where his will dated 31 AUG 1749 was proved 26 MAR 1750.[12]
B22. WILLIAM ALEXANDER, b. c.1708 in Somerset Co., Md., m. c.1727 to Agnes (who some have mistakenly believed to be Agnes Alexander, daughter of William Alexander II above and his wife Catharine Wallace).

---

[1] Parran, Series II, p. 59.
[2] Somerset Co., Md. Judicial Records, 1696-1698, p. 25.
[3] MDSA, Somerset Co., Md. Liber O11 IKL, fol. 3.
[4] Ibid.
[5] MDSA, Maryland Wills, Liber 29, fol. 267, will of Mathew Alexander, dated 1 DEC 1753, prov. 12 JUN 1754, which mentions his brother Arthur Alexander who has a lot in Charles Town; also see Cecil Co., Md. Wills, Liber BB2, fol. 137.
[6] Joseph Alexander (c. 1660-1730), a tanner, purchased on 14 MAY 1714 land on the Big Elk River in Cecil Co., Md. from Thomas Stevenson, called "New Munster," hence the beginning of the root of the "Alexander Family of New Munster."
[7] Cecil Co., Md. Deeds, Bk. 3, p. 206, Thomas Stevenson to Elias Alexander, dated 15 AUG 1718.
[8] Worth S. Ray, The Mecklenburg Signers and Their Neighbors (reprint ed; Baltimore: Genealogical Publishing Co., Inc., 1982).
[9] Frederick Co., Md. Accounts, Bk. 35, fol. 83.
[10] Maryland Inventories, Liber 47, fol. 68, amount £91.17.6.
[11] Lancaster Co., Pa. Deeds, Bk. 7, p. 146.
[12] York Co., Pa. Wills, Bk. A1, p. 10; also see Cecil Co., Md. Deeds, Bk. 7, p. 146, referring to Lancaster Co., Pa.

His will dated 22 MAR 1772[1] in Mecklenburg Co., N.C., was prov. 6 APR 1772 in Mecklenburg Co., exec. by son Adam Alexander, wits. Joseph Kennedy and Elias Alexander. Children:

+   B221.   (Col.) ADAM ALEXANDER, b. 24 SEP 1728 in Somerset Co., Md., m. 4 AUG 1752 to Mary Shelby. He d. 13 NOV 1798 in Clear Creek Section of Mecklenburg Co., N.C., bur. Rock Springs graveyard there.

    B222.   (Capt.) CHARLES ALEXANDER, SR. "the signer," b. 4 JAN 1730 in Somerset Co., Md., will dated 28 JAN 1801,[2] naming wife "Jean," m. (1) Susan Polk, m. (2) Jean (   ), d. c.1801 in Mecklenburg Co., N.C. Seven known children.

    B223.   WILLIAM ALEXANDER, served in the Maryland militia of 1748, perhaps d. 1760 in Talbot Co., Md.,[3] may have m. Hannah (   ). His will dated 17 DEC 1758, prov. 7 MAR 1760, wit. George Parratt and Peter Comerford, filed in Talbot Co., Md.[4] The will mentions wife Hannah who also left a nuncupative will written in 1761.[5] Children:

        B2231. REBECCA ALEXANDER.

        B2232. MARY ALEXANDER.

        B2233. NANCY ALEXANDER.

        B2234. WILLIAM ALEXANDER, b. 1751 (age 12 in 1763), a carpenter and joiner.[6]

    B23.   FRANCIS ALEXANDER, named in his brother Jedediah Alexander's 1749 will.

    B24.   ESTER/ESTHER ALEXANDER, named in her brother Jedediah Alexander's 1749 will.

    B25.   MARY ALEXANDER, named in her brother Jedediah Alexander's will.

    B26.   ELIJAH ALEXANDER, d. 1785 intestate in Mecklenburg Co., N.C., m. Lavinia (   ).

    B27.   MARGARET ALEXANDER, m. John Fleniken.[7]

    B28.   ISAAC ALEXANDER, b. 1715 at Slate Hill, Cecil Co., Md. (now Lancaster Co., Pa.), d. c.1793 in Washington Co., Pa. where his will is dated 29 JAN 1793, m. Elizabeth Bradley. Children:

        B281.   HENRY ALEXANDER, of Lancaster Co., Pa.

        B282.   ISAAC ALEXANDER.

        B283.   CATHERINE ALEXANDER.

        B284.   ANN ALEXANDER, m. Abel Johnson, a Quaker from England.

        B285.   ESTER/ESTHER ALEXANDER.

        B286.   REBECCA ALEXANDER.

        B287.   JOSEPH ALEXANDER.

        B288.   ALEXANDER ALEXANDER.

+   B29.   ABRAHAM ALEXANDER, b. 9 DEC 1718 in Cecil Co., Md., d. 22 APR 1786 in Charlotte, Mecklenburg Co., N.C., bur. Sugaw[8] Creek Cem. of that county, m. Dorcas (Amelia Wilson?), b. 14 MAR 1734, d. 23 MAY 1800.

    B2(10).   ANDREW ALEXANDER, b. 1718, d. 1786.[9]

    B2(11).   ZEBULON ALEXANDER, b. 7 DEC 1720 in Chester Co., Pa., d. 1784 in Mecklenburg Co., N.C., served for North Carolina in the Rev. War, will dated 3 MAR 1784,[10] prov. SEP 1784, exec. wife Jane and son-in-law John McCree, wit. Abram Alexander, Mathew Bryan, Jr., and Hezekiah Alexander. He m. in 1743 to Jane/Jean McClung. Children:[11]

        B2(11)1.   MARY IRWIN ALEXANDER, b. 1754, received £0.5.00 in her father's 1784 will.

        B2(11)2.   RUTH ALEXANDER, b. 1756, received £0.10.00 in her father's 1784 will, m. John McCree.

        B2(11)3.   HANNAH ALEXANDER, b. 1761, received a horse and saddle in her father's 1784 will, d. 1788 in Mecklenburg Co., N.C., m. Thomas Greer, b. 1744, d. testate in 1828.[12]

        B2(11)4.   PHINEUS ALEXANDER, b. 1762, received £0.10.00 and a crosscut saw in his father's 1784 will.

        B2(11)5.   ABEL ALEXANDER, b. 1764, inherited his father's plantation on Sugaw Creek called *Indian Land* for which Zebulon obtained *a petten* [patent] *years agoe*.

        B2(10)6.   [William] ZEBULON ALEXANDER, b. 1768, inherited half of the plantation on which his father was residing at the time of death in 1784, the other half to go to his brother Zenor.

---

[1] Mecklenburg Co., N.C. Wills, Bk. A, p. 6.

[2] Mecklenburg Co., N.C. Wills, Bk. A, p. 43.

[3] Ferguson.

[4] MDSA, Original Wills Box 1, folder 37; Maryland Wills, Liber 30, fol. 853, with executor as Howell Powell, a Quaker.

[5] MDSA, Original Wills Box 1, folder 38; Maryland Wills, Liber 31, fol. 288; Maryland Inventories and Accounts, Liber 74, fol. 195.

[6] Maryland Accounts, Bk. 50, p. 189, dated 5 DEC 1763, age 12 in 1763; Talbot Co., Md. Deeds, Bk. 23, p. 252, dated 9 AUG 1787.

[7] Robert B. Powers, A Record of My Maternal Ancestors (Delaware, Ohio, 1966), p. 4.

[8] Also seen as Sugar Creek.

[9] Brent H. Holcomb, Mecklenburg Co., N.C. Abstract of Early Wills, 1763-1790 (Greenville, S.C.: By the Author, 1980), p. 1.

[10] Mecklenburg Co., N.C. Wills, Bk. A, p. 4.

[11] Genealogy of James Alexander, Pennsylvania G.R.C., 1982, at the D.A.R. Library in Washington, D.C.

[12] A Bible of the Alexander Greer Family is held by the Jackson-Madison County Library in Tennessee; also see Mecklenburg Co., N.C. Wills, Bk. A, p. 161.

B2(11)7.   ZENOR [or Zenas] ALEXANDER, b. 1771, inherited half of his father's plantation in 1784.

B2(11)8.   DEBORAH ALEXANDER, b. 1767, d. 1821, m. 1785 to Jesse Clark, b. 1756 in Pa., d. 1835 in N.C. Child:

B2(11)81.   WILLIAM L. CLARK, b. 1788, m. Dian Manley.

B2(11)9.   TIRZAH ALEXANDER, b. 1769, received a horse and saddle in her father's 1784 will.

B2(11)(10). MARTHA ALEXANDER, inherited her father's plantation called *Gum Swamp* along with a Negro girl named Hannah, in her father's 1784 will.

B2(12). EZRA ALEXANDER, b. 26 FEB 1739 in Cecil Co., Md., m. Mary Polk, b. 1744, d. 8 SEP 1814 at age 70y. Ezra d. 6 JUL 1800 in Mecklenburg Co., N.C., bur. with his wife in the Polk Family Cem. near Pineville, N.C.[1] Ezra left a will dated 16 FEB 1798, prov. in Mecklenburg Co., N.C.[2] Known children:[3]

B2(12)1.   ELEAZER ALEXANDER, b. 23 NOV 1763, d. 6 OCT 1810, bur. Alexander Family Cem. off Beach Croft Rd. between Spring Hill and Sparkman's Store at Theta, Maury Co., Tenn., m. c.1788 to Margaret Carter, b. 19 SEP 1770, d. 27 JAN 1858 (tombstone broken), bur. Alexander Family Cem.,[4] daughter of Robert Clark and Margaret Bronson, and granddaughter of Daniel Clark and Elizabeth Pannil of Virginia.[5] Seven known children.[6]

B2(12)2.   JAMES ALEXANDER, b. 1765, one of the executors of his father's will, d. 15 OCT 1804, age 39y, bur. in Polk Family Cem. nr. Pineville, N.C. Child:

B2(12)21.   CLARISSA HARLOW ALEXANDER, d. 24 APR 1794, bur. in Polk Family Cem.

B2(12)3.   DORCAS ALEXANDER.

B2(12)4.   ABDON ALEXANDER, b. c.1770, a patriot of the War of 1812.

B2(12)5.   AUGUSTUS ALEXANDER, b. 20 AUG 1772, d. 25 SEP 1849 in Mecklenburg Co.,[7] bur. Sharon Presbyterian Church Cem., Charlotte, N.C., m. (1) Dorcas[8] Culp, b. 11 FEB 1779, d. 20 SEP 1836, bur. Sharon Presbyterian Church Cem., m. (2) 14 FEB 1839 to Sarah Glass, b. 1791, d. 23 JUL 1865. Thirteen known children.[9]

B2(12)6.   PARIS ALEXANDER, b. 17 SEP 1775, m. Dinah Eugenia Neely, b. 21 AUG 1777, removed to Madison Co., Tenn.

B2(12)7.   REDEMPTA ALEXANDER.

B2(12)8.   POLLY ANN ALEXANDER, b. 10 OCT 1781, d. 5 DEC 1851, bur. Six Mile Cem., m. 22 JUL 1802 to John Culp, b. 1784, d. 7 OCT 1842, bur. Six Mile Cem., Lancaster Co., S.C.

B2(12)9.   PEGGY HENDERSON ALEXANDER, d. 9 MAY 1774, age 1, bur. in Polk Family Cem.

B2(13). ARTHUR ALEXANDER, removed to Anson Co., N.C., m. Margaret Wilson [or Wallace],[10] and left a will dated 16 DEC 1763 in Anson (now Mecklenburg) Co., N.C. [Ferguson], prov. APR 1764, exec. by his brother Ezra Alexander, as wit. by James Alexander, Abraham Alexander and Ezekiel Wallace.[11] Children:

B2(13)1.   ELIAS ALEXANDER, received £5 and his father's silver buckle in his father's 1763 will.

B2(13)2.   MARY ALEXANDER.

B2(13)3.   ANN ALEXANDER, according to her father's 1763 will, to be cared for by her uncle Abraham Alexander.

B2(14). (Col.) ELIAS ALEXANDER, JR.,[12] b. 1747 in Md., will dated 16 MAR 1818,[13] d. 1818 in Rutherford Co., N.C., bur. near Forest City, N.C., served in the Rev. War, m. c.1770 to Nancy Agnes "Annie" McCall, c.1752-c.1826.[14] Children:[15]

B2(14)1.   ANNIE ALEXANDER, b. 1771, d. 1841, m. Stephen Campbell, 1770-1846.

B2(14)2.   FRANCIS R. ALEXANDER, b. 11 MAR 1772 in Rutherford Co., N.C., m. 24 JUL 1799 in Lincoln Co., N.C. to Lavina Magness, d. 1845.

B2(14)3.   THOMAS ALEXANDER, b. 1774.

---

[1] Huntsville, Ala. Library, filing case, Alexander Family.
[2] Mecklenburg Co., N.C. Wills, Bk. A, p. 14.
[3] Ferguson.
[4] Marise P. Lightfoot, They Passed This Way: Maury County, Tennessee Cemetery Records (1964), p. B73.
[5] Mrs. Frank M. Angellotti, The Polks of North Carolina and Tennessee, p. 10.
[6] Huntsville, Ala. Library, filing case, Alexander Family, Letter of Jeannette Osteen; Maury County, Tennessee Historical Society, Maury County Cousins, p. 525; Angellotti, p. 10.
[7] Mecklenburg Co., N.C. Wills, Bk. A, p. 164.
[8] Her tombstone engraving reads Doreus Alexander.
[9] D.A.R. Magazine, p. 909.
[10] Settlement of the estate of Arthur Alexander of Anson Co., N.C. by Ezra Alexander and Margaret Wilson, late Margaret Alexander, executors, July 1777.
[11] Mecklenburg Co., N.C. Wills, Bk. A, p. 9.
[12] The American Monthly Magazine, by Eliza Oliver Denniston, Vol. XLI (July-November 1912), p. 176; lengthy biographical sketch.
[13] Rutherford Co., N.C. Wills, Bk. C, p. 101.
[14] Pennsylvania G.R.C., 1982, p. 4, at the D.A.R. Library, Washington, D.C.
[15] D.A.R. Grandfather Ser. II, VI, 1966, at the D.A.R. Library, Washington, D.C.

B2(14)4. ALSTON ALEXANDER, b. 1776.

B2(14)5. Infant ALEXANDER.

B2(14)6. (Maj.) ROSS ALEXANDER, b. 1780, d. intestate in 1849, bur. in New Bethel Baptist Church Cem., Forest City, Rutherford Co., N.C., m. Maria Waters.

B2(14)7. JANE ALEXANDER, b. 1 MAY 1783, d. 13 MAR 1864, m. 1804 in Lincoln Co., N.C. to Vardry McBee, Jr., b. 19 JUN 1775, d. 23 JAN 1864; both bur. Christ Episcopal Church, Greenville, S.C. Nine known children.[1]

B2(14)8. MARGARET ALEXANDER, b. 1785, m. David Rhinehart. One daughter known.

B2(14)9. WILLIAM ALEXANDER, b. 1789, served in War of 1812.

B2(14)(10). ELIAS ALEXANDER, III, b. 1792, d. 1879 unmarried.

B2(14)(11). JAMES TAYLOR ALEXANDER, b. 1794, m. Harriet Clark.

B2(14)(12). MARTHA "Patsey" ALEXANDER, b. 1797, m. 31 JAN 1815 in Rutherford Co., N.C. to Jacob Fisher.

B221. Adam Alexander
(1728-1798)

Adam Alexander, son of William Alexander and Agnes (   ), was born September [28], 1728, near Princess Anne, Somerset County, Maryland.

He was married August 4, 1752 to Mary Shelby, daughter of Evan Shelby and Catherine Davies, who was born August 8, 1735 in Holston, Maryland. Adam and Mary were members of the Rock Spring Presbyterian Church. He was a judge, and served for North Carolina in the Revolutionary War.[2] Adam was also found to be the sheriff of Mecklenburg County,[3] and was one of the signers of the Mecklenburg Declaration of Independence in 1775.

Adam Alexander died intestate on November 13, 1798 in the Clear Creek Section of Mecklenburg County, North Carolina, aged 70y 7d, and was buried in the Old Rock Springs Cemetery located 7 miles east of Charlotte, North Carolina.[4] Many of this family were buried at Philadelphia Church located 2 miles from Rock Spring.

Mary Alexander died November 26, 1813, age 78y 3m, in Mecklenburg County, North Carolina, and was buried in Rocky Spring Meeting House burial ground at Mint Hill, N.C.

Known children of Adam Alexander and Mary Shelby, all born in Clear Creek Section of Mecklenburg County, North Carolina:[5]

B2211. ISAAC S. ALEXANDER, b. 7 JUN 1756, d. 2 SEP 1823 in Mecklenburg Co., N.C., m. Ruth Reese, b. 1753, d. 26 OCT 1825, both bur. Sugaw Creek Presbyterian Church Cem.

B2212. CATHERINE ALEXANDER, b. c.1759, m. before 1779 to John McCoy, b. 1753.

B2213. ADAM RANKIN ALEXANDER, m. Leah Reagan. One known child.

B2214. CHARLES TAYLOR ALEXANDER, b. 9 AUG 1764, d. 26 AUG 1828, m. 21 DEC 1796 in Cabarrus Co., N.C. to Margaret Means, b. 30 DEC 1777, d. 17 JUL 1845; both bur. Philadelphia Presbyterian Church Cem. at Mint Hill, N.C. Nine known children.

B2215. EVAN SHELBY ALEXANDER, lawyer, b. 1767 in Mecklenburg Co., N.C., attended Princeton Univ. in 1787, served in the 10th Congress from 24 FEB 1806 to 3 MAR 1809, d. 28 OCT 1809, unmarried.[6]

B2216. SARAH SHELBY ALEXANDER, b. 1777, d. 11 OCT 1842, m. John Springs, son of Capt. Richard Springs/Springsteen (b. 27 OCT 1751, d. 5 JUN 1818). Two known children.

B2217. SUSAN ALEXANDER, m. James Oliver Wiley II, grandson of David Wiley. One known son, Moses Wiley.

B2218. MARY "Polly" ALEXANDER, b. 1778, d. 19 AUG 1838, m. Dr. Cunningham Harris, b. 31 AUG 1768, d. 10 JAN 1814; both bur. at Rocky River Presbyterian Church Cem., Cabarrus Co., N.C.

---

[1] Worth S. Ray, Tennessee Cousins (1950, reprint Baltimore: Genealogical Pub. Co., 1989), p. 108.

[2] J.B. Alexander, History of Mecklenburg County, North Carolina, 1740-1900, p. 788, at D.A.R. Library in Washington, D.C.

[3] Ancestral Records and Portraits (Grafton Press, N.Y., 1910), Vol. 1, p. 127.

[4] There is also a memorial marker at the Philadelphia Presbyterian Church at Mint Hill, Mecklenburg Co., N.C.

[5] J.B. Alexander, History of Mecklenburg County, North Carolina, 1740-1900, p. 788; Ferguson Appendix.

[6] Biographical Dictionary of the American Congress, 1774-1949 (Washington: U.S. Gov. Printing Office, 1950), p. 769.

B29. Abraham Alexander
(1718-1786)

Abraham Alexander, son of Elias Alexander and Sophia Alexander, was born December 9, 1718 in Cecil County, Maryland, and was born and raised in the house of his maternal grandfather, Major John Davidson who was one of the signers of the Mecklenburg Declaration of Independence.[1] He removed c.1746 to Catawba County, North Carolina, about 3 miles northeast of Charlotte, at Alexander's Mill.[2] He was married c.1749 to Dorcas (   ) thought by some to be Dorcas Amelia Wilson.

Abraham Alexander served in the Revolutionary War, and while chairman of the Mecklenburg Convention of the 19th and 20th of May 1775, was a signer of the Declaration of Independence while residing in Mecklenburg County, North Carolina. He was a justice of the peace, and was an elder of the Presbyterian Church.

Abraham Alexander died April 23, 1786 in Charlotte, Mecklenburg County, North Carolina, and was buried in Sugaw Creek Presbyterian Church graveyard in that county,[3] near the more recent site of the Charlotte Country Club.[4] Abraham's will was dated April 12, 1786 and was filed in Mecklenburg County, North Carolina.[5]

Dorcas Alexander, born March 14, 1734, died aged 66 on May 28, 1800 and was buried in the Sugaw Creek Presbyterian Church graveyard. Another source provides Dorcas' death date as 28 MAY 1778 aged 67y,[6] but this seems improbable, as her will was dated February 29, 1800 and was filed in Mecklenburg County, North Carolina.[7]

Known children of Abraham Alexander and Dorcas [Amelia Wilson?]:[8]

B291. (Dr.) ISAAC ALEXANDER, b. FEB 1750, poss. in N.J., d. 13 JAN 1812 in Camden, S.C., m. (1) unknown, m. (2) 14 DEC 1788 to Mrs. Margaret B. Smith, and m. (3) 5/15 JUL 1807 to Sarah Thornton, d. 9 DEC 1863. Two known children.[9]

B292. ELIZABETH ALEXANDER, b. 19 FEB 1755, d. 20 OCT 1826, m. her cousin (G151.) WILLIAM SAMPLE ALEXANDER, son of Hezekiah Alexander and Mary Sample, d. 26 OCT 1820, age c.70y.

B293. ABRAHAM ALEXANDER, b. 6 MAR 1762, d. 11 MAR 1829, m. (1) 6 MAR 1787 to Margaret Harris, b. 23 SEP 1763, d. 12 JAN 1806, m. (2) 5 MAR 1808 to Jane McCorkle, b. 15 JUN 1773, d. 4 FEB 1834.

B294. MARK "Marcus" ALEXANDER, b. 6 JUN 1766, d. 23 OCT 1795.

B295. NATHANIEL ALEXANDER, b. 3 JUL 1767, d. 5 FEB 1808, bur. Sugaw Creek Presbyterian Church Cem., m. 24 MAY 1794 to Jane Harris, b. 16 APR 1770. Child:

B2951. MARY WILSON ALEXANDER, m. Nicholas R. Morgan.

B296. JOAB ALEXANDER, a county magistrate, b. 9 FEB 1769, d. 21 MAR 1828, bur. Sugaw Creek Presbyterian Church, m. Joannah/Hannah Wallace, b. 1769, d. 3 APR 1823. Nine known children.

B297. EZRA ALEXANDER, b. 3 DEC 1772, d. 12 JAN 1791, bur. Sugaw Creek Presbyterian Church, reportedly *commanded a company in Col. William Davidson's battalion under General Rutherford, against the Tories assembled at Ramsour's Mill, near the present town of Lincolnton.*[10]

B298. CYRUS ALEXANDER, b. 9 JAN 1779, m. 20 MAR 1797 in Mecklenburg Co., N.C. to Rebecca Arthur, d. intestate on 24 MAY 1799, bur. Sugaw Creek Presbyterian Church. Marriage bonded by Josiah Alexander, wit. by Isaac Alexander. Two children named in the 1800 will of Dorcas Alexander.

---

[1] C.L. Hunter, <u>Sketches of Western North Carolina</u> (Raleigh, 1877; reprint ed., Baltimore: Genealogical Publishing Co., Inc., 1990), p. 40.
[2] <u>Parran</u>, p. 68.
[3] Tombstone, Sugaw Creek Presbyterian Church graveyard; *Let me die the death of the righteous, and let my last end be like his.*
[4] D.A.R. Library, Washington, D.C., filing case, Alexander Family.
[5] Mecklenburg Co., N.C. Wills, Bk. A, p. 1.
[6] <u>Genealogy of James Alexander</u>, by Pennsylvania D.A.R. Genealogical Records Committee, 1982, p. 3.
[7] Mecklenburg Co., N.C. Wills, Bk. A, p. 3.
[8] <u>Ferguson</u>.
[9] Annie K. Ingram, *The Six Alexanders Who Signed the Mecklenburg Declaration of Independence*, <u>D.A.R. Magazine</u>, Vol. 86, No. 5, p. 908.
[10] <u>C.L. Hunter</u>, p. 57.

C. ELIZABETH (ALEXANDER) WALLACE
(c.1650-)

Elizabeth Alexander, born c.1650, probably in County Donegal, Ireland, is believed to have been a daughter of William Alexander of Eredy, County Donegal, Ireland. She was married before 1665 in North Ireland to Matthew Wallace,[1] "yeoman," son of John Wallace and Margaret Thomson. Matthew Wallace had a brother John *of Manoakin River, Maryland* who left a will in Somerset County in 1685.[2]

Matthew and Elizabeth moved through Somerset County, Maryland to Cecil County, Maryland by 1707 where she died.

Probable children of Matthew Wallace and Elizabeth Alexander:[3]

C1.   HANNAH WALLACE, b. c.1665 in Raphoe Parish, Ireland.

C2.   SAMUEL WALLACE, b. c.1667 in Raphoe Parish, Ireland, resided in Kent Co., Md. in 1711, rem. to Calvert Co., Md. by 1718, m. Frances Young, daughter of Arthur Young of Calvert Co., Md. Child:

   C21.   ANN WALLACE.

C3.   JAMES WALLACE, b. c.1669 in Raphoe Parish, Ireland, removed to Prince Georges Co., Md. by 1691, m. 2 FEB 1720 in St. Stephens Parish of Cecil Co., Md. to Sarah McKnitt, daughter of John McKnitt and Martha Dale.

C4.   MATTHEW WALLACE, JR., b. 1672 in Somerset Co., Md., d. 3 MAY 1751 in New Munster, Cecil Co., Md. (later part of Chester Co., Pa.), bur. at Head of Christiana Church Cem. in New Castle Co., Del., m. his cousin (F3.) SARAH ALEXANDER, daughter of Samuel Alexander and Mary Taylor, bur. in Frederick Co., Md. Children:

   C41.   JAMES WALLACE, rem. to Kent Co., Md., will dated 31 JAN 1741 in Kent Co., Md.,[4] m. Elizabeth Hart, sister of Robert Hart. Children:

      C411.   MARGARET WALLACE.

      C412.   MARY WALLACE.

      C413.   SARAH WALLACE.

   C42.   MATTHEW WALLACE, III, b. 1712, d. 1792, m. his cousin JANE ALEXANDER, rem. to Mecklenburg Co., N.C. where bur. in Sugaw Creek Presbyterian Church at Charlotte, N.C.

   C43.   WILLIAM WALLACE, lived on Manokin River in Somerset Co., Md., heir of friend Peter Kizey in will of 8 OCT 1715 in which he inherited 50-acre tract called *Chance*.[5]

   C44.   JOSEPH WALLACE, b. c.1720, left will dated 19 FEB 1781, proved in April 1781 in Mecklenburg Co., N.C.,[6] m. Margery (   ). Children:

      C441.   WILLIAM WALLACE.

      C442.   EDWARD R. WALLACE.

      C443.   SAMUEL WALLACE.

      C444.   ELIZABETH WALLACE.

      C445.   ANN WALLACE.

   C45.   GEORGE WALLACE.

   C46.   MARY WALLACE, m. her cousin (D5.) MARK ALEXANDER, son of James and Mary Alexander, *q.v.*

   C47.   ALEXANDER WALLACE.

   C48.   EZEKIEL WALLACE.

   C49.   JOHN WALLACE.

C5.   RICHARD WALLACE, b. c.1672 in Somerset Co., Md., d. after 5 MAY 1744 in Somerset Co., Md., m. Grace White, daughter of John White of Somerset Co., Md., removed to Prince Georges Co., Md., was a legatee in the will of James Williams in 1691. Ten children.

C6.   JANE WALLACE, b. c.1674 at Manokin Hundred, Somerset Co., Md., d. c.1698, m. 28 MAR 1693[7] in Somerset Co., Md. as second wife of John McKnitt,[8] b. c.APR 1660, d. 23 DEC 1714 in Elk River, Cecil Co., Md. Children:[9]

   C61.   MARGARET McKNITT, b. 26 DEC 1693, d. 1736, bur. Head of Christiana Church Cem., New Castle Co.,

---

[1] Alexander Kin, Vol. 2, p. 301.

[2] Ray, p. 298.

[3] Genealogy of James Alexander, Pennsylvania G.R.C., 1982, at the D.A.R. Library, Washington, D.C.

[4] Maryland Wills, Liber 22, fol. 333, dated 31 JAN 1740/1, prov. 3 APR 1741.

[5] Ray, p. 297.

[6] Mecklenburg Co., N.C. Wills, Bk. F, pp. 223-4; also see Alexander Kin, Vol. 1, p. 70.

[7] Pennsylvania Genealogical Magazine (Philadelphia, Pa.: The Genealogical Society of Pennsylvania), Vol. XVI (Oct. 1948), p. 77.

[8] MDSA, Somerset Co., Md. Records, Liber IKL, fol. 169.

[9] Genealogy of James Alexander, Pennsylvania G.R.C., 1982, at D.A.R. Library, Washington, D.C.

Del., m. 1714 to her cousin (G5.) JAMES ALEXANDER, son of Joseph Alexander and Abigail McKnitt, *q.v.*

C62.   WILLIAM McKNITT, b. c.1696, d. 1747 in Dorchester Co., Md., m. Elizabeth (   ). Child:
        C621.   ANN McKNITT.

C63.   JANE/JEAN McKNITT, b. c.1698, m. her cousin (F6.) ANDREW ALEXANDER, son of Samuel Alexander and Ann Taylor. Andrew purchased land from John McKnitt III in Cecil Co., Md. on 14 JUN 1745.[1]

C7.   CATHARINE WALLACE, b. c.1676 in Somerset Co., Md., d. there before 2 MAR 1734, m. her first cousin WILLIAM ALEXANDER II, son of William Alexander I and Ann Liston, *q.v.*

C8.   WILLIAM WALLACE, b. c.1678.

C9.   DAVID T. WALLACE, b. 1680 in Somerset Co., Md., d. c.1751 in Murderkill, Kent Co., Del.

C(10).   ROBERT WALLACE, b. c.1681 in Somerset Co., Md.

C(11).   JOHN WALLACE, b. 24 JUN 1687 in Manokin Hundred of Somerset Co., Md.,[2] removed to Prince Georges Co., Md. by 1691, then to Cecil Co., Md.,[3] m. 24 FEB 1736 in St. Stephens Parish of Cecil Co., Md., to Mary Hollins.

C(12).   DOROTHY WALLACE, b. c.1689 in Somerset Co., Md., d. c.1747, m. her cousin (I2.) JOHN McKNITT, son of John McKnitt and Jane Alexander, b. 8 SEP 1687 in Worcester Co., Md., d. before June 1733 in Bohemia Manor of Cecil Co., Md.

C(13).   ANN WALLACE, b. c.1690 in Somerset Co., Md., m. her maternal 1st cousin (B3.) ARTHUR ALEXANDER, son of Andrew Alexander and Jane McKnitt, *q.v.*

C(14).   ISABELLA WALLACE, b. c.1690, d. 22 DEC 1779 in Chester Co., Pa.

C(15).   THOMAS WALLACE, SR., b. c.1708 in Somerset Co., Md., m. _____ Fleming, sister of Lodovic Fleming.

---

[1] Cecil Co., Md. Deeds, Bk. 6, p. 480.
[2] MDSA, Somerset Co., Md. Records, Bk. IKL.
[3] Alexander Kin, Vol. 2, p. 297.

D. JAMES ALEXANDER
(c.1660-after 1736)

James Alexander, "the weaver," was born c.1660 in County Donegal, Ireland, is thought to be a son of William Alexander of Eredy, County Donegal, Ireland. James Alexander was "transported" in 1678 to Somerset County, Maryland.[1] He died some time after 1736 in New Munster, Cecil County, Maryland.

In 1714, James Alexander sold part of Milford Hundred to William Semple of Chester County, Pennsylvania,[2] and was involved in a border dispute between the states of Maryland, Delaware and Pennsylvania as settled by the Mason-Dixon line. James Alexander married Mary (   ). One source gives her name as Mary Steele, daughter of John Steele,[3] who died some time before 1714, but she more appropriately has been found to be the wife of James Alexander, son of Samuel Alexander and Ann Taylor.

Possible children of James Alexander, Sr. and Mary (   ):

D1.   DAVID ALEXANDER, "the weaver" and also a farmer, b. c.1680 in Somerset Co., Md., was an Elder in Head of Christiana Church, New Castle Co., Del., which was founded in 1708. Name of wife unknown. He died c.1740 and his son Aaron Alexander began disposing of his property by 1749. David's widow may have remarried, but not to John Dobbin as some researchers have claimed. Children:
   D11.   AARON ALEXANDER, b. c.1718.
   D12.   ANN ALEXANDER, b. c.1720, m. Gilbert Clark, son of Alexander Clark.[4]
   D13.   JAMES ALEXANDER, b. c.1724, d. 1781, mentioned in his brother William Alexander's 1805 will in Mecklenburg Co., N.C., res. on Mallard Creek there, m. Elizabeth (   ), a widow by October 1781.
   D14.   EZEKIEL ALEXANDER, SR., b. c.1726, d. testate 27 JAN 1811,[5] age 85, m. Martha (   ); both bur. in the oldest cemetery at Sugaw Creek Presbyterian Church. Children:
       D141.   EZEKIEL ALEXANDER, JR., b. 1767, d. September 1836, age 69, m. Nancy (   ); bur. in the second cemetery at Sugaw Creek Presbyterian Church.
       D142.   WALLACE ALEXANDER, perhaps b. 1769, d. 1825, age 56, bur. Sugaw Creek Presbyterian Church Cem.
       D143.   JAMES TAYLOR ALEXANDER, b. 1772/7, d. 12 JUN 1825, age 48, bur. Sugaw Creek Presbyterian Church Cem.
       D144.   SARAH ALEXANDER, m. Richard Robison.
       D145.   DEBORAH ALEXANDER, m. Robert Robison, d. by 1797.
   D15.   WILLIAM ALEXANDER, blacksmith, b. c.1728, d. testate 23 OCT 1805,[6] age 77, m. Rebecca Brown, res. on Mallard Creek in Mecklenburg Co., N.C. Child:
       D151.   WILLIAM ALEXANDER, JR., "Blind Billy," b. 1779, m. Mary Henderson, daughter of Andrew Henderson and Elizabeth Robison.
       D152.   DANIEL ALEXANDER, inherited his father's mill.
       D153.   JOSIAH ALEXANDER, inherited his father's land north of the Mill Branch.
       D154.   REBECCA ALEXANDER, m. Charles Richmond.
       D155.   RUTH ALEXANDER.
D2.   JAMES ALEXANDER, JR., b. c.1690, on the rent roll of New Munster, Cecil Co., Md. for 1738, sold property in Cecil Co. on 13 AUG 1740,[7] m. to (1) Sophia (   ),[8] and m. (2) Rachel (   ) by time of a patent on 19 JUL 1779.[9] Child:
   D21.   DAVID ALEXANDER. It is believed he married Susannah (   ). On 13 JUN 1758, Isaac Alexander and David Miller, both of New Castle upon Delaware, sold for £70, 125 acres of *Hispaniola* and *Bullen's Range* to David and Susannah Alexander of Cecil Co., Md.[10] In 1760, Robert Husbands was apprenticed to learn the shoemaker trade from David Alexander, long a resident of Cecil Co.[11] On 23 OCT 1769, his cousin (F11.) JOSEPH ALEXANDER, son of James Alexander and Mary Steele, of Augusta Co., Va., sold

---

[1]   Index of Early Settlers to Maryland, Vol. 1, from an unidentified location.
[2]   Cecil Co., Md. Deeds, Bk. 5, p. 97.
[3]   Pennsylvania Genealogical Magazine (Philadelphia, Pa.: The Genealogical Society of Pennsylvania), Vol. XVI (Oct. 1948), p. 87.
[4]   North Carolina Colonial Records, Vol. 5, p. 1197.
[5]   Mecklenburg Co., N.C. Wills, Bk. A4, p. 17, dated 22 AUG 1810, proved in court term January 1811.
[6]   Mecklenburg Co., N.C. Wills, Bk. A15, p. 44, dated 6 AUG 1804, proved in court term October 1805.
[7]   Cecil Co., Md. Deeds, Bk. 6, p. 19.
[8]   Cecil Co., Md. Deeds, Bk. 6, p. 19.
[9]   Cecil Co., Md. Deeds, Bk. 14, p. 327.
[10]   Cecil Co., Md. Deeds, Bk. 9, p. 23.
[11]   Cecil Co., Md. Court Orders, Bk. 1759-1760, p. 503.

to him two tracts of land called *Sligo* and *Alexandria*, while a resident of Cecil Co., Md.[1]

D3.   MOSES ALEXANDER, b. c.1693 in Somerset Co., Md., of age of majority before 1714 when he was party to a deed with his father in Cecil Co., Md.[2] for part of the *New Munster* tract, d. testate in 1762 in New Munster, Cecil Co., Md.,[3] bur. Head of Christiana Church Cem. at Newcastle Co., Del., will mentions friends and executors Theophilus and Amos Alexander, inventory signed by William Longwell. Moses and Mary made a deed of Milford Hundred in 1735,[4] sold land to John McCoy in 1740. Moses Alexander m. Mary Wallace, daughter of Jane Wallace,[5] b. 1700, d. 25 OCT 1758 aged 58y, bur. Head of Christiana Church Cem. near Newark, Del. Children:

D31.   NATHANIEL ALEXANDER, b. 1714 in Md., of Cabarrus Co., N.C., on Rocky River in 1751, had a mill, d. 1767, letters of admin. granted 22 JUL 1767, m. Elizabeth (   ). He received £0.15.00 in his father's 1762 will.

D32.   ABRAHAM ALEXANDER, b. 1717, received £0.15.00 in his father's 1762 will.

D33.   PRISCILLA ALEXANDER, b. c.1720, inherited her father's Bible in his 1762 will, m. (1) to John White, m. (2) to William Longwell. After she d., he m. (2) 9 DEC 1756 to Margaret Glenn.[6] William left a will dated 13 JAN 1790, prov. 24 APR 1790 in Cecil Co., Md. Three known children.[7] Child:

D331.   HANNAH WHITE, received £20 in her grandfather's 1762 will.

D34.   JAMES ALEXANDER, b. c.1722, rem. from Cecil Co., Md. to Lancaster Co., Pa. before 1767, to Shenandoah Valley c.1747, then on to Mecklenburg Co., N.C. by 1750 where he had 640 acres on upper Cathey's Creek, d. there 1753. Child:

D341.   WILLIAM ALEXANDER, m. Araminta (   ) who gave land for church at Elkton, Md. in 1741, mentioned in Rowan Co., Tenn. deeds.[8] Child:

D3411.   JAMES ALEXANDER, teacher in Rowan Co., Tenn. before the Rev. War, m. Mary (   ).

D35.   ZEBULON ALEXANDER, b. 1727, listed as the fifth of ten children in his father's will of 2 FEB 1762 whereby he received £0.15.00, rem. to Mecklenburg Co., N.C. He m. (1) Hannah Hodgson, d. c.1772, d/o Phineas Hodgson of *Pleasant Gardens* in Chester Co., Pa.;[9] m. (2) to Jane McClung. Zebulon made a will in 1784 filed in Mecklenburg Co., N.C. Child:

D351.   ZEBULON ALEXANDER, JR.

D36.   MARK ALEXANDER, b. c.1730 in Cecil Co., Md., merchant of Baltimore, Md. by 1756, d. without issue by APR 1797. *Alexander was jailed for at least two months in 1787 as an insolvent debtor.*[10]

D37.   MOSES ALEXANDER, b. 1733, perhaps confused with (D54.) Col. MOSES ALEXANDER, son of Mark Alexander and his wife Mary Wallace.

D38.   (Lieut.[11]) DANIEL ALEXANDER, "youngest son" in his father's 1762 will, b. in Cecil Co., Md., rem. to Mecklenburg Co., N.C., a joiner and planer, will dated 25 MAR 1776, prov. APR 1777 in Mecklenburg Co., N.C.,[12] wit. by Benjamin Alexander, Edward Giles (jurat) and Andrew Alexander. He inherited all his father's real and personal estate in Cecil Co., Md. by the 1762 will, but it was soon sold.[13] Daniel was an Elder of Poplar Creek Presbyterian Church, and owned land on Mallard Creek in Mecklenburg Co., N.C. He m. Prudence (   ),[14] thought to be a daughter of James Alexander and Rachel (   ).[15] Children:[16]

D381.   JAMES ALEXANDER, b. 24 OCT 1742, d. during Rev. War., will dated 25 DEC 1779, prov. APR 1781[17], wit. by Andrew Alexander (jurat), Benjamin Alexander and Andrew Alexander, m. Rachel

---

[1] Cecil Co., Md. Deeds, Bk. 11, p. 462.

[2] Cecil Co., Md. Deeds, Bk. J.D. 2, pp. 280-83, dated 18 MAY 1714, between Thomas Stevenson of Bucks Co., Pa. of the one part [because he is moving], and Matthew Wallace, yeoman, James Alexander [Allexander], farmer, Arthur Alexander, farmer, David Alexander, weaver, James Alexander, weaver, *and his son Moses Alexander*, and Joseph Alexander, farmer, and his son James Alexander, of the other party; *their share of* land on the east side of Elk River in Cecil Co., Md.

[3] Maryland Wills, Liber 31, fol. 820, will of Moses Alexander, dated 2 FEB 1762, prov. 1 DEC 1762, wit. William Frier, Joseph Cannon, Sarah Craige; also see Cecil Co., Md. Wills, Bk. 32, p. 620; also see Cecil Co., Md. Bonds, Bk. 3, p. 139.

[4] Cecil Co., Md. Deeds, Bk. 5, p. 97; Deed Bk. 5, p. 235.

[5] The will of Jane Wallace in Cecil Co., Md., in 1736, mentions daughter Mary Alexander.

[6] Old Sweeds Church Register, Wilmington, Del., p. 709.

[7] Virginia Historical Society (VHS), Mss1:K5823a, Alexander family No. 2.

[8] Rowan Co., N.C. Deeds, Bk. III, pp. 21, 495.

[9] Alexander Kin, Vol. 2, p. 364.

[10] Papenfuse, p. 103.

[11] North Carolina Colonial Records, Vol. 22, p. 396.

[12] Mecklenburg Co., N.C. Wills, Bk. I, p. 23, executor James Alexander.

[13] Cecil Co., Md. Deeds, Bk. 3, p. 129.

[14] Some researchers speculate her maiden name may be Anderson, as son William is known to have used William Anderson to be set apart from other William Alexanders in the area. The will of Prudence Alexander was proved 22 OCT 1800.

[15] Frederick A. Virkus, Compendium of American Genealogy, Vol. VI, p. 248.

[16] Alexander Kin, Vol. 2, p. 501.

[17] Parran, p. 67.

( ). Three known children.[1]

D382. (Lieut.) WILLIAM ALEXANDER, b. 30 JAN 1745 in Salisbury, Cecil Co., Md., m. c.1765 to Esther Brown,[2] and d. on 31 MAY 1820 in Maury Co., Tenn., bur. Ebenezer Presbyterian Church Cem. William was reportedly appointed by the Province of North Carolina to establish a public factory for making muskets and bayonets for the Continental Army,[3] and was a patriot of the Rev. War for N.C. for which he was allotted 1,000 acres by the Congress of N.C. in 1787. Esther, b. 23 SEP 1745 [or 29 OCT 1745], d. Friday, 17 OCT 1823 at 3:00, aged 78y 10d, bur. Reese's Chapel/Ebenezer Presby. Ch. Cem. of Maury Co., Tenn. Nine known children, including Silas Alexander of Fayette and Maury Cos. in Tenn.[4]

D383. STEPHEN ALEXANDER, "Captain" in the Rev. War, b. 16 JUN 1749 in Cabarrus Co., N.C., d. testate 26 JUN 1831 in Cabarrus Co., N.C.,[5] m. 18 SEP 1771 to Martha Wilson, daughter of Zaccheus Wilson of Ireland, b. 30 MAR 1754 in Anson Co., N.C., d. 4 JAN 1844 in Cabarrus Co., N.C.[6] Stephen was an executor of his father's 1776 will. Thirteen known children.

D384. MATTHEW ALEXANDER, b. c.1751, inherited his father's plantation by the 1776 will, along with 56 acres located between that of William Alexander and James Scott, m. Elizabeth ( ), rem. to Sumner Co., Tenn., d. 5 SEP 1823 testate.[7]

D385. MARGARET ALEXANDER, m. 1 APR 1789 to her cousin Francis Alexander.

D386. JOSIAH ALEXANDER, b. SEP 1755, received £100 and a negro girl named Tandy by his father's 1766 will, d. 6 DEC 1817, m. Mildred Orr, b. 6 SEP 1762, d. 12 OCT 1815. Four known children.

D387. HEZEKIAH ALEXANDER, b. post 1756, by his father's 1766 will for which he was executor, inherited 150 acres which adjoined that of his brother Stephen Alexander, poss. m. Elizabeth Johns(t)on.

D39. MARY ALEXANDER, b. 1738, m. c.1765 in Baltimore, Md. to Capt. James Cox, a tailor of Baltimore, d. 1777.[8] She left a will dated 2 FEB 1790, prov. 23 FEB 1790 in Baltimore, Md., men. niece Mary Dysart.[9] Mary received £30 in her father's 1762 will.

D3(10). RUTH ALEXANDER, b. 1740, m. James Dysart/Dizard/Dyzzart. Child:

D3(10)1. MARY DYSART.

D4. SOPHIA ALEXANDER, b. c.1697, d. after 1755 in Cecil Co., Md. when she deposed that James Alexander was her father and James Alexander, Jr. was her brother,[10] m. John Garner.

D5. MARK ALEXANDER, b. c.1700, lived in Baltimore, Md., agent of Lord Baltimore, mem. Committee of Safety, m. his paternal 1st cousin once removed (C46.) MARY WALLACE, daughter of Matthew Wallace, Jr. and Sarah Alexander. In 1750 he res. Cabarrus Co., N.C. (later Mecklenburg). Some have dubbed this the *Caledon Branch* of the Alexander Family.

D51. DAVID ALEXANDER, easily confused with (D17.) DANIEL ALEXANDER.

D52. MARY ALEXANDER.

D53. NATHANIEL ALEXANDER.

D54. (Col.) MOSES ALEXANDER, blacksmith and first sheriff of Mecklenburg Co., N.C., b. 1725 in Cecil Co., Md., lived in Salisbury Dist., d. intestate in 1771 in Mecklenburg Co., N.C., m. c.1753 to his cousin Sarah Taylor Alexander, daughter of William Alexander and Jane Taylor,[11] 1733-1813. She m. (2) Gen. John Smith, son of Robert Washington Smith. Children:[12]

D541. (Dr.) NATHANIEL ALEXANDER, b. 5 MAR 1756 in Concord, Mecklenburg Co., N.C., d. testate 7 MAR 1808 in Salisbury, N.C.,[13] bur. in Presbyterian Church Cem. of Charlotte, N.C., m. Margaret Polk Brevard, daughter of Ephraim Brevard and Margaret Polk, d. 8 NOV 1808 in Charlotte, N.C., bur. in Presbyterian Church Cem. there. Nathaniel was governor of N.C. from late 1805 to 1 DEC 1806.[14] No known issue.

D542. MARK ALEXANDER, b. 1757/60, d. intestate in 1824, m. (1) MAY 1789 to Lucy Bugg, daughter of Jacob Bugg, m. (2) Elizabeth ( ), served in Rev. War, merchant in Mecklenburg Co., N.C. Five known children.

[1] Also see Alexander Kin, Vol. 2, p. 502.
[2] Sometimes seen referred to as Mary Brown.
[3] Perry, p. 11.
[4] Marise Parrish Lightfoot, Let the Drums Roll, p. 51.
[5] Caburrus Co., N.C. Wills, Bk. 5, p. 180.
[6] D.A.R., Applications, Series 3.
[7] Sumner Co., Tenn. Wills, Bk. 2, p. 2, dated 24 MAR 1823.
[8] Papenfuse, p. 103.
[9] Baltimore Co., Md. Wills, Bk. 4, p. 409.
[10] Cecil Co., Md. Land Commissions, Bk. 2, p. 57.
[11] Alexander Kin, Vol. 2, p. 501.
[12] Ibid.
[13] Mecklenburg Co., N.C. Wills, Bk. A, p. 24.
[14] Earley Winfred Bridges, Masonic Governors of North Carolina (Greensboro, N.C., 1937), p. 131.

D543. JANE ALEXANDER, b. 1761, d. c.1834, m. (1) to William Locke, m. (2) to Richard Trotter. One known daughter.

D544. WILLIAM LEE SAMPLE ALEXANDER, known as "Lawyer Billy," b. 1 NOV 1765 in Mecklenburg Co., N.C., d. 16 MAR 1806, member of the Society of the Cincinnati, m. Elizabeth Henderson. Six known children.

D545. WALLACE ALEXANDER, lawyer, b. 8 FEB 1767, d. 15 MAR 1804, m. 28 MAR 1797 to Ann Nancy Dobson, daughter of Capt. Dobson. Six children.

D546. SARAH TAYLOR ALEXANDER, b. 1769?, m. Archibald Henderson, son of Judge Richard Henderson of Hanover Co., b. 7 AUG 1768 in Granville Co., N.C.[1], d. 1822, res. Salisbury. Three known children.[2]

D547. Possibly MOSES ALEXANDER, JR., d. in the Rev. War.

D55. MARK ALEXANDER, b. 1730, taxed as a bachelor in Baltimore, Md. in 1756, age 26y, served in the Rev. War at Brandywine and Germantown. Child:

D551. MARK ALEXANDER, lawyer in Mecklenburg Co., Va., served in Rev. War.

Other Possible Children of James Alexander, Sr.:

D6. JOHN ALEXANDER, witnessed the 1727 will of his uncle Samuel Alexander.

D7. JOSEPH ALEXANDER, m. Margaret (   ), left will dated 23 OCT 1769 in Cecil Co., Md.,[3] sold land with his son James to Mary Alexander on 18 DEC 1719.[4] Child:

D71. JAMES ALEXANDER.

D8. FRANCIS ALEXANDER.

---

[1] Jo White Linn, Gray Family and Allied Lines, 1976, p. 167.
[2] Lucy Henderson Horton, Family History (Franklin, Tenn.: Press of the News, 1922), p. 285.
[3] Cecil Co., Md. Wills, Bk. 11, p. 125.
[4] Cecil Co., Md. Deeds, Bk. 3, p. 282.

E. FRANCIS ALEXANDER
(c.1654-1701)

Francis Alexander, was born c.1654 in Raphoe Parish of County Donegal, Ireland, and believed to be a son of William Alexander of Eredy, County Donegal, Ireland. He is known to have a wife named Rebecca (   ). Francis Alexander died before March 21, 1701, at Manokin Hundred in Somerset County, Maryland, when a bond was issued to his widow Rebecca as the administratrix of his estate, with Paule Henry as security.[1] An inventory of the estate was presented to court by appraisers Lawrance Ryley and Peter Camell.[2] Some time passed while the estate was being settled, because as late as 1704, the court summoned Rebecca to appear and render her account of the estate.[3]

   Possible child of Francis Alexander and Rebecca (   ):

+   E1.   HENRY ALEXANDER, SR., b. c.1680, perhaps m. Rachel (   ), and d. before March 1727 in Manokin Hundred of Somerset Co., Md.[4]

E1. Henry Alexander, Sr.
(c.1680-c.1727)

Henry Alexander is thought to be a son of Francis Alexander by his wife Rebecca. Henry Alexander was surety for his mother in October 1701.[5] His wife was Rachel (   ), and nothing further is known about her. On June 11, 1712, he purchased from George Taylor and wife Comfort Anderson, a 300-acre tract called *Golden Quarter* and tract *Ripley*,[6] and the deed mentioned that Francis Alexander was deceased.

   Between March 18, 1717 and November 22, 1718, Henry Alexander was party to a suit with John Hampton.[7] In 1718, Henry Alexander still owned *Golden Quarter* tract in Somerset County, Maryland. On September 17, 1718 he witnessed in Somerset County, Maryland the will of William Bedder, Sr.[8]

   On April 11, 1721, Henry Alexander appraised the estate of Jonathan Hudson.[9] On August 7, 1721, Henry Alexander appraised the estate of Nathaniel Ennis,[10] whose will dated December 18, 1720 was proved April 4, 1721 in Somerset County, Maryland.[11] On September 15, 1721, Henry Alexander appraised the estate of Jeremiah Poynter,[12] whose will was dated January 27, 1720/1 and was proved April 10, 1721.[13]

   On March 20, 1727/8, Henry Alexander's widow Rachel Alexander, administratrix, filed bond, and made final estate return of August 20, 1729 in Worcester County, Maryland.[14]

   Known children of Henry Alexander, Sr. and wife, possibly Rachel (   ):

E11.   SARAH ALEXANDER, m. William Franklin. On 17 SEP 1747, William Franklin and wife Sarah, the daughter of Henry Alexander, sold 222 acres of *Golden Quarter* to John Newbold.

E12.   HENRY ALEXANDER, JR., d. intestate c.1747 in Worcester Co., Md. May be the same who patented land there, called *Addition* in 1741 and *Freeman's Adventure* in 1741.

---

[1]   Maryland Testamentary Proceedings, Bk. 19A, p. 59, session 21 MAR 1701.
[2]   Maryland Testamentary Proceedings, Bk. 19A, p. 24, session 13 OCT 1707; also see Maryland Inventories and Accounts, Liber 21, fol. 53 for an undated inventory by appraisers Lawrance Riley and Peter Camell.
[3]   Maryland Testamentary Proceedings, Bk. 20, p. 65, session 24 JUL 1704.
[4]   Ruth T. Dryden, Worcester Co., Md. Deeds, p. 260.
[5]   Maryland Testamentary Proceedings, Bk. 19A, p. 65.
[6]   Somerset Co., Md. Deeds, Liber CD, fol. 815.
[7]   Lankford, p. 3.
[8]   Maryland Calendar of Wills, Vol. 14, p. 192.
[9]   Somerset Co., Md. Inventories, Liber JW15.
[10]   Ibid.
[11]   Maryland Calendar of Wills, Vol. V, p. 63; Maryland Wills, Liber 16, fol. 501.
[12]   Somerset Co., Md. Inventories, Liber JW15.
[13]   Maryland Wills, Liber 17, fol. 14; Maryland Calendar of Wills, Vol. V, p. 69.
[14]   Maryland Testamentary Proceedings, Bk. 28, pp. 192, 293, 433.

F. SAMUEL ALEXANDER
(c.1657-1733)

Samuel Alexander, Sr., born c.1657 in Raphoe Parish, County Donegal, Ireland,[1] is thought to be a son of William Alexander of Eredy, County Donegal, Ireland. Samuel Alexander was living in Somerset County, Maryland as early as 1680.[2] About 1684, he was married, probably in Somerset County, to Mary Taylor, daughter of George Taylor and Comfort Anderson.[3] Comfort Anderson was the daughter of William Anderson, and a sister of Naomi Anderson who married Reverend Francis Makamie, pioneer missionary and preacher in Virginia and on the Eastern Shore.[4] Mary Taylor was born c.1655 and died c.1733.

On January 21, 1716, Samuel Alexander witnessed the will of William Gyliot in Somerset County, Maryland which was proved March 20, 1716.[5]

By 1713, Samuel Alexander was living in Cecil County, Maryland. He lived on a tract he called *Sligo* which was 200 acres in Bohemia Manor of Cecil County, surveyed for him on May 8, 1713, patented December 10, 1714.[6] On November 13, 1720, Samuel was appointed attorney for Griffith Jones, then of Albemarle County, North Carolina.[7] *On 13 JUN 1723, Richard Thompson deeded to Samuel Alexander and Peter Bouchelle, 1 acre of land for the use of the Presbyterian Congregation to erect [thereon] a meeting house' for which an annual rent of one ear of Indian corn was to be paid, if lawfully demanded.*[8]

Samuel Alexander also owned several other tracts: 130-acre *Alexandria*[9] surveyed for him and John Holtham on January 19, 1720 and patented to sons Martin and Francis Alexander on November 4, 1732; also 868-acre *Hispaniola* that was surveyed for William Richardson in 1720 and purchased in 1724; and 129-acre *Bullen's Range* in 1723. Afterwards he is shown on the Cecil County Rent Roll for taking ownership from William Richardson on March 30, 1724.

Samuel's will was dated March 9, 1730, and proved June 14, 1733 in Cecil County.[10] His wife Mary was named; she and his son Andrew were made executors. On April 10, 1733, Mary, relict, petitioned the court to be excused as executor *by reason of old age*.[11] Sons Francis and Martin witnessed the will, while Andrew confirmed the inventory made by them in November 1733. Samuel Alexander and his wife are buried in Bethel Cemetery of Chesapeake City, Maryland.[12]

Known children of Samuel Alexander, Sr. and Mary Taylor:

+ F1. JAMES ALEXANDER, farmer, b. 1 JAN 1685 in Annemessix, Somerset Co., Md.,[13] d. 1717 in Cecil Co., Md., m. Mary Steele.[14]
+ F2. MARTIN ALEXANDER, b. 18 MAR 1687 in Annemessix, Md.,[15] m. (1) unknown, m. (2) Susannah Foster, and d. 1751 in Cecil Co., Md.
   F3. SARAH ALEXANDER, b. 28 AUG 1690 in Pocomoke, Somerset Co., Md. (now in Worcester Co.),[16] m. her cousin (C4.) MATTHEW WALLACE, JR., and had ten children, *q.v.*
+ F4. FRANCIS ALEXANDER, weaver, b. 28 MAR 1693 in Annemessix, Md.,[17] d. 1760 at *Carroll's Delight* of Frederick Co., Md., m. (1) Martha Blair, m. (2) Jane (   ).
   F5. MARY ALEXANDER, b. 1695 in Pocomoke, Somerset Co., Md., inherited land called *Alexandria* after her mother's death, m. (1) in 1727 to Thomas Craig[18] of Bohemia Manor, Md., and m. (2) by 1750 to _____ Lowry/Lowrey. Mary Lowry and her six daughters were mentioned in Martin Alexander's 1750 will.
+ F6. ANDREW ALEXANDER, of *Bullen's Range* in Cecil Co., b. 1697 in Pocomoke, Md., may have m. (1) his cousin (C63.) JEAN McKNITT, daughter of John McKnitt and Jane Wallace, but known to m. Sarah (   ), and d. 1782 in Mecklenburg Co., N.C.

---

1 Alexander Kin, Vol. 1, p. 6, the authors theorize that Samuel Alexander and his father were born in Scotland.
2 Somerset Co., Md. Judicial Records, 1680-1690, p. 160.
3 Frances Alexander Butterworth, A Family of the House of Alexander (1909), gives father as George Taylor, while others have stated Elias Taylor.
4 Frederick A. Virkus, Compendium of American Genealogy (1930), Vol. III, p. 176.
5 Maryland Calendar of Wills, Vol. IV, p. 43.
6 Maryland Land Patents, Liber EE6, fol. 185.
7 Somerset Co., Md. Deeds, Liber JK, 1719-1722, fol. 99.
8 Butterworth, p. 12.
9 Ibid.
10 Cecil Co., Md. Wills, Bk. 20, p. 707; Maryland Wills, Liber 20, fol. 706.
11 Cecil Co., Md. Wills, Bk. AA, p. 29.
12 Parran, p. 63.
13 Somerset Co., Md. Records, Liber IKL, fol. 3.
14 Mrs. Butterworth, in her book on the Alexanders, has Mary Steele as the wife of Francis Alexander, not James Alexander.
15 Somerset Co., Md. Records, Liber IKL, fol. 3.
16 Ibid., fol. 4.
17 Ibid.
18 Cecil Co., Md. Wills, Bk. 20, p. 707.

F7. SAMUEL ALEXANDER, JR., b. 1699 in Pocomoke, Md., will prov. 21 JAN 1784 in Mecklenburg Co., N.C.,[1] m. Mary (   ), left will dated 9 MAR 1730, res. in Cecil Co., Md. in 1724, and at *Enderly Farm* near Charlotte, N.C. Samuel served in the Rev. War and taken prisoner at Camden, S.C. at age 78y.[2] Child:

F71.   SAMUEL ALEXANDER III, a captain in the Rev. War. Child:

F711.   SAMUEL ALEXANDER IV, res. at Enderly Farm near Charlotte, N.C., m. Sarah (   ), will wit. James McGilleb and John Alcorn (jurat), with executors as his wife Sarah and Samuel Pickens. Five known children.

F1. James Alexander, Sr.
(1685-c.1717)

James Alexander, Sr., a carpenter and farmer, son of Samuel Alexander and Mary Taylor, was born January 1, 1685 in Annemessix (a Quaker settlement), Somerset County, Maryland. He was married to Mary Steele [Steel], daughter of John and Mary Steele of New Castle County, Delaware, as evidenced by the will of John Steele dated April 20, 1751, proved May 1, 1751, which mentions son Moses Steele, son James Steele, and daughter Mary, the wife of James Alexander.[3]

James Alexander, carpenter, died in the area of New Munster, Cecil County, Maryland.[4] His will dated is July 12, 1717 and is on file in Cecil County,[5] Maryland and a copy in New Castle County, Delaware.[6] In the 1717 will, the testator mentioned that John Steel, yeoman of New Castle County, Delaware, was his father-in-law. John Garner, in his will of 1734, leaves money to the *children of James Alexander by Mary Steel*.

As seen earlier, James was dead before Thomas Stevenson conveyed an additional 903 acres to the Alexanders on August 15, 1718, his widow Mary received his share.[7] In his will he appointed his *father-in-law John Steele of New Castle County, Delaware*, wife Mary and *brother Francis Alexander of Cecil County, weaver* his executors. Samuel Alexander, probably his father and <u>not</u> his brother, witnessed the will.

On December 19, 1719, Joseph Alexander and his son James Alexander, both of New Munster, Cecil Co., because they are moving, gave a quit claim to Joseph Alexander, John Alexander, and Francis Alexander, sons of James Alexander, carpenter, late of New Munster, deceased, and to his widow Mary Alexander for their interests in 316 acres of land in New Munster bought by James Alexander, carpenter, from Thomas Stevenson and confirmed by Stevenson to the children of the widow of the said James Alexander by deed of August 15, 1718.[8] One of the witnesses to this deed was James Alexander (evidently James "the weaver").

In his will, James Alexander, carpenter, distinctly stated that his plantation contained 316 acres, and that size of tract is what his wife and sons sold.

Known children of James Alexander, Sr. and Mary Steele:

F11.   JOSEPH ALEXANDER, carpenter, of *Sligo* tract in Cecil Co., Md., b. c.1713/4 in Cecil Co., rem. to New Castle Co., Del. where on 12 DEC 1740 he and his wife deeded land to Adam Wilson of New Castle Co. Joseph then rem. to Augusta Co., Va. where he is found in records as late as 1774. It is believed his wife's name was Margaret (   ). On 23 OCT 1769, Joseph Alexander of Augusta Co. sold for £7.10 two tracts of land called *Sligo* and *Alexandria* in Cecil Co., Md. to his cousin (D2.) DAVID ALEXANDER, son of James and Mary (   ) Alexander, of Cecil Co., Md.,[9] *q.v.*

F12.   JOHN ALEXANDER.

F13.   MOSES ALEXANDER, wit. the 1734 will of John Garner in Cecil Co., Md.,[10] perhaps d. 1762 in Cecil Co., Md., reportedly married his cousin (F28.) SARAH ALEXANDER, daughter of Martin Alexander and Mary Taylor, *q.v.*

F14.   JAMES ALEXANDER, JR., perhaps the same James Alexander who was executor to the 1734 will of John Garner of Cecil Co., Md. in 1725.[11]

[1] Mecklenburg Co., N.C. Wills, Bk. A, p. 36.
[2] Hugh McCall, <u>History of Georgia ...</u> (Atlanta, Ga.: Cherokee Publishing Co., 1969), p. 327.
[3] Cecil Co., Md. Wills, Bk. G, p. 468.
[4] Some researchers have concluded he was a weaver, and was bur. in Bethel Cem. of Chesapeake City, Cecil Co., Md.
[5] Cecil Co., Md. Wills, Bk. 18, p. 416.
[6] New Castle Co., Del. Wills, Bk. C, p. 103.
[7] Cecil Co., Md. Deeds, Bk. 2, p. 280; Deed Bk. 3, p. 212, dated 15 AUG 1718, recorded 10 FEB 1718/9 by attorney; also see Bk. 3, p. 282, dated 18 DEC 1719.
[8] Cecil Co., Md. Deeds, Bk. 3, p. 282, dated 18 DEC 1719.
[9] Cecil Co., Md. Deeds, Bk. 11, p. 462.
[10] Maryland Calendar of Wills, Vol. V, p. 204, will of John Garner, dated 7 MAR 1723/4, prov. 22 OCT 1725.
[11] Maryland Calendar of Wills, Vol. V, p. 204, will of John Garner, dated 7 MAR 1723/4, prov. 22 OCT 1725.

F15. FRANCIS ALEXANDER, b. c.1715 in New Castle Co., Del., m., perhaps secondly[1] on 12 MAR 1776 to Eleanor Simonton of "White Clay Creek Hundred," served in the Rev. War, and signed 29 JUN 1778 as the fourth on the certified list of persons who have taken the oath of fidelity before Thomas James, Esquire.[2] He resided in Cecil Co., Md. where his will was dated 18 JAN 1781, prov. 9 APR 1781 in Pencader Hundred of New Castle Co., Del.[3] Eleanor's will, dated 12 JAN 1807, was filed in New Castle Co., Del.[4] Children, order uncertain:[5]

F151. BENJAMIN ALEXANDER, b. 1758 in Elkton, Cecil Co., Md., d. after 1819 near Wilmington, Del., m. 17 MAR 1803 in Cecil Co., Md. to Rebekah Woodland McClure. He was a private in the Rev. War, serving with Capt. Isaac Lewis' Company.[6]

F152. WILLIAM ALEXANDER, b. 21 APR 1759 in New Castle Co., Del., m. by Rev. John Murray on 11 MAR 1779 to Jane (Throckmorton?) Alexander, b. 24 OCT 1748. William was guardian to his brother Jesse Alexander. William left a will dated 23 SEP 1836, prov. 10 AUG 1840 in Centre Co., Pa. William d. 3 AUG 1840, bur. Old Unionville Cem. nr. Unionville, Centre Co., Pa.[7] Jane d. 30 JUN 1825 aged 76y 8m 6d, bur. Old Unionville Cem. Four known children.[8]

F153. FRANCES "Fanny" ALEXANDER, m. John Aiken who was declared administrator of the estate of Francis Alexander.[9]

F154. MARY ALEXANDER, m. John Bouldin.

F155. ISAAC ALEXANDER, m. Jane Steele, d. 1785 in New Castle Co., Del. Isaac left a will dated 6 SEP 1784, prov. 17 DEC 1785 there in Pencader Hundred.[10] Jane (sometimes Jean), was a daughter of Margaret *of Pencader Hundred in New Castle Co. Del.*, and left a will dated 12 FEB 1795, prov. 10 MAR 1795 in Cecil Co., Md.,[11] wit. Samuel Ireland and Nicholas Chambers. The will of Margaret Steele dated 23 SEP 1780, prov. 2 OCT 1780 in New Castle Co., Del., men. dau. Jane Alexander and son-in-law Isaac Alexander. Six known children.

F156. JESSE ALEXANDER, made a ward of his brother William Alexander on 5 APR 1785 [perhaps in Cecil Co., Md.].

F157. SUSANNA ALEXANDER, b. 1779, m. "Hance" Hanson, was under the guardianship of Andrew Foster when her father died.[12]

F2. Martin Alexander
(1687-1751)

Martin Alexander, son of Samuel Alexander and Mary Taylor, was born March 18, 1687 in Annemessix, Somerset County, Maryland. He is believed to have married more than once, but the known wife is Susannah Foster, daughter of James Foster and Elizabeth Bouldin[13] of *Jones Green Spring* plantation in Maryland.[14] The plantation adjoined *Knowlwood*, a large plantation exchanged many times by the Alexander Family. Martin Alexander witnessed the will left by James Foster dated April 12, 1748 which named daughter Susannah Foster.[15] James and Elizabeth Foster were buried in Huntersville, North Carolina.

Martin is known to have had two properties; his *Sligo* estate, and the *Alexandria* estate[16] in Cecil County, Maryland, which in part he received from his father on September 1, 1723.[17] Martin wrote a will dated March 18, 1750 in Cecil County, which was proved August 16, 1751.[18]

---

[1] Butterworth, states that he m. (1) to Martha Blair.
[2] Edward Webb Cooch, Battle of Cooch's Bridge, p. 109.
[3] New Castle Co., Del. Wills, Bk. L, p. 229.
[4] New Castle Co., Del. Wills, Bk. Q, p. 37.
[5] D.A.R. Library, Grandfather Papers, Index.
[6] Delaware Archives, Vol. 3, p. 109.
[7] New Munster, subject filing case, at the Maryland Historical Society, Baltimore, Md.
[8] History of Centre County, Pennsylvania, p. 174.
[9] New Castle Co., Del. Orphans Court, Bk. F, p. 246.
[10] New Castle Co., Del. Wills, Bk. M, p. 162, admin. by Peter Williams.
[11] Cecil Co., Md. Wills, Bk. FF6, p. 17.
[12] Cooch, p. 257.
[13] Maryland Wills, Liber 25, fol. 339, will of James Foster, dated 12 APR 1748, mentions the his wife's uncle, James Boulding.
[14] Frances Alexander Butterworth, Alexander Family (Chicago, Ill., 1909), p. 20.
[15] Maryland Wills, Liber 25, fol. 339, will of James Foster, dated 12 APR 1748, prov. 10 MAY 1748.
[16] Mrs. Ralph W. Van Valin, History of James Alexander. Martin Alexander and Francis Alexander patented the tract Alexandria on 4 NOV 1732.
[17] Cecil Co., Md. Deeds, Bk. 4, p. 75.
[18] Cecil Co., Md. Wills, Bk. 2, p. 106; Maryland Wills, Liber 28, fol. 155.

Possible children of Martin Alexander, order uncertain:

F21. AARON ALEXANDER,[1] SR., b. c.1711 in Pocomoke, Worcester Co., Md., m. (1) Eleanor (   );[2] (2) Jean Brown Ross, widow of Isaac Ross, b. 1713 in Pocomoke, d. 1766; m. (3) Mary (   ), d. post 1771. Aaron d. c.1772 in Mecklenburg Co., N.C., as his will on file there is dated 15 NOV 1771, prov. 1772.[3] Known children:[4]

    F211. AARON ALEXANDER, JR., b. 1761 in Pocomoke, d. testate c.1806 in Mecklenburg Co., N.C.[5]

    F212. DANIEL [or David] ALEXANDER, b. 1763 in Pocomoke, d. testate 1776 in Mecklenburg Co., N.C., m. Prudence Alexander, d. 25 MAR 1776 in Cabarrus Co., N.C. Seven known children.

    F213. JOHN BROWN ALEXANDER, b. 1765 in Pocomoke, m. 1 AUG 1786 to Barbara King, of Scotland.

F22. DAVID ALEXANDER, SR., b. Pocomoke, served in the Rev. War, m. to Elizabeth Caldwell. David d. in Mecklenburg Co., N.C., where his will was dated 31 MAY 1796.[6] He inherited half the plantation where his father lived when he wrote his will in 1750. Children:

    F221. JOEL ALEXANDER, d. before 1833 in Rutherford Co., Tenn.

    F222. THOMAS ALEXANDER, unlocated by 1796.

    F223. DAVID ALEXANDER, JR., b. 25 DEC 1772 in Cecil Co., Md., m. (1) Ann Caldwell, rem. to N.C., m. (2) in 1811 to Mary Frances Rankin, rem. to Ky. where he died c.1833. Thirteen known children.

    F224. ISAAC ALEXANDER, in Ala. in 1794. Seven known children.[7]

    F225. EPHRAIM ALEXANDER, believed to have married twice, removed to Knoxville, Tenn.

    F226. MARY ALEXANDER, removed to Rutherford Co., Tenn. m. (1) _____ Haley, m. (2) _____ Burke.

    F227. SARAH ALEXANDER, b. 1774 in Cecil Co., Md., d. 23 JAN 1869, bur. Alexander Cem. of Crescent, Rutherford Co., Tenn., m. 14 AUG 1800 in Mecklenburg Co., N.C. to her first cousin (F231.) DANIEL ALEXANDER, son of James and Anna (   ) Alexander, q.v. One known child.[8]

    F228. FRANCES "Fanny" ALEXANDER, m. her cousin James Alexander, removed to Rutherford Co., Tenn. Two known children.

    F229. JAMES ALEXANDER, men. in his father's 1796 will.

F23. JAMES ALEXANDER, b. 1724, m. Anna (   ), received £20 in his father's 1751 will. Child:

    F231. DANIEL ALEXANDER, b. 23 JAN 1773 in Md., founded the town of Alexandria, Tenn., d. 20 OCT 1857 in Rutherford Co., Tenn., bur. in Alexander Family Cem. at Crescent, Tenn., m. 14 AUG 1800 in Mecklenburg Co., N.C. to his first cousin (F227.) SARAH ALEXANDER, daughter of David Alexander and Elizabeth Caldwell, rem. to Murfreesboro, Tenn.

F24. AMOS ALEXANDER, b. 1738 in Cecil Co., Md., d. 7 DEC 1813 in Mecklenburg Co., N.C., bur. Baker Family Cem. near Gilead Associate Reformed Presbyterian Church of Huntersville, Iredell Co., N.C., m. 1771 in Cecil Co., Md. to Susannah Johnston who died after 1813, as her will is filed in Mecklenburg Co., N.C.,[9] and was buried at Baker Cem. Amos Alexander served in the Rev. War, for Salisbury Dist. of N.C. He lived 4½ miles from Beattie's Ford. His will was filed 7 DEC 1813.[10] Children:

    F241. MARY ALEXANDER, b. 1780, d. 1830, m. Eli Conger, b. 1775, d. 1834 in Butts Co., Ga. Six known children.

    F242. JOSIAH MARTIN ALEXANDER, d. intestate. One known child.

    F243. EPHRAIM K. ALEXANDER, b. 25 JAN 1783, d. 2 JAN 1847 in Hickman Co., Tenn., m. Margaret Price.

    F244. ELI ALEXANDER, b. 6 DEC 1784 in Mecklenburg Co., N.C., left a will there,[11] d. 26 JUL 1834 in Mecklenburg Co., N.C., bur. Gillead A.R.P. Church Cem. of Huntersville, N.C., m. 21 DEC 1808 there to Margaret C. Alcorn (bondsman Ephraim Alexander), daughter of John and Rebecca Alcorn, b. 5 FEB 1786 in Ireland, d. 3 AUG 1873 in Mecklenburg Co., N.C., bur. Gilead A.R.P. Church Cem. Nine known children.[12]

    F245. REBECCA ALEXANDER, m. _____ Oils.

    F246. EZEKIEL ALEXANDER. One known child.

---

[1] Some researchers have placed this Aaron Alexander as the son of David Alexander (d. c.1740).
[2] Mecklenburg Co., N.C. Deeds, #2719, p. 312, Elinor relict of Aaron deeds 212 acres to James Alexander.
[3] Mecklenburg Co., N.C. Wills, Bk. A, p. 10.
[4] LDS family group sheet, as submitted by Miss Sidney Meeker of Jackson, Tenn.
[5] Mecklenburg Co., N.C. Wills, Bk. A, p. 50.
[6] Mecklenburg Co., N.C. Wills, Bk. A, p. 41.
[7] Butterworth, p. 15.
[8] Alexander Kin, Vol. 2, p. 378.
[9] Mecklenburg Co., N.C. Wills, Bk. A, p. 63.
[10] Mecklenburg Co., N.C. Wills, Bk. A, p. 63.
[11] Mecklenburg Co., N.C. Wills, Bk. G, p. 181.
[12] Genealogy of James Alexander, Pennsylvania G.R.C. (1982), at D.A.R. Library, Washington, D.C.

F247. MINTY [or Araminta] ALEXANDER.
F25. REBECCA ALEXANDER, m. Thomas Morgan, b. Bucks Co., Pa., rem. to Orange Co., N.C., then to Savannah, Ga. where he died in 1778. Four known children, including:
F251. NANCY MORGAN, m. Benjamin Hart.
F26. ELI ALEXANDER, of tract *Bullen's Range*, b. 1717, d. April 1785 in Cecil Co., Md., m. Tamazon Ford, daughter of Richard B. Ford. Tamazon d. c.1823 in Cecil Co., Md. In his father's 1751 will, Eli inherited lands purchased from Thomas Stratton. Eli left a will dated 31 MAR 1785 in Cecil Co., prov. 26 APR 1785, wit. Jeremiah Taylor, Isaac Taylor, and William Price, Jr.[1] Tamazon left a will dated 5 DEC 1822, prov. 25 JAN 1823, wit. Benjamin Pearce, Sr., William Boulden and Margaret Pearce.[2] Children:
F261. JOSIAH ALEXANDER, inherited tract *Bullen's Range* by his father's 1785 will.
F262. RICHARD FORD ALEXANDER. In 1793, he was a gentleman of New Castle Co., Del., and sold for £175 to Richard Harding, of Elkton, Md., a part of *Hispaniola* and *Bullen's Range* which he had inherited from his father.[3] About 1799 he res. in Casho Co., N.C.
F263. HARMON ALEXANDER, b. c.1773 in St. Stephens Parish of Cecil Co., Md., d. testate[4] OCT 1826 in York Co., S.C., served in the War of 1812, m. Catherine J. (   ), will dated 11 MAY 1844, prov. 10 DEC 1844.[5] By his father's 1785 will he inherited all land purchased of Caleb Alexander which was part of *Knowlwoods*, rem. 1799 to Casho Co., N.C. Six children mentioned in his will.
F264. LEVI ALEXANDER.
F265. JEREMIAH ALEXANDER, b. 4 JUL 1763 in Md., res. Morgan Co., Ala. bet. 1832-3, served in the Rev. War,[6] d. 26 JAN 1847 in Walker Co., Ala., bur. Old Zion Cem. of Jasper, Ala.
F266. HEZEKIAH ALEXANDER.
F267. ARAMINTA ALEXANDER, m. 12 MAR 1795 by William Duke in Cecil Co., Md. to Thomas Beedle.
F268. SUSANNAH ALEXANDER, b. c.1736.
F269. LYDIA ALEXANDER, b. c.1740.
F26(10). STEPHEN ALEXANDER.
F27. JOSIAH ALEXANDER, m. Elizabeth (   ), d. Mecklenburg Co., N.C., left a will dated 28 JUN 1776,[7] wit. George Ross, Jean Braden and Rebecca Morgan, with his brother Aaron Alexander as executor. Children:
F271. JOSIAH ALEXANDER, inherited his father's plantation.
F272. DEBORAH ALEXANDER.
F273. ALEXANDER ALEXANDER.
F274. MARY ALEXANDER.
F275. ELIZABETH ALEXANDER.
F276. SQUIRE ALEXANDER.
F28. SARAH ALEXANDER, b. 1733 in Cecil Co., Md., d. 1813 in Cabarrus Co., N.C., m. her cousin (F13.) MOSES ALEXANDER, son of James Alexander and Mary Steele, *q.v.*
F29. MOSES ALEXANDER, b. poss. 1737 in Pocomoke, Md., d. 1781 in N.C., m. Jane Taylor, served in the Rev. War as a private for N.C. In his father's 1750 will, Moses inherited land in New Castle Co., Del., provided he pay his brother Aaron Alexander £15 at age 21.

F4. Francis Alexander
(1693-1760)

Francis Alexander, son of Samuel Alexander and Mary Taylor of Somerset County, Maryland, was born there on March 28, 1693 in Annemessix, Somerset County, Maryland.[8] He was a weaver, as claimed in his will dated August 27, 1760, that was recorded in Frederick County, Maryland,[9] as witnessed by John Ralston, John Hart and John Agnew.[10]

---

[1] Cecil Co., Md. Wills, Bk. EE5, p. 55.
[2] Cecil Co., Md. Wills, Bk. A8, p. 104.
[3] Butterworth, p. 38.
[4] York Co., S.C. Wills, Bk. G, p. 215; Case 7, file 76.
[5] York Co., S.C. Wills, Bk. 3, p. 107; Case 1, file 1205.
[6] National Archives, Revolutionary War Pensions, File #S31515.
[7] Mecklenburg Co., N.C. Wills, Bk. A, p. 11.
[8] Somerset Co., Md. Records, Liber IKL.
[9] Frederick Co., Md. Wills, Bk. A1, p. 143; Maryland Wills, Liber 31, fol. 130.
[10] Maryland Wills, Original Wills, Box 2, folder 25.

Francis married Jean [or Jane] (   ),[1] and is known to have owned property tracts named *Carroll's Delight* in Frederick County, Maryland, and *Alexandria* in Cecil County, Maryland. Jean [or Jane] died July 12, 1771 in Frederick County, Maryland, or just over the state line in what is now Adams County, Pennsylvania. Both Francis and Jean are buried in Lower Marsh Creek graveyard, Adams County.

Francis was executor of his brother James Alexander's will, dated July 12, 1717,[2] and his name is found in various court and land records of Cecil County, Maryland as late as January 1734. In September 1754, he executed power of attorney to his brother Andrew Alexander[3] to sell his land *Francis' Marsh* on Long Creek. He described his residence as *Carroll's Delight* near Marsh Creek in the County of York, Province of Pennsylvania.

Known children of Francis Alexander and Jean/Jane (   ), order uncertain:

F41.   HANNAH ALEXANDER, m. William Blair, as indicated her father's will in Frederick Co., Md.[4]
F42.   JOHN ALEXANDER, a soldier of the Rev. War, b. 1733 in Pa., d. c.1814 in Knox Co., Tenn., m. before 1765 to Agnes Craighead, daughter of Rev. Alexander Craighead, rem. from either Lancaster, Pa. or Rockbridge Co., Va. where Rev. Craighead was preaching, to res. 1783 on Big Limestone Creek, now Washington Co., Tenn. His sister Naomi and husband followed. In his father's 1760 will, John received the works of authors Homer and Nero, and all his father's tobacco. Children:[5]
    F421.   AGNES ALEXANDER, m. L.E. Newton.
    F422.   FRANCIS ALEXANDER, m. Jane Adair.
    F423.   MARY ALEXANDER, m. Adam Rankin.
    F424.   RHODA ALEXANDER, b. 1758, d. 1823, m. 20 MAR 1793 in Washington Co. TN to James Rodgers, b. 1758, d. 1817; both bur. Lebanon-in-the-Forks Cem., Knox Co., Tenn.
    F425.   JOHN ALEXANDER, m. 16 MAR 1792 in Greene Co., Tenn. to Thurzy Bridges.
    F426.   JACOB ALEXANDER, m. Mary Trotter.
    F427.   HANNAH ALEXANDER, b. c.1768, d. 13 JUL 1822 at Cotton Port, Limestone Co., Ala., bur. Hayden Cem., New Hope, Madison Co., Ala., m. 26 MAR 1791 in Washington Co., Tenn. to William DeWoody, b. 1754 in Ire., d. 1818, bur. Hayden Cem. Eight children.
    F428.   AMELIA ALEXANDER, m. 13 FEB 1796 in Washington Co., Tenn. to Benjamin McNutt, bur. McNutt Family Cem. near Knoxville, Tenn.
    F429.   ELIZABETH BROWN ALEXANDER, b. c.1772, d. 16 NOV 1865 at Greenville, Tenn., bur. Old City Cem. there, m. 10 SEP 1801 in Washington Co., Tenn. to Joseph Rogers Brown, b. 9 AUG 1767, d. 1 NOV 1845; both bur. Old Harmony graveyard of Greene Co., Tenn.
    F42(10).   TABITHA ALEXANDER, b. c.1777, d. 19 MAR 1844 at Greenville, Tenn., m. 6 OCT 1806 in Greene Co., Tenn. to Joel Dryden, b. 1774, d. 1825; both bur. Old Harmony graveyard of Greene Co., Tenn.
    F42(11).   DAVID ALEXANDER, m. Margaret Brown.
F43.   NAOMI EMMA "Emmie" ALEXANDER, b. 13 DEC 1736, d. 10 SEP 1813, bur. Lebanon-in-the-Fork Presbyterian Church Cem. of Knox Co., Tenn.,[6] m. 24 SEP 1761 to Reynolds Ramsey, b. 24 OCT 1736 [in Ireland, Scotland (or New Castle Co., Del. as on tombstone)], d. MAR 1816, bur. Lebanon-in-the-Fork Presbyterian Church Cem. Reynolds Ramsey reportedly fought in the French and Indian War in 1755[7] and served with Gen. Washington at Trenton and Princeton during the Rev. War [tombstone]. After marriage the couple rem. to York Co. (now Adams), Pa., six or eight miles west of Gettysburg, and erected a merchant mill on Marsh Creek, later known as Millers Town.[8] After their sons had left Pennsylvania, they sold the mills and moved to Gettysburg which had been founded by Samuel Gettys, who was first married to Reynolds Ramsey's sister Isabella.[9] About 1808 they moved to Knox Co., Tenn., and lived first near Ebenezer Church of which their son Samuel Graham Ramsey was pastor, later moving to Swan Pond near Knoxville, Tenn. where the Ramsey House is currently restored and open to the public. Children:
    F431.   FRANCIS ALEXANDER RAMSEY, b. 31 MAY 1764 near Gettysburg, Pa., d. of malaria on 5 NOV 1820 in Knoxville, Tenn., m. (1) 7 APR 1789 to his cousin (G192.) MARGARET ALEXANDER, b. 3 APR 1766, d. of consumption on 7 JUL 1805 at Swan Pond, eldest daughter of John McKnitt Alexander and Jane

[1] Author Worth Ray in his Tennessee Cousins, p. 217, suggests Francis was first married to Martha Blair. That Francis Alexander was son of Samuel Alexander's brother James Alexander.
[2] New Castle Co., Del. Wills, Bk. C1, p. 103.
[3] Cecil Co., Md. Deeds, Bk. 8, p. 312.
[4] Frederick Co., Md. Wills, Bk. A1, p. 143, William Blair was an executor of the 1760 will of Francis Alexander.
[5] Alexander Kin, Vol. 2, pp. 406-7.
[6] Jeannette Tillotson Acklen, Tennessee Records (1976), p. 135.
[7] William S. Jarnagin, A Genealogical Chart of the Alexander-Ramsay/Ramsey Family of Scotland & America (Concord, Mass.: Walden Press, 1976).
[8] Willie Reeves Hardin Bivins, The Family of Reynolds Ramsey (Oklahoma City, 1987), p. 1.
[9] Bivins, p. 1.

Bean [or Bain] of Mecklenburg Co., N.C., *q.v. Francis Alexander Ramsey arrived on the western border of N.C. in 1783. His uncle, John Alexander, had invited him to come live with them on Big Limestone Creek, in present-day upper East Tennessee. He was then 19 years old, well educated, and had with him his horse, surveyor's chain and compass. In August 1783, he went with Robert Love, James White and others on a journey to explore the French Broad River to its junction with the Holston and on down the Tennessee River to where it joined the Little Tennessee. They were looking for good places to locate in the unexplored wilderness. James White chose the spot where he later founded Knoxville; F.A. Ramsey entered a claim for land at the junction of the French Broad and Holston Rivers, planning to build there later. In October of 1783 he entered 400 acres on the Big and Little Limestone creeks and was appointed surveyor of Washington County. Soon after he was married and set up house on his 400-acre tract on Little Limestone, near Jonesboro in Washington Co., N.C. (later in TN). After removing to Knox Co. in 1792 and being appointed by Gov. Blount as Clerk of Superior Court of the Hamilton District, F.A. Ramsey built a log home on his land near the fork of the Holston and Tennessee rivers and called it "Swan Pond." He later had the pond drained and built a stone home.* F.A. Ramsey m. (2) in AUG 1806 to Mrs. Ann Agnew Fleming, d. DEC 1816, daughter of Judge Agnew, m. (3) on 3 APR 1820 to Mrs. Margaret Christian Russell Cowan Humes, b. 15 JUN 1777, d. 10 APR 1854, daughter of Andrew Russell and Margaret Christian, grand-daughter of Gen. William Christian and Mary Campbell. Her first husband was James Cowan, d. 1801, and she m. 1802 to Thomas Humes, d. 1816.[1] Seven known children.[2]

F432. JOHN RAMSEY, d.y.

F433. WILLIAM RAMSEY, believed to have d. in Ga. c.1826, m. Martha Ochiltree,[3] line sketched forward in Bivins, pp. 37-39.

F434. SAMUEL GRAHAM RAMSEY, b. 20 OCT 1771 in York Co. (now Adams), Pa., d. of hemorrhage of the lungs which terminated in dropsy, 5 JUL 1817 in Knox Co., Tenn., a minister and educator of Knox County, m. 24 FEB 1797 to Elizabeth Christian Fleming Allen, widow of Rev. Carey Allen, daughter of Gen. William Fleming.

F435. AMELIA NAOMI RAMSEY, b. York Co. (now Adams), Pa., d. from convulsions resulting from childbirth about a year after her second marriage, bur. Ebenezer Churchyard, m. (1) James King, rem. to Knox Co., Tenn., m. (2) (   ) Taylor.[4]

F44. MARY ALEXANDER, m. by 1748 to _____ Boulden [or Boulding], inherited the book "Saints Everlasting Rest" by Mr. Richard Baxter in her father's 1760 will.

F45. PHEBE ALEXANDER, m. by 1748 to _____ Patton, inherited the works of Bishop Hopkins in her father's 1760 will.

F46. MARK ALEXANDER.

F47. ISAAC ALEXANDER, rem. to Washington Co., Tenn.

F48. ISABELLA ALEXANDER, m. _____ Patton.

F49. JACOB ALEXANDER, yeoman, of Cecil Co., Md., d. by 24 MAY 1748 when his estate inventory was filed by his widow,[5] m. on 20 FEB 1744 in New Castle Co., Del. to Rebecca Booth. Child:

F491. CALEB ALEXANDER, b. c.1747 (age 2 in 1749), d. after 1784 in Cecil Co., Md.[6]

F6. Andrew Alexander
(1696-1782)

Andrew Alexander, son of Samuel Alexander and Mary Taylor of Somerset County, Maryland, was born 1697 in Pocomoke, Maryland. He was an attorney, and may have married (1) his cousin (C63.) JEAN McKNITT, daughter of John McKnitt and Jane Wallace. To support the opinion that Andrew's wife was Jean McKnitt one may consider the purchase on June 14, 1745 by Andrew Alexander of land tract *Glasgow* from John McKnitt III that had been part of the lands of John McKnitt, Sr. in Cecil County, Maryland.[7] Andrew is known to have married Sarah (   ), and died in 1782 in Mecklenburg County, North Carolina.

His will was proved May 29, 1782 in Mecklenburg County,[8] as witnessed by Zaccs. Wilson, Edward Giles and Abram Alexander.

---

[1] Bivins, pp. 3-4.
[2] Ray, p. 217; Bivins, pp.3-4.
[3] Hesseltine, p. 2.
[4] Bivins, p. 86.
[5] Maryland Inventories and Accounts, Liber 40, fol. 221. Next of kin are Phebey Patton and Mary Boulden.
[6] Cecil Co., Md. Land Commissions, Bk. 3, p. 30.
[7] Cecil Co., Md. Deeds, Bk. 6, p. 480.
[8] Mecklenburg Co., N.C. Wills, Bk. A, p. 37.

Children of Andrew Alexander:

F61.   JOHANNA ALEXANDER, received one cow and calf in her father's 1782 will.
F62.   MOSES ALEXANDER, b. 8 MAR 1739, lived on Mallard Creek near Hopewell Church in Mecklenburg Co., N.C., m. Martha Kirkham/Kirkman, b. 24 DEC 1751. In his father's 1782 will, Moses received a smooth boar gun, a book called "Ambrous Looking to Jesus," and a share in his father's stile and crosscut saw. Children:[1]

    F621.   ANDREW ALEXANDER, b. 14 OCT 1770, m. Prudence Alexander, daughter of James Alexander, granddaughter of Daniel Alexander.
    F622.   AMBROSE ALEXANDER, b. 4 AUG 1772, likely in Cabarrus Co., N.C., d. testate on 1 FEB 1843 in Cape Girardeau Co., Mo., bur. Pleasant Hill Cem., m. 15 AUG 1806 in Cabarrus Co., N.C., to Ellen Query, daughter of Alexander Query and Peggy McCord. Eight known children.
    F623.   MOSES ALEXANDER, b. 30 DEC 1774, m. (1) 28 JAN 1800 in Mecklenburg Co., N.C. to Elizabeth Orr, daughter of Nathan Orr, and m. (2) to Matilda McCaleb.
    F624.   SIDNEY ALEXANDER (twin), b. 29 AUG 1777, m. 7 DEC 1799 in Cabarrus Co., N.C. to Robert Query.
    F625.   URIAH ALEXANDER (twin), b. 29 AUG 1777, m. 18 JAN 1804 in Cabarrus Co., N.C. to Nancy Query, rem. to Tenn.
    F626.   HEZEKIAH ALEXANDER, b. 1779.
    F627.   JAMES ALEXANDER, b. 2 FEB 1780, killed as a boy.
    F628.   BENJAMIN ALEXANDER, b. 18 MAY 1784, d. testate[2] 17 MAR 1861, m. 27 JUN 1808 in Cabarrus Co., N.C. to Mary "Polly" Alexander, d. 12 JUL 1853, aged 68y, daughter of Stephen Alexander. Eleven known children.[3]
    F629.   [WILLIAM] ABNER ALEXANDER, b. 27 NOV 1786, d. testate 30 MAY 1868, aged 81y 7m 3d, elder of Mallard Creek Presby. Church, will 23 NOV 1865,[4] m. 9 SEP 1811 in Cabarrus Co., N.C. to Elizabeth Monteith, from Ireland, d. 11 JAN 1871. Four known children.
    F62(10).   AMZI ALEXANDER, b. 1788, m. 16 APR 1806 to Martha Robinson.
    F62(11).   EZRA ALEXANDER, b. 19 JUN 1792, d. of small pox as infant.
F63.   BENJAMIN ALEXANDER, in his father's 1782 will, received a rifle and a pot.
F64.   ANDREW ALEXANDER, of Coddle Creek, N.C., inherited his father's plantation. Perhaps he was the same Andrew Alexander who was b. 14 MAR 1749, d. 25 FEB 181?, and was first m. to his cousin Margaret Alexander (23 APR 1759-12 DEC 1790), and m. (2) to Mary Patterson, b. 9 AUG 1752.[5] If this is true, the following children:

    F641.   MATTHEW ALEXANDER, b. 23 FEB 1779.
    F642.   SOLOMON ALEXANDER, b. 7 AUG 1782, d. 10 JUN 1787.
    F643.   MAYBEN ALEXANDER, b. 29 OCT 1788.
    F644.   JAMES MADISON ALEXANDER, b. 4/12 JUN 1790, d. 28 SEP 1852/9, m. (1) 30 OCT 1825 to Prudence Cole, b. 22 MAR 1805, d. 16 MAY 1840, m. (2) Martha (   ), b. 9 JUN 1804. Nine known children.
    F645.   MARGARET ALEXANDER, b. 15 NOV 1792.
    F646.   AMZI C. ALEXANDER, b. 10 NOV 1795.
    F647.   ANDREW ALEXANDER, b. 15 SEP 1797.
    F648.   WASHINGTON ALEXANDER, b. 25 DEC 1799.
    F649.   NELSON G. ALEXANDER, b. 25 MAY 1802.
F65.   ISAAC ALEXANDER, of Mecklenburg Co., N.C.

[1] J.E. Flow, Alexander Family, at D.A.R. Library, Washington, D.C.
[2] Cabarrus Co., N.C. Wills, Bk. 2, p. 90.
[3] Alexander Kin, Vol. 2, p. 399.
[4] Mecklenburg Co., N.C. Wills, Bk. J, p. 255.
[5] Stripes (Texas Genealogical Quarterly), Vol. VI-2, June 1966.

G. JOSEPH ALEXANDER
(c. 1659-c.1730)

Joseph Alexander, was born c.1659 in Raphoe Parish, County Donegal, Ireland, thought to be a son of William Alexander of Eredy, County Donegal, Ireland. One family tradition was that he came to America on the ship *Welcome* in 1679.[1]

He was known as "Joseph, the tanner" as he referred to himself in his will dated December 17, 1725, filed December 30, 1726, which was proved March 9, 1730 in Cecil County, Maryland. The will was witnessed by Ann Taylor, widow, "Irish" John Dale, and John [McKnitt] (Jr.).[2]

On May 14, 1714, Joseph Alexander purchased property in the *O'Dwire Tract* on the Big Elk River in Cecil County, Maryland from Thomas Stevenson. Because the tract was referred to as "New Munster," Joseph became known as the progenitor of the "New Munster Alexanders."

He was first married c.1675 in Somerset County, Maryland to Jane McKnitt, born c.1653 in Ireland, died by March 1729/30 in Chester County, Pennsylvania (formerly part of the New Munster Tract in Cecil County, Maryland), daughter of John McKnitt and Elizabeth Wallace. Joseph Alexander married second to Abigail McKnitt, sister of his first wife. The McKnitt Family was closely related to the Alexanders of New Munster, as well as to the family when they migrated to Mecklenburg County, North Carolina.

Known children of Joseph Alexander and his first wife Jane McKnitt:

G1.   SOPHIA ALEXANDER, b. 26 FEB 1680 in Somerset Co., Md., d. after 13 DEC 1726 in Slate Hill, Cecil Co., Md. (now in Lancaster Co., Pa.), m. her paternal 1st cousin (B2.) ELIAS ALEXANDER, son of Andrew Alexander and Ann Taylor, *q.v.*

G2.   FRANCIS ALEXANDER, b. c.1689, d. 1781 in Mecklenburg Co., N.C.

G3.   JANE ALEXANDER, b. c.1691, m. Alexander McCoy, as indicated in her father's will.

G4.   ABIGAIL ALEXANDER, b. c.1693, d. 1781 in Mecklenburg Co., N.C., m. Francis Clapham, as indicated in her father's will.

+   G5.   JAMES ALEXANDER, yeoman, b. c.1695 in Cecil Co., Md., m. (1) to (C61.) MARGARET McKNITT, daughter of John McKnitt and Jane Wallace, had land in Mecklenburg Co., N.C., d. 1779 in Cecil Co., Md., see below.

G5. James Alexander
(c.1695-1779)

James Alexander, yeoman, son of Joseph Alexander "the tanner" and yeoman, was born c.1695 in Manokin Hundred of Cecil County, Maryland. About 1713, he married Margaret McKnitt, daughter of John McKnitt and Jane Wallace, who was reportedly born December 26, 1693 in Manokin, Somerset County, Maryland,[3] and was dead by 1745. By 1746, he married secondly to Abigail (   ).

I have found it said that he was one of his Lordship's justices in 1723, and a coronet in a troop commanded by Capt. Thomas Johnson in 1740.[4] It has been said he was a ruling elder of the New Castle Presbyterian Church in 1725,[5] and frequently after that in those of the Synod of Philadelphia.[6] In a deed dated August 22, 1740, James Alexander, a farmer of Cecil County, and his sister Sophia Alexander, sold a 184-acre tract (the same which his father Joseph had purchased in 1718 from Thomas Stevenson).[7]

James Alexander's will was dated June 17, 1772 in Cecil County, Maryland, where it was proved May 31, 1779.[8] In it he made clear that he was a property owner in Mecklenburg County, North Carolina. He served in the Revolutionary War.[9] We note here too that because the state line of Pennsylvania changed in 1732, it is often difficult to provide accurate locations for events for this family.

---

[1] Alexander Kin, Vol. 1, p. 8.
[2] Cecil Co., Md. Wills, Bk. CC3, p. 23; Maryland Wills, Liber 20, fol. 235.
[3] Letter, Bob Cooney, January 1986.
[4] Delaware G.R.C., 1952, Vol. 4, p. 64, at D.A.R. Library, Washington, D.C.
[5] Ray, Mecklenburg Signers.
[6] S.A. Perry, Alexander Family Records, undated and unreferenced manuscript at the Denver Public Library, Denver, Colo.
[7] Cecil Co., Md. Deeds, Bk. 6, p. 16.
[8] Cecil Co., Md. Wills, Bk. CC3, p. 100.
[9] Parran, p. 59.

Known children of James Alexander and his first wife Margaret McKnitt:[1]

G11.   THEOPHILUS ALEXANDER, a blacksmith, b. 13 MAR 1714/5 in Cecil Co., Md., d. 7 AUG 1768 in Cecil Co.,[2] bur. Head of Christiana Church Cem. near Newark, Del., m. Catharine Wallace. After he died, Catherine rem. to North Carolina, d. 1775, as her will was dated 20 JUL 1775 and filed in Mecklenburg Co.[3] Theophilus Alexander's will was dated 20 FEB 1768, proved 19 AUG 1768, by which he left his wife Catherine the sum of £120. Children, order uncertain:

    G111.   (Rev.) JOSEPH ALEXANDER, inherited £20 and his father's land in North Carolina, m. Martha Davies, rem. to Bullocks Creek, S.C.

    G112.   MARGARET [Ann] ALEXANDER, received £10 in her father's 1768 will, d. 1802, bur. Hopewell Presbyterian Church Cem., Mecklenburg Co., N.C., m. James Cannon, b. 1731, d. testate 8 SEP 1784.

    G113.   SOPHIA ALEXANDER, received £7 in her father's 1768 will, m. John Sharp.[4] Children:
        G1131. ARAMINTA SHARP.
        G1132. LEVINA SHARP.

    G114.   KEZIA ALEXANDER, b. 1740, received £65 in her father's 1768 will, m. 1768 in Elton, Md.[5] to Joseph Young.

    G115.   GEORGE ALEXANDER, inherited his father's plantation which was willed to Theophilus Alexander by his grandfather James Alexander, m. Margaret Harris, left a will of 1776 in Mecklenburg Co., N.C. He was reportedly in the Rev. War. One known son.

    G116.   CATHERINE ALEXANDER, received £65 by her father's 1768 will, m. (G172.) EZEKIEL SHARP, son of James Sharp and Jemima Alexander.

    C117.   ANN [Polly] ALEXANDER, m. Joseph Cannon.

G12.   JEMIMA ALEXANDER, b. 10 FEB 1715/6, d.y. in Cecil Co., Md.

G13.   EDITH ALEXANDER, b. 10 JAN 1718, d.y. in Cecil Co., Md.

G14.   KEZIAH ALEXANDER, b. 9 MAY 1720, d. c.1750/1, bur. in York Co., Pa., m. Walter Sharp.

+ G15.   HEZEKIAH ALEXANDER, b. 13 JAN 1722 in Cecil Co., Md., d. 10 JAN 1801 or 16 JUL 1801, a signer of the Mecklenburg Declaration, m. c.1749 to Mary Sample, daughter of William and Esther Sample.

G16.   EZEKIEL ALEXANDER, b. 17 JAN 1725 in Cecil Co., Md., by the 1772 will he inherited his father's land on Long Creek in Mecklenburg Co., N.C. He may be the same who left a will dated 12 APR 1786 in Onslow Co., N.C., which was proved JUL 1786,[6] and that mentioned wife Esther (   ) who died in 1790, as her will was dated 5 OCT 1790 and proved 14 OCT 1790 in Onslow Co., N.C. Children:

    G161.   JOSEPH ALEXANDER, d. 1789, will dated 14 DEC 1790, filed in Onslow Co., N.C., m. Sarah (   ).

    G162.   ANN ALEXANDER.

    G163.   CATHERINE ALEXANDER.

    G164.   HANNAH ALEXANDER, m. _____ Pickett.

    G165.   MARY ALEXANDER, m. John James.

    G166.   JAMES ALEXANDER.

G17.   JEMIMA ALEXANDER, b. 9 [or 7] JAN 1727 in Cecil Co., Md., m. 1752 to James Sharp of Cecil Co., d. c.1759, son of Thomas (d. 1749) and Isabella Sharp of Cecil Co.[7] She d. 1 SEP 1797 in Mecklenburg Co., N.C. where she was bur. in Sugaw Creek Presbyterian Church Cem. Six children listed in the appendix of the Ferguson Family Genealogy at D.A.R. Library in Washington, D.C.:[8]

    G171.   ISABELLA SHARP, b. 8 JUL 1745, d. 1829, m. 22 DEC 1762 to Rev. Thomas Price, d. 27 APR 1799 in Lincoln Co., N.C., bur. Bethel Cem. of Clover, York Co., S.C.

    G172.   EZEKIEL SHARP, b. 14 JAN 1748, d. 14 JAN 1828 in Wilson Co., Tenn., m. (G116.) CATHERINE ALEXANDER, daughter of Theophilus Alexander, q.v. Children:
        G1721. JEMIMA ALEXANDER SHARP, b. 20 MAY 1781 in Mecklenburg Co., N.C., d. 7 OCT 1825 in Wilson Co., Tenn., q.v., m. 1 DEC 1803 in Wilson Co., Tenn. to (G1(15)3.) ABNER ABRAHAM

---

[1] Also see J.B. Alexander, Biographical Sketches of the Early Settlers of the Hopewell Section (Mecklenburg Co., N.C., 1897). Also Letter from Bob Cooney, Jr., of Nashville, Tenn., dated 15 JAN 1986.
[2] Maryland Wills, Liber 36, fol. 570, will of Theophilus Alexander, dated 20 FEB 1768, proved 19 AUG 1768.
[3] Mecklenburg Co., N.C. Wills, Bk. A, p. 16.
[4] Annapolis, Md. copy of Will Bk. 36, p. 570.
[5] L.D.S., International Genealogical Index.
[6] Onslow Co., N.C. Wills, Bk. L, p. 58.
[7] Ray, Mecklenburg Signers, p. 524, provides the husband of Jemima Alexander as Thomas Sharp, Jr., and gives children as: William Sharp, b. 13 DEC 1742 in Cecil Co., Md., John Sharp, James Sharp, Joseph Sharp, and Samuel Sharp. The Register of Maryland Historic Families gives that Thomas Sharp is a son of John Sharp.
[8] Ingram, p. 312. Letter from Bob Cooney, Jr., Nashville, Tenn., dated 15 JAN 1986.

ALEXANDER, b. 10 AUG 1778 in Cecil Co., Md., d. 1857.

G1722. JOSEPH ALEXANDER FIELDING SHARP.

G173. PRISCILLA SHARP, b. 1 SEP 1750, d. 13 MAY 1838, bur. Centre Presbyterian Church, Iredell Co., N.C., m. Lewis John Jetton, b. 24 JAN 1749, d. 21 SEP 1826. Twelve known children.[1]

G174. JOHN SHARP, b. 28 APR 1753, d. 1 NOV 1824, bur. Sharp Family Cem., Rutherford Co., Tenn., m. Martha Young.

G175. JAMES SHARP, b. 1754, d. 1811, bur. on farm at Stones River, Rutherford Co., Tenn., m. Rachel Cannon. Nine known children.

G176. SARAH SHARP, b. 16 SEP 1755, d. 16 SEP 1794, unmarried, bur. Sugaw Creek Presbyterian Church Cem. in Mecklenburg Co., N.C., *dau. of James and Jemima* on her tombstone.

G18. AMOS ALEXANDER, SR., b. 13 JAN 1728/9 in Cecil Co., Md.,[2] m. c.1750 in Cecil Co. to Sarah Sharp, and d. APR 1780 in Cecil Co. His will dated 15 JUL 1779, was wit. by Robert Willson, William Johnston, Hezekiah South and Joseph Alexander, and proved 8 MAY 1780 in Cecil Co.[3] Sarah, a daughter of James and Jemima Sharp,[4] was b. 1732 in Cecil Co., d. early in 1802 there, buried with husband in Head of Christiana Presbyterian Church, 2 miles from Newark, Del. Sarah left a will dated 26 OCT 1801 which was proved 6 APR 1803, as witnessed by Josiah Alexander and John Scott.[5] Amos was known to be a patriot of the Rev. War,[6] serving as a justice of the peace and a magistrate.[7] Children:

G181. WALTER ALEXANDER, b. 10 APR 1751 in Cecil Co., Md., d. at Valley Forge, Pa. after 11 MAY 1778 when administration papers were initiated for his estate in Cecil Co., m. 1773 to Eleanor Evans, b. 1752 in Cecil Co., daughter of Robert Evans (1711-1755) and Margaret Kirkpatrick, of Milford Hundred. Robert Evans was a son of John Evans (d. 1738) and wife Jean Moore (d. 1751) of West Nottingham Twp., Chester Co., Pa., and Margaret Kirkpatrick was a daughter of John Kirkpatrick of East Nottingham Twp., Chester Co., Pa. Walter Alexander was buried at Head of Christiana Presbyterian Church Cem. One known son, Robert Alexander.

G182. PRISCILLA ALEXANDER, b. 28 MAY 1753, d. FEB 1817, m. (1) in 1774 to her cousin Isaac Alexander, and m. (2) Robert Longwell, b. 1855, d. 1813.

G183. RACHEL ALEXANDER, b. 23 MAY 1755, d. 1817, received £1,600 in her father's will, m. (1) her first cousin Capt. Isaac Alexander, m. (2) _____ Longwell, and removed to Penns Valley, Pa.[8]

G184. JEMIMA ALEXANDER, b. 1757, d. 1840, m. 1778 to Alexander Reed, son of John Reed.

G185. RUTH ALEXANDER, b. 26 MAY 1759, d. 1842, m. c.1779 to Andrew Wallace, of Baltimore, Md., and received £1,400 by her father's 1780 will.

G186. MARY ALEXANDER, b. 6 AUG 1761 in Cecil Co., Md., d. 1 JAN 1820 there, m. 20 FEB 1782 to John Evans, b. 8 MAY 1760 in Cecil Co., d. 3 MAR 1823.[9] She received £1,600 by her father's 1780 will. One known daughter:

G1861. SARAH EVANS, who m. Robert Gallaher.

G187. DORCAS ALEXANDER, b. 23 SEP 1763, d. 1818, m. 8 OCT 1790 in Cecil Co., Md. to Henry McCoy, of Philadelphia, Pa., res. Alexandria, Va. Dorcas received £1,600 by her father's 1780 will.

+ G188. AMOS ALEXANDER, JR., b. c.1762/6 in Cecil Co., Md., removed to Alexandria, Va., married twice.

G189. SARAH ALEXANDER, b. 19 MAY 1769, d. 28 OCT 1827, m. 3 JAN 1793 to Robert Hodgson, of Chester Co., Pa. She received £1,600 by her father's 1780 will.

G18(10). MARK ALEXANDER, b. 13 NOV 1771, d. intestate[10] on 1 OCT 1802 at Elkton, Md. after a severe illness of 24 days,[11] merchant of Alexandria, Va., m. 12 APR 1798 by Rev. Cosden in Cecil Co., Md. to Elizabeth Gilpin, of Cecil Co., rem. to Alexandria, Va.

G18(11). MARGARET GILPIN ALEXANDER (twin), b. 9 JUL 1774, m. 15 MAR 1797 in Cecil Co., Md. to her cousin James Alexander. Margaret received £1,600 by her father's 1780 will.

G18(12). JAMES ALEXANDER (twin), b. 9 JUL 1774, d. 1865, m. Mary Clendenin, of Harford Co., Md.

+ G19. JOHN MCKNITT ALEXANDER, b. 6 JUN 1733 in Cecil Co., Md., d. 10 JUN 1817 in Mecklenburg Co., N.C., bur. Hopewell Presbyterian Church Cem., m. SEP 1762 in Pa. to Jean Bain/Bean/Bane.

G1(10). MARGARET ALEXANDER, b. 6 JUN 1736 in Cecil Co., Md., d.y.

---

[1] See Bible record of the Lewis John Jetton Family, Tennessee State Library and Archives, Nashville, Tenn.

[2] D.A.R. Magazine, Vol. 1952, p. 312.

[3] Cecil Co., Md. Wills, Bk. CC3, p. 141.

[4] Daughter of Thomas Sharp, will prov. 1749, and wife Isabel, per Delaware G.R.C. (1952), Vol. 4, p. 64.

[5] Cecil Co., Md. Wills, Bk. FF6, p. 275.

[6] D.A.R. Magazine (Oct. 1930), pp. 620-2.

[7] Maryland Archives, Vol. 21, p. 249.

[8] G.R.C. (1954), General Lafayette Chapter, p. 77, at D.A.R. Library, Washington, D.C.

[9] D.A.R. membership application, #554025, of Mary L. Rossland Hermanson.

[10] Alexandria, Va. Wills, Bk. A, administration by Elizabeth Alexander, 7 DEC 1802.

[11] Alexandria Advertiser, 4 OCT 1802.

Children of James Alexander and his second wife Abigail (   ):

G1(11).   ELIZABETH ALEXANDER, b. 17 NOV 1746, d. testate on 1 AUG 1822,[1] aged 75y 9m, bur. Hopewell Presbyterian Church Cem. in Mecklenburg Co., N.C., m. 1766 to William A. Sample, d. SEP 1791, aged nearly 55y, bur. Hopewell Presbyterian Church Cem., son of William Sample and Esther Garrison. Children:[2]

    G1(11)1.   ABIGAIL SAMPLE, b. 16 DEC 1763, m. Thomas Dickson [Dixon] who d. 1827 testate in Rutherford Co., Tenn.[3]

    G1(11)2.   ESTHER SAMPLE, b. 17 NOV 1765, d. 25 MAR 1818, m. as 2nd wife of John Carothers, d. testate 28 FEB 1838 in his 83rd year; both bur. in Steel Creek Presbyterian Church Cem. of Charlotte, Mecklenburg Co., N.C.

    G1(11)3.   MARY SAMPLE, b. JUL 1768 in Mecklenburg Co., N.C., d. in N.C., m. her cousin James Alexander.

    G1(11)4.   JAMES SAMPLE, b. 14 FEB 1770 in Mecklenburg Co., N.C., d. testate[4] 7 JAN 1853, bur. Hopewell Presbyterian Church Cem., m. Martha Robison.

    G1(11)5.   JEMIMA SAMPLE, b. FEB 1772 in Mecklenburg Co., N.C., bur. Hopewell Presbyterian Church Cem., m. 15 MAR 1796 to Andrew Berry [or Barry].

    G1(11)6.   ANN SAMPLE, b. JAN 1776 in Mecklenburg Co., N.C., d. 29 MAY 1830, bur. Hopewell Presbyterian Church Cem., m. 4 APR 1804 to John Henderson.

    G1(11)7.   JOSEPH R. SAMPLE, b. NOV 1777 in Mecklenburg Co., N.C., d. testate[5] 4 AUG 1842, bur. Sugaw Creek Presbyterian Church Cem. of Mecklenburg Co., N.C., m. 4 FEB 1801 to Elizabeth Robison.

    G1(11)8.   JANE BAIN SAMPLE, b. 7 JAN 1780 in Mecklenburg Co., N.C., d. 20 MAY 1850 in Bartow Co., Ga., m. 22 DEC 1803 to Andrew Moore. Nine children.

G1(12).   ABIGAIL ALEXANDER, b. 24 MAY 1748, d. 23 SEP 1817, bur. at Hopewell Presbyterian Church Cem., Mecklenburg Co., N.C., m. Capt. Francis Bradley. Capt. Bradley, b. 1743, fought in McIntyre's skirmish and was killed by Torries[6] on 14 NOV 1780 at the age of 37 years, and buried in Hopewell Presbyterian Church Cem.[7] Known children:

    G1(12)1.   JAMES BRADLEY.
    G1(12)2.   REBECCA BRADLEY.
    G1(12)3.   JOHN MCKNITT BRADLEY.
    G1(12)4.   ELIZABETH BRADLEY, b. 1776, d. 19 AUG 1817, bur. Hopewell Presbyterian Church Cem.
    G1(12)5.   ESTHER BRADLEY.

G1(13).   MARGARET ALEXANDER, b. 30 APR 1750, d. after 1772 in Rutherford Co., Tenn., m. Ezekiel [Beaty] McCoy.[8] Known children:

    G1(13)1.   JAMES MCCOY.
    G1(13)2.   ESTHER MCCOY, m. 25 JAN 1792 in Mecklenburg Co., N.C. to Asahel Boggs.
    G1(13)3.   ABIGAIL MCCOY, b. 1774, d. 1800, m. 13 MAR 1792 in Mecklenburg Co., N.C. to David Parks.
    G1(13)4.   JOHN MCCOY, m. 1798 in Mecklenburg Co., N.C. to Esther Frazier.
    G1(13)5.   HENRY MCCOY.

G1(14).   JOSIAH ALEXANDER, b. 3 AUG 1752 in Cecil Co., Md., d. after 1772, name of wife unknown. Possible child:

    G1(14)1.   AZARIAH ALEXANDER, b. 1780, m. 16 NOV 1802 in Mecklenburg Co. NC to Fanny Alexander, as bonded by Ephraim Alexander and witnessed by Isaac Alexander. Azariah had a great grandson Casper C. Phillips of Meridian, Miss.

G1(15).   EZEKIEL ALEXANDER, b. 21 OCT 1754 in Cecil Co., Md., inherited his father's land on Long Creek in Mecklenburg Co., N.C. by the will in 1772, d. 18 AUG 1832 in Wilson Co., Tenn., m. c.1773 to Jemima Esther McCoy, d. after 1832 in Wilson Co., Tenn. Known children:[9]

    G1(15)1.   JAMES ALEXANDER, b. 16 JUN 1774.

---

[1] Mecklenburg Co., N.C. Wills, Bk. E, p. 109.
[2] Mecklenburg Signers, p. 533.
[3] Rutherford Co., Tenn. Wills, Bk. 7, p. 300.
[4] Mecklenburg Co., N.C. Wills, Bk. I, p. 205.
[5] Mecklenburg Co., N.C. Wills, Bk. H, p. 103.
[6] Letter, Jeannette Osteen, filed in subject Alexander Family at Huntsville, Ala. Library.
[7] Mecklenburg Signers.
[8] Reference of a John McCay, Vol. 6, folio 16, 22 AUG 1740, Cecil Co., Md. Some researchers have John McCay as the husband of Margaret Alexander, as in Cecil Co., Md. we find a will dated 24 FEB 1783 for John McCay that mentions sons-in-law George and Josiah Alexander, and friend Hezekiah South, along with grandson Henry McCay.
[9] Ferguson Appendix, and Grandfather Papers at D.A.R. Library, Washington, D.C.; Alexander Kin, Vol. 2, p. 375.

G1(15)2.   JEAN ALEXANDER, b. 25 FEB 1776.

G1(15)3.   ABNER ABRAHAM ALEXANDER, b. 10 AUG 1778, m. (1) 1 FEB 1803 in Wilson Co., Tenn. to (G1721.) JEMIMA ALEXANDER SHARP, b. 20 MAY 1781, d. 7 OCT 1825, m. (2) Margaret Cummings, d. 7 OCT 1825. Six known children.[1]

G1(15)4.   BEATY ALEXANDER, b. 21 SEP 1780.

G1(15)5.   LYDIA ALEXANDER, b. 2 MAR 1784, m. 1 APR 1809 in Wilson Co., Tenn. to Andrew Morrison, as bonded by Ezekiel Alexander.

G1(15)6.   JOSIAH ALEXANDER, b. 7 MAY 1785.

G1(15)7.   JOHN MCKNITT ALEXANDER, b. 20 MAY 1787.

G1(15)8.   EZEKIEL ALEXANDER, b. 22 DEC 1789 in Mecklenburg Co., N.C., will DEC 1835, prov. 20 APR 1836,[2] m. 8 OCT 1810[3] in Wilson Co., Tenn. to Mary "Polly" Cooper, b. 20 MAY 1788 in Va., d. 2 JUN 1865 in Cannon Co., Tenn. He served in the War of 1812 under Col. Raulston and Capt. Black, for which he enlisted 13 NOV 1814. Nine known children.

G1(16).   GEORGE ALEXANDER.

G188. Amos Alexander, Jr., Mayor of Alexandria, Virginia
(c.1762-1826)

Amos Alexander, Jr., was a merchant and, perhaps most notably, a mayor of the city of Alexandria, Virginia. He was a son of Amos Alexander, Sr. and Sarah Sharp of Cecil County, Maryland.[4]

    Amos Alexander was married at least twice in Alexandria, and also he may have been married before moving there. It appears he removed from Maryland to Fairfax County, Virginia previous to September 29, 1795 when he purchased Alexandria lots from George Coryell and his wife Ann.[5]

On November 3, 1796,[6] Amos Alexander purchased for £100 additional property at 805 Duke Street in Alexandria (on which now stands a 3 story wood frame house) from William Cash, Jr. and his wife Mary.

On May 6, 1797, Amos Alexander, along with William Newton of Fairfax County, purchased a 352-acre parcel in Hampshire County, Virginia from John Thomas Ricketts and wife Mary. The grantors may have been Amos' future in-laws, as his wife's maiden name was Ricketts.

On October 11, 1797, at *Cameron*, [Cameron Mills[7]] the seat of John Thomas Ricketts, Amos Alexander, Jr. was married by Rev. James Muir[8], to Miss Ann Ricketts.[9]

On February 15, 1798, George Summers of Alexandria certified that an election had been held on the second Tuesday of February, inst., which elected, among others, Amos Alexander as town recorder.[10]

In 1799, Amos Alexander possessed a lot on the northeast corner of King and Washington streets in Alexandria, which later in 1807 was purchased by Robert Young.[11] The 1799 tax list for Alexandria reflects that Amos Alexander was a merchant, with wife, one child, and four slaves (1 over 16 years, 3 under 16 years).[12] On September 20, 1799, Amos Alexander of Fairfax County purchased property from William Whan of Montgomery County Maryland.

On September 28, 1799, Amos Alexander of Alexandria wrote a letter to the Governor of Virginia requesting *as many copies of the revised code as can be spared for the use of the authorities of Alexandria.*[13] He was an elected mayor of Alexandria from February 1800 to February 1801.[14]

When the 1800 tax list was prepared for Alexandria, Amos Alexander was taxed for owning one coach.[15] Along with William Hartshorne, he was executor of the estate of Daniel Curtin, and an estate appraisal was made March 6,

---

[1] Alexander Kin, Vol. 2, p. 375; citing Charlotte, N.C. Public Library, Stafford Notebooks, pp. 97-8.

[2] Mecklenburg Co., N.C. Wills, Bk. E, p. 153.

[3] Edythe Rucker Whitley, Marriages of Wilson County, Tennessee, 1801-1850 (Baltimore: Genealogical Publishing Co., Inc., 1981), p. 9; bondsman Abraham Cooper.

[4] I present an unusual amount of information here, as I collected it over several decades of research in the Alexandria, Va. area.

[5] Alexandria, Va. (Hustings) Deeds, Bk. G, 1795-1796, pp. 188-197.

[6] Alexandria, Va. (Hustings) Deeds, Bk. H, 1795-1797, pp. 357-62.

[7] John Stump and John Rickets purchased part of "Cameron Mills" in 1791 from William Bird. John Ricketts' interest was conveyed to David Ricketts in 1806.

[8] Rev. James Muir (b. 12 APR 1757 in Catrine, Scotland; d. 8 AUG 1820 at Colross in Alexandria), was pastor of the Old Presbyterian Meeting House of Alexandria from MAY 1789 until his death, son of Rev. Dr. George Muir and Tibbie Wardlaw [William Randolph Sengel, Can These Bones Live? (Kingsport Press, 1973), p. 39], m. 28 FEB 1783 in Bermuda to Elizabeth Wellman.

[9] Alexandria Times, Vol. 1, No. 161, 13 OCT 1797, p. 3.

[10] Minutes of Alexandria City Council (1792-1800), manuscript at Alexandria Library, p. 237.

[11] Ethelyn Cox, Historic Alexandria, Virginia: Street by Street (Alexandria: Historic Alexandria Foundation, 1976), p. 68.

[12] Virginia Genealogist, Vol. 4, p. 121.

[13] Calendar of Virginia State Papers, Vol. 9, p. 49.

[14] Cox, p. 31.

[15] Virginia Genealogist, Vol. 4, p. 17.

1800.[1] About this time, Amos Alexander can be found as part of the Alexandria City Council proceedings.[2] Also, by March 1, 1800, land records in Alexandria confirm the wife of Amos was named Ann.[3] Wife Ann is also reflected in land records about this time when the couple cleared notes Amos Alexander had which were held by the Bank of Alexandria, involving Francis Peyton, and partners Charles Bennett and John Watts, merchants of the business *Bennett and Watts*.[4]

On September 2, 1800, Amos Alexander witnessed an indenture in Alexandria between Thomas Herbert and wife Jane, and William Hepburn and John Dundas, merchant partners.[5] On September 6, 1800, Amos Alexander, mayor of Alexandria, wrote a letter to the Governor of Virginia, reporting: *There have been some cases of yellow fever in the town; but only of such persons as brought it with them from Norfolk. Several have died at the quarantine station.*[6]

On October 20, 1801, an inventory of the effects of John Pennoyer, deceased, was filed by Amos Alexander who was *foreman of the Coroners Inquest.*[7]

The 1803 tax register of Alexandria reflects that Amos Alexander was taxed for at least three properties:[8] (1) a brick structure at King and Washington streets; (2) a 1-acre lot with a small frame structure at Washington and Wythe streets; and (3) a vacant lot at Duke and Columbus streets. On September 10, 1803, Amos Alexander was appointed to be Inspector of Flour for Alexandria in place of Daniel Douglas, deceased,[9] and two days later Amos Alexander appointed Jesse Wherry to be his assistant in that capacity.[10]

Ann Alexander died Monday morning, January 16, 1804, in the 31st year of her age—*she has left a disconsolate husband and three small children.*[11]

Amos Alexander was remarried, January 10, 1805, by Rev. James Muir to Miss Eliza Wroe,[12] who was under 21 years of age, a daughter of Absolem Wroe, as bonded by his father Amos Alexander, and as confirmed in Alexandria deeds.[13] Eliza Alexander was alive as late as November 18, 1814.[14]

Amos Alexander was a member of Alexandria Brooke Lodge 47 from which he was delegated on December 11, 1810 to Brooke Lodge 2 of Alexandria, which belonged to the District of Columbia. Masonic records[15] reveal he served in a number of Masonic positions: 1812-13, 1816 as Deputy Grand Master; 1814, 1817 as Grand Master; 1814 to 1818 as Worshipful Master; 1821 as Junior Warden; 1822 as Senior Warden.

On January 1, 1814,[16] William S. Moore and Catharine his wife of the Town of Alexandria in the District of Columbia, conveyed to Charles Alexander of the county of Alexandria, for $400, annuity and rent of $66.66 of a 1-acre lot bounded by Washington, Wythe, and St. Asaph streets. The lot had been devised unto Amos Alexander, merchant, by Charles Alexander, Sr. of *Preston* and Frances his wife on May 17, 1798.[17]

On December 6, 1816,[18] Amos Alexander purchased a parcel from Thomas Swann, which was partitioned to William Hodgson and wife Portia and had been conveyed to Swann in 1807.

On August 29, 1821, an announcement appeared in the Alexandria Gazette that *the creditors of Amos Alexander are hereby requested to bring in their claims to the subscriber, properly authenticated, on or before the 8th day of November next, otherwise they may be by law, debarred from any benefit of his estate;* signed Isaac Robbins, trustee.[19]

Based on his newspaper obituary,[20] it is known that Amos died September 9, 1826 in his 56th year, and was buried in a Masonic Cemetery next to the Grand Lodge of the District of Columbia. It has been suggested his grave may have been removed to the Masonic section of Congressional cemetery of Washington DC. The actual grave location has not been found.

[1] Alexandria, Va. Wills, Bk. A, pp. 39 (inv. 6 MAR 1800), 41, 44-5, 63; Will Bk. C, pp. 184, 280.
[2] Minutes of Alexandria City Council, manuscript at Alexandria Library.
[3] Alexandria, Va. Deeds, Bk. D, p. 214, recorded 15 DEC 1802; Deed Bk. D, p. 336, rec. 29 MAR 1803.
[4] Alexandria, Va. (Corporation Court) Deeds, Bk. M (1799-1800), pp. 430-37.
[5] Alexandria, Va. Deeds, Bk. A, p. 35; rec. 14 APR 1801.
[6] Calendar of Virginia State Papers, Vol. 9, p. 137.
[7] Alexandria, Va. Wills, Bk. A, p. 47.
[8] 1803 Tax Register of Alexandria, manuscript at Alexandria Library.
[9] Alexandria, Va. Deeds, Bk. G, p. 396, rec. 23 DEC 1803; oath taken 12 SEP 1803.
[10] Alexandria, Va. Deeds, Bk. G, p. 397, rec. 12 DEC 1803.
[11] Alexandria Advertiser, 17 JAN 1804.
[12] Alexandria Advertiser, 11 JAN 1805; bond in Arlington Co.
[13] Alexandria, Va. Deeds, Bk. K, p. 33, dated 13 JUN 1805, rec. 27 JUN 1805.
[14] Alexandria, Va. Deeds, Bk. X, p. 426, recorded 28 NOV 1814.
[15] Telephone Conversation (Stu Minor, 10/22/90); Grand Lodge of the District of Columbia.
[16] Alexandria, Va. (Corporation Court) Deeds, Bk. AA, pp. 330-36.
[17] Alexandria, Va. (Hustings Court) Deeds, Bk. K No. 2 (1798), pp. 471-75. Then on 18 MAR 1800 conveyed and assigned by Charles Alexander, Sr. (1737-1806) and Frances his wife to the son Charles Alexander, Jr. (c.1774-1814) of *Mt. Ida*, the latter whom made conveyance on 10 FEB 1811 to William S. Moore, as recorded in the Office of the Circuit Court of the District of Columbia at Alexandria.
[18] Alexandria, Va. Deeds, Bk. C No. 2, p. 408; rec. 7 DEC 1816.
[19] Alexandria Gazette (Alexandria, 29 AUG 1821), p. 1.
[20] Alexandria Gazette (Alexandria, 11 SEP 1826), p. 3.

Probable children of Amos Alexander, Jr., mayor of Alexandria:

G1881. WILLIAM HENRY ALEXANDER, b. c.1798, prob. in Alexandria, Va., d. suddenly on 15 OCT 1824[1] in his 27th year, near Port Royal, Caroline Co., Va. His obituary indicates that as the *eldest son of Amos Alexander, Esq. and lately Deputy Inspector of Flour in this town.*

G1882. JAMES S. ALEXANDER, b. 1799, prob. in Alexandria, Va., d. 9 OCT 1822 in Kingston, Jamaica, aged 23y.[2]

G1883. SARAH A. ALEXANDER, m. by bond dated 23 SEP 1819 in Alexandria Co., D.C. to James Cloud.

G1884. WALTER W. ALEXANDER, b. 1805, "third son," d. after suffering from yellow fever for nine days, 15 JUL 1829 in New Orleans, La., in his 24th year, bur. Girod Cem. there.[3]

G1885. AMOS MARK ALEXANDER, b. c.1808 in Alexandria, Va., d. 18 DEC 1850 in his 42nd year, in Wakulla Co., Fla. at the residence of Mr. William Walker,[4] leaving a wife and three children. He was living in Alexandria, D.C. at the time of the 1820 census,[5] but rem. to Florida c.1825 where he was listed on the 1840 Federal census for Leon Co., Fla.,[6] and at Port of St. Marks on the census taken 17 OCT 1850 (p. 254) as a merchant, with wife Rebecca (poss. Allen), age 27 in 1850, b. S.C. On the 1860 Federal census for Newport, Wakulla Co., Fla. (p. 899), Rebecca is residing with the family of Lucius M. Allen of S.C. and his wife Mariah E., while Amos is residing with the family of Rev. William T. Duvall.

G1886. Possibly ALBERT R.[7] ALEXANDER, b. c.1815 in Md. (age 35 in 1850), printer, resided in Leon Co., Fla. when the 1840 Federal census was taken.[8] The family was enumerated 17 OCT 1850 on the Federal census for Port of St. Marks, Wakulla Co., Fla. (p. 254, family #60). Albert m. 6 JUN 1839 in Leon Co. FL by R.B. Kerr, M.G. to Sarabell Walker, b. c.1822 in S.C. Two known children.

G15. Hezekiah Alexander
(c.1722-1801)

Hezekiah Alexander, son of James Alexander and Margaret McKnitt, was born January 13, 1722[9] in or near Cecil County, Maryland (some accounts give birthplace as Pennsylvania). He was married by license dated June 12, 1752 in Pennsylvania,[10] as granted by acting Governor James Hamilton, to Mary Sample, daughter of William Sample of Ayshire, Scotland and wife Esther Garrison of Cecil County, Maryland.

It has been claimed that Hezekiah purchased c.1745 a tract of land, possibly 500 acres, in Cumberland County (now Franklin), Pennsylvania. In 1773 he is said to have sold this tract to Richard Bard, and on this property was constructed a stone house known later as "Bard's Mansion," which some suspect may have actually been built by Hezekiah Alexander.

Mary (Sample) Alexander was born 1735 in North Carolina, died May 17, 1805, aged 71 years, and was buried beside her husband in Sugaw Creek Presbyterian Church churchyard. She left a will dated September 30, 1803, which was witnessed by John Davis, James Moore and John Orr.[11]

About 1754 the couple moved to Sugaw Creek, approximately 4 miles from Charlotte in Mecklenburg County, North Carolina. It is known Hezekiah purchased land c.1764 near the Catawba River in the Piedmont area of North Carolina. On May 13, 1765, Hezekiah Alexander, blacksmith, and Mary his wife of Pennsylvania and New Castle, sold to Moses Ferguson, School Master of Mecklenburg County, their 180-acre tract situate on the west side of the Catawba River on both sides of Allison's Creek. On January 22, 1767, Hezekiah *of New Castle, Pennsylvania* purchased from William Menter of Mecklenburg for £80 lawful money of North Carolina, a 400-acre tract situate on the north side of the Broad River on *a large creek that runs in about 5 or 6 miles above Second Broad River.* Hence, in 1767 he owned a 600-acre plantation in Mecklenburg County, and for £80 gained possession of what was later known as the *Rock House* tract on July 19, 1769 in a deed from his brother John McKnitt Alexander, tailor, in which he was penned as a blacksmith. Hezekiah subsequently purchased for £100 on April 23, 1771 another 370 acres from his brother John McKnitt Alexander, situate on both sides of Long Creek. The house called *Rock House* was completed in 1774 when it was occupied by the family. In April of that year he purchased two tracts on McAlpine Creek

---

[1] *Alexandria Gazette* (Alexandria, 23 OCT 1824), p. 3.
[2] *Alexandria Gazette* (Alexandria, 19 DEC 1822), p. 3.
[3] *Alexandria Gazette* (Alexandria, 13 AUG 1829), p. 3.
[4] *Alexandria Gazette* (Alexandria, 21 DEC 1850), p. 2.
[5] U.S. 1820 District of Columbia Census, p. 196, city of Alexandria.
[6] U.S. 1840 Florida Census, Leon Co., p. 64, no township listed.
[7] Perhaps initial stands for Ricketts.
[8] U.S. 1840 Florida Census, Leon Co., p. 63, no township listed.
[9] Tombstone, Sugaw Creek Presbyterian Church graveyard; *In memory of Hezekiah Alexander, Who departed this life July 16th, 1801, Aged 73 years.*
[10] *Pennsylvania Genealogical Magazine* (Philadelphia, Pa.: The Genealogical Society of Pennsylvania), Vol. 32, p. 71.
[11] Mecklenburg Co., N.C. Wills, Bk. A, p. 47.

from the Flaniken Family, a 208-acre one from Jane Flaniken, and another of 190 acres from John Flaniken.

On January 17, 1775, Hezekiah Alexander, along with other justices of Mecklenburg County, paid 20 shillings to the Commissioners of Charlotte for construction of the public jail on Lot No. 37 which was bound by Trade Street. Alexander was elected a member of the Provincial Congress from Mecklenburg County which met at Halifax on November 12, 1776[1]. On October 15, 1778, for £0,30 annually, he purchased Lot No. 60 on the East Side of Tryon Street in Charlotte, from Thomas Polk, Ephraim Brevard and James Jack.

Hezekiah Alexander died July 16, 1801 in Mecklenburg County, North Carolina, and was buried in Sugaw Creek Presbyterian Church graveyard there. His will that was filed in Mecklenburg County was dated August 8, 1796, and was witnessed by James Orr, Nathan Mitchell and William Sample Allen. It had one codicil dated January 28, 1797.[2]

Known children of Hezekiah Alexander, order uncertain:

G151. WILLIAM SAMPLE ALEXANDER, b. c.1751 in N.C., d. 26 OCT 1826 in his 75th year, bur. Rocky River Presbyterian Church Cem. of Cabarrus Co., N.C., m. (1) in 1770 to his cousin (B292.) ELIZABETH ALEXANDER (b. 19 FEB 1755, d. 29 NOV 1796, bur. Rocky River Presbyterian Church Cem.), daughter of Abraham Alexander and Dorcas [perhaps Wilson], q.v., m. (2) c.1797 to Sarah Rodgers, d. 27 NOV 1799, m. (3) c.1820 to Martha Nichols, b. 1792, d. 9 SEP 1853. William served in the Rev. War as a supplier and wagon master. His will prov. 15 JAN 1827 in Cabarrus Co.[3] Fifteen known children.

G152. (Dr.) JAMES R[ANKIN?] ALEXANDER, b. 23 NOV 1756 in Cecil Co., Md., d. 11 MAR 1836 in Allen Co., Ky., bur. Allen (prev. Warren) Co., Ky., m. 26 NOV 1789 in Mecklenburg Co., N.C. to Dorcas Garrison, b. 23 JUN 1766, d. 28 JAN 1852. As a resident of Cecil Co., Md., James enlisted 1 AUG 1776 in Co. of Capt. Walter Alexander, son of his uncle Amos,[4] and was discharged 1 DEC 1776, after which he returned to N.C. Ten known children.

G153. SILAS ALEXANDER, b. 1758/9 in N.C., d. intestate 27 OCT 1831, aged 72y, bur. Sharon Presbyterian Church Cem.[5] located at 5201 Sharon Road in Charlotte, N.C., m. c.1790 to Mary "Polly" (   ), b. 1764, d. 12 OCT 1833. His tombstone mentions he was a soldier of '76. Seven known children.[6]

G154. ESTHER ALEXANDER, b. 28 SEP 1762 in N.C., d. 12 SEP 1829, bur. Pleasant Prairie Cem. of Coles Co., Ill., m. 4 MAR 1786 by Rev. James McRee of Presbyterian Church of Mecklenburg Co. NC to Samuel Garrison, b. 24 AUG 1762, d. 27 MAR 1833, soldier of the Rev. War. Eight known children.

G155. MARY "Polly" ALEXANDER, b. c.1764/5 in N.C., d. before the 1796 will of Hezekiah, m. Col. Charles "Devil Charley" Polk who accidentally shot her dead while cleaning his gun. After Mary's death Polk tried unsuccessfully to marry his sister-in-law Kezia, and may have removed to S.C. Two known children.

G156. HEZEKIAH ALEXANDER, b. 13 JAN 1767 in N.C., d. post 1839, prob. bur. in Providence Presbyterian Church Cem. of Charlotte, N.C., m. c.1792 to Patsy (   ). By 1796, res. on McAlpins Creek in Mecklenburg Co., N.C. Nine known children.

G157. AMOS ALEXANDER, b. 13 MAY 1769, prob. Mecklenburg Co., N.C., d. intestate 25 JAN 1847, aged 77y 9m 12d, bur. Sugaw Creek Cem. No. 2, m. 23 DEC 1797 in Mecklenburg Co., N.C. to Mildred Orr, b. 1772, d. 1828, daughter of William Orr and Rebecca Montgomery. His obituary reveals that *he was a useful and much respected member of society and had been for more than thirty years an elder in the Presbyterian Church at Sugaw Creek.* Marriage bondsman Isaac Campbell, witness Isaac Alexander. Five known children.

G158. JOEL ALEXANDER, b. 26 APR 1773, d. intestate 17 MAY 1825, aged 52y 21d, m. c.1800 to Ruth (   ),[7] who could not read nor write, d. 26 DEC 1825; both bur. Sugaw Creek Cem. No. 2. Eight known children.

G159. KEZIA ALEXANDER, b. 1774, d. 1819, at one time betrothed to Charles Polk. She left a will dated 5 JUN 1819[8] in which she described herself as *Sick and weak state of health.* Her estate inventory was conducted 2 DEC 1819. Two known children.

G15(10). OSWALD ALEXANDER, a farmer and planter, b. 16 SEP 1775 at *Rock House* in Mecklenburg Co., N.C.,d. suddenly 11 DEC 1826, prob. bur. Sugaw Creek Cem. No. 2, m. (1) on 19 SEP 1799 to Sarah Sample, b. 16 JUL 1768, d. 6/16 MAR 1808, he m. (2) on 9 MAR 1809 in Mecklenburg Co. to Hannah Park(s), b. 1 JUL 1789, d. 9 FEB 1823, aged 33y 5m, bur. Sugaw Creek Cem. No. 2, he m. (3) on 17 OCT 1826 in Mecklenburg Co. to Mary Moore, b. 1797, d. 19 MAR 1847, daughter of James Moore. The widow Mary married twice after Oswald's death: m. (1) to William Lucky, then m. (2) to Thomas J. Grier,

---

[1] C.L. Hunter, p. 42.
[2] Mecklenburg Co., N.C. Wills, Bk. A, fols. 20-4.
[3] Cabarrus Co., N.C. Minutes of the County Court of Pleas and Quarter Sessions, Vol. 4, back.
[4] D.A.R. Patriot Application.
[5] Records of this cemetery note he was the first burial there.
[6] Ingram, p. 900.
[7] There is a rather unclear tombstone in Sugaw Creek Cem. for Ruth Alexander, who d. 26 DEC 1825, age 72.
[8] Mecklenburg Co., N.C. Wills, Bk. A, p. 53.

d. testate[1] 1872. Nine known children.[2]

G15(11).　JOSEPH ALEXANDER, b. 26 AUG 1776, d. 15 DEC 1851,[3] bur. Benton Cem., Polk Co., Tenn., m. Elizabeth McReynolds,[4] b. 1780, d. 20 MAY 1856, bur. Benton Cem. Ten known children.

G19. John McKnitt Alexander
(1733-1817)

John McKnitt Alexander, son of James Alexander and Margaret McKnitt, was born June 6, 1733 in the northeastern part of Cecil County, Maryland, near the Pennsylvania state line. It has been said he removed to Mecklenburg County, North Carolina about 1754.[5] He was married in September 1762 to Jean Bain [or Jane Bean], daughter of William Bain of East Nottingham , who was born c.1740 near Philadelphia, in Chester County, Pennsylvania. The couple settled in Hopewell congregation area of Mecklenburg County. It has often been found that John was a tailor and farmer, and he served in the Revolutionary War.

Apparently John McKnitt Alexander prospered in his business and soon became wealthy and an extensive landholder, *and rising in the estimation of his fellow citizens, was promoted to the magistracy and the Eldership of the Presbyterian Church. He was a member of the Provincial Assembly in 1772, and one of the Delegates to the Convention which met at Hillsboro*[6] on August 21, 1775.

John McKnitt Alexander wrote his will July 2, 1807, and subsequently made two codicils on November 3, 1812 and April 30, 1813. He died at the age of 84 years on July 10, 1817 in Mecklenburg County, North Carolina, and was buried in Hopewell Presbyterian Church Cemetery, located about 10 miles north of Charlotte, North Carolina.[7] Jean Alexander died March 16, 1789, also in Mecklenburg County, and was also buried in Hopewell Cemetery.

Children of John McKnitt Alexander and Jean Bain:

G191.　WILLIAM BAIN ALEXANDER, b. 25 APR 1764 in Mecklenburg Co., N.C., d. testate[8] 23 JAN 1844 and, being Presbyterian, was buried in Hopewell Presbyterian Churchyard of Mecklenburg Co., m. 25 AUG 1791[9] to Violet Davidson, a daughter of Maj. John Davidson (b. 1736 in Pa.[10]) and Violet Winslow Wilson (1741-1818), daughter of Samuel Wilson, Sr. (d. testate[11] on 13 MAR 1778 in his 68th year). William B. Alexander reportedly owned nearly 6,000 acres in Mecklenburg Co. Violet d. 26 OCT 1821 and was also buried at Hopewell. Twelve known children.

G192.　MARGARET McKNITT "Peggy" ALEXANDER, b. 3 APR 1766, d. 7 JUL 1805, bur. First Presbyterian Church Cem. of Knox Co., Tenn.,[12] m. 7 APR 1789 in Adams Co., Pa. to her cousin (F431.) FRANCIS ALEXANDER RAMSEY, b. 31 MAY 1764 in Adams Co., Pa. After Peggy died, F.A. Ramsey m. (2) AUG 1806 to Ann Agnew who d. DEC 1816, bur. First Presbyterian Church Cem. Seven known children.[13]

G193.　JEAN "Polly" BAIN ALEXANDER, b. 6 JUL/AUG 1768, d. 18 MAY 1816, bur. Providence Presbyterian Church Cem. of Charlotte, N.C., m. Rev. James Wallis (b. 1762, d. testate 1819 in Wilkes Co., N.C.[14]), pastor of Providence Church. He was bur. at Providence Church. Six known children.[15]

G194.　ABIGAIL BAIN ALEXANDER, b. 25 NOV 1770, d. 14 MAY 1802, bur. Hopewell Presbyterian Church Cem. of Huntersville, Mecklenburg Co., N.C., m. c.1792 as the first wife of Rev. Samuel Craighead Caldwell of Hopewell and Sugaw Creek Presbyterian Church, b. 10 JUL 1768, d. 25 AUG 1824, son of Dr. David Caldwell and wife Rachel Craighead (m. 1766), daughter of Rev. Alexander Craighead of Guilford, N.C.[16] Two known children.

---

[1] Mecklenburg Co., N.C. Wills, Bk. K, p. 89.
[2] Mecklenburg Signers, p. 394.
[3] Ingram, p. 312.
[4] Bruce Hodgson Stribling, Striblings of Walnut Hill and Related Families (1979), p. 15.
[5] Rumple, p. 271.
[6] C.L. Hunter, p. 43; Rumple, p. 271, and the Mecklenburg Convention on 20 MAY 1775.
[7] Rev. William Henry Foote, Sketches of North Carolina (New York NY, 1846), p. 201. "John McKnitt Alexander who departed this life July 10th, 1817, aged 84; p. 204, he m. c. 1759 Jane Bane of Pa.; p. 481, "bones of Black Billy Alexander" lie in Sugaw Creek Cemetery."
[8] Mecklenburg Co., N.C. Wills, Bk. H, p. 162.
[9] Mecklenburg Signers, pp. 323, 335, 384.
[10] C.L. Hunter, p. 49.
[11] Mecklenburg Co., N.C. Wills, Bk. G, p. 57.
[12] Tennessee Records, p. 135.
[13] Ingram, p. 847.
[14] Wilkes Co., N.C. Wills, Bk. 3, p. 169.
[15] Sketches of North Carolina.
[16] Rev. James Geddes Craighead, The Craighead Family (1876), p. 78.

G195. (Dr.) JOSEPH MCKNITT ALEXANDER, b. 28 APR 1774, d. testate[1] 17 OCT 1841 at *Rosedale*, bur. Hopewell Presbyterian Church Cem. of Huntersville, Mecklenburg Co., N.C., m. 3 AUG 1797 to Dovey Wilson Winslow, b. 16 MAY 1776, d. 6 SEP 1801, bur. Hopewell Presbyterian Church Cem., daughter of Col. Moses Winslow and wife Jean Osborne. One known child:

G1951. (Dr.) MOSES WINSLOW ALEXANDER, b. 1798, d. 1845.

---

[1] Mecklenburg Co., N.C. Wills, Bk. H, p. 57.

H. JOHN ALEXANDER
(c.1662-after 1735)

John Alexander, born c.1662 in Raphoe Parish of County Donegal, Ireland,[1] is thought to be a son of William Alexander of Eredy, County Donegal, Ireland. John Alexander was married c.1692 in Annemessix, Maryland to Mary Barbary. They resided in Somerset County, Maryland. He was a party to a suit *Wm. Parker agt. John Alexander, def.*, with Andrew Alexander attending for four days.[2] It is not known whether he moved with others to Cecil County, Maryland or if he left the county, as no definite information can be found.

A John Alexander witnessed the Cecil County deed of Thomas Stevenson to James Alexander, weaver, on August 15, 1718; it being the first record found of a John Alexander in that county.

Known and possible children of John Alexander and Mary Barbary:

H1.   ESTHER ALEXANDER, b. 18 MAY 1693 in Pocomoke, Somerset Co., Md.[3]
H2.   HENRY ALEXANDER.

---

[1] Gus Skordas shows a John Alexander, transported in 25 APR 1679 on the ship *Globe*.
[2] Somerset Co., Md. Judicial Records, 1696-1698, p. 25.
[3] Somerset Co., Md. Records, Liber IKL/O11, 1714-1715, p. 4.

I. JANE (ALEXANDER) McKNITT
(c.1665-1693)

Jane Alexander, was born c.1665 in Raphoe Parish of County Donegal, Ireland, thought to be a daughter of William Alexander of Eredy, County Donegal, Ireland. About 1683, perhaps in County Donegal, Ireland, Jane Alexander was married to John McKnitt, Jr., a son of John McKnitt and Elizabeth Wallace. The couple first resided in Somerset County but removed to Cecil County, Maryland. Jane McKnitt died March 28, 1693 back in Manokin Hundred of Somerset County, Maryland.

After her death, John McKnitt married (secondly) to Jane Wallace, then after her death to Martha Dale. John McKnitt died December 23, 1714 in Cecil County, Maryland. His brother-in-law Samuel Alexander was surety for a bond to widow Martha McKnitt and son John McKnitt to administer the estate of John McKnitt [Macknit], deceased.[1]

Known children of John McKnitt, Jr. and first wife Jane Alexander:[2]

I1. ROBERT McKNITT, b. 4 JUN 1685 at Manokin, Somerset Co., Md., will, prov. 7 APR 1769, in New Castle Co., Del., men. his wife Isabella (   ), sons Moses and Alexander, and his grandchildren Isabella and William Nevins. If correctly identified, it follows that he had received his share of his father's property during his father's lifetime, and having removed outside the jurisdiction of the Maryland courts, his next younger brother qualified in his stead in 1714/15 as administrator of their father's estate.[3] Children:
  I11.   MOSES McKNITT.
  I12.   ALEXANDER McKNITT.
  I13.   Daughter McKNITT, m. _____ Nevins.
I2. JOHN McKNITT, III, planter, b. 8 SEP 1687 in Somerset Co., Md., d. between 14 APR 1733 and 13 JUN 1733 in Cecil Co., Md., m. his cousin (C(12.)) DOROTHY WALLACE, who m. (2) Robert Patton, brother of John and House Patton. Children:
  I21.   DANIEL McKNITT, *likely never to be capable of maintaining himself.*
  I22.   JOHN McKNITT, IV, *who inherited his [father's] lands, and who died testate[4] in 1747* in Guilford Co., N.C.
  I23.   MARY McKNITT, b. c.1714, m. c.1733 to Adam Brevard, b. c.1712, d. c.1733 in Worcester Co., Md.
  I24.   HANNAH McKNITT.
  I25.   ALEXANDER McKNITT, of Guilford Co., N.C., b. c.1715, d. testate[5] there c.1775.
  I26.   JAMES McKNITT, of Mecklenburg Co., N.C., letters of administration 16 APR 1765 granted to Robert McKnitt and wife Catherine (   ).
I3. KATHERINE McKNITT, b. 10 AUG 1689 in Somerset Co., Md., d. c.1734 in Cecil Co., Md., m. 1711 to John Brevard, res. Cecil Co., Md. Children:
  I31.   ADAM BREVARD, b. c.1712, d. testate in Worcester Co., Md., will dated 6 NOV 1782, prov. 15 JUL 1783.
  I32.   JOHN BREVARD, JR., b. c.1714, rem. to Iredell Co., N.C., d. 1790 age 75 in Rowan Co. (now Iredell) NC, m. Jane McWhorter, b. c.1716, d. 1800, daughter of Hugh McWhorter of Pencader Hundred, New Castle Co. DE, d. testate, will 17 FEB 1749, prov. 6 MAR 1749.
  I33.   BENJAMIN BREVARD, b. c.1720, d. c.1793 testate in Cecil Co., Md.
  I34.   ELIZABETH BREVARD, b. c.1722.
  I35.   ROBERT BREVARD, of Rowan Co., N.C.
  I36.   ZEBULON BREVARD, b. 24 MAR 1724, m. 7 MAR 1754 to Ann Templeton, b. NOV 1733.
I4. MARY McKNITT, b. 26 FEB 1691/2 at Manokin Hundred in Somerset Co., Md., d. at Elk River, Cecil Co., Md., m. c.1708 to Thomas Powell, b. 1689, d. before 1726 in Worcester Co., Md.

---

[1] Maryland Testamentary Proceedings, Bk. 22, p. 475, session 30 JUL 1715, exhibited from Cecil Co., Md.
[2] Pennsylvania Genealogical Magazine (Philadelphia, Pa.: The Genealogical Society of Pennsylvania), Vol. XVI, Oct. 1948, p. 83.
[3] Ibid.
[4] Guilford Co., N.C. Wills, Bk. A, p. 250.
[5] Guilford Co., N.C. Wills, Bk. A, p. 253.

Benjamin Alexander

Benjamin Alexander, was married to Susan Polk,[1] b. Cumberland Co., Pa., daughter of William Polk, probably b. at *White Hall* in Maryland, and d. c.1753 west of the Yadkin River in North Carolina. The wife of William Polk was Margaret Taylor. Children of Benjamin Alexander and Susan Polk:

a. William "Black Billy"[2] Alexander, b. 1749 in Bucks Co., Pa.,[3] d. 19 DEC 1836, res. in Cabarrus Co., N.C. and served in several capacities during the Rev. War. His wife was Rebecca (   ). Children:

   a1. Daniel Alexander, b. 5 MAR 1757 in Mecklenburg Co., N.C., m. 11 JUN 1800 in Mecklenburg Co. (as bonded by Andrew Wallace) to Susannah Shelby, rem. to Hardeman Co., Tenn., then back to Mecklenburg Co., N.C. where he died. During the Rev. War he served in his father's company in 1778 and that of Capt. Thomas Alexander in 1780. Five known children.

   a2. William Alexander, b. 1760, m. either JUN 1783 in Mecklenburg Co., N.C. or 3 OCT 1787 in Tyrell Co., N.C. to Sarah Alexander, rem. to Maury Co., Tenn. where he received a pension based on services during the Rev. War.

   a3. Josiah Alexander.

   a4. Rebecca Alexander.

b. (Maj.) Thomas Alexander, b. 1753, d. 1844,[4] m. Jane Morrison, daughter of Neil Morrison.[5] In 1775, Thomas first entered into service as a private in Capt. John Spring's company, *and marched to the head of the Catawba River, to assist in protecting the frontier settlements, then greatly suffering from the murderous and depredating incursions of the Cherokee Indians.*[6] Child:

   b1. Margaret Alexander, m. Robert Wilson, son of Samuel Wilson, Sr. and his third wife Margaret Jack.[7]

c. (Capt.) Charles Alexander, b. 4 JAN 1755 in Mecklenburg Co., N.C.[8] He first enlisted as a private in JUL 1755 in the company of Capt. William Alexander, and Col. Adam Alexander's regiment. By 1814, he rem. to Giles Co., Tenn. (now Lincoln Co.), and in 1833 to Maury Co., Tenn. where he died.

d. Susan Alexander.

e. Benjamin Alexander.

f. Taylor Alexander.

Henry Alexander

Henry Alexander, d. testate before 3 APR 1694 when his will was proved in Talbot Co., Md.,[9] m. Margaret (   ), who after Henry's death m. (2) to Timothy Lane. Margaret d. before January 1697 in Talbot Co. Children:

a. John Alexander, b. before 1673.

b. Elizabeth Alexander, b. before 1675, m. Pierce Fleming.[10] She inherited tract *Kingstown* by her father's 1693 will.

c. Katherine Alexander, b. after 1676.

---

[1] Mrs. Frank M. Angellotti, <u>Polks of North Carolina and Tennessee</u>, p. 4.

[2] Apparently called such from being the reputed leader of a small band of ardent patriots who in 1771 blackened their faces and destroyed the king's powder on its way to Hillsboro [<u>C.L. Hunter</u>, p. 115].

[3] <u>C.L. Hunter</u>, p. 115.

[4] <u>Charlotte Journal</u>, 17 JAN 1845.

[5] <u>Mecklenburg Signers</u>, pp. 504, 508.

[6] <u>C.L. Hunter</u>, p. 113.

[7] <u>C.L. Hunter</u>, p. 87.

[8] <u>C.L. Hunter</u>, p. 117.

[9] Maryland Wills, Liber 7, fol. 36, dated 13 MAR 1693, proved 3 APR 1694, wit. by Joseph James, the will constitutes his widow Margaret as executrix; also see Maryland Testamentary Proceedings, Bk. 15C, p. 146, session 12 NOV 1694.

[10] Talbot Co., Md. Deeds, Bk. 14, p. 168, dated 20 JUL 1736.

John Alexander of Talbot County, Maryland

John Alexander [or Allexander], d. 7 DEC 1708 in St. Stephen's Parish of Talbot Co., Md. He may have m. Mary ( ), who as the administratrix of John Alexander, late of Talbot Co., who m. 20 DEC 1710 to Philip Kersey.[1] Children:
a. Henry Alexander,[2] b. 2 FEB 1690 in St. Peter's Parish, Talbot Co., and prob. the same who in 1768 deeded to William Martin several tracts in Talbot Co., Md.: 250a called *Alexander's Chance*, 100a called *Wales*, 180a called *Lowe's Good Luck*,[3] and 50a called *Irish Freshes*.[4] He may have m. Hannah Parrot, daughter of Francis Parrott of Talbot Co., Md., who d. testate in 1761 and mentioned his daughter Hannah Alexander.[5]
b. Naomi Alexander, b. 16 JAN 1693 in St. Peter's Parish.
c. Elizabeth Alexander, b. 2 FEB 1696 in St. Peter's Parish.

John Alexander of Lincoln County, Tennessee

John Alexander, reportedly from Chester County, Pennsylvania (and possibly a descendant of John Alexander and Margaret Glasson/Gleason), was m. c.1754 in what is now Iredell Co., N.C. to Rachel Davidson, sister of Samuel Davidson and eldest daughter of John Davidson. He resided in the Pennsylvania area then removed to Rowan Co., N.C., then later to Lincoln Co., Tenn. where he resided during the Revolutionary War. He was at Kings Mountain in 1780, Crowder's Creek in 1781, and ultimately removed to Tennessee.[6] Children:
a. James Alexander, of the Rev. War, b. 23 DEC 1756 at Buffalo Creek in Mecklenburg (now Rutherford) Co., N.C., d. testate[7] 28 JUN 1844 in Bee Tree Creek of Buncombe Co., N.C., bur. in Robert Patton burying ground but removed to Bee Tree,[8] m. 19 MAR 1782 at Allison Creek in York District of S.C. to Rhoda Cunningham. Rhoda, b. 15 OCT 1763 in Lancaster Co., Pa., d. 29 JAN 1848 at Bee Tree Creek, bur. Piney Grove Presbyterian Church Cem., daughter of Humphrey Cunningham and Rhoda Summerville. James bur. Robt. Patton's Meeting house and body moved to Piney Grove Presbyterian Church. They lived in an area at the mouth of the Bee Tree Creek known as the "Swannanoa Settlement." Ten known children.[9]
b. Thomas Alexander, d. in Williamson Co., Tenn., m. Elizabeth Davidson, daughter of Maj. William Davidson,[10] rem. to Harpeth River near Nashville, Tenn.

Thomas Alexander of Talbot County, Maryland

Thomas Alexander, Sr. devised to his wife Hannah his plantation at Piny Point. He died testate on November 6, 1681 in Talbot County, Maryland,[11] married to Hannah ( ), who, as relict and executrix of Thomas Alexander, married (2) on January 1, 1682 to William Holland.[12] Widow Hannah [or sometimes read as Susannah] married (3) by 1709 to Thomas Tate when she conveyed the *Cardiffe* tract to her son Thomas Alexander, Jr.[13] Children:
a. John Alexander, under age in his father's 1681 will, planter, d. testate before 18 APR 1740 in Talbot Co., Md.,[14] m. (1) Hannah (as named in his father's will), m. (2) to Alie [also Alce or Alse] Sulivant, d. DEC 1826 in St. Peter's Parish. In 1726, John Alexander and wife Alse deeded a 46-acre portion of tract *Wales* in Talbot Co., Md. to Samuel Dickinson, merchant.[15] John Alexander m. (3) on 16 JAN 1730 in St. Peter's Parish to Ann [or Amy or

[1] Maryland Inventories and Accounts, Liber 32, fol. 88.
[2] Maryland Calendar of Wills, Vol. VII, p. 184; Maryland Wills, Liber 21, fol. 628. Henry Alexander is mentioned in the will of Philip Kacey, planter of Talbot Co., Md., made 13 MAR 1735, prov. 28 JUN 1736, in which the testator makes legacy to Henry son of John Alexander, and also mentions that after his wife Mary Kacey, the residue of his estate is to be divided between John Alexander and Edmond Karey.
[3] Talbot Co., Md. Deeds, Bk. 13, p. 70, dated 25 MAY 1723, John Alexander bought tract Lowe's Good Luck from Nicholas Lowe.
[4] Talbot Co., Md. Deeds, Bk. 19, p. 487, dated 30 MAR 1768, states Henry Alexander is son of John Alexander.
[5] Maryland Wills, Originals at the Maryland State Archives, Box 19, folder 19, Francis Parrott, proved 23 JUN 1761.
[6] F.A. Sondley, History of Buncombe County, North Carolina, p. 742.
[7] Buncombe Co., N.C. Wills, Bk. A, p. 105.
[8] F.A. Sondley, Alexander-Davidson Family Reunion, Swannanoa, N.C., August 26, 1911, p. 28.
[9] Heritage of Old Buncombe County, North Carolina, 1981, Vol. 1, pp. 133-134, includes his portrait.
[10] William Davidson remained in the "Swannanoa Settlement" on the farm which he settled in 1785, and died there 16 MAY 1814 where buried. His wife was Margaret McConnell [also see F.A. Sondley, My Ancestry (1930), p. 108].
[11] Maryland Wills, Liber 2, fol. 172, will of Thomas Alexander, dated 23 NOV 1681, proved 7 MAR 1682, wit. John Price, Robert Fowler; date of death of 3 NOV 1681 comes from estate appraisers in 1682 [Maryland Inventories and Accounts, Liber 7C, fol. 1]; also see Maryland Testamentary Proceedings, Bk. 12B, p. 14, session 1 APR 1682 for the will of Thomas Alexander being presented to court.
[12] Maryland Inventories and Accounts, Liber 36, fol. 247; also see Maryland Testamentary Proceedings, Bk. 13, p. 9, session 28 FEB 1682.
[13] Talbot Co., Md. Deeds, Bk. 11, p. 90, dated 19 JUL 1709, her name may have been Susannah, as by 1709, Susannah, widow of Thomas Alexander had m. Thomas Tate, and sold tract Cardiffe to her son Thomas Alexander.
[14] Maryland Wills, Liber 22, fol. 195, will of John Alexander, dated 5 MAR 1739, proved 18 APR 1740, mentions wife Ann Alexander.
[15] Talbot Co., Md. Deeds, Bk. 13, p. 277, dated 2 AUG 1726.

Naomi] Mackey, who after his death m. on 3 JUN 1740 in St. Peter's Parish, Talbot Co. to William Alexander. Children:

  a1. Mary Alexander, b. 22 DEC 1731 in St. Peter's Parish, Talbot Co., Md.
  a2. Henry Alexander, b. 28 NOV 1734 in St. Peter's Parish.
b. Edward Alexander, under age in his father's 1681 will.
c. Mary Alexander, m. Edward Cary, d. testate before 18 APR 1740.[1]
d. Susanna Alexander, under age in her father's 1681 will.
e. Thomas Alexander, Jr., b. c.1682,[2] inn holder in 1713, m. Mary (   ). In 1702, Thomas Alexander and his wife Mary deeded to John Wilson a 150-acre tract called *Highfield's Addition*, in Talbot Co.[3] In 1709, Thomas Alexander and his wife Mary deeded to Thomas Taylor a 400-acre tract called *East Ottwell*, in Talbot Co.[4] In 1726, Thomas Alexander, Sr. and Thomas Alexander, Jr., carpenters, deeded to Thomas Bosman a tract called *Cardiffe* in Talbot Co., Md.[5] After Thomas Alexander, Jr. died, his widow Mary m. (2) by 14 MAR 1732 to Philip Casey. Children:[6]

  e1. Thomas Alexander, III, b. 17 MAY 1703, bapt. 1 AUG 1703, inherited the rights to tract *Cardiffe* in 1709 by his grandmother Hannah Tate,[7] perhaps the same Thomas Alexander who m. 23 JAN 1728 in St. Peter's Parish of Talbot Co. to Susannah Ford. An estate inventory was filed in Talbot Co. on 13 JAN 1746, naming a minor son John Alexander and next of kin Mary James and Rigby Foster.[8]
  e2. John Alexander, alive in 1732 when Philip Casey and his wife Mary deeded to William Mackey their rights in land at the head of Dividing Creek.[9]
  e3. Keturah Alexander.
  e4. Mary Alexander.

---

[1] Maryland Wills, Liber 22, fol. 194, will of Edward Cary, planter, dated 17 FEB 1740, proved 18 APR 1740.
[2] In his father's will he may be the child the testator called "the child my wife now carries."
[3] Talbot Co., Md. Deeds, Bk. 9, p. 155, dated 16 MAR 1702.
[4] Talbot Co., Md. Deeds, Bk. 11, p. 124, dated 19 JUL 1709.
[5] Talbot Co. Deeds, Bk. 13, p. 348, dated 17 MAR 1726.
[6] Talbot Co. Guardianships, Bk. A, August Court 1748.
[7] Talbot Co. Deeds, Bk. 11, p. 90, dated 19 JUL 1709.
[8] Talbot Co. Inventories, Bk. 34.
[9] Talbot Co. Deeds, Bk. 13, p. 781, dated 14 MAR 1732.

SELECTED BIBLIOGRAPHY

Acklen, Jeannette Tillotson, <u>Tennessee Records</u> (Baltimore: Genealogical Publishing Co., 1976).

Alexander, J.B., <u>Biographical Sketches of the Early Settlers of the Hopewell Section</u> (Mecklenburg, N.C., By the Author, 1897).

Alexander, Virginia W. and Charles C. Alexander, <u>Alexander Kin</u> (Columbia, Tenn.: Privately Printed; 1964), Two Volumes.

Angellotti, Mrs. Frank M., <u>The Polks of North Carolina and Tennessee</u> (Easley, S.C.: Southern Historical Press, 1984).

<u>Archives of Maryland</u> (Baltimore, Md.: Maryland Historical Society, 1883).

<u>Biographical Dictionary of the American Congress, 1774-1949</u> (Washington: U.S. Government Printing Office, 1950).

Bivins, Willie Reeves Hardin, <u>The Family of Reynolds Ramsey</u> (Oklahoma City: By the Author, 1987).

Bridges, Earley Winfred, <u>Masonic Governors of North Carolina</u> (Greensboro, N.C.: By the Author, 1937).

Bruce, Philip Alexander, <u>History of Virginia</u> (Chicago and New York: The American Historical Society, 1924). Six Volumes.

Butterworth, Frances Alexander, <u>Records of a Family of the House of Alexander</u> (Chicago, Ill.: By the Author, 1909).

<u>Calendar of Virginia State Papers</u> (New York: Kraus Reprint Corp., 1968). Eleven Volumes.

Chalkley, Lyman, <u>Chronicles of the Scotch-Irish Settlement in Virginia, Extracted from the Original Court Records of Augusta County, 1745-1800</u> (Baltimore: Genealogical Publishing Co., 1965). Three Volumes.

Cooch, Edward Webb, <u>Battle of Cooch's Bridge, Delaware</u> (Wilmington, Del.: W.N. Cann, Inc., 1940).

Cotton, Jane Baldwin, <u>Maryland Calendar of Wills</u> (Baltimore: Kohn & Pollock, c.1901-1904), Eight Volumes [series continued by Family Line Publications]

Couper, William, <u>History of the Shenandoah Valley</u> (New York: Lewis Publishing Co., 1952). Three Volumes.

Cox, Ethelyn, <u>Historic Alexandria, Virginia: Street by Street</u> (Alexandria: Historic Alexandria Foundation, 1976).

Craighead, James Geddes, Rev., <u>The Craighead Family</u> (Philadelphia: By the Author, 1876).

Craun, Victor S., <u>Craun Family in America and Its Connection With Other Families</u> (By the Author, 1950).

Culton, Sarah Alexander, <u>A Documentary of Scotch-Irish Alexander Family History: The People, Places and Events Before 4000 B.C. to 2005 A.D., Third Edition</u> (Colville, Wash.: By the Author, 2005).

Dorman, John Frederick, Editor, <u>The Virginia Genealogist</u> (Washington, D.C. and Falmouth, Va.: By the Compiler, 1957-).

Douglas, Robert, Sir, <u>The Peerage of Scotland</u> (Edinburgh, 1813). Two Volumes.

Dryden, Ruth T., <u>Land Records of Worcester County, Maryland, 1666-1810</u> (San Diego: By the Author, 1987).

Foote, William Henry, Rev., <u>Sketches of North Carolina</u> (New York: R. Carter, 1846).

Goeller, Mildred Searson, <u>The Steeles of Steeles Tavern, Virginia</u> (Ripplemead, Va.: By the Author, 1974).

Hamlin, Charles Hughes, <u>The Thacker Genealogy, 1635-1870</u> (Richmond: By the Author, 1964).

Heritage of Old Buncombe County, North Carolina (Asheville, N.C.: Old Buncombe County Genealogical Society, 1981; Winston-Salem, N.C.: Hunter Publishing Co., 1987).

History of Saline County, Missouri (St. Louis: Missouri Historical Co., 1881).

Holcomb, Brent Howard, Mecklenburg County, North Carolina, Abstract of Early Wills, 1763-1790 (Greenville, S.C.: By the Author, 1980).

Holsinger, Paul G., Descendants of David Holsinger of Virginia (Ann Arbor, Mich.: Edward Brothers, 1969).

Horton, Lucy Henderson, Family History ... (Franklin, Tenn.: Press of the News, 1922).

Houston, Florence A.W., Maxwell History and Genealogy (Indianapolis, Ind.: Press of C.E. Pauley, Indianapolis Engraving Co., 1916).

Howe, Henry, Historical Collections of Virginia (Charleston, S.C.: Babcock & Co., 1845).

Hunter, C.L., Sketches of Western North Carolina (Raleigh, 1877; reprint ed., Baltimore: Genealogical Publishing Co., 1990).

Ingram, Annie K. Blythe, *The Six Alexanders Who Signed the Mecklenburg Declaration of Independence*, D.A.R. Magazine (Vol. 86, No. 5, May 1952).

Jamagin, William S., A Genealogical Chart of the Alexander-Ramsay/Ramsey Family of Scotland & America (Concord, Mass.: Walden Press, 1976).

Lankford, Wilmer O., They Lived in Somerset County, Maryland, 1700-1725 (Princess Anne: Manokin Press, 1991).

Leonard, John W., The Book of St. Louisans (St. Louis: The St. Louis Republic, 1906).

Lightfoot, Marise Parrish, They Passed This Way: Maury County, Tennessee Cemetery Records (1964).

Lightfoot, Marise Parrish, Let the Drums Roll : Veterans and Patriots of the Revolutionary War who Settled in Maury County, Tennessee (Columbia, Tenn. : Maury County Historical Society, 1976).

Link, Paxson Rude, The Link Family ... (Paris, Ill.: By the Author, 1951).

Linn, Jo White, Gray Family and Allied Lines (Salisbury, N.C.: By the Author, 1976).

Maryland Historical Magazine (Baltimore: Maryland Historical Society, 1906-).

May, George Elliott, Port Republic: The History of a Shenandoah Valley River Town (Staunton: Lot's Wife Publishing, 2001).

McCall, Hugh, History of Georgia ... (Atlanta, Ga.: Cherokee Publishing Co., 1969).

McCue, John Nolley, The McCues of the Old Dominion (Mexico, Mo.: Missouri Printing & Publishing Co., 1912).

Papenfuse, Edward C., et al., A Biographical Dictionary of the Maryland Legislature, 1635-1789 (Baltimore: Johns Hopkins University Press, 1979). Two Volumes.

Parran, Alice Norris, Register of Maryland's Heraldic Families, 1634-1935 (Baltimore: H.G. Roebuck & Son, c.1935-1938), Two Volumes.

Pennsylvania Genealogical Magazine (Philadelphia, Pa.: The Genealogical Society of Pennsylvania), Vol. XVI (October 1948), pp. 85-90.

Pennsylvania Genealogical Records Committee, Genealogy of James Alexander (D.A.R. Library, 1982).

Pippenger, Wesley E., Pippenger and Pittenger Families (Baltimore: Gateway Press, 1988).

Portrait and Biographical Record of Lafayette and Saline Counties, Missouri (Chicago: Chapman Brothers, 1893).

Powers, Robert B., A Record of My Maternal Ancestors (Delaware, Ohio: By the Author, 1966).

Ray, Worth Stickley, The Mecklenburg Signers and Their Neighbors (Baltimore: Genealogical Publishing Co., 1962).

Ray, Worth Stickley, Tennessee Cousins: A History of Tennessee People (reprint ed.: Baltimore: Genealogical Publishing Co., 1989).

Rogers, Charles, Rev., Memorials to the Earl of Stirling and of the House of Alexander (Edinburgh, 1877), Two Volumes.

Rumple, Jethro, The History of Presbyterianism in North Carolina (Reprinted from the North Carolina Presbyterian, 1878-1887 (Richmond: The Library of Union Theological Seminary in Virginia, 1966).

Sondley, Forster Alexander, History of Buncombe County, North Carolina (Spartanburg, S.C.; reprint ed., 1977).

Stribling, Bruce Hodgson, Striblings of Walnut Hill and Related Families (1979).

Torrence, Clayton, Old Somerset on the Eastern Shore of Maryland (Richmond: Whittet & Shepperson, 1935).

Virginia Auditor of Public Accounts, Virginia Militia in the War of 1812: from rolls in the Auditor's Office (Baltimore: Genealogical Publishing Co., 2001). Two Volumes.

Virkus, Frederick Adams, Compendium of American Genealogy (Chicago: A.N. Marquis, 1925), Six Volumes.

Whitney, Alethea Helen, A History of the Manokin Presbyterian Church, Princess Anne, Maryland, 1672-1980 (Denton: The Baker Printing Co., 1981).

A

Abbas
Barbara J. (Severin) 92
Ella (Brinston) 92
James Craig 92
James Leroy 92
James Shultz 92
LeRoy Edward 92
Mary Ann 92
Mary L. (Pippenger) . . 80, 92
Pamela Suzanne 92

Abston
Alta 88
Howard T. 88
Patricia Ann 88

Accomack Co., Va. . . . 1, 4, 11,
15, 116

Adair
Jane 133

Adams
Eliza J. 41
Adams Co., Pa. . 133, 134, 144
Lower Marsh Creek Cem.
. . . . 133

Adel, Ga. 32
Afton, Va. 56

Agnew
Ann 144
John 132
Judge 134

Ahlefeld
Carolyn E. (Ailshie) 38
Mitch 38

Aiken
Frances (Alexander) 130
John 130

Ailshie
Archie Monroe 38
Asie 38
Bessie (Wampler) 38
Carolyn Elizabeth 38
Dorothy A. (Dukes) 38
Sharon Janice 38

Airs
Thomas 12
Albemarle Co., N.C. 7, 128
Albemarle Co., Va. . 11, 15, 16,
18, 19, 47, 56, 57, 98, 99,
104
Charlottesville . . . 59, 69, 110
Covesville 48, 56
Fredericksville Parish 98
Liberty Baptist Church Cem.
. . . . 56
Scottsville 1
Shadwell 69
Stony Point 56

Albertville, Ala. 109
Albuquerque, N.M. . . . 81
Alconbury, Eng. 107

Alcorn
John 129, 131
Margaret C. 131
Rebecca ( ) 131
Alex, Okla. 82

Alexander
Aaron 123, 131, 132
Aaron Bowman 112
Abdon 118
Abel 117
Abigail 116, 136, 139
Abigail ( ) 136, 139
Abigail (McKnitt) . . . 4, 116,
122, 136
Abigail A.E. (Minger) . 23, 24,
26-28, 30, 33, 34
Abigail Bain 144
Abner 135
Abner Abraham 137, 140
Abraham . . . 117, 118, 120,
124, 143
Abram 117, 134
Ada A. 110
Adam 116, 117, 119, 148
Adam Rankin 119
Agnes 8, 116, 133
Agnes ( ) 116, 119
Agnes S. (Katzer) . . . 33
Albert Charles 34
Albert R. 142
Aleath V. (Leonard) . . . 62
Alexander 117, 122, 132
Alice Cornelia 48, 63, 68
Alie (Sulivant) 149
Alma ( ) 27
Alston 119
Amanda E. (Potter) 25
Ambrose 135
Amelia 133
Amos 124, 131, 138, 143
Amos M. 142
Amos Mark 142
Amos, Jr. 138, 140-142
Amzi 135
Amzi C. 135
Anadel (Vines) 109
Andrew . 2, 4, 116, 117, 122,
124, 128, 133-136
Andrew Charles 110
Andrew Jackson 25
Anita Ruth 67
Ann 117, 118, 123, 137
Ann (Bevans) . 1, 15, 18, 19,
23, 40, 43, 46, 47, 57, 71,
99

Ann (Caldwell) 131
Ann (Liston) . . . 4, 6, 7, 9, 122
Ann (Mackey) 149, 150
Ann (Ricketts) 140
Ann (Taylor) . . . 4, 116, 122,
123, 136
Ann W. (Roberts) 20, 23, 24,
35, 36, 38
Anna ( ) 131
Anna (Moore) 113
Anna Mae 39
Annabelle (Vansant) 28
Annie 118
Annie Amelia 73, 85
Araminta 132
Araminta ( ) 124
Arnold 26
Arnold D. 28
Arthur 26, 116, 118, 122
Asa 15, 16, 19, 99
Augustus 118
Azariah 139
Bailey Lynn 111
Barbara (Huff) 114
Barbara (King) 131
Barbara (Spaulding) 111
Barbara A. (Silvy) 23
Barbara Ann 23
Beaty 140
Belle 25
Benjamin 124, 130, 135,
148
Bernice Louella 27
Bertha Irene 73, 96
Bettie 54
Bettie Lee 68, 69
Betty Berry 111
Betty Jane 108
Betty L. (Deplue) 28
Betty Lee 48, 63
Beverly Elaine 28
Black Billy 148
Bonnie L. 114
Brett Hunter 108
Brigid Rose 109
Brownie Belle 107
C.W. 54
Caleb 132, 134
Caroline Virginia 63
Carolyn M. 114
Carrie (Sheets) 113, 115
Catharine 67
Catharine (Wallace) 6-9,
116, 122, 137
Catherine 117, 119, 137
Catherine Emaline 106
Catherine J. ( ) 132
Catherine L. 113

Cecile (Shively) 27
Charles . . . 18, 117, 141, 148
Charles B. 59
Charles E. 114
Charles Homer 62
Charles L. 25
Charles Newton . . . 25, 27, 28
Charles Taylor 119
Charles William . . 18, 48, 58,
                              62
Charles, Sr. 117
Charlotte Ellen 108
Christine Marie 67
Clarence B. 59
Clarence M. 113
Clarissa Harlow 118
Clayton Philip 111
Cleo 115
Clyde Wilbur 34
Connie (Kimble) 33
Connie Levada 109
Corina B. (Caylor) 39
Cyrus 120
Dana 67
Daniel . . 123-125, 131, 135,
                             148
Daniel Gary 109
Darrell Jay 34
Darrell S. 113
David 99, 104, 106, 111,
        112, 123, 125, 129, 131,
                             133
David Beydler 109
David Craun 107
David D. 114
David Stickley 106, 112
David Thomas 110
David William 111
Dawn 34
Deborah . . 34, 118, 123, 132
Deborah S. (Bowman) . . . 108
Dedrie 34
Delilah Ellen 104
Della Pearl 34
Denise 34
Dianah E. (Neely) 118
Donald L. 114
Donald Lee 34
Donna S. (Coffman) 107
Dorcas 118, 138
Dorcas ( ) 117, 120
Dorcas (Culp) 118
Dorcas (Garrison) 143
Dorcas (Wilson) 120
Dorcas A. (Wilson) . 117, 143
Doris (Huffman) 109
Doris (Pearl) 112
Doris G. (Allen) 109
Dorothy 28
Dorothy A. (George) . . 44, 46

Dorothy R. 114
Dorthea (Caulfield) 3
Douglas W. 113
Douglas Wade 109
Dovey W. (Winslow) 145
Drew L. 34
Duane Francis 28
Edith 137
Edith Blanch 28
Edith May 34
Edith Myrtle 26
Edith R. 115
Edith R. (Wilburn) 34
Edward 150
Edwin Glenn 114
Effie C. (Bussert) 34
Elaine (Bowling) 34
Eleanor ( ) 131
Eleanor (Evans) 138
Eleanor (Simonton) 130
Eleanor Tull 19, 20, 40
Eleazer 118
Eli 131, 132
Elias . . 8, 116-118, 120, 136
Elias, III 119
Elias, Jr. 118
Elijah 117
Eliza (Wroe) 141
Eliza H. (Guthrey) . 48, 65, 66
Elizabeth . . 4, 7-9, 120, 121,
        132, 139, 143, 148, 149
Elizabeth ( ) 123-125,
                             132
Elizabeth (Alexander) . . 120,
                             143
Elizabeth (Bradley) 117
Elizabeth (Caldwell) 131
Elizabeth (Davidson) 149
Elizabeth (Dunavant) . . 1, 18,
                         58, 71
Elizabeth (Gilpin) 138
Elizabeth (Henderson) . . 126
Elizabeth (Johnson) 125
Elizabeth (McReynolds) . 144
Elizabeth (Monteith) 135
Elizabeth (Orr) 135
Elizabeth (Robertson) . . 8-10
Elizabeth Ann . . . 20, 23, 35,
                             46
Elizabeth B. (Jesser) . . 48, 62
Elizabeth Brown 133
Elizabeth Garnet 67
Elizabeth Lee 67
Ella (Millard) 26
Ella M. (Millard) 34
Ellen Delilah 104
Elmo Gibson 48, 58
Elmo Walter 34
Elsie (Crim) 111
Elsie Viola 27

Elva F. (Simmons) 109
Elvin G. 113
Elvin Gardell, Jr. 113
Elvin Gardell, Sr. 113
Emaline 115
Emily (Woodson) 71
Emma (Diehm) . . 25, 27, 28
Emma Cora Alice 111
Emma J. (Bateman) . . 57, 58
Emma Jane 1, 48, 60
Emma Leola 72, 73, 94
Ephraim 131, 139
Ephraim K. 131
Eric Alan 108
Erin Victoria 111
Ester 117
Esther 143, 146
Esther ( ) 137
Esther (Brown) 125
Ethel W. 25
Eva B. (Craun) 109
Evan Shelby 119
Evelyn Mae 113
Ezekiel . . . 131, 137, 139, 140
Ezekiel, Jr. 123
Ezekiel, Sr. 123
Ezra 118, 120, 135
Family 1, 2, 125, 130
Fannie E. (Jones) 25, 26
Fanny 139
Fanny (Alexander) 139
Flora Grace 26
Flossie Abigail 33
Flossie Catherine 115
Frances 130
Frances ( ) 34, 141
Francis . . 2, 4, 117, 125-130,
               132, 133, 136
Francis Leroy 28
Francis R. 118
Franklin R. 110
Freddie 54
Gabriel Dean 113
Gail (Altenburg) 114
Gail Charlene 110
Geneva L. (Bateson) . . . 28
George 137, 140
George Newton 39
George Washington . . 26, 33
Gertrude 39
Gladys Alberta 113
Glen Brown 107
Gordon Weinburg 112
Grace (Cook) 114
Grace M. (Geuy) 27
Gregg Allen 109
Gunivere (Arey) 113
Gwenneth Lou 33
Hallah Franklin 111
Hannah 117, 133, 137

Hannah ( ) 117, 149
Hannah (Hodgson) 124
Hannah (Park) 143
Hannah (Parrot) 149
Hannelore B. (Keller) 59
Harmon 132
Harold Jay 33
Harold P. 113
Harriet (Clark) 119
Harriet A. 44
Harry Joseph 33
Harry Lowell 33
Harry Wilson 111
Hattie (Hooke) 111
Heather Adele 108
Helen (Fitzpatrick) 109
Helen Lavesta 34
Helen Louise 39
Helen Virginia 111
Henriette Catherine . . . 73, 95
Henry 99, 117, 127, 146,
148-150
Henry Thomas 34
Henry, Jr. 127
Henry, Sr. 127
Hezekiah 117, 120, 125,
132, 135, 137, 142, 143
Hilda L. 113
Hobart Link 115
Homer B. 112
Homer Birely 112
Homer Jesser 62
Howard Oscar 113
Hugh Lee 107
Ina Florence 26
Ina Mae 85
Inez E. (Barker) 73, 80
Infant . . 25, 67, 106, 108, 119
Irene M. 110
Irenus Bedford 113
Isaac . . . 117, 120, 123, 130,
131, 134, 135, 138, 139,
143
Isaac S. 119
Jacob 39, 133, 134
James . . . 2, 4, 7, 8, 68, 117,
118, 121-124, 126, 128, 129,
131-133, 135-139, 142, 144,
146, 149
James David 111
James Dixon 67
James E. (Selman) 107
James Franklin 25, 48
James Harvey 67
James Madison 135
James Newton 38, 39
James R. 143
James Robert 111
James S. 142
James Taylor 119, 123

James W. 19, 72
James Wallace 115
James Washington . . 19, 20,
48, 71-74, 78, 82, 85, 91, 94-
96
James William 39, 111
James, Jr. 123
James, Rev. 2, 7
Jane . . . 5, 7, 119, 121, 122,
126, 136, 147
Jane ( ) 128
Jane (Adair) 133
Jane (Bean) 133, 144
Jane (Harris) 120
Jane (Kennedy) 16
Jane (McClung) . . . 117, 124
Jane (McCorkle) 120
Jane (McKnitt) 116, 122,
136
Jane (Morrison) 148
Jane (Steele) 130
Jane (Taylor) 125, 132
Jane (Throckmorton) 130
Janet (Myers) 108
Jared C. 19, 106
Jared Craun 16, 19, 71, 106,
107
Jean 140
Jean ( ) 117, 133
Jean (Bain or Bean) 138
Jean (Brown) 131
Jean (Dekker) 67
Jean (McKnitt) 128
Jean Bain 144
Jedediah 116, 117
Jemima 137, 138
Jemima (McCoy) 139
Jemima A. (Sharp) 140
Jemima E. (McCoy) 139
Jennifer L. 113
Jennifer Marie 108
Jenny (Null) 112
Jeremiah 132
Jesse 130
Jill Lynn 108
Joab 120
Joan D. 114
Joannah (Wallace) 120
Joel 131, 143
Johanna 135
Johanna L. 114
John 2, 5, 9-12, 15, 57, 116,
126, 129, 133, 134, 146,
148-150
John Adam 107
John B. 131
John Bevans . 20, 23, 24, 35,
36, 38
John Brown 107, 131
John Edward 111

John Franklin 23
John H. 106
John Henry . . . 104, 106, 107
John Joseph 25, 26
John Leslie 109
John M. 138
John McKnitt . 133, 138, 140,
142, 144
John R. 114
John Seaver 67
John Sheldon . 10-12, 15, 18,
57, 99
John Whitlock 67
John Will 44, 46
John, of Eredy . . . . . vii, 2-4
Joseph 4, 116, 117, 122,
123, 126, 129, 136-138, 144
Joseph Alfred 114
Joseph Clayton 27
Joseph Donald 39
Joseph McKnitt 145
Joseph Moore 112
Joseph Moore, II 112
Joseph Moore, Jr. 112
Joseph Moore, Sr. 112
Josiah . . 120, 123, 125, 132,
138-140, 148
Josiah Martin 131
Juanita (Day) 25
Judy 67
Judy (Fischer) 110
June (Merrell) 109
Karl R. 106, 111
Karl R., Jr. 106
Karl Russell, III 111
Karl Russell, Jr. 111
Karl Russell, Sr. 111
Kathaleen (Borden) 114
Katherine 148
Katherine E. (LaFollette) . . 39
Kathleen 67
Kathryn (Racer) 107
Keith Michael 108
Kenneth 25
Kenneth Woodrow 33
Keturah 150
Kezia 137, 143
Keziah 137
Kimberly 67
Larabe 28
Larry Joe 28
Lavina (Magness) 118
Lavinia ( ) 117
Leah (Fleming) . . 11, 12, 15,
18, 99
Leah (Reagan) 119
Leanah 110
Lee A. 110
Lena (Young) 114
Lena M. (Walthall) 26, 33

157

Leroy 28
Leslie Craun 109
Levi 132
Lillian J. (Johnson) 34
Linda (Carlson) 112
Lindberg C. 114
Lisa D. (Miller) 108
Lisa F. (Townsen) 112
Lisa Renee 108
Liston 1, 7-9
Lois (Dixon) 67
Lois (Wine) 114
Lorene E. (Husted) 34
Lori Jo 28
Lorna (Martin) 33
Louis Carl 26
Louis Fry 72, 73, 80, 85
Louisa (Forqueran) 71
Lucinda Ann 112
Lucinda Mae 23
Lucinda Margaret 107
Lucy (Bugg) 125
Lucy (Meyerhoeffer) 114
Lula (Michael) 58
Lula A. (Michael) 58
Lula B. 58
Lurty James 104, 113
Luther David 114
Lyda Elizabeth 110
Lydia 132, 140
Madeline (Miller) 113
Madeline (Roach) 114
Madge Maupin 112
MaDora (Jordan) 111
Marbaret B. ( ) Smith . . 120
Marceline Emma 68
Margaret . 20, 117, 119, 125,
         133, 135, 137-139, 148
Margaret ( ) 126, 129,
                             148
Margaret (Alexander) . . 125,
                             135
Margaret (Brown) 133
Margaret (Carter) 118
Margaret (Cummings) . . . 140
Margaret (Gleason) 149
Margaret (Harris) . . . 120, 137
Margaret (McKnitt) 122, 136,
                   137, 142, 144
Margaret (Means) 119
Margaret (Polk) 125
Margaret (Price) 131
Margaret (Stickley) . 99, 104,
               106, 111, 112
Margaret (Wilson) 118
Margaret Ann 105
Margaret C. 110
Margaret Catherine 113
Margaret E. (Shufflebarger)
         107

Margaret G. (Alexander)
         138
Margaret Gilpin 138
Margaret McKnitt 144
Margaret P. (Brevard) . . . 125
Margie (Hensley) 112
Marguerite (Dougherty) . . 111
Maria ( ) 67
Maria (Waters) 119
Mariam (Shaw) 3, 4
Marie (Laughtin) 108
Marie (Luker) 67
Marie Delaino 115
Marie T. (Desoulets) 109
Marion H. 99
Marion Harold . . 99, 104, 115
Marion Richard 114
Mark . . . 120, 121, 124-126,
                   134, 138
Mark Davis 34
Marshall Huffman 109
Martha 118, 119
Martha ( ) 123, 135
Martha (Blair) 128, 133
Martha (Davies) 137
Martha (Kirkham) 135
Martha (Nichols) 143
Martha (Robinson) 135
Martha (Robison) 139
Martha (Wilson) 125
Martha Alice 113
Martha J. (Patterson) 23, 38,
                             39
Martha M. (Gover) 73, 82
Martin 128-131
Mary   8, 9, 67, 117-119, 125,
     128, 130-135, 137, 138, 143,
                             150
Mary ( ) . . 4, 72, 121, 123,
         124, 129, 131, 149, 150
Mary (Alexander) 135
Mary (Barbary) 5, 146
Mary (Clendenin) 138
Mary (Cooper) 140
Mary (Croushorn) 113
Mary (Dupree) 111
Mary (Henderson) 123
Mary (Hodnett) 112
Mary (Jordan) 111
Mary (Maupin) 112
Mary (Moore) 143
Mary (Polk) 118
Mary (Reed) 113
Mary (Rice) . . 20, 72, 82, 85,
               91, 94-96
Mary (Sample) 120, 137,
                   139, 142
Mary (Shelby) 117, 119
Mary (Sheldon) . 9, 10, 12, 15
Mary (Shull) 115

Mary (Sorrells) 113
Mary (Steele) . 123, 128, 129,
                             132
Mary (Taylor) . . . 4, 121, 128-
               130, 132, 134
Mary (Trotter) 133
Mary (Wallace) 121, 124
Mary Alice . . . 71-73, 82, 113
Mary Ann . 25, 28, 29, 48, 59,
                             109
Mary E. (Link) 106, 112
Mary E. (Prentice) 26
Mary Elizabeth 43, 106
Mary F. (Rankin) 131
Mary Frances 43, 107
Mary G. (Hedrick) 108
Mary Gibson 66
Mary Irwin 117
Mary Louis 114
Mary M. (Palmer) 23
Mary Ruth 34
Mary S. (Jordan) . . . 104, 111
Mary Sheldon 20
Mary Wilson 120
Matilda (McCaleb) 135
Matthew 116, 125, 135
Matthew David 110
Matthew Robert 108
Mattie (Troyer) 113
May (Sanders) 33
Mayben 135
Maybeth (Ramsey) 114
Megan 28
Melvin Harry 114
Mervin Racer 107
Michael Gordon 108
Mike Hays 33
Mildred (Orr) 125, 143
Millie (Loveless) 25
Millie Myrtle 28
Minnie (Bowman) 112
Minor H. 112
Minor Mervin 112
Minty 132
Miss 16
Molly Snell 112
Moses 1, 7-10, 124, 125,
               129, 132, 135
Moses Harvey . . . 47, 48, 54,
                   65, 66
Moses Harvey, Jr. 66
Moses Liston . . 1, 20, 43, 46,
                   47, 56
Moses Winslow 145
Moses, Jr. 126
Myrtie (Berry) 111
Nancy 16, 67, 117
Nancy ( ) 123
Nancy (Goodman) 59
Nancy (Hamilton) 20

Nancy (Query) 135
Nancy A. (McCall) 118
Nancy E. (Chaney) 110
Nancy F. (Hamilton) 43
Nannie 72
Nannie (Ashley) 72
Naomi 133, 149
Naomi Emma 133
Naomi Jane 113
Nathaniel 116, 120, 124, 125
Neil Wade 108
Nelson G. 135
Nelson John Robert 114
Nettie (Calvert) 62
Nettie B. 110
Neva Virginia 109
Nicole Michelle 67
Nina Lee 71, 73, 91
Nora 25
Norma Gene 107
Oscar Vastine 113
Oswald 143
Otto 25
Otto Laverne 34
Paige (Snell) 112
Pamela (Miller) 34
Paris 118
Patricia (Loving) 112
Patricia (Nevius) 111
Patricia Ann 67
Patsy ( ) 143
Paul Gardner 114
Pauline 112
Peggy (Eutsler) 114
Peggy Henderson 118
Peggy Y. (Long) 108
Peyton 63
Phebe 134
Phineus 117
Phyllis (Lambert) 114
Phyllis Pauline 113
Polly Ann 118
Priscilla 124, 138
Priscilla (Alexander) 138
Prudence 131, 135
Prudence ( ) 124
Prudence (Alexander) . . 131, 135
Prudence (Cole) 135
Rachel 138
Rachel ( ) . . . 123, 124, 127
Rachel (Alexander) 138
Rachel (Arnold) 26
Rachel (Davidson) 149
Ray Elgin 28
Raymond Galen 27
Raymond Robert 113
Reba (Cash) 113
Reba V. (Sandy) 108

Rebecca 117, 123, 131, 132, 148
Rebecca ( ) . . . 4, 127, 148
Rebecca (Allen) 142
Rebecca (Arthur) 120
Rebecca (Booth) 134
Rebecca (Brown) 123
Rebecca Frances 105
Rebecca Jordan 112
Rebecca Stacy 67
Rebekah W. (McClure) . . 130
Rebertha V. 110
Reda F. 114
Redempta 118
Retta Irene 26
Reuben 16, 19, 99, 104
Rhoda (Cunningham) . . . 149
Rhoda Lynn 28
Richard B. 59
Richard Brian 111
Richard Brown 59
Richard F. 113, 132
Richard Ford 132
Richard John 67
Robert 138
Robert Bowman 112
Robert David 114
Robert Donald 108
Robert Ellis 104, 111
Robert Elmer 26
Robert Stephen 112
Robert Wayne 108
Roberta Stephanie 112
Rosa E. (Davis) 73, 85
Rosa L. 114
Rosa Lee 62
Rosanna (McCracken) . . 116
Roscoe V. 114
Ross 119
Rudolph B. 107
Rudolph Bell 109
Ruth 117, 123, 125, 138
Ruth ( ) 143
Ruth (Reese) 119
Ruth (Sheets) 62
Ruth Ann 114
Ruth E. (Stansbury) 66
Ruth Virginia 66
Sally (Streiber) 67
Samantha ( ) 71, 78
Samuel 2, 4, 7-9, 16, 19, 99, 121-123, 126, 128-130, 132-134
Samuel Perry 26
Sandra L. (Stroberg) 109
Sarabell (Walker) 142
Sarah . 15, 16, 121, 123, 125, 127-129, 132, 138, 148
Sarah ( ) . 9-11, 128, 129, 134, 137

Sarah (Alexander) . 129, 132, 148
Sarah (Black) 114
Sarah (Egger) 25
Sarah (Fleming) 12, 15
Sarah (Glass) 118
Sarah (Rodgers) 143
Sarah (Sample) 143
Sarah (Sharp) 138, 140
Sarah (Smith) . . . 16, 99, 104
Sarah (Thornton) 120
Sarah A. 142
Sarah A. (Maxwell) . . 20, 47, 48, 56, 57, 59, 60, 62, 63, 65, 68
Sarah Agnes 106
Sarah Beth 107
Sarah Catherine . 71, 72, 78, 80
Sarah E. (Craun) . . . 104, 106
Sarah Elizabeth 26, 30
Sarah Jean 67
Sarah Lynn 67
Sarah M. (Reid) 25, 26
Sarah Margaret 48, 60
Sarah R. (Huffman) 107
Sarah Seymour 66
Sarah Shelby 119
Sarah Taylor 125, 126
Scott Barry 110
Sharon B. (Wine) 114
Shelby (Jones) 113
Shelby J. 114
Sidney 135
Silas 125, 143
Solomon 135
Sophia . . 116, 120, 125, 136, 137
Sophia ( ) 123
Sophia (Alexander) . . 8, 116, 120
Squire 132
Stanley Roller 114
Stephen 125, 135
Susan 119, 148
Susan (Monroe) 28
Susan (Polk) 117, 148
Susan Jane 23, 36
Susan R. (Horn) 39
Susanna 130, 150
Susannah 132
Susannah ( ) 123
Susannah (Ford) 150
Susannah (Foster) 128
Susannah (Johnston) . . . 131
Susannah (Shelby) 148
T.W. 54
Tabitha 133
Tamazon (Ford) 132
Tammy Lavonna 109

Tanya Marie 111
Taylor 148
Thelma D. (Kelley) 107
Theophilus 124, 137
Theresa (Pietropouli) 67
Therese F. (Schleper) 66
Thomas .. 118, 131, 148, 149
Thomas Jefferson 26, 34
Thomas S. 20
Thomas W. 58
Thomas Woodward .. 48, 57, 58
Thomas, III 150
Thomas, Jr. 150
Thurzy (Bridges) 133
Tirzah 118
Todd Wayne 34
Todd William 108
Trent Lee 34
Uriah 135
Vanessa 34
Velma Elizabeth 33
Vicki (Lockhart) 33
Viola (Graham) 113
Violet (Davidson) 144
Virginia Amelia 67
Virginia Joyce 113
Virginia Maude 26
Wallace 123, 126
Walter W. 142
Walter, Capt. 143
Washington 135
Wendy Denise 107
Whitfield 28
Wilbur David 113
Willam Benjamin 72
William . 1, 2, 7, 9, 15, 18, 19,
    23, 40, 43, 46, 47, 57, 71,
    99, 116, 117, 119, 123-125,
        130, 138, 148-150
William B. 144
William Bain 144
William Benjamin . 18-20, 35,
    36, 43, 47, 48, 54, 56, 57,
    59, 60, 62, 63, 65, 68, 71,
        74
William Brown 18
William D. 114
William David 27
William Dudley 108
William Guthrey 66, 67
William Henry 142
William I 4-7, 9, 122
William II 6-9, 122
William Lee Sample 126
William Louis 34
William Newell 26
William Noel 109
William O. 114

William, of Eredy .. 4, 6, 116,
    121, 123, 127, 128, 136,
        146, 147
William Otterbein 25
William Sample 120, 143
William Whitfield . 23, 24, 26,
    27, 30, 33, 34, 36
William Woodward .. 58, 59, 71
William Zebulon 117
William, II 6
William, Jr. 7, 123
Willie (Garrett) 111
Williiam Abner 135
Williiam Benjamin 54
Zebulon 117, 124
Zebulon, Jr. 124
Zenor 118
Alexandria City, Ala. ... 112
Alexandria Co., D.C. 141
    Mt. Ida 141
    Preston 141
Alexandria, Tenn. 131
Alexandria, Va. 19, 33, 59,
    109, 138, 140-142
    Alexandria Library 140
    Bank of Alexandria 141
    Brooke Lodge 2 141
    Brooke Lodge 47 141
    Chapman's Ferry 18
    Colross 140
    Inspector of Flour 141
    Old Presbyterian Meeting
        House 140
Alleghany Co., Va. 44
    Covington 58
Allen
    Barbara Marie 80
    Brittany 97
    Carey 134
    Doris G. 109
    Dorothy 29
    Elizabeth C. (Fleming) ... 134
    George W. 19, 47
    Lucius M. 142
    Mariah E. ( ) 142
    Mary E. Brown 109
    Rebecca 142
    Richard E. 97
    Rita M. (Corteville) 97
    Roscoe Miller 109
    Velma Pearl 91
    William Sample 143
Allen Co., Ky. 143
Allison
    O.E., Rev. 37
Allison's Creek 142
Altenburg
    Gail 114
Amelia C.H., Va. 35

Americus, Kan. 27
Amyx
    Ethel W. (Alexander) 25
    Fred S. 25
    Freda S. 25
    May (Alexander) .. 25, 27, 28
    Millie M. (Alexander) 28
    Shouse M. 28
    Shouse Morton 28
Anderson
    Comfort 127, 128
    Cornelius 6
    Florence 28
    Naomi 128
    William 116, 128
Anderson Co., Kan. 27
    Garnett 25, 26, 33
    Greeley 33, 35, 38
    Greeley Cem. 25, 39
Angelotti
    Mrs. Frank M. 118
Annemessix, Md. 128-130,
        132, 146
Anson Co., N.C. 118, 125
Antill
    Ruth Ann 35
Antonio, Tex. 85
Antrim
    Capt. 57
Apache, Colo. 69
Applegate
    Emma 41
    H. 41
    T. 41
Ardmore, Okla.
    Ardmore Memorial Hospital
        82
    Rose Hill Cem. 82
Arey
    Gunivere 113
Argenbright
    Don Martin 113
    Phyllis P. (Alexander) ... 113
Armentrout
    Elsie (Thacker) 41
    Helen (Alexander) 111
    William Preston 111
Armstrong
    Arthur 98
    James 98
    Jane (Kincaid) 98
    Nancy 98
Arnett
    Andrew 2
    William 2
Arnold
    Gail M. Stuart 108
    Rachel 26
Arthur
    Rebecca 120

Ashbacker
  Regina Margaret 33
Ashland, Kan. 34
Ashley
  Nannie 72
Atchison Co., Kan.
  Atchison 37
Atherton, Calif. 73
Atlanta, Ga. 87
Augusta Co., Va. . . 11, 12, 15,
      16, 19, 23, 44, 47, 56-59,
      104-107, 113, 123, 129
  Alexander Casket & Furniture
      Co. 43
  Augusta Memorial Park . . 113
  Augusta Stone Presbyterian
      Church Cem. 115
  Back Creek 43
  Basic City 19, 41
  Coiner's Store 56
  Deerfield 107
  Doom's Station 59
  Fishersville . . 44, 57, 62, 113
  Ft. Defiance 114, 115
  Greenville 69
  Greenville Dist. 99
  King's Daughters Hospital
      114
  Locust Springs 68
  Lyndhurst 43, 44, 46
  Middlebrook 110
  Moffat's Creek 35
  Mountain View Cem. 56,
      105
  Mt. Pisgah Cem. . . . 104-106
  Mt. Sidney 46, 104, 105,
      107, 112-114
  Mt. Solon 108
  Naked Creek 105, 110
  New Hope 46, 56
  Old Providence Church . . . 63
  Piedmont 56
  Salem Lutheran Church Cem.
      . . . . . . 104-107, 110-113
  Sangerville 109
  South River Dist. 44
  South River Twp. 43
  Spottswood 113
  Springhill 114
  St. Michaels Reformed Church
      Cem. 107, 110
  Staunton . . . 43, 44, 61, 107,
      108, 113, 115
  Staunton Bar Association
      107
  Stonewall 105
  Verona 108
  Waynesboro . 15, 16, 18, 19,
      43, 44, 47, 48, 54, 56-58, 60,
      62, 63, 65, 68, 69, 71, 72,

      78, 85, 104, 108, 109, 113,
      114
  Waynesboro Community
      Hospital 113
  Weyers Cave . . 71, 107, 109,
      110, 114
Ault
  David Leonard 31
  Elizabeth E. (Hathaway) . . 31
  Leonard Fay 31
  Vonna L. (Samuelson) . . . 31
Aurora, Ark. 37
Aurora, Colo. 86
Austin, Tex. 81
Ayshire, Scot. 142

B

Baber
  Betty G. (Good) 113
  Carolyn (Blackwell) 113
  Ernest G. 113
  Ernest N. 113
  Hilda (Alexander) 113
  Richard 113
  Stephen G. 113
  Vicki L. 113
Bacigalupo
  Betty 63
  James 62
  James Alexander 63
  Mary L. (Boro) 62
  Maybelle E. ( ) 63
  Rosa L. (Alexander) 62
  Vincent David 62
  William Vincent 63
Back Creek, Va. 43
Baggett
  Denver Enos 82
  Franchelle 82
  Lynn Richard 82
  Mary L. (Gilliam) 72, 82
Bain
  Jean 138, 144
  William 144
Bakersfield, Mo. 39
Bakewell
  Gertrude Elizabeth 67
Ball
  William 98
Baltimore Co., Md. 7
Baltimore, Md. . 110, 111, 124-
      126, 138
  Maryland Historical Society
      130
Bangor, Wales 107
Barbary
  Mary 5, 146
Barber
  Mabel Deater 29
  Marian Estella 29

Bard
  Richard 142
Barille
  Dorothy (Alexander) 114
  John J. 114
Barker
  Inez Ellen 73, 80, 85
  James Franklin 80, 85
  Joseph V. 78
  Martha M.J. (Bell) 78
  Martha T. (Molden) . . . 80, 85
  Samuel T. 72, 78
  Sarah C. (Alexander) . . . 72
Barnes
  Keith, Jr. 68
  Keith, Sr. 68
  Sara (Crutcher) 68
Barnett
  Joan L. (Day) 92
  Randall David 92
Barrett
  Henriette C. (Alexander) . . 73
  John G. 95
  John Joseph 73
  Mae 95
Barton Co., Mo. 91
Bartow Co., Ga. 139
Bash
  Doris A. (Dukes) 38
  Robert Henry 38
Basic City, Va. 19, 41
Bastian
  Mr. 33
  Violet (Sullins) 33
Bastian, Va. 107
Bateman
  Elijah 57
  Emma Jane 48, 57, 58
  Isabella M. (Hamilton) . . . 57
  Isabelle M. 57
  Maggie B. 58
Bates Co., Mo. 78
  Hume 33
Bateson
  Geneva Leola 28
  Jasper Newton 28
Bath Co., Va. 98
  Falling Spring Valley 98
  Green Valley 98
  Warm Springs 98, 108
Baton Rouge, La. 81
Battle of Fredericksburg . . . 23
Battle of Winchester 68
Baumgarten
  Barbara A. (Sebastian) . . . 87
  Deborah Lynn 87
  Michael Duayne 87
  Robert George 87
Baxter
  Richard 134

Bayless
  Carla Jo 32
  Carol K. (Carver) 32
  Cathy Elaine 32
  Cathy Sue 32
  Cleora Elaine 32
  Joan ( ) 32
  Keven James Martin 32
  Lawrence Clarence 32
  Lawrence Robbert, III 32
  Lawrence Robert, Jr. 32
  Lawrence Robert, Sr. 32
  Orpha A. (Hammond) 32
  Pamela S. (Garrett) 32
  Robin Carol 32
Baylor
  David 105
  Helen Sands 105
  Rebecca E. (Landes) . . . 105
Beagle, Kan. 25-28, 33
Bean (see Bain)
  Jane 133, 144
Beard
  Rev. 57
  William 11
Beattie's Ford, N.C. 131
Beaver
  Nellie 38
Beckham Co., Okla.
  Elk City 81
  Sayre 87
Bedder
  William, Sr. 127
Beddow
  William 99
Beedle
  Araminta (Alexander) . . . 132
  Thomas 132
Beery
  Hannah R. 112
Bell
  Amy (Markwell) 92
  Amy Frances 92
  Berwin Irving 86, 92
  Berwyn Warren 92
  Corrine K. (Muir) 92
  Cynthia G. (Plattner) 92
  Deborah P. (Perkins) 92
  Diana L. (Giffin) 92
  Harlee 92
  Ida 110
  Irving 92
  Jeannine Lee 86, 92
  Jeff Alan 92
  John Irving 92
  Kim ( ) 92
  Martha M.J. 78
  Mick Aaron 92
  Mildred I. (Pippenger) . . . 86, 92

  Terry Lynn 92
  Thomas Lynn 92
Bellier
  Augustine 33
Bellows
  Harriett Odessa 82
Belton, Mo. 96, 97
Belvue, Kan. 31
  Greenwood Cem. 31
Bennett
  Charles 141
  Harriett Elsaba 91
Benthall
  Ada C. (Edwards) 69
  Anne Edwards 69
  Henen Christian 69
Berkeley, Calif. 73
Bermuda, W.I. 140
Berrien Co., Mich.
  Sawyer 94
Berry
  Andrew 139
  James 111
  Jemima (Sample) 139
  Mr. 112
  Myrtilla Susan 111
  Naomi ( ) 111
  Rebecca C. (Thacker) . . . 42
  Roberta (Alexander) . . . 112
  William 42
Bethlehem, Pa. 60
Bevans (see Bibbins)
  Ann . . . 1, 15, 18, 19, 23, 40, 43, 46, 47, 57, 71, 99
  Eleanor (Tull) 15, 18, 57
  Family 1
  John 15, 18, 57
  Margaret (Price) 18
  Mary (Dewry) 18
  Rowland 15, 18
  Sarah 8
  Thomas 18
Beverley
  Robert 4
Beymer
  Phebe Ann 28
Bibbins (see Bevans)
  Ann 18
  John 18
Bibbins Landing, Md. 18
Bibbins Point, Md. 18
Billings
  Benjamin 9
Birch Tree, Mo. 94
Bird
  Jacqueline (Snow) 60
  John Woodbridge 60
  Mary J. (Chambers) . 43, 47, 54, 60
  Peyton 60

  Robert Montgomery 60
  William 140
Black
  Adelina Sarah 114
  Capt. 140
Blacksburg, Va. 59, 110
Blackwell
  Carolyn L. 113
Blain
  Elizabeth 41
Blair
  Hannah (Alexander) 133
  Martha 128, 133
  William 133
Bland Co., Va.
  Bastian 107
Bledsoe
  John Quincy 27
  Marvin E. 27
  Thurman L. 27
Blount
  Gov. 134
Blue Hills, Mo. 87
Blue Mound, Kan. 81
Blue Springs, Mo. 86, 88
Bodkin
  Delilah 35
Boggs
  Asahel 139
  Esther (McCoy) 139
Bonita, Calif.
  Glen Abbey Memorial Park 82
Bonner Springs, Kan. 33
Boone Co., Ind. 24, 25
  Crawfordville 28
  Jamestown 25
Boone, N.C. 88
Booth
  Rebecca 134
Boots
  Margaret (Bruce) 81
Borden
  Kathaleen 114
Boro
  Mary L. 62
Borzonosca, Italy 63
Boston, Mass. 18
Bouchelle
  Peter 128
Boulden
  Mary (Alexander) 134
  William 132
Bouldin
  Elizabeth 130
  John 130
  Mary (Alexander) 130
Boulding
  James 130
Bourbon Co., Kan. 78, 81

Bowen
  Family 94
Bowers
  Derias Wayne 92
  Janice L. (Day) 92
  Kristina Dee 92
Bowes
  Janet Lynn 96
  Karl 96
  Larry Joe 96
  Larry Lynn 96
  Lori Diane 96
  Ruth A. (O'Neill) 96
  Stelline ( ) 96
  Terri 96
Bowles
  Ida 87
Bowling
  Ben 34
  Elaine 34
  Iva (Sawyers) 34
Bowman
  Belle (Alexander) 25
  Benjamin 112
  Catherine ( ) 112
  Charles 25
  Deborah Susan 108
  Edith B. (Alexander) 28
  Elba Clark 28
  Goldie 25
  Hannah R. (Beery) 112
  Henry 25
  Minnie B. 112
  Samuel R. 112
Bowman, Ga. 60
Boyd
  Jane 47, 56
  Rebecca 47, 48, 56
Braden
  Jean 132
Bradley
  Abigail (Alexander) 139
  Elizabeth 117, 139
  Esther 139
  Francis 139
  James 139
  John McKnitt 139
  Rebecca 139
Bradshaw
  Susan Jewett 85
Breckenridge, Mo. 32
Breedlove
  Lena Virginia 44
Brenner
  Esther E. 31
Brevard
  Adam 147
  Benjamin 147
  Elizabeth 147
  Ephraim 125, 143

Jane (McWhorter) 147
John 147
John, Jr. 147
Katherine (McKnitt) 147
Margaret (Polk) 125
Margaret Polk 125
Mary (McKnitt) 147
Robert 147
Zebulon 147
Bridge Port, Kan. 37
Bridges
  Thurzy 133
Bridgewater, Va. 106-108,
                              113
  Oak Lawn Cem. 41
Brinston
  Ella 92
Bristol, Tenn. 108
Broad River 142
Broadwater
  Betty (Sheldon) 11, 15
  James 11
Brockus
  Anna M. (Alexander) 39
  Betty J. (Richey) 39
  Bryan 39
  Clifford Wayne 39
  Della (Bickerstaff) 39
  Delores Jean 39
  Eldon Eugene 39
  Eldon Ray 39
  Eli 39
  Eunice (Finch) 39
  Jim 39
  Martha Emiline 39
  Mary (Holloway) 39
  Nancy Sue 39
  Nellie Marie 39
  Norman James 39
  Richard Dale 39
  Roger Newton 39
  Ronald Wayne 39
  Rose F. (Henry) 39
  Thomas 39
  Thomas B. 39
  Thomas Newton 39
  Tonya 39
Bronson
  Margaret 118
Brooklyn, N.Y. 65
Brova
  Ida 94
Brown
  Anna A. (Morrow) 81
  Barbara Dell 81
  David 81
  Elizabeth B. (Alexander)
      133
  Ernest Carlee 81
  Esther 125

Frances L. (McCleron) . . . 81
Gay L. 81
Gay Lee 81
Harvey Joe 32
Imogene (Mills) 81
Infant 81
Jean 131
Jennifer 81
Jessie B. 81
Jessie Bernice 81
Joseph Rogers 133
Julia Ann 81
Katherine 96
Leslie Jean 81
Mable Margaret 31
Margaret 83, 110, 133
Mary E. 109
Nellie V. (Paddock) 81
Omer 78
Omer F. 81
Omer Frankliln, Sr. 81
Omer Franklin, Jr. 81
Rebecca 123
Tracy D. (Erecius) 32
William Thomas 81
Brown Co., Ohio
  Mt. Orab 38
Brownsburg, Va. 23
Brownsville, Pa. 41
Brubeck
  Edith (Alexander) 115
Bruce
  "E." Delbert 81
  Ann 81
  Charles Delbert 81
  Delbert 81
  Donald 81
  Helen (Murray) 81
  Jack Allen 81
  Jessie (Brown) . . . 65, 78, 81
  Julia Ann 81
  Kimberly 81
  Margaret 81
  Mary Ann 81
  Mikaela Mitchell 81
  Philip A. 104
  Rebecka Jean 81
  Robert 81
  Robert Franklin 81
  Ruth 81
  Stephanie (Gautreau) 81
Bryan
  Mathew, Jr. 117
Bryant, Ind. 28, 29
Bucks Co., Pa. 132, 148
Bugg
  Jacob 125
  Lucy 125
Bullard
  Henry 9

Bullocks Creek, S.C. 137
Buncombe Co., N.C.
   Bee Tree Creek 149
   Swannanoa Settlement . . 149
Burkdoll
   Anna F. (Shofner) 36
   Betty Jean 36
   Flora M. (Hopwood) 35
   Francis Alonzo 35
   John Elwin 36
   John William 35
   Lloyd Francis 36
   Margaret (Needham) 35
   Virginia L. (Vaughn) 36
Burke
   Mary (Alexander) 131
Burton
   Charles D. 91
   Clara T. 91
   John 44
   Martha ( ) 44
   Mary ( ) 4
   Susan 44
   William 4
Busch
   Jessica Lee 28
   Rhonda L. (Alexander) . 28
   Steven 28
   Steven Alexander 28
Bussert
   Effie Corrine 34
Butler Co., Mo.
   Poplar Bluff 86
Butts Co., Ga. 131
Byers
   Sadie 105
   Stella Catherine 105
Byrd
   Barbara 40

C

C.S.A.
   Alexander, James W. 72
   Alexander, John F. 23
   Alexander, John W. 44
   Alexander, Thomas W. . . . 57
   Alexander, William B. 47
   McCormick, Horatio T. . . . 68
   Walton, John N. 98
Cabarrus Co., N.C. . . 119, 124,
      125, 131, 132, 135, 148
   Rocky River Presbyterian
     Church Cem. 119, 143
Caldwell
   Abigail B. (Alexander) . . . 144
   Ann 131
   David 144
   Elizabeth 131
   Emma 39
   John 7, 8

Rachel (Craighead) 144
Samuel Craighead 144
Caldwell, Idaho
   Memorial Park Hospital . . . 85
Calhoun, Mo. 86
California 26
Calvert
   James 62
   Mary (Croft) 62
   Nettie 62
Calvert Co., Md. 121
Camden, S.C. 120, 129
Camell
   Lawrance 127
   Peter 127
Cameron
   Beatrice R. (Haller) 31
   John Gordon 31
   John Mitchell 31
   John Scott 31
   Steven Lee 31
   Valorie L. (Samuelson) . . . 31
Camp Chase, Ohio 72
Campbell
   Annie (Alexander) 118
   Frank 80
   Isaac 143
   Katherine (Riley) 69
   Mary 134
   Nellie Riley 69
   Stephen 118
   William 69
Cannon
   Ann (Alexander) 137
   James 137
   Joseph 137
   Margaret (Alexander) . . . 137
   Rachel 138
Cannon Co., Tenn. 140
Cape Girardeau Co., Mo. . . 135
Cardinal
   Donald 36
   O'Della (Vint) 36
Caricofe
   Catherine Susan 41
   Goldie Raymond 41
Carlson
   Linda 112
Caroline Co., Va.
   Port Royal 142
Carothers
   Esther (Sample) 139
   John 139
Carroll Co., Ind.
   Delphi 30
Carroll's Delight 133
Carruth
   Elizabeth 69
Carter
   Alma 59

Charles D. 59
Lucy (Dufner) 59
Margaret 118
Carver
   Carol Kay 32
   Carroll Kemper 32
   Cleora M.S. ( ) 32
   Frances Elaine 32
   Mabel F. (McCain) 32
   Virgile Bell 32
Cary
   Edward 150
   Mary (Alexander) 150
Cary, N.C. 69
Casey
   Mary ( ) 150
   Philip 150
Cash
   Mary ( ) 140
   Reba F. 113
   William, Jr. 140
Casho Co., N.C. 132
Cass Co., Minn. 72
Cass Co., Mo. 35
   Belton 96
   Harrisonville 35
Catawba Co., N.C. 120
   Alexander's Mill 120
Catawba River 142, 148
Catling
   Amanda A. 56
   Betsy 56
   Eleanor (Tull) 15, 57
   Eliza 56
   Elizabeth ( ) 57
   Family 1
   Joshua 18, 57
   Joshua M. 15
   Joshua Merrill 15, 18, 57
   Julia A. 56
   Mary 57
   Thomas 56
   Tracey (Tressco) 57
Catrine, Scot. 140
Caulfield
   Dorthea 3
   James, Rev. 3
Caylor
   Corina Belle 39
Cearlock
   Diane 68
Cecil Co., Md. . . 1, 4, 5, 7, 116-
    118, 120-126, 128-132, 134,
    136-140, 142-144, 146, 147
   Alexandria 124, 128-130,
                 133
   Big Elk River 116, 136
   Bohemia Manor 122, 128
   Bullen's Range 128, 132
   Elk River 121, 147

Elkton 130
Francis' Marsh 133
Glasgow 134
Hispaniola 128, 132
Long Creek 133
Manokin Hundred 136
New Munster . 121, 123, 124,
129, 136
O'Dwire Tract 136
Salisbury 125
Slate Hill 136
Sligo 124, 128-130
St. Stephens Parish . . . 121,
122, 132
Cedar Grove Mills, Va. 24
Cedar Vale, Kan. 38
Centre Co., Pa.
Old Unionville Cem. 130
Unionville 130
Cepeda
Charles 67
Kathleen (Alexander) 67
Chambers
Claude Caesar 60
Edith (Whitlock) 46, 47
Edith R. (Whitlock) . . . 18, 60
Eliza J. (Roberts) 60
Emma J. (Whitlock) . . 19, 43
Mary Jane 47, 54, 60
Nicholas 130
Robert G. 60
Chambersburg, Ill. 37
Chancellor
Janet L. (Bowes) 96
Kenneth 96
Chaney
Nancy Elizabeth 110
Chapman
Alfred 19
Chariton Co., Mo.
Keytesville 82
Charles
E. 46
Charles Co., Md. 18
Charleston, Va. 71
Charlotte, N.C. . . . 2, 117, 119-
121, 129, 142-144
Presbyterian Church Cem.
. . . . 125
Public Library 140
Sharon Presbyterian Church
Cem. 118
Steel Creek Presbyterian
Church Cem. 139
Charlottesville, Va. . 58, 59, 69,
110
Meadows Presbyterian Church
. . . . 69
University of Virginia Hospital
. . . . 59, 69

Chase
Ida B. 36
Cherokee Indians 148
Cherryvale, Kan. 26
Fairview Cem. 26, 34
Sunset Retreat Nursing Home
. . . . 34
Chesapeake Bay 7, 18
Chesapeake City, Md.
Bethel Cem. 128
Chester Co., Pa. . . 1, 117, 121-
123, 136, 138, 144, 149
East Nottingham Twp. . . . 138
West Nottingham Twp. . . 138
Cheverly, Md. 110
Chicago, Ill. 86
Chickasha, Okla. 83
Chitwood
Cecile (Shively) 27
Christian
Hugh A. 114
Lola L. 114
Margaret 134
Mary (Campbell) 134
Reda (Alexander) 114
William 134
Chula Vista, Calif. 72, 82
Clan MacAlister 2
Clapham
Abigail (Alexander) 136
Francis 136
Clare Co., Mich.
Clare 25, 29
Clare, Mich. 25, 29
Claremore, Okla. 37
Woodlawn Cem. 37
Clark (see Clarke)
Alexander 123
Ann (Alexander) 123
Carole 97
Daniel 118
Deborah (Alexander) 118
Dian (Manley) 118
Elizabeth (Pannil) 118
Gilbert 123
Harriet 119
J., Prof. 65
Jesse 118
John 57
Margaret (Bronson) 118
Robert 118
William L. 118
Clark Co., Kan.
Ashland 34
Clark Co., Nev.
Las Vegas 38
Clarke (see Clark)
Brett Thomas 88
James Granville, Jr. 88
James Granville, Sr. 88

James Steven 88
Jane Leigh 88
John Kevin 88
Judith Alta 88
Madeline L. (McLaughlin)
. . . . 72, 82, 88
Marilyn ( ) 88
Mr. 54
Patricia A. (Abston) 88
Clarkson
James 99
Maria (Wood) 99
Clarksville, Tenn. 108
Claxton
Allen E. 40
Lucy (Denton) 40
Clayton, Mo. 66
Clem
Jos. 54
Clendenin
Mary 138
Cleveland
Rev. 56
Clifton
Darrell 29
Evelyn W. (Guy) 29
Gladwin 29
Mary J. (Guy) 29
Clinedinst
Charles Gates 61
Mary B. (Whitlock) 61
Clinton, Mo. 19, 94
Cloud
James 142
Sarah (Alexander) 142
Sarah A. (Alexander) 142
Clover Hill, Va. 40, 41
Clover, S.C. 137
Cochran
Carla J. (Bayless) 32
Julian Michael 32
Lark 32
Michael Dean 32
Sarah J. 113
Sybil Emma 33
Wanda (Hill) 32
Cocke
A.R., Rev. 54, 58
John H. 99
Coddle Creek, N.C. 135
Coffman
Donna Stuart 107
Katie 41
Coiner
Gabriel Dewitt 105
Lucy A. (Wine) 105
Mary L. (Faber) 59
Vastine 59
Cole
Prudence 135

Coleman
  Barbara (Fath) 68
  Caleb Berrien 68
  Cody Ray 68
  Craig Berrien 68
  Hal Berrien 68
  Lauren Nicole 68
  Timothy Dean 68
  Tracy Lee 68
  Vicki (Shaw) 68
  Virginia D. (Theis) 68
  Zachary 68
Coles Co., Ill.
  Pleasant Prairie Cem. . . . 143
Collins
  Mr. 39
  Nancy S. (Brockus) 39
Colne, Eng. 92
Colorado 25
Columbia, Md. 110
Columbia, Mo. 87
Comerford
  Peter 117
Concord, N.C. 125
Conger
  Eli 131
  Mary (Alexander) 131
Connelly
  Margaret 86
Cook
  Edgar G. 44
  Elizabeth 30
  Grace P. 114
  Miss 28
  Mr. 44
Cooke Co., Ga.
  Adel 32
Cooper
  Mary 140
Copeland
  Catherine 25
  John 25
  Nora (Alexander) 25
  Winifred 25
Coppedge
  Mary Leota 82
Corbin
  Betty (Sheldon) 11
  Peter 11
  William 11, 15
Corning, Kan. 31
Corteville
  Alberta (O'Neill) 97
  Alberta I. (O'Neill) 97
  Brian Kenneth 97
  Carole (Clark) 97
  Colleen Patricia 97
  Drucilla (Matiecawiez) 97
  Elizabeth 97
  Jacque (McDonald) 97

  James Thomas 97
  Joseph Michael 97
  Kathleen Teresa 97
  Leonie (Van Dew) 97
  Lianne (Curtis) 97
  Olivia 97
  Pamela Michelle 97
  Rita Maureen 97
  Thomas Michael 97
  Timothy John 97
  Victor 97
  William Donald 97
  William Joseph 97
  William Patrick 97
Coryell
  Ann (   ) 140
  George 140
Cosden
  Rev. 138
Cottman
  Benjamin 8
Cotton Port, Ala. 133
Cottrell
  Arthur 31
  Esther E. (Brenner) 31
County Armagh, Ire. 91
County Cork, Ire. 96
County Donegal, Ire. . . 2, 6, 7,
  116, 121, 123, 127, 128,
  136, 146, 147
  Balleighan 3
  Clonmany Parish 3
  Raphoe Parish 3
  Taghboyne Parish 3
Covesville, Va. 48, 56
Covington, Va. 58, 108
  Cedar Hill Cem. 58
Cowan
  James 134
  Margaret C. (Russell) . . . 134
Cox
  James 125
  Julia A. (Brown) 81
  Mary (Alexander) 125
Coyner's Store, Va. 56
Craig
  Mary (Alexander) 128
  Thomas 128
Craighead
  Agnes 133
  Alexander, Rev. 133, 144
  Rachel 144
Craun
  C. Randolph 110
  Catharine 104, 105
  Catherine 106, 112
  Charles Homer 110
  Daniel Harvy 106
  Eva 110
  Eva Blanch 109

  Fleta (Null) 109
  Granville 110
  Ida (Bell) 110
  James W. 110
  John 110
  Lee A. (Alexander) 110
  Lucinda (Wise) 106
  Lutie (Wineberg) 110
  Margaret (Brown) 110
  Neoma (Rimel) 110
  Richard F. 110
  Ruby 110
  Samuel H. 109
  Samuel Henry 109
  Sarah Elizabeth . . . 104, 106,
    107
Crawford
  John 7
Crawford Co., Kan.
  Pittsburg 33
  Topeka 86
Crawfordville, Ind. 28
Creager
  C.E., Rev. 36
Crescent, Tenn.
  Alexander Family Cem. . . . 131
Crim
  Anna (   ) 111
  Elsie P. 111
  William 111
Crimora, Va.
  Mountain View Cem. 105
  Trinity Lutheran Church . . 104
Crissman
  James Edward 108
  Kathryn A. (Moats) 108
Croft
  Mary 62
Crouse
  A.L., Rev. 44
Croushorn
  James William 105
  Lucy A. (Wine) 105
  Mary 113
Crowley
  Mary 66
Crutcher
  Annie 68
  Benjamin James 68
  Bettie (Davis) 68
  David 68
  Diane (Clearlock) 68
  Donald Eugene 68
  Doris (Sullivan) 68
  Elizabeth Harris 68
  Eugene Long 68
  James Alexander, Jr. 68
  James Alexander, Sr. 68
  Janet Dale 68
  Kari Nicole 68

Katherine 68
Marceline E. (Alexander) . . 68
Patrick Joseph 68
Paul Anthony 68
Rachel 68
Ralph 68
Rebecca 68
Robert Donald 68
Robert Paul 68
Roy 68
Ruth ( ) 68
Sara 68
Susan Margaret 68
Cuddy
  Leonard 33
  Marvin W. 33
  Velma E. (Alexander) 33
Culp
  Dorcas 118
  John 118
  Polly A. (Alexander) 118
Cumberland Co., Pa. 142,
                              148
Cumberland Co., Va. 65
Cunningham
  Humphrey 149
  James 2
  Rhoda 149
  Rhoda (Summerville) . . . 149
Curryville, Ind. 29
Curtin
  Daniel 140
Curtis
  Lianne 97

D

Daintry 7, 8
Dalby
  Daima Melinda 113
Dale
  John 136
  Martha 121, 147
Dallas, Tex. 87
Dancaster
  Della (Bickerstaff) 39
Dannatt
  Maude Ethel 86
Daugherty
  Mary Ann 42
Davidson
  John 120, 144, 149
  Margaret (McConnell) . . . 149
  Mr. 19
  Rachel 149
  Samuel 149
  Violet 144
  Violet W. (Wilson) 144
  William 120, 149
Davies (see Davis)
  Catherine 119

Martha 137
Davis (see Davies)
  Bettie 68
  Campbell Robert 23, 35
  Edmund 19
  Edmund, Capt. 19
  Electa May 35
  Elizabeth A. (Alexander) . . 23
  Ellis 35
  Gov. 62
  John 142
  Rosa E. 73, 85
  Sallie ( ) 35
  Virginia C. 35
Davison
  Chester Leland 91
  Velma P. (Allen) 91
  Zora Eileene 91
Day
  Beulah (Wagner) 92
  Dorothy Hollen 86, 92
  Edward 7
  Elijah 92
  Harold Leslie 92
  Harold Leslie, Jr. 92
  Janice Leann 92
  Joan Louise 92
  Juanita 25
  Mary A. (Abbas) 92
  Mary Elizabeth 36
Dayton, Ohio 92
Dayton, Va. . . . 40, 42, 107, 110
  Pleasant View Mennonite Cem.
  41
Dean
  Carl R., Sr. 41
  Norma J. (Thacker) 41
Decatur, Ill. 35
Deepwater, Mo. 94
Deerfield, Va. 107
Dekker
  Jean 67
Delaware 123
Delaware, Ohio 54
Delker
  Deanna Kay 31
  Dorothy (Graves) 31
  Lester 31
Delphi, Ind. 30
Denton
  Alice F. 40
  Charles Lee 40
  Charley 40
  Elizabeth J. (Kersh) 40
  Emma S. (Huffman) 40
  James William 40
  Lillian Virginia 40
  Lucy 40
  Mary A. (Thacker) 40
  Mary J. 40

Selah F. 40
Denver, Colo. 91
  Denver Public Library . . . 136
Deplue
  Adolph 28
  Betty Lee 28
  Claudia (Plumlee) 28
Depriest
  Mary 60
Desoulets
  Marie Theresa 109
Detamore
  Rebecca C. (Thacker) 42
  St. Clair 42
Detroit, Mich.
  Grace Hospital 95
Dewey
  Oscar 81
DeWoody
  Hannah (Alexander) 133
  William 133
Dewry
  Mary 18
Dickinson
  Samuel 149
Dickson
  Abigail (Sample) 139
  Thomas 139
Diddle
  D.E. 46
  F. 46
  Mary Gertrude 46
Diehm
  Emma 25, 27, 28
  Fred 27
  Mary ( ) 27
  Mary Elizabeth 33
Disosway
  John Justice 69
  Rebecca A. (McCormick) . 69
Dixon
  Lois 67
Dobbin
  John 123
Dobbs
  Ashley Lynn 87
  Dillon 87
  Kiplin 87
  Wanda K. (McLaughlin) . . . 87
Dobson
  Ann N. (Dobson) 126
  Ann Nancy 126
  Capt. 126
Doom's Station, Va. 59
Dorchester Co., Md. 1, 9
Doris 87
Dorman
  Charity 11
  John 9
  Mary (Sheldon) 11

Matthew 11
Michael 15
Nehemiah 10
Sarah (Gray) 10
Sarah (Sheldon) 11
Dougherty
  Marguerite 111
Douglas
  Amy Janelle 81
  Daniel 141
  Gay (Brown) 81
  Gay L. (Brown) 81
  Gregory 81
  Larry D. 81
  Larry Daniel 81
  Rev. 57
  Ronald 81
Douglas Co., Kan.
  Lawrence 25, 27, 28
Douglas Co., Nebr.
  Omaha 87
Downs
  Elizabeth (Whitlock) 61
Driver
  Bonnie (Puffenbarger) . . . 114
  Phillip 114
  Zola Adaline 37
Dryden
  Joel 133
  Ruth T. 127
  Tabitha (Alexander) 133
Dublin, Ire. 97
DuBose
  Joyce Marie 32
Dufner
  Lucy 59
Duke
  William 132
Dukes
  Alice M. (Stringer) 38
  Anna May 37
  Barbara Jean 38
  Betty Jean 38
  Donald Lee 38
  Doris Ann 38
  Dorothy Aileen 38
  Earl Hand 37
  Fern 37
  George F. 38
  Gerald Dennis 38
  Gertrude 38
  Harold Ellis 37
  Harold Paul 38
  Henry Sylvester 36
  Howard Henry 37
  John William 37
  Kenneth Paul 38
  Larry Eugene 38
  Lena ( ) 38
  Marjorie L. (Locke) 38

Marvin Hardin 38
Mary B. (Ernest) 37
Mary J. (Killough) 37
Maxine (Oliver) 38
May (Hume) 37
Mayfred Ethel 38
Nellie (Beaver) 38
Patrick Joseph 37
Stephen 36
Susan ( ) 36
Susan J. (Alexander) . 23, 25,
                              36
Viola F. (Hand) 36
Walter Henry 38
Wayne Edward 38
William 37
William Bernard 37
William H. 23
William Henry 23, 36
Dulaney
  William 7
Dull
  Betsy 67
  John Scott 67
  Judy (Alexander) 67
  Tom 67
Dumbell
  Marceline E. (Alexander) . . 68
  Ralph H. 68
Dumfries, Va. 108
Dunavant
  Elizabeth 1, 58, 59
  Elizabeth (Jenkins) 59
  Joseph S. 59
  Joseph Samuel 59
  Melissa (Lamar) 59
  Ollie Brown 59
Duncan
  Bettie June 35
Dundas
  John 141
Dunmore
  John 23
Dupree
  Mary 111
Duvall
  William T., Rev. 142
Dwyer
  Winifred Catherine 30
Dysart
  James 125
  Mary 125
  Ruth (Alexander) 125

E

Earls of Stirling 1
Earlysville, Va. 68, 69
East Chicago, Ill. 31
Edinborough, Scot. 1
Edna, Kan. 30

Edscorn
  Carol A. (Sordillo) 86
  Christopher 87
  Christopher Mark 86
  David Alexander 87
  Dorothy E. (McLaughlin) . . 86
  Joseph 87
  Julie Ann 87
  Kenneth Charles 86
  Luke Vincent 87
  Marielle 87
Edwards
  Ada Cornelia 69
  Eunice E. (McNutt) 33
  James Harvey 33
  Violet Norma 33
Egger
  Sarah 25
El Paso, Tex. 59
Elbert Co., Va.
  Bowman 60
Eldred
  J.W., Rev. 37
Elk City, Okla. 81
Elk Co., Kan.
  Howard 26
Elk Rapids, Mich. 26, 29
Elkton, Md. 124, 130, 138
Elliott
  Fred 29
  Nadean L. (Guy) 29
Ellis
  Gertrude (Dukes) 38
  Jessie 80
  Mollie (Ham) 80
  Mollie Ham 80
  Newton 38
  William 80
Elliss
  Leroy L. 38
  Sharon J. (Ailshie) 38
Ellisville, Mo. 97
Elmwood, Nebr. 80
Emporia, Kan. 34, 37
England 117
Englewood, Colo. 91
Enid, Okla. 107
Ennis
  Nathaniel 127
Enoch
  Ella Mae 82
Enser
  Mary 12
Erecius
  Dorothy D. (Holmes) 32
  Linda ( ) 32
  Richard Andrew, Jr. 32
  Richard Andrew, Sr. 32
  Tracy Dawn 32
Eredy, Ire. 2, 116

Ernest
Mary Bridget 37
Errigal Parish, Ire. 3
Essex Co., Va.
Tappahannock . . . . . vii, 108
Eureka, Kan. 26
Eutsler
Peggy 114
Evans
Bertha Alma 35
Delores J. (Brockus) 39
Eleanor 138
Jean (Moore) 138
John 138
Margaret (Kirkpatrick) . . . 138
Mary (Alexander) 138
Mr. 39
Robert 138
Sarah 138
Evanston, Ill. 92
Evansville, Ind. 80
Everest, Kan. 36
Evers
Ella Dorothy 41
Everson
Mr. 96
Nancy L. (O'Neill) 96
Ewing
S.P. 82
Excelsior Springs, Mo. 80
Eye
W.D., Rev. 112
Eynon
Esther Maud 80
John 72, 78, 80
Sarah C. (Alexander) 72, 78, 80

F

Faber (see Fauber)
Ada (McCormick) 59
Ada McCormick 59
Charles Maxwell 59
Dorothy (Winn) 59
Edwin McFaddin 59
Harold 59
Harold Hamilton 59
Lucille 59
Mary Lucille 59
Maxwell 59
Sara 59
William 59
William F. 59
Faber, Va. 56
Fairfax Co., Va. 140
Cameron 140
Cameron Mills 140
Vienna 112
Fairfield, Va. 113

Fairman
Charles E., III 30
Charles E., Jr. 30
Charles E., Sr. 30
Mary (Marshall) 30
Virginia E. (Scott) 30
Fairmount, Mo. 85
Falk
Dana Lynn 32
Danny Eugene 32
Danny Eugene, Jr. 32
Louella L. (Lawbaugh) . . . 32
Veronica L. (Wellington) . . 32
William Francis 32
Farran
Kimberly L. 28
Fath
Barbara 68
Fauber (see Faber)
Alma (Carter) 59
Charles Maxwell 59
Elizabeth (Harnes) 59
Ella (Williams) 59
Joseph 59
Joseph Everett 59
Lottie H. 18
Lottie Hildreth 18, 59, 72
Mary A. (Alexander) . . 48, 59
Mollie 54
Rodger W. 59
Stuart 59
William Franklin 48, 59
Fauquier Co., Va. 105
Faye
Irene L. (McCormick) 91
John Daniel Heavner 91
Jon David McCormick 91
Nina S. (Pippenger) 91
Wendy Sue 92
Fayette Co., Pa.
Brownsville 41
Fayette Co., Tenn. 125
Feagans
Georgia S. (McLaughlin) . . 87
Michael 87
Feet
D., Rev. 111
Ferguson
Doris 87
Evelyn (Walker) 87
John 71
Moses 142
Walter Edwin 87
Ferril
Jesse J. 78
Finch
Eunice 39
Finley
Devin William 32
Dylan Thomas 32

Gervaise S. (White) 32
Robert Craig 32
Ryan Patrick 32
Theresa A. (Holmes) 32
William Brian 32
Fischer
Judy 110
Fisher
Jacob 119
Martha (Alexander) 119
Fishersville, Va. . . . 44, 57, 62
Fitzpatrick
Helen L. 109
Flaniken
Family 143
Jane 143
John 143
Fleming
Ann (Agnew) 134
Elizabeth (Alexander) . . . 148
Leah 12, 15, 18, 99
Lodovic 122
Miss 122
Pierce 148
Sarah 12, 15
William 15, 134
Flemmings
Elizabeth 23
Fleniken
John 117
Margaret (Alexander) . . . 117
Flenniken
John 116
Fletcher
Dorothy (Alexander) 28
Mr. 28
Ted 28
Flow
J.E. 135
Fogle
George 25
Millie (Loveless) 25
Fontana, Kan. 26, 36
Foote
William H., Rev. 56
William Henry 4
Ford
Caroline Fulton 30
Richard B. 132
Susannah 150
Tamazon 132
Ford Co., Kan. 38
Forest City, N.C. 118
New Bethel Baptist Church
Cem. 119
Forqueran
John 71
Louisa 71
Sarah (Miller) 71

Foster
  Andrew 130
  Elizabeth (Bouldin) 130
  James 130
  Rigby 150
  Susannah 128, 130
Foster City, Calif. 110
Foster, Mo.
  Salem Cem. 78
Fountaine
  Mary 18
Foust
  Elizabeth 59
Fowler
  Robert 149
Fox
  Charles 86
  David Edgar 86
  Frances (Miller) 86
  Karen K. (Searcy) 86
  Kelli Kristen 86
  Kimberly Kay 86
France 18
Franklin
  Sarah (Alexander) 127
  William 127
Franklin Co., Ind. 30
Franklin Co., Kan.
  Lane . . 26, 33, 35, 36, 38, 39
  Lane Cem. 35, 39
  Ottawa 36, 39
  Potawatomie Twp. 38
  Pottawatomie Twp. 35
  Princeton 35, 36, 39
  Richmond 39
  Wellsville 34
Franklin Co., Pa. 142
Franklin, W.Va. 41
Frazier
  Esther 139
Frederick Co., Md. . . 116, 121,
                      132, 133
  Carroll's Delight 128, 133
Frederick Co., Va. 111
  Carter Hall 112
  Stephens City 112
Freed
  Cheryl Ruth 31
  Kathy (Kendall) 31
  Ronald 31
Freeman
  Joseph 10
  William 10
  Winfield 95
Freeman's Discovery 11
French
  Charlotte E. (Alexander)
    108
  Dawn Gay 108
  Herbert Winston 108

Kelly Joe 108
Kirk Lee 108
Linda M. (Peay) 108
Scott Winston 108
French and Indian War . . . 133
French Broad River 134
Fresno, Calif. 110
Friedens, Va. 40
Fries
  Jefferson 41
  Martha (Thacker) 41
  Martha E. (Thacker) 41
Frontenac, Kan. 28
Frost
  Donna 87
Fry
  Amy Michele 108
  Douglas Page 108
  Elizabeth Harriet 106
  Erin Renee 108
  Jane 98
  John 98
  Kathryn A. (Moats) 108
  Mary F. ( ) 98
Ft. Defiance, Va. 114
Ft. Leavenworth, Kan. 37
Ft. Meade, Md. 110
Ft. Scott, Kan. 27, 81
  Mercy Hospital 81
Ft. Sill, Okla. 30
Fulks Run, Va. 109
Fulton, Kan. 81
Funkhauser
  Margaret 87

G

Gallaher
  Robert 138
  Sarah (Evans) 138
Gallia Co., Ohio 25
  Gallipolis 25, 27
Gallipolis, Ohio 25, 27
Gardner
  Charlotte 29
Garner
  John 125, 129
  Sophia (Alexander) 125
Garnett, Kan. . . . 25, 26, 33, 35
  Arkhaven Nursing Home . . 27
Garrett
  Alexander 98
  James 32
  Pamela Sue 32
  Phylenna (Hawkins) . . . 111
  Virginia (Sands) 32
  Virginia Dean 30
  William H. 111
  Willie Odessa 111
Garrison
  Dorcas 143

Esther 139, 142
Esther (Alexander) 143
Samuel 143
Gates
  Exira 35
Gautreau
  Stephanie 81
Gentry
  David 56
  Jane (McCue) 56
George
  Dorothy A. 44, 46
Georgia 134
Germany 58, 62
Gettys
  Isabella (Ramsey) 133
  Samuel 133
Gettysburg, Pa. 133
Geuy
  Grace Marie 27
Gibson
  Capt. 47
  Janet Catherine 107
Giffin
  Diana Lynn 92
  Dorothy ( ) 92
  Everett 92
Giles
  Edward 124, 134
Giles Co., Tenn. 59, 148
Gilliam
  Charles Edward 82
  Edward Marshall 73, 82
  Ella M. (Enoch) 82
  Emma Pauline 82
  Family 82
  Harriet O. (Bellows) 82
  James Sanders 82
  Judith A. (Woodson) 82
  Martha (Martin) 82
  Martha M. (Gover) 73
  Mary Louise 72, 82
  Ralph Edward 82
  Sallie Eulalia 82
  Walter Harvey 82
  William Richardson 82
Gilliam, Mo. 82
Gillie
  Thomas 7, 8
Gilpin
  Elizabeth 138
Gladdy
  Cora 106
Glass
  Sarah 118
Gleason
  Margaret 149
Glendale, Calif. 36
Glenn
  Frances Jane 56

Margaret 124
Gnefken
  Bernard W., Rev. 38
Godard
  George 7
Goeller
  Mildred Searson 69
Golliday
  Liney 43
Goochland Co., Va. 40
Good
  Betty Gail 113
  Catharine 105
  Colleen D. 28
  Daima M. (Dalby) 113
  Debbie (Huffer) 113
  Donald Alfred 113
  Doris (   ) 113
  Eva L. (Wonderly) 113
  Gary Alexander 113
  M. Gertrude 41
  Martha (Alexander) 113
  Martin Luther 113
  Martin Luther, Jr. 113
  Martin Luther, Sr. 113
  Mary J. (Sheets) 113
  Mrs. William 82
  Norman Eugene 113
  Samuel David 113
Good's Mill, Va. 58
Goodman
  Nancy 59
Gover
  Martha Mae 73, 82
  Mary (Rice) . . 20, 72, 73, 82,
                  85, 94-96
  Walter 20, 72, 73, 82
Governor of Virginia . . 140, 141
Grabill
  Fannie 40
  Frances E. (Thacker) 41
  John Henry 41
  Mary Ellen 41
Grady Co., Okla.
  Alex 82
  Chickasha 83
Graham
  Pamela S. (Garrett) 32
  Robert 32
  Viola 113
Grand Co., Mich.
  Elk Rapids 26
Grandstaff
  Julia A. 105
Grandview, Mo. 85, 96
Granville Co., N.C. 126
Grass
  Frederick 16
  Nancy (Alexander) 16
  William R. 16

Graves
  Dorothy 31
Gray
  Elizabeth (   ) 10
  Family 10
  Joseph 10
  Rebecca 10
  Sarah 10
  Westcot 10
  William 10, 11
Grayville, Ill. 46
Greeley, Kan. . . . 25, 27, 33, 35
  Greeley Cem. 38
Green
  Mary 29
Greene Co., Tenn. 133
  Old Harmony Cem. 133
Greene Co., Va.
  Ruckersville 69
  Stanardsville 112
Greenhorne, Colo. 69
Greenville, Del.
  Memorial Gardens Cem. . . 60
Greenville, Okla. 82
Greenville, S.C.
  Christ Episcopal Church
                              119
Greenville, Tenn. 133
Greenville, Va. 69
Greenwood Co., Kan.
  Eureka 26
Greer
  Hannah (Alexander) 117
  Thomas 117
Grier
  Mary (Moore) 143
  Thomas J. 143
Griffin
  John 8
Grimes
  Mrs. S.H. 73
  S.H. 73
Groah
  Ann 112
Grottoes, Va. 109, 111
Guilford Co., N.C. 147
Guilford, N.C. 144
Guinn (see Gwinn)
  Mrs. 72
Gutchine
  John 2
Guthrey
  Eliza 65, 66
  Eliza H. 48
  Elizabeth (Hawkins) 65
  Elizabeth (Palmer) 65
  John 65
  John Garnett 65
Guy
  Audrey Virginia 29

Barbara Jane 29
Betty Lee 29
Carol (Van Collie) 29
Charles Kenneth 29
Clem V. 25
Clemeth Valandingham . . 25,
                          28, 29
Donald Edwin 29
Dorothy (Allen) 29
Dorothy E. (Hibner) 29
Elain J. (Love) 29
Evelyn Winifred 29
Gay Janette 29
Gerald Warner 29
Harold 39
Harriet Jean 29
Helen Irene 29
Helen L. (Alexander) 39
Infant 29
Irma Beverly 29
Jack Kinsey 29
Jean (Zimmerman) 29
Joan Pearl 29
Kristy Kay 30
Lester 29
Mabel D. (Barber) 29
Mable (   ) 29
Marian E. (Barber) 29
Mary (Green) 29
Mary (Jaenicki) 29
Mary A. (Alexander) . . 25, 29
Mary Jane 29
Matilda L. (LaCure) 29
Maurice Leroy 29
Maurice Manning 29
Melba Esther 29
Mildred C. (Kinsey) 29
Nadean Lucille 29
Nancy Marie 29
Patsy Lou 29
Pauline (McDonald) 29
Pearl Sadie 29
Phebe A. (Beymer) 28
Ray Alexander 29
Richard Calvin 29
Robert Dale 29
Rodney Earl 30
Ruth Ellen 29
Samuel D. 28
Samuel Earl 29
Samuel Earl, Jr. 29
Sandra Lee 29
Shirley Jean 29
Shirley M. (Rhody) 29
Sue Ann 29
Vanessa (Yankee) 30
Virginia Ann 29
William Keith 29
Gwinn (see Guinn)
  C.D. 73

171

Lydia E. Neff 72
Marian Thomas 73
Nannie Alexander 72
Thomas Wilhite 72
Wilbur 73
William Madison 73
Gyliot
William 128

H

Hackensack, Minn. 72
Haith
William 9
Haley
Mary (Alexander) 131
Haller
Beatrice Rachel 31
Ham
Mollie 80
Hamilton
Isabella M. 57
James, Gov. 142
John 2, 43
Nancy 20
Nancy F. 43
Hamilton Co., Ohio
Mill Creek Twp. 16
Hammarlund
Cheryl R. (Freed) 31
Daniel Charles 31
Howard Henry 31
Lillie B. ( ) 31
Lois M. (Stambaugh) 31
Oscar 31
Scott Robert 31
Theodore Emmett 31
Hammond
Elizabeth Pauline 82
Emma P. (Gilliam) 82
Harry 82
Lela Mae 87
Orpha Ada 32
Hampshire Co., Va. 140
Hampshire Co., W.Va. 111
Hampton
John 127
Hampton, Va. 109
Hand
Fidelia S. ( ) 36
J.W. 36
Viola Frances 36
Hanson
Barbara J. (Guy) 29
Hance 130
Jack 29
Susanna (Alexander) . . . 130
Hardeman Co., Tenn. 148
Hardin
Beatrice Mona 92

Harding
Richard 132
Harford Co., Md. 138
Harmon
Thomas, Rev. 24
Harnes
Elizabeth 59
Harnsberger
Stephen 23, 40
Harper
Albert Goodrich 30
Linda Sue 30
Mariam 96
Virginia D. (Garrett) 30
Harpeth River 149
Harris
Cunningham 119
Jane 120
John 15
John, Jr. 15
Lois 38
Margaret 120, 137
Mary (Alexander) 119
William H. 48
Harrisonburg, Va. . . 41, 46, 58,
107, 108, 111
East Lawn Memorial Gardens
. . . . 41
Weavers Mennonite Church
Cem. 41
Harrisonville, Mo. 35, 92
Harshbarger
Dallas William 105
Jesse L. 105
Margaret (Wine) 105
Hart
Benjamin 132
Elizabeth 121
John 132
Nancy (Morgan) 132
Robert 121
Hartshorne
William 140
Harvey Co., Kan.
Newton 37, 38
Hathaway
Elizabeth Ethel 31
Hawkins
Eliza E. (Hayden) 65
Elizabeth 65
Elizabeth Seymour 65
Joseph Sexton 65
Phylenna 111
Hay
Emma 58
Hayden
Eliza Myrick 65
Haynes
Shirley 82

Hays
Connie (Kimble) 33
Haysville, Kan.
Green Meadows Nursing Home
. . . . 37
Hayzlett
Hillard J. 40
Heatwole
Peggy (Thacker) 41
Heckman
Martha E. (Brockus) 39
Perry W. 39
Hedrick
Joseph Paul 108
Mary G. 108
Mary Graham 108
Rebecca Grace 108
Stephanie (Swecker) 108
Hegarty
Kathleen T. (Corteville) . . . 97
Michael Edward 97
Helms
Sally 16
Hemp
Katie 105
Henderson
Andrew 123
Ann (Sample) 139
Archibald 126
David 67
Elizabeth 126
Elizabeth (Robison) 123
Erin 67
Helen S. (Baylor) 105
John 139
Mary 123
Richard 126
Sarah L. (Alexander) 67
Sarah T. (Alexander) 126
Wale Guy 105
Henderson, Tenn. 82
Hendrix
Amanda E. (Potter) 25
Joseph A. 25
Henrico Co., Va. 20, 23
Henry
Helen L. (Alexander) 34
James F. 34
Paule 127
Rose Finch 39
Henry Co., Mo.
Calhoun 86
Hensley
Margie 112
Norma J. (Thacker) 41
Rome Benjamin 41
Hepburn
William 141
Herbert
Jane ( ) 141

Thomas 141
Hermanson
   Mary L. (Rossland) 138
Herrick
   Jeffrey P. 112
   Molly S. (Alexander) 112
Herring
   Amanda A. (Catling) 56
   Thomas D. 56
Herrmann
   Christal Laine 30
   George 30
   Peggy L. (Morris) 30
Hevener
   Carolyn (Alexander) 114
   Roy E. 114
Hibner
   Dorothy Evelyn 29
Hickman Co., Tenn. 131
Hickman Mills, Mo. 96
   St. Catherine's Church . . . 97
Higginbotham
   Ann Cameron 67
   Bruce Sala 67
   Elizabeth Bruce 67
   Erin 67
   Kent Richard, Jr. 67
   Kent Richard, Sr. 67
   Melody ( ) 67
   Sarah J. (Alexander) 67
High Point, N.C. 111
Highland Co., Va. . . 35, 36, 110
Hill
   Wanda 32
Hirni
   Clifford Ray 34
   Esperanza G. (Tafoya) . . . 34
   Mary R. (Alexander) 34
   Mary Ruth 34
   Phyllis Ann 34
   Raymond Hadley 34
   William Antone 34
Hobbs
   Absolom 11
Hodgson
   Hannah 124
   Portia ( ) 141
   Robert 138
   Sarah (Alexander) 138
   William 141
Hodnett
   Gaines 112
   Mary 112
Hoffman
   Benjamin 107
Hogshead
   Hunter 56
   Mollie ( ) 56
Hoisington, Kan. 25

Holbrook
   J.H. 19
   Judith 19
   Selah 19
Holder
   Lawrence 92
   Matthew 92
   Melissa 92
   Pamela S. (Abbas) 92
Holland
   Hannah ( ) 149
   William 149
Hollaway
   Cleo (Alexander) 115
   Howard J. 115
Hollins
   Mary 122
Holloway
   Mary 39
Holmes
   Cynthia Marie 32
   Dorothy Dell 32
   Joyce M. (DuBose) 32
   Mary (McCain) 31
   Michelle Lynn 32
   Robert Keith 32
   Sarah Ruth 32
   Sherri Rae 32
   Terry Wesley 31
   Theresa Ann 32
   Thomas Ray 32
   William Dale 31
Holsinger
   David 112
Holston River 134
Holston, Md. 119
Holtham
   John 128
Home City, Kan. 31
Homer City, Pa. 58
Homes
   Edward 2
Hook
   Emma (Van Lear) 111
   Hattie Virginia 111
   John Calvin 111
Hoone
   E.W., Rev. 72
Hoover
   E.J. (Shuey) 105
   R.D. 105
   Roberta 105
Hopkins
   Bishop 134
Hopwood
   Charles 35
   Flora May 35
   Ida M. (Vint) 35
   John Platt 35
   Juanita Esther 35

Mexa Eva 35
Ruth A. (Antill) 35
Horn
   Emma (Caldwell) 39
   George Washington 39
   Susan R. 39
Horton
   Lucy Henderson 126
Hot Springs, Ark. 96
Hottinger
   Arlon 115
   Marie (Alexander) 115
Houff
   Bertie 106
   Elizabeth M. 105
Houston, Tex. 31, 32
Howard, Kan. 26
Howe
   Henry 71
Hoy
   Isaac 19
Hudson
   Jonathan 127
   Laura A. (Link) 106
   Paul C. 106
   Virginia C. 105
Huff
   Barbara A. 114
Huffer
   Debbie 113
Huffman
   Brown M. 107
   Doris Ann 109
   Emma Susan 40
   Mary M. (Landes) 107
   Sarah Rebecca 107
Hulvey
   B. 105
   Dora Lula 105
   Elizabeth M. (Hulvey) . . . 105
Hume
   Mary (Winegar) 37
   May 37
   William Angel 37
Hume, Mo. 33
Humes
   Thomas 134
Hunt
   Edwin, Jr. 66
   Mary Frances 66
   Mary G. (Alexander) 66
Hunter
   E. Pearl 38
Huntersville, N.C. . . . 130, 131,
                        144
Hunting Quarter 6, 7
Huntingdon, W.Va. 59
Huntsville, Ala. 109, 118
Hurtford Co., N.C. 69

Husbands
  Robert 123
Husted
  Lorene Elizabeth 34
Hutchens
  Clarence E. 114
  Sandra (Ramsey) 114
Hutchinson, Kan. 37
Hyattsville, Md. 91

I

Illinois 30
Independence, Mo. . . 35, 80, 85,
          87, 94, 96, 97
  Independence Sanitarium
          . . . . 80, 85, 86
  Mt. Washington Cem. 80
  Woodlawn Cem. 86, 87
India 86
Indian Harbour Beach, Fla.
          109
Indian Territory 82
Iredell Co., N.C. 149
  Baker Family Cem. 131
  Centre Presbyterian Church
          138
  Gilead A.R.P. Church . . . 131
  Huntersville 131
Ireland . . 86, 125, 131, 133, 135
  Clonmany Parish 3
  Conleigh Parish 2
  County Donegal . . . 2, 3, 6, 7
  Eredy 2
  Letterkenny 6
  Raphoe Parish 2-4
  Raymoghy Parish 2
  Samuel 130
  Taghboyne Parish 2, 3
  Ulster 2
Irwin
  Dorothy J. (Tarver) 33
  Mr. 33
Ishmael
  Alma 80
Israel
  George W. 46

J

Jack
  James 143
  Margaret 148
Jackson
  Bessie 46
  Edwin Andrew 43, 46
  Elizabeth A. (Alexander) . 20,
          46
  George 105
  George Kemper 46
  Lucy A. (Wine) 105
  Mary E.M. 46
  Mary G. (Diddle) 46
  Willis 19, 20, 46
Jackson Co., Kan.
  Leavenworth 87
Jackson Co., Mo. 86
  Independence 35, 85
  Kansas City . . 26, 28, 30, 32,
          85
Jaenicki
  Mary 29
Jaffrey, N.H. 86
James
  Daisy 26
  John 137
  Mary 150
  Mary (Alexander) 137
  Rachel (Arnold) 26
  Thomas 130
James River 1, 18
Jameson
  A.H. 57
Jamestown, Ind. 25
Jamison
  Eugene 81
  Jennifer Louise 81
  Karen Ann 81
  Mary A. (Bruce) 81
  Sharon Kay 81
Jarvis
  Mr. 36
Jasper, Ala.
  Old Zion Cem. 132
Jay Co., Ind.
  Bryant 28, 29
Jeffries
  Marguerite 37
Jenkins
  Elizabeth 59
Jennings
  Mary (Speece) 56
Jesser
  Elizabeth B. 48, 62
  Elsie 58
  Emma 58
  Emma (Hay) 58
  Emma L. 58
  Fred 58
  Fred C. 58
  Jacob F. 58
  John 58, 62
  Lula (Alexander) 58
  Margaret 58
  Richard 62
  Rosa (Kohler) 58, 62
Jetton
  Lewis John 138
  Priscilla (Sharp) 138
Johnson
  Abel 117
  Ann (Alexander) 117
  Deanna K. (Delker) 31
  Don 31
  Elizabeth 125
  Lillian Jean 34
  Thomas 136
Johnson City, Tenn. . . . 46, 59,
          63
Johnson Co., Kan. 37
  Oceltree 31
  Olathe 33, 85
  Overland Park 33
Johnston
  Susannah 131
  William 138
Jones
  Ada Carolyn 86
  Danny Edward 108
  Dawn G. (French) 108
  Fannie E. 25
  Fannie Eva 25, 26
  Griffith 7, 128
  John 116
  Mary ( ) 7, 10
  Maude E. (Dannatt) 86
  Melba E. (Guy) 29
  Philip 10
  Richard Isham 29
  Robert Lee 86
  Shelby J. 113
  William 11
Jonesboro, Tenn. 134
Jordan
  Kelli K. (Fox) 86
  MaDora 111
  Mary Susan 104, 111
  Robert Dean 86
Judd
  Michaell 7

K

Kacey
  Mary ( ) 149
  Philip 149
Kahoka, Mo. 35
Kalamazoo, Mich. 78
Kanawha Co., W.Va. . . . 46, 71
  Cabin Creek 46
Kanawha Salines, W.Va. . . 71,
          74
Kansas City, Kan. . . . 25, 31-33,
          37, 85, 87, 91, 94, 95
  Berean Baptist Church . . . 32
  Dorothy J. (Tarver) 33
  Highland Park Cem. . 26, 30-
          33
  Kansas University Medical
    Center 35
  Memorial Park Cem. 36
  Mt. Hope Cem. 36

Providence Hospital 32
Washington Ave. Methodist Church 37
Kansas City, Mo. .. 26, 28, 30, 32, 33, 37, 65, 71-73, 78, 80, 81, 85-88, 92, 94-97
Baptist Medical Center ... 80
Bethany Baptist Church .. 86
Budd Park Christian Church 85-87
Calvary Cem. 97
Christ the King Catholic Church 97
Elms Nursing Home 86
Elmwood Cem. 72, 96
Floral Hills Cem. . 32, 33, 35, 92
Forest Hill Cem. 96, 97
J.W. Wagner Funeral Home 48, 72
Kansas City General Hospital 94, 95
Kaw River 92
Kaw Twp. 85
Linwood Methodist Church 86, 87
McGilley Memorial Chapels 72
Memorial Park Cem. 92
Montgomery Wards 85
Mt. Moriah Cem. . 80, 86-88, 91, 96
Mt. Washington Cem. 94
Nora-Rae Restorium 36
Peltzman Bottle Co. 91
Pioneer Insurance Co. ... 86
Research Hospital 80
Research Medical Center 87, 97
St. Joseph's Hospital .. 86, 88
St. Luke's Hospital 96
St. Mary's Catholic Cem. ... 95
St. Mary's Hospital 94
Union Cem. 26
Union Station 95
University of Kansas Medical Center 80
Woodlawn Cem. 87
Kansas University 31
Karey
    Edmond 149
Katzer
    Agnes Sophia 33
Keagy
    Elizabeth (Denton) 40
    Lillian V. (Denton) 40
    Louis J. 40
    Margaret E. (Skelton) 40
    Winfred Denton 40

Kechi, Kan.
    Kechi Cem. 37
Keller
    Hannelore Brigitte 59
    Rebecca 104
    Samuel W., Rev. 38
Kelley
    Thelma Dorothy 107
Kemper
    Benjamin F. 19
    Judith (Holbrook) 19
Kencht
    Anna 96
Kendall
    Kathy 31
Kennedy
    Elizabeth (Stickley) 104
    Jane 16
    Joseph 117
    Peter 104
    Stuart 16
Kenner
    Winder 13
Kent Co., Del.
    Murderkill 122
Kent Co., Md. 121
Kentucky 131
Kerr
    R.B., Rev. 142
Kersey
    Mary ( ) 149
    Philip 149
Kersh
    Elizabeth Josephine 40
Kesterson
    Elizabeth 98
    Francis M. 98
    John 98
    Mary (Walton) 98
    Sarah E. 98
    William 98
Kettering, Ohio 92
Keytesville, Mo. 82
Kice
    Nancy 44
Killiam
    Jacob, Rev. 104, 106
Killough
    Aaron Bilderback 37
    Annie E. (Miller) 37
    Mary Joy 37
Kimball
    Betty J. (Burkdoll) 36
    Harold Dean 36
    Janet Elaine 35
Kincaid
    Helen (Simmons) 110
    Stacel 110
King
    Alma (Ishmael) 80

Amelia N. (Ramsey) 134
Barbara 131
Barbara M. (Allen) 80
Charles R. 80
Daniel R. 72, 78, 80
David 80
Ernest Clinton 80
Ernest D., Jr. 80
Ernest D., Sr. 80
Ernest James 80
Eva G. 80
Evelyn P. (Lask) 80
Floyd A. 80
Francis Marion 80
Inez E. (Barker) ... 73, 80, 85
Jack 80
James 80, 134
Jesse D. 80
Jessie (Ellis) 80
Lester Glen 80, 85
Lorene Estella 80
Lucille G. (Milling) 80
Margaret (Reed) 80
Mary Ellen 35
Nehemiah 8
Patricia (Pow) 80
Robert 80
Robert E. 80
Sarah C. (Alexander) . 72, 80
Virginia 80
Kingston, Jamaica 142
Kinney
    Nicholas C. 15
Kinsey
    Audrey V. (Guy) 29
    Charlotte (Gardner) 29
    Clark Allen 29
    Hattie (Plank) 29
    Hattie J. (Plank) 29
    Jay 29
    Mildred Cleo 29
    Roy Enos 29
    Samuel A. 29
    Shirley (Shear) 29
Kintyre, Scot. 2
Kirkham
    Martha 135
Kirkpatrick
    John 138
    Margaret 138
Kirkwood, Mo. 86
Kizey
    Peter 121
Knight
    Anna (Dukes) 36, 37
    Anna M. (Dukes) 23, 37
    Donald Wayne 37
    Fred Henry 37
    John J. 37
    John Jordan 37

John William 37
Joyce Ann 37
Zola A. (Driver) 37
Knox Co., Tenn. 133, 134
   Ebenezer Church 133
   First Presbyterian Church
   144
   Lebanon Church Cem. . . . 133
Knoxville, Tenn. . 28, 131, 133,
                           134
   McNutt Family Cem. 133
Kohler
   Rosa 58, 62
Korea 39
Krause
   Edward Herman 83
   Edward Raymond 83
   Margaret (Brown) 83
   Willa C. (McClintock) 83
Kuching, Malaysia 85
Kugler
   Frances E. (Carver) 32
   Malcolm 32
Kunkle
   Emma (Jesser) 58

L

Labette Co., Kan. 78
   Parsons 34
LaCrosse, Wisc. 33
LaCure
   Elizabeth E. (Sackett) 29
   Louis 29
   Matilda Leone 29
LaDue, Mo. 81
Lafayette, La. 28
LaFollette
   Katherine E. 39
Lain
   Kay 37
Laing
   Margaret 61
LaJunta, Colo. 26
Lake Co., Ind.
   East Chicago 31
Lamar
   Elizabeth (Foust) 59
   James L. 59
   James Larkin 59
   Melissa 59
Lambert
   Phyllis R. 114
Lancashire, Eng. 92
Lancaster Co., Pa. . . . 98, 116,
              117, 124, 149
   Slate Hill 117, 136
Lancaster Co., S.C.
   Six Mile Cem. 118
Lancaster Co., Va. 4
Lancaster, Pa. 133

Landall
   Robert 8
Landers
   Maud M. 63
   Willie Maude 63
Landes
   Charles Stuart 105
   Daisey Pearl 106
   Ellen D. (Alexander) 104
   Emaline (Alexander) 115
   Emma Pearl 105
   Infant 105
   John Alexander 105
   Josephine 115
   Laura Frances 104
   Luella M. (Moore) 105
   Martha Florence 105
   Mary Margaret 107
   Mr. 115
   Nancy Margaret 104
   Nora (Rimel) 105
   Ora 106
   Rebecca Ellen 105
   Sadie (Byers) 105
   Sarah Jane 105
   Wallace Valentine 105
   William Austin 104
   William K. 105
Lane
   Margaret ( ) 148
   Timothy 148
Lane, Kan. . 23, 26, 27, 33, 35,
               36, 38, 39
   Lane Cem. 26, 39
   Quaker Cem. 26, 27
   Spring Grove Friends Church
   26
Lankaitis
   Dungale Sophi 31
Las Animas, Colo. 81
Las Vegas, Nev. 38
   Paradise Memorial Gardens
   38
   Sunrise Hospital 38
Lask
   Evelyn Pearl 80
Lathrop
   James W. 36
   Naomi E. (Vint) 36
Laughtin
   Marie 108
Lawbaugh
   Louella Lee 32
Lawrence
   Elisha 116
Lawrence, Kan. 25, 27, 32
   Memorial Park Cem. 28
   Mt. Calvary Catholic Cem.
   28

Laws
   Agnes (Alexander) 8
   John 8
   Sarah (Bevans) 8
   William 8
Lawton, Okla. 30
Leavenworth Co., Kan. 35
   Leavenworth 96
Leavenworth, Kan. . . 28, 87, 96
Lecuyer
   Lucien 29
Lee's Summit, Mo. 87, 91
Leicester, Eng. 69
Leich
   George 2
Lenapah, Okla. 37
   Mt. Washington Cem. 37
Lennox
   George Carson 69
   Katherine E. (McCormick)
   69
Leon Co., Fla. 142
Leonard
   Aleath V. 62
   Mrs. Alice 29
Lewis
   A.D., Rev. 36
   Isaac, Capt. 130
Lexington, Mo. 35
   Macpelah Cem. 18
Lexington, Va. 38, 72
Lightfoot
   Marise P. 118
Limestone Co., Ala.
   Cotton Port 133
Lincoln Co., N.C. . . . 118, 119,
                      137
Lincoln Co., Tenn. . . . 148, 149
Lincoln, Nebr. 87
Lincolnton, N.C.
   Ramsour's Mill 120
Lindsborg, Kan.
   Elmwood Cem. 37
   Smoky Hill Cem. 37
Link
   Annie (Van Lear) 106
   Bertie (Houff) 106
   Catharine (Craun) . 104, 105
   Catherine (Craun) . . 106, 112
   Catherine E. (Alexander)
   106
   Daniel Melanchton 106
   Daniel W. 104-106, 112
   David Daniel 106
   Elizabeth H. (Fry) 106
   Elwood 113
   Julia Frances 105
   Laura Agnes 106
   Laura F. (Landes) 104
   Martin Luther 104

Mary (Alexander) 113
Mary Emily 106, 112
Linn
   Jo White 126
Linn Co., Kan. . . 25-28, 30, 34,
                           78
   Blue Mound 81
   Centerville Cem. 28
   Lettel Cem. 78
   Liberty Twp. 25, 36
   Mound City 39, 81, 85
   Parker 25-27, 33, 34
   Pleasanton . . 33, 78, 80, 81,
                           85
   Pleasanton Cem. . . 78, 80, 81
   Potosi Twp. 78
   Woodland Cem. 81
Linn Co., Mo.
   Woodland Cem. 81
Liston
   Ann 4, 6, 7, 9, 122
   Victoria ( ) 6
   William, Rev. 6
Little Tennessee River 134
Littleton, Colo. 91
   St. James Presbyterian Church
                           91
Lobban
   Martha Jane 56
   Sarah A. (McCue) 56
   William 56
Loch
   Mary Eva 36
Locke
   Jane (Alexander) 126
   Marjorie Lucille 38
   William 126
Lockyear
   Loranelle L. (Schultz) 80
   Ralph 80
Locust Springs, Va. 68
Londonderry, Ire. 2, 69
Long
   Peggy Yvonne 108
Longwell
   Margaret (Glenn) 124
   Mr. 138
   Priscilla (Alexander) . . . 124,
                          138
   Rachel (Alexander) 138
   Robert 138
   William 124
Lord Baltimore 125
Los Angeles, Calif. 80
Louisiana Purchase 18
Louisville, Ky.
   Fourth Street Methodist Church
                           58
Love
   Elain Joyce 29

Robert 134
Love Co., Okla. 82
   Marietta 82
Loveless
   John H. 25
   Susan ( ) 25
Loving
   Patricia 112
Lowry
   Mary (Alexander) 128
   Mr. 128
Lucas
   Christopher Wesley 91
   Logan James 91
   Rachel (Pippenger) 91
Lucky
   Mary (Moore) 143
   William 143
Ludlow, Mo. 80
   Monroe Cem. 80
Luker
   Marie 67
Luray, Va. 44, 58, 107
Lynchburg, Va.
   Guggenheim Nursing Home
                           59
   Spring Hill Cem. 59
Lyndhurst, Va. 43, 44, 46
Lyon Co., Kan. 27
   Americus 27
   Emporia 34

M

MacAlister
   Alexander 2
   Charles 2
   John 2
Machaffie
   Bruce 66
   Terri (Shapiro) 66
Machet
   Elizabeth W. 56
Mackey
   Ann 150
   William 150
Macon Co., Ill. 36
Madison Co., Ala.
   Hayden Cem. 133
   New Hope 133
Madison Co., Tenn. 118
Maginnis
   Margaret 10
Magness
   Lavina 118
Makamie
   Francis, Rev. 128
   Naomi (Anderson) 128
Makin Co., Ill. 35
Malloy
   Family 95

Fritz 95
   Mae (Barrett) 95
Malonis
   Joe 29
   Nancy M. (Guy) 29
Manchester, Eng. 78
Maness
   Carl Christy 85
   Carla Dianne 85
   Ina M. (Alexander) 85
   Maryla Ann 85
Manhattan, Kan. 30, 31
   Sunset Cem. 30
Manley
   Dian 118
Mann
   Gay J. (Guy) 29
   Roger 29
Manokin River 7
Manwell
   Jack Dempsey 29
   Shirley J. (Guy) 29
Maple Hill, Kan. 31
Maquoketa, Iowa 65
Marchand
   Adel 31
Mariage
   Sandra L. (Guy) 29
   Tracey 29
Marietta, Okla. 28, 82
   Lakeview Cem. 28, 82
Markwell
   Amy 92
Marshall
   Mary 30
Marshall, Mo. . . 19, 48, 54, 65,
                 66, 71, 72, 78
   Fray & Alexander 66
Martin
   Frances E. (Carver) 32
   George H. 104
   George H., Rev. 104
   Jason Karl 32
   John 32, 33
   Lorna 33
   Martha 82
   Michael 32
   Regina M. (Ashbacker) . . . 33
   Robin Elaine 32
   William 149
Martinsville, Va. 58
Maryland 1, 123
   Eastern Shore 1, 2
   Jones Green Spring 130
   Knowlwood 130
   Manoakin River 121
   Somerset County 2
Mathews
   Charles W. 56
   Eleanor 48, 56

Eliza (Catling) 56
Mathias
    Mrs. Virgil 42
Mathias, W.Va 42
Matiecawiez
    Drucilla 97
Matile
    Bernice L. (Alexander) . . . 27
    Jake 27
Maupin
    Mary Laura 112
Maury Co., Tenn. . . . 118, 125,
                      148
    Alexander Family Cem. . . 118
    Ebenezer Presbyterian Church
      Cem. 125
Maxwell
    Anna 48, 56
    Bezaleel 47, 48, 56
    Eliza 56
    Elizabeth 56
    Ella 56
    James 47, 56
    Jane (Boyd) 47, 56
    John Harvey 56
    Mary (McCue) 56
    Mary (Speece) 56
    Mary A. (McCue) 47
    Moses 47, 56
    Rebecca (Boyd) . . 47, 48, 56
    Sally (Page) 56
    Sarah A. 20
    Sarah Ann . . . 20, 47, 48, 56,
       57, 59, 60, 62, 63, 65, 68
McAlpine Creek 142
McBee
    Vardry, Jr. 119
McCain
    Dorothy Faye 33
    Elizabeth (Cook) 30
    Ethel Lillian 30
    Infant 31
    Irene 31
    Mabel Fern 32
    Mary 31
    Sam R. 26
    Samuel Ramsey 26, 30
    Sarah E. (Alexander) . . 26, 30
    William 30
McCaleb
    Matilda 135
McCall
    Nancy Agnes 118
McClain Co., Okla.
    McCurdy Clinic 82
McCleron
    Frances Louise 81
McClintock
    James Walter 82
    Mary L. (Coppedge) 82

Rex Wilford 82
Sallie E. (Gilliam) 82
Willa Claire 83
McClung
    Jane 117, 124
McClure
    Rebekah Woodland 130
McClurg
    Barbara Jean 38
    E. Pearl (Hunter) 38
    Mayfred E. (Dukes) 38
    Wavil Dow 38
    William Harvey 38
McCollough
    Corina B. (Caylor) 39
McConnell
    Margaret 149
McCord
    Daniel 36
    Mary E. (Day) 36
    Mary Etta 36
McCorkle
    Jane 120
McCormick
    Robert 69
    Ada 59
    Alice C. (Alexander) . 48, 63,
                       68
    Anne E. (Benthall) 69
    Bettie L. (Alexander) . . 68, 69
    Betty L. (Alexander) . . 48, 63
    Cyrus 19
    Eliza V. (Organ) 68
    Elizabeth (Carruth) 69
    Fred A. 62
    Frederick Alexander 69
    Frederick Campbell . . 68, 69
    Hazel (Patrick) 69
    Horatio Thompson . . 48, 54,
                63, 68, 69
    Irene Lavelle 91
    James 69
    Katherine Elizabeth 69
    Keith Steele 69
    Martha (Sanderson) 69
    Mary (Steele) 69
    Mr. & Mrs. 54
    Mrs. E.V. 54
    Nellie R. (Campbell) 69
    Patricia 69
    Rebecca Anne 69
    Robert 69
    Sarah (Steele) 69
    Steele S. 63
    Thomas 69
    Virginia (Organ) 63
    W.H. 54
    William 69
    William H. 48
    William Holcome 63, 68

William Steel(e) 63, 68
William Thompson 69
Willie M. (Landers) 63
McCoy
    Abigail 139
    Alexander 136
    Catherine (Alexander) . . . 119
    Dorcas (Alexander) 138
    Esther 139
    Esther (Frazier) 139
    Ezekiel 139
    Henry 138, 139
    James 139
    Jane (Alexander) 136
    Jemima E. 139
    Jemima Esther 139
    John 119, 124, 139
    Margaret (Alexander) . . . 139
    Margaret Funkhauser 87
McCracken
    Rosanna 116
McCrary
    Catherine 41
McCree
    John 117
    Ruth (Alexander) 117
McCue
    Anna (Maxwell) 48
    Bazaleel 56
    Charles 48, 56
    Cyrus 56
    Eleanor (Mathews) . . . 48, 56
    Elizabeth 56
    Elizabeth W. (Machet) 56
    Frances (Winebarger) 56
    Frances J. (Glenn) 56
    James Wakefield 56
    Jane 56
    John 48, 56
    John, Rev. 56
    Martha J. (Lobban) 56
    Mary 48, 56
    Mary Ann 47
    Robert 56
    Sarah A. 56
    Simson ( ) 56
    William Boyd 56
McCulland
    Jean 69
McCullough
    Robert 16
    Robert, Capt. 16, 19
McCullough's Mills 19
McCurdy
    James W. 72, 73
    Nannie (Alexander) 72
    W.E. 73
McCutchan
    Frank, Rev. 68

McDonald
Jacque 97
Joyce (Alexander) 113
Mr. 113
Pauline 29
McEntyre
Gerald Scott 30
John Gerald 30
John Guy 30
Mary Delana 30
Virginia 30
Virginia E. (Scott) 30
Winifred C. (Dwyer) 30
McGaheysville, Va.
Mt. Olivet Cem. 41
McGilleb
James 129
McGinnis
Dorothy Alice 87
McKenney
Family 43
McKinley
President 54
McKnitt
Abigail 4, 116, 122, 136
Alexander 147
Ann 122
Catherine (   ) 147
Daniel 147
Dorothy (Wallace) . . 122, 147
Elizabeth (   ) 122
Elizabeth (Wallace) 136,
147
Hannah 147
Isabella (   ) 147
James 147
Jane 116, 122, 136
Jane (Alexander) . . . 5, 7, 122
Jane (Wallace) . . . 121, 128,
134, 136, 147
Jean 128, 134
John . . . 5, 7, 121, 122, 128,
134, 136, 147
John IV 147
John, III 147
John, IV 147
John, Jr. 136, 147
Katherine 147
Margaret 121, 136, 137,
142, 144
Martha (Dale) 121, 147
Mary 147
Miss 147
Moses 147
Robert 147
Sarah 121
William 122
McLaughlin
Annie A. (Alexander) . . 73, 85
Carol S. (Peggs) 87

Charles Louis 87
Charles Peake 73, 85
Charles William 87
David Lee 87
Doris (Ferguson) 87
Dorothy A. (McGinnis) . . . 87
Dorothy Eleanor 86
Dorothy H. (Day) 86, 92
Evelyn Denice 87
Georgia Sue 87
Jeanette (Sheets) 87
Jeannine L. (Bell) 86
Jennifer (   ) 87
John Henry 85
Kelly Marie 87
Lela M. (Hammond) 87
Leslie Carol 92
Madeline Louise 88
Marguerite Evelyn 87
Margye Ann 87
Michael David 87
Mildred Amy 86
Norman Alexander . . 86, 92
Norman Eugene 86, 92
Sarah Ann 87
Susan J. (Bradshaw) 85
Wanda Kay 87
William Jewel 87
McLean
Patricia (McCormick) 69
Robert 69
McMillen
George 87
Madeline Rose 87
Margaret Ann 87
Sarah A. (McLaughlin) . . . 87
McMullen
Aldine K. 42
Leola D. 42
Mary A. (Daugherty) 42
Mary A. (Moubray) 42
Stephen 42
McNutt
Amelia (Alexander) 133
Benjamin 133
Eunice Ethel 33
McQuain
Elizabeth 35
McRee
James, Rev. 143
McReynolds
Elizabeth 144
McWhorter
Hugh 147
Jane 147
Means
Margaret 119
Mecklenburg Co., N.C. . . . 117,
118, 120, 123-125, 128, 129,

131, 132, 134-137, 139, 143,
147-149
Cathey's Creek 124
Clear Creek 117, 119
Concord 125
Enderly Farm 129
Gum Swamp 118
Hopewell Church 135
Hopewell Presbyterian Church
Cem. . . 137-139, 144, 145
Huntersville 144, 145
Indian Land 117
Long Creek . . . 137, 139, 142
Mallard Creek 123, 124,
135
McAlpins Creek 143
Mint Hill 119
Philadelphia   Presbyterian
Church 119
Providence   Presbyterian
Church Cem. 143, 144
Provincial Congress 143
Rock House 142, 143
Rock Spring 119
Rock   Spring   Presbyterian
Church Cem. 119
Rock Springs Cem. 117
Rocky Spring Meeting House
. . . . 119
Rosedale 145
Sharon   Presbyterian   Church
Cem. 143
Steel   Creek   Presbyterian
Church Cem. 139
Sugaw Creek 117
Sugaw Creek Cem. 117
Sugaw Creek Cem. No. 2
. . . . 143
Sugaw   Creek   Presbyterian
Church 123
Sugaw   Creek   Presbyterian
Church Cem. 119-121,
137-139, 142, 143
Mecklenburg Co., Va. 126
Mecklenburg   Declaration   of
Independence . . 119, 120,
137
Mecklenburg, N.C. 4
Melton
Edward Blair, Jr. 112
Edward Blair, Sr. 112
James Allen 112
Mary Lee 112
Pauline (Alexander) 112
Menstrie, Scot. 1
Menter
William 142
Meridian, Miss. 139
Merrell
June Victoria 109

Messmer
 Anna (Kencht) 96
 Charles E. 96
 Margaret Kate 96
Meyer
 Dana (Alexander) 67
 George 67
Meyerhoeffer
 Lucy V. 114
Miami Co., Kan. 35
 Beagle 25-28, 33
 Beagle Cem. 33
 Lane 26, 39
 Lane Cem. 39
 Mound Twp. 36
 Osawatomie . . 27, 33, 36, 37
 Osawatomie Cem. 27, 33
 Paola 26, 33, 35
 Quaker Cem. 26
 Spring Grove Friends Church
  26
Miami, Fla. 36
Miami, Kan.
 Osawatomie Cem. 33
Miami, Mo. . 65, 72, 73, 78, 80,
  82, 85, 91, 94
Michael
 Deanna Lynn 109
 Jeannie Sue 109
 John P. 109
 John Paul 109
 Lula A. 58
 Lula Ann 58
 Mary (Pence) 58
 Mary F. (Pence) 58
 Neva V. (Alexander) 109
 Sallie Dale 109
 William H. 58
 William Henry 58
Mickel
 Gwenneth L. (Alexander) . 33
 Roger 33
Middlebrook, Va. 110
Midlothian, Va. 110
Milbourn
 Thomas 18
Milburn
 Kitturah 15
Millard
 Ann (Smith) 34
 Ella 26
 Ella May 34
 Ransom H. 34
Miller
 Annie Elizabeth 37
 Carolyn Jean 39
 David 123
 Donald Eugene 39
 Ermel Ernest 94
 Ernest Alva 39

 Frances 86
 John George, III 85
 Lisa Dawn 108
 Madeline 113
 Maryla A. (Maness) 85
 Nellie M. (Brockus) 39
 Pamela 34
 Rick Allen 94
 Samuel 23
 Shirley M. (Teft) 94
Millers Town, Pa. 133
Milling
 Lucille Georgia 80
Mills
 Alexander 8
 Esther 8
 Hannah 8
 Imogene 81
 John 8
 Lucy Wyatt 57
 Mary 8
 Mary (Alexander) 8
 Mary (Catling) 57
 Nathaniel 8
 Rebecca 8
 Robert 8
 Zachariah 57
Milvane, Kan. 33
Milwaukee, Wisc. 83
Minger
 Abigail A.E. . . 23, 24, 26-28,
  30, 33, 34
 Joseph 24
 William 24
Mings
 Ruth (Bruce) 81
Minnich
 Allison 87
 Rachel 87
 Richard Earl 87
Mint Spring, Va. 43
Mitchell
 Mikaela 81
 Nathan 143
Moats
 Brownie B. (Alexander) . . 107
 John Leon 108
 Karissa Dawn 108
 Kathryn Arlene 108
 Lerty Leon 107
 Sarah P. (Michael) 108
Moffat's Creek, Va. 35, 36
Molden
 Martha Tryphena 80, 85
Monroe
 Betty Jeanne 31
 Charles Arden, Jr. 31
 Charles Arden, Sr. 31
 Emma C. (Potts) 31
 George 31

 Irene (McCain) 31
 James Franklin 30-32
 Susan 28
Monteith
 Elizabeth 135
Montgomery
 Rebecca 143
Montgomery City, Mo. 80
Montgomery Co., Kan.
 Cherryvale 26, 34
Montgomery Co., Md. 140
Montgomery Co., Tex. 39
Montrose, W.Va. 98
Moore
 Andrew 139
 Anna Laura 113
 Catharine ( ) 141
 Flossie (Alexander) 115
 James 142, 143
 Jane B. (Sample) 139
 Jean 138
 Josephine (Landes) 115
 Luella M. 105
 Mahrlin Alexander 115
 Mary 143
 Rebecca Ann 98
 Robert L. 115
 Rollie Omega 115
 William S. 141
Morehead, Kan. 34
Morgan
 Mary W. (Alexander) 120
 Nancy 132
 Nicholas R. 120
 Rebecca (Alexander) . . . 132
 Thomas 132
Morgan Co., Ala. 132
Morgan Co., Mo.
 Versailles 81
Morris
 Emma P. (Gilliam) 82
 Jayme (Queen) 81
 Peggy Lou 30
 Ted G. 82
 Tommie 81
Morrison
 Andrew 140
 Jane 148
 Lydia (Alexander) 140
 Neil 148
Morrow
 Anna Alice 81
Moser
 Deanna L. (Michael) 109
 Eugene Paul, II 109
 Eugene Paul, III 109
 Sarah Elizabeth 109
Moses
 Charles 43
 Charles N. 43, 46

Elwood Lester 44
Emma J. (Sweet) 44
Infant 44
LenaV. (Breedlove) 44
Leonard Houston 44
Lina Lee 43
Mamie E. (   ) 44
Samuel M. 44
Willie Franklin 44
Mosley
  Carl 32
  Mabel F. (McCain) 32
Moswell
  Dorothy J. (Tarver) 33
  Mr. 33
Moubray
  Benjamin W. 42
  Lena (Myers) 42
  Lydia C. (Thacker) 40, 42
  Mary Alice 42
  William Otterbine 42
Mound City, Kan. . . . 65, 81, 85
  Woodland Cem. 81
Mount
  Mrs. R.L. 36
Mt. Ayr, Iowa 92
Mt. Clinton, Va. 41, 42
Mt. Crawford, Va. . . . 107, 108,
                                114
  St. Jacobs Spaders Lutheran
    Church Cem. 40
Mt. Jackson, Va. 108
Mt. Orab, Ohio 38
Mt. Sidney, Va. . . . 46, 104, 105,
                107, 112-114
Mt. Solon, Va. 107, 108
Mt. Waterman, Calif. 31
Muir
  Albert 92
  Corrine Kay 92
  Elizabeth (Wellman) 140
  Frances (   ) 92
  George, Rev. 140
  James, Rev. 140, 141
  Tibbie (Wardlaw) 140
Mulberry Hill Farms 88
Muncie
  Bessie 35
Murderkill, Del. 122
Murphy
  Adel (Marchand) 31
  Melva Olive 31
  Mose 31
Murray
  Ann (Sheldon) 11
  Charles 81
  Helen 81
  James 11
  John, Rev. 130
  Suzie (West) 81

Mustoe
  Anthony 98
Myers
  Janet Louise 108
  Lena 42

N

Naked Creek, Va. 105
Nashville, Tenn. 149
  Tennessee State Library and
    Archives 138
National Casket Co. 58
Nazer
  Betty Louise 80
  Lorene E. (King) 80
  Randall Robert 80
Needham
  Juanita E. (Hopwood) 35
  Margaret 35
  Stephen D. 35
Neely
  Dinah Eugenia 118
Neff
  Lydia E. 72
Nelson Co., Va. 47, 48, 56
  Faber 56
  Rock Spring Cem. 56
Nelson, Eng. 92
Nemaha Co., Kan.
  Corning 31
  Seneca 31
Neosho Co., Kan.
  Morehead 34
Nevada, Mo. 96
Nevins
  Isabella 147
  Mr. 147
  William 147
Nevius
  Patricia 111
New Albana, Miss. 110
New Castle Co., Del. . . . 123,
                129, 130, 132-134
  Head of Christiana Church
    123
  Head of Christiana Church
    Cem. . . 121, 124, 137, 138
  Pencader Hundred 130
New Castle Presbyterian Churc
    . . . . h136
New Castle, Pa. 142
New Haven, Conn. 35
New Hope, Va. 19, 46, 56
New Jersey 120
New London, Conn. 108
New Market, Va. 47, 57
New Melle, Mo. 68
New Munster, Md.   1, 116, 123,
                                129
New Orleans, La. 142

Girod Cem. 142
Newark, Del. 124
Newbold
  John 127
Newburn, N.C. 69
Newcastle Co., Del.
  Head of Christiana Church
    Cem. 124
Newman
  Judge 81
Newport News, Va. . . . 108, 109
Newport, Fla. 142
Newport, Va. 36
Newsham
  Beatrice M. (Hardin) 92
  David Grant 92
  Grant 92
  Michael Anthony 92
  Roy 92
  Wendy S. (Faye) 92
Newton
  Agnes (Alexander) 133
  L.E. 133
  William 140
Newton, Kan. 37, 38, 92
Nichols
  Martha 143
Niederman
  Ann C. (Higginbotham) . . . 67
  Emily 67
  Jerry 67
  Matthew 67
  Sarah 67
  Tobias 67
Noelle
  Bryce Alexander 87
  Donna (Frost) 87
  Jason Tyler 87
  Julie A. (Edscorn) 87
  Leo J. 87
  Robert Leo 87
Norfolk Co., Va. 7
Norfolk, Va. 58
North
  Rebecca 37
North Carolina 119
North Mountain, Va. 41
North Platte, Nebr. 109
Northumberland Co., Va. . . . 9,
                                11, 57
Northup
  Dorothy 112
Nowata Co., Okla.
  Lenapah 37
Null
  Fleta 109
  Jenny 112

181

O

O'Hara
  Marguerite (Jeffries) 37
  T.E. 37
O'Malley
  Bill 34
  Helen L. (Alexander) 34
O'Neill
  Alberta Irene 97
  Barney Clayton 96
  Bertha I. (Alexander) . . 73, 96
  Emmet Claiborn 96
  Helen Marie 96
  James Emmet 73, 96
  James Patrick 96
  John Edward 96
  Katherine (Brown) 96
  Margaret K. (Messmer) . . . 96
  Mariam (Harper) 96
  Nancy Lou 96
  Ruth Ann 96
  Thomas 96
Ocala, Fla. 58
Oceltree, Kan. 31
Ocheltree
  Martha R. 114
Ochiltree
  Martha 134
Ohio 24
Oils
  Rebecca (Alexander) . . . 131
Oklahoma 38
Oklahoma City, Okla. 27
Olathe, Kan. 33, 85
Old Providence, Va. 54
Oliver
  Maxine 38
Omaha, Nebr. 80, 87
  Hill Crest Memorial Park . . 80
Onslow Co., N.C. 137
Orange Co., N.C. 132
Organ
  Eliza Virginia 68
  Virginia 63
Orr
  Elizabeth 135
  James 143
  John 142
  Mildred 125, 143
  Nathan 135
  Rebecca (Montgomery) . . 143
  William 143
Osawatomie, Kan. . 27, 33, 35-
                              37, 81
  Green Valley Cem. 35
Osborne
  Jean 145
Otero Co., Colo.
  LaJunta 26

Ottawa, Kan. 35, 36, 39
  Crestview Nursing Home . 39
Overland Park, Kan. . . . 33, 81,
                              87
  Shawnee Mission Medical
  Center 81
Ozark Co., Mo.
  Bakersfield 39
Ozark, Ark. 36

P

Packer
  Ernie 29
  Pearl S. (Guy) 29
Paddock
  Amanda (Shields) 81
  George Henry 81
  Nellie Victoria 81
Page
  Sally 56
Page Co., Va.
  Luray 44, 107
Painter
  Phebe 44
  Rev. 112
Palmer
  Charles Henry 91
  Elizabeth 65
  Harriett (Bennett) 91
  Harriett E. (Bennett) 91
  Jacob 23
  Marguerite Pearl 91
  Mary M. 23
Palo Alto, Calif. 72, 73
Pannell
  Mrs. Arron 62
Pannil
  Elizabeth 118
Paola, Kan. 26, 27, 33, 35
Paris, Ill. 87
Park
  Hannah 143
Parker
  Lee 2
  William 146
Parker, Kan. 25-28, 33, 34
  Highland Cem. 25, 26
  Liberty Twp. 34
Parks
  Abigail (McCoy) 139
  David 139
Parratt
  George 117
Parrish
  Bonnie (Alexander) 114
  Howard 114
Parrot
  Francis 149
  Hannah 149

Parrott
  Francis 149
Parsons
  David 23
Parsons, Kan. 34
Patrick
  Hazel 69
Patterson
  John 44
  Joseph 44
  Martha E. (Stanton) 44
  Martha J. 23
  Martha Jane 23, 38, 39
  Percy A. 44
  Phebe (Painter) 44
Patton
  Dorothy (Wallace) 147
  House 147
  Isabella (Alexander) 134
  John 147
  Mr. 134
  Phebe (Alexander) 134
  Robert 147, 149
Paul
  Arthur 35
  Bessie (Muncie) 35
  Exira (Gates) 35
  Ida M. (Vint) 35
  Lewis 35
  William Clyde 35
Pearce
  Benjamin, Sr. 132
  C.V., Rev. 38
  Margaret 132
Pearl
  Ann (Groah) 112
  Anna ( ) 35
  Clinton Augustus 35
  Doris Lucinda 112
  Joseph 112
Peay
  Linda Michelle 108
Peculiar, Mo. 92
Peggs
  Carol Sue 87
Pence
  Mary F. 58
  Mary Frances 58
Pendleton Co., Va. 35
Pennoyer
  John 141
Penns Valley, Pa. 138
Pennsylvania . . . 62, 118, 123,
                        136, 142, 144
Perdue
  James O. 114
  Joan (Alexander) 114
Perkins
  Deborah Patricia 92

Perry
  S.A. 136
Perry Co., Ohio
  Pisgah Cem. 41
Persons
  John 7
Peterman
  Ida Mae 28
Petersburg, Va. 4
Petersburg, W.Va. 112
Peterson
  Carl 37
  Fern (Dukes) 37
  Kay (Lain) 37
  Rebecca (North) 37
  Sharlene D. (Savage) 37
  Wallace W. 37
  Warren Henry 37
  Wendell Charles 37
Petoskey, Mich. 29
Pettis Co., Mo.
  Sedalia 30
Peyton
  Francis 141
Philadelphia, Pa. . 58, 91, 136,
                            144
Phillips
  Casper C. 139
  Thomas 8
Pickens
  Samuel 129
Pickett
  Hannah (Alexander) 137
  Mr. 137
Piedmont, Va. 56
Pietropouli
  Theresa 67
Pineville, N.C.
  Polk Family Cem. 118
Piplico
  Joseph 69
  Katherine E. (McCormick)
         69
Pippenger
  Charles Wesley 91
  Charley Wesley 91
  Daniel C. 72
  John Wesley 73, 91
  Malissa M. (Pippinger) . . . 91
  Marguerite (Palmer) 91
  Marguerite P. (Palmer) . . . 91
  Marjorie Jeanne 71, 91
  Mary Lee 80, 92
  Mildred Irene . . 71, 80, 86, 92
  Nina L. (Alexander) . . . 71, 73
  Nina Sue 91
  Patrice 91
  Rachel 91
  Simon Peter 91
  Wesley Eugene 91, 92

  Z. Eileene (Davison) 91
Pippinger
  Malissa Malvina 91
Pirkey
  Alice F. (Denton) 40
  Robert E. 40
Pittsburg, Kan. 33
Plank
  Hattie 29
  Hattie J. 29
Platt
  Bernice ( ) 86
  Marce Lynn 86
  Raymond 86
Plattner
  Charles W. 92
  Cynthia Gail 92
Pleasant Hill, Mo. 88, 92
Pleasanton, Kan. . . 33, 78, 81,
                            85
  Littell Cem. 85
  Pleasanton Cem. 85
Plumlee
  Claudia 28
Pocomoke, Md. 128, 129, 131,
                 132, 134, 146
Polk
  Charles 143
  David 8
  Devil Charley 143
  Kezia 143
  Kezia (Alexander) 143
  Margaret 125
  Margaret (Taylor) 148
  Mary 118
  Mary (Alexander) 143
  Susan 117, 148
  Thomas 143
  William 148
Polk Co., Tenn.
  Benton Cem. 144
Pollitt
  Thomas 8
Ponotoc, Miss. 92
Poplar Bluff, Mo. 86
Port Republic, Va. . 15, 19, 23,
          40, 47, 57, 104, 111, 112
  Sons of Temperance 46
Port Royal, Va. 142
Porter
  Hugh 10
  McKemmey 11
  William 10
Potomac River 19
Pottawatomie Co., Kan.
  Belvue 31
  Greenwood Cem. 31
  Kaw Twp. 31
  Wamego 31

Potter
  Amanda Elizabeth 25
  Uriah 25
Pow
  Patricia 80
Powell
  Howell 117
  Mary (McKnitt) 147
  Thomas 147
Poynter
  Jeremiah 127
Prat
  Mary D. (McEntyre) 30
  Paul David 30
Prentice
  Mary E. 26
Price
  Isabella (Sharp) 137
  John 149
  Margaret 18, 131
  William, Jr. 132
Prince Edward Co., Va. 82
Prince Georges Co., Md. . 121,
                            122
Prince William Co., Va.
  Dumfries 108
  Quantico 109
Princess Anne Co., Va. 7
Princess Anne, Md. 7, 119
Princeton University 119
Princeton, Kan. 35, 36
  Princeton Cem. 39
Princeton, N.J. 133
Providence 11
Pueblo Co., Colo.
  Pueblo 26
Pueblo, Colo. 26, 27
  Imperial Gardens Cem. . . . 27
  Mountain View Cem. 26
Puffenbarger
  Bonnie 114
  David 115
  Mary (Alexander) 114
Pulaski, Tenn. 59
Pulaski, Va. 58
Pumphry
  Eva (Craun) 110
  John 110
Purcell, Okla. 82
Putnam Co., Va. 25, 26
Putnam Co., W.Va. 24, 71
  Alexander-Amos Cem. . . . 71

Q

Quantico, Va. 109
Queen
  Barbara D. (Brown) 81
  Barry 81
  James Richard 81
  Jayme 81

Query
Alexander 135
Ellen 135
Nancy 135
Peggy (McCord) 135
Robert 135
Sidney (Alexander) 135
Quincy, Ill. 95

R

Racer
Kathryn 107
Radford, Va. 54, 63
Ragan
Edith M. (Alexander) 26
Romullus 26
Ralston
John 132
Ramsey
Amelia Naomi 134
Ann (Agnew) 134, 144
Elizabeth C. (Fleming) . . . 134
Francis Alexander . 133, 134,
144
Isabella 133
J.G.M. 4
Johanna (Alexander) 114
John 134
Margaret (Alexander) . . . 133
Margaret C. (Russell) . . . 134
Margaret C.R.C. 134
Margaret M. (Alexander)
. . . . 144
Martha (Ochiltree) 134
Maybeth L. 114
Naomi E. (Alexander) . . . 133
Reynolds 133
Samuel Graham . . . 133, 134
Sandra L. 114
William 134
William L. 114
Rankin
Adam 133
Mary (Alexander) 133
Mary Frances 131
Rantoul, Kan. 39
Raphoe Parish, Ire. . 2-4, 121,
127, 128, 136, 146, 147
Raphoe, Ire. 7
Rapid City, Mich. 29
Raulston
Col. 140
Ray
Worth S. 116
Raymond
Jonathan 7
Raymond, Mo. 97
Raymore, Mo. 92, 97
Raytown, Mo. . . 86, 91, 92, 97

Reagan
Leah 119
Reed
Alexander 138
Andrew 105
Jemima (Alexander) . . . 138
John 105, 138
John W. 113
Julia (Smith) 105
Julia A. (Grandstaff) . . . 105
Luther Hamilton 105
Margaret 80
Martha F. (Landes) 105
Mary B. 113
Sarah E. (Wine) 105
Sarah J. (Cochran) 113
Rees
Lewis 85
Reese (also see Rice)
J.R. 23
Ruth 119
Reeves
Anita R. (Alexander) 67
Clint 67
Reid
Sarah M. 25
Sarah Martha 25, 26
Reno Co., Kan.
Hutchinson 37
Revolutionary
War 117
Revolutionary War . . . 91, 118-
120, 124-126, 129-133, 136-
138, 143, 144, 148, 149
Rhinehart
David 119
Margaret (Alexander) . . . 119
Rhody
Shirley May 29
Rice
Mary . 72, 73, 82, 85, 91, 94-
96
Richard
Asa, Rev. 114
Richardson
William 128
Richey
Betty Jo 39
Richmond
Charles 123
Rebecca (Alexander) . . . 123
Richmond, Kan. 39
Richmond, Va. . 58, 62, 63, 65,
108, 110
Camp Carter 16, 19
Ricketts
Ann 140
David 140
John T. 140
John Thomas 140

Mary ( ) 140
Ridgeway
Philip 91
Riley
Katherine 69
Riley Co., Kan.
Manhattan 30
Rimel
Charles 110
Neoma 110
Nora 105
Roach
Madeline 114
Roanoke, Va. . . . 58, 108, 109,
112
Evergreen Burial Park . . . 109
Robbins
Isaac 141
Roberts
Ann W. . . 20, 23, 24, 35, 36,
38
Curtis 98
Eliza J. 60
Robertson
Elizabeth 8-10
Robinson (see Robison)
Martha 135
Mary (Speece) 56
Mr. 56
Robison (see Robinson)
Andrew 15
Deborah (Alexander) . . . 123
Elizabeth 123, 139
Martha 139
Richard 123
Robert 123
Sarah (Alexander) 123
Rochester, Minn. 83
Rockbridge Baths, Va. . . . 39
Rockbridge Co., Va. . . . 23, 35,
36, 38, 133
Brownsburg 23
Cedar Grove Mills 24
Emanuel Cem. 23
Fairfield 113
Lexington 35, 38, 72
Rockbridge Baths 39
Walker's Creek . . . 23, 35-38
Walker's Creek Twp. 23
Zack 23
Rockingham Co., Va. . . 19, 41,
43, 44, 46, 57, 71, 99, 105,
106
Arrey Family Cem. 40
Beaver Creek Brethren Cem.
. . . . 41
Bridgewater . . . 107, 108, 113
Clover Hill 40, 41
Cook Creek 104
Dayton 107, 110

Dayton Cem. 40-42
Friedens 40
Friedens U.C. Cem. 40
Friedens United Church of
    Christ Cem. 40
Fulks Run 109
Good's Mill 58
Grottoes 109, 111
Harrisonburg . 107, 108, 110-
    112
McGaheysville 41
Mill Creek Church of the
    Brethren Cem. 108
Mt. Crawford . . 40, 107, 108,
    114
North Mountain 41
Ottobein Cem. . . . 40, 41, 110
Port Republic . 15, 19, 23, 40,
    46, 47, 57, 104, 108, 111,
    112
Port Republic Cem. 112
Rockingham Memorial Hospital
    . . . . 107, 112
Singers Glen 41, 42
Singers Glen Cem. 42
St. John's Lutheran Cem.
    42
St. Michaels Reformed Church
    Cem. 106, 110
Timberville 108, 114
Rodgers
    Sarah 143
Rogers
    Charles 2
    James 99
    Margaret (Wood) 99
    Margaret L. (Wood) 99
Rogers Co., Okla.
    Claremore 37
Rokiawakin River 7
Rosedale, Kan. 80
Ross
    George 132
    Isaac 131
    Jean (Brown) 131
    Judith Mooney 31
Rowan Co., N.C. . . . 147, 149
Rowan Co., Tenn. 124
Ruckersville, Va. 69
Russell
    Andrew 134
    Margaret (Christian) 134
    Margaret Christian 134
Rutherford
    Doris A. (Dukes) 38
    Ernest L. 38
    Gen. 120
Rutherford Co., N.C. . . 118, 119
    Buffalo Creek 149

Rutherford Co., Tenn. 131,
    139
    Alexander Family Cem. . . 131
    Crescent 131
    Sharp Family Cem. 138
    Stones River 138

S

Sackett
    Elizabeth Esther 29
Saginaw, Mich. 29
Salina, Kan. 31, 37
    Asbury Hospital 37
Saline Co., Kan.
    Salina 37
Saline Co., Mo. . . 18, 47, 69, 80
    bounty land 19
    Gilliam 72
    Jefferson Twp. 72
    Marshall . . 19, 48, 54, 65, 66,
        71, 72, 78
    Miami . 65, 72, 73, 78, 80, 82,
        85, 91, 94
    Miami Twp. 72, 73
    Salt Pond Twp. 71
    Slater 72
Salisbury
    Betty L. (Theis) 67
    Faith Elizabeth 67
    Garth David 68
    Garth Delmar 67
    John Theis 68
Salisbury, Md. 8, 125
Salisbury, N.C. 125
Salt Lake City, Utah 108
Sample
    Abigail 139
    Ann 139
    Elizabeth (Alexander) . . . 139
    Elizabeth (Robison) 139
    Esther 137, 139
    Esther (Garrison) . . . 139, 142
    James 139
    Jane Bain 139
    Jemima 139
    Joseph R. 139
    Mary 120, 137, 139, 142
    Sarah 143
    William 139, 142
    William A. 139
Samuel
    Valorie Leigh 31
Samuelson
    Eben 31
    Judith M. (Ross) 31
    Mable M. (Brown) 31
    Marvin Lee 31
    Melanie Sue 31
    Scott Eben 31
    Shirley A. (Scott) 31

    Vonna Lynn 31
San Diego Co., Calif. 36
    Chula Vista 82
San Diego, Calif. 36, 82
    El Camino Cem. 82
San Francisco, Calif. . . . 73, 92
San Jose, Calif.
    Alta Mesa Cem. 73
    Willow Brae Sanitarium . . . 73
San Mateo, Calif. 73
San Pedro, Calif. 31
Sanders
    Dorothy D. (Holmes) 32
    Lester Eugene, Jr. 32
    Lewis M. 33
    May 33
    Rex Keith 32
    Sybil E. (Cochran) 33
Sanderson
    Martha 69
Sandidge
    M.C., Rev. 78
Sands
    Virginia 32
Sandy
    Reba Virginia 108
Santa Clara Co., Calif. 73
Santa Clara, Calif. 81
Sasebo, Japan 109
Savage
    Sharlene Dee 37
Savannah, Ga. 132
Sawyer, Mich. 94
Sawyers
    Iva 34
Sayre, Okla. 87
Schleper
    Therese F. 66
Schlotter
    Patsy L. (Guy) 29
    Thomas Clark 29
Schreckhire
    J.M., Rev. 23, 36
Schultz
    Betty L. (Nazer) 80
    Clifford Glen 80
    Loranelle Louise 80
    Melora Ann 80
    Scott Andres 80
    Susan Eileen 80
Schumacher
    George Gilbert 86
    Kimberly K. (Fox) 86
Scotland 2, 7, 86, 131, 133
Scott
    Alice D. (Teed) 30
    Christal L. (Herrmann) . . . 30
    Ethel L. (McCain) 30
    Georgia M. (Sherrill) 30
    Haley Nicole 30

Henry C. 30
James 125
Jennifer Rebecca 30
John 138
John Frederick 30
John Frederick, III 30
John Frederick, IV 30
John Frederick, Jr. 30
Kathryn E. ( ) 30
Linda S. (Harper) 30
Robert Gregory, Jr. 30
Robert Gregory, Sr. 30
Shirley Ann 31
Virginia Elizabeth 30
William C. 56
Scottsdale, Ariz. 86
Scottsville, Va. 1
Scranton, Iowa 38
Seaman, Kan. 29
Searcy
Ada C. (Jones) 86
Alanna Kiersten 86
Claire L. (Ward) 86
Karen Kay 86
Michael Ward 86
Mildred A. (McLaughlin) . . 86
Milton Norman 86
Robert Eugene 86
Robert Gayle 86
Robert Henry 86
Robert Keith 86
Sarah (Wallace) 86
Sarah Ann 86
Timothy Lee 86
Wakefield Paul 86
Seattle, Wash. 87, 110
Sebastian
Barbara Ann 87
Gail (Tatum) 88
Jerry Van 88
Loren Lee 88
Marguerite E. (McLaughlin)
. . . . 87
Van Dulare 87
Secrist
Aaron Daniel 109
Alvin Delmas 109
Derek Anthony 109
Erica Michelle 109
Mary A. (Alexander) 109
Sedalia, Mo. 30, 92
Sedgwick Co., Kan. 37
Sedgwick 38
Wichita 36-38
Sedgwick, Kan. 38
Hillside Cem. 38
Selman
James Ella 107
James Wilson 107
Seneca, Kan. 31

Sengel
William Randolph 140
Severin
Barbara Jean 92
Shadwell, Va. 69
Shapiro
Bryan 66
Ernest 66
Jesse Maxwell 66
Joan ( ) 66
Justin 66
Kevin 66
Mary (Crowley) 66
Mary F. (Hunt) 66
Michael Guthrey 66
Nicholas Gleyre 66
Nicolas Joseph 66
Sandra (Wise) 66
Sonam 66
Terri 66
Sharp
Araminta 137
Catherine (Alexander) . . . 137
Ezekiel 137
Isabella 137
Isabella ( ) 137
James 137, 138
Jemima ( ) 138
Jemima (Alexander) 137
Jemima Alexander . 137, 140
John 137, 138
Joseph 137
Joseph A.F. 138
Keziah (Alexander) 137
Levina 137
Martha (Young) 138
Priscilla 138
Rachel (Cannon) 138
Samuel 137
Sarah 138, 140
Sophia (Alexander) 137
Thomas 137
Walter 137
Shaults
Drew A. 87
James 87
Kelly M. (McLaughlin) . . 87
Kyle R. 87
Shaver
Edward J. 40
Mary J. (Denton) 40
Shaw
Jennie 112
Mariam 3, 4
Vicki 68
Shawnee Co., Kan.
Topeka 30
Shawnee, Okla. 86
First Baptist Church 86

Shea
Corky 92
Mary A. (Abbas) 92
Shear
Shirley 29
Sheets
Carrie R. 115
Carrie Rebecca 113, 115
Charles 113
George Emory 106
Jeanette 87
Mary Jane 113
Mary K. (Wine) 106
Ruth 62
Sarah (Wine) 113
Shelby
Catherine (Davies) 119
Evan 119
Mary 117, 119
Susannah 148
Sheldon
John 10, 11, 15
Mary 9-12
Mary ( ) 10, 11
Sarah 11
Sheldon's Addition 11
Shelley
Bessie Marie 94
Sam 94
Shenandoah Co., Va. 72
Edinburg 109
Mt. Jackson 108
Wheatfield 111
Woodstock 108, 109
Shenandoah Valley . . . 18, 124
Sherrill
Caroline F. (Ford) 30
George Hartley 30
Georgia Maxine 30
Shields
Amanda 81
ships
Desire 18
Globe 146
Welcome 136
Shively
Cecile 27
Shoemaker
Barbara (Thacker) 41
Shofner
Anna Faye 36
Shrewsbury, Mo. 87
Shuey
E.J. 105
Shufflebarger
Margaret Ellen 107
Shull
Mary 115
W.J., Rev. 37

Sibert
   Doris A. (Huffman) 109
Siebenmorgen
   Anthony Charles 87
   Georgia S. (McLaughlin) . . 87
   Timothy 87
Silver Spring, Md. 92
Silvy
   Barbara Ann 23
   Elizabeth (Flemmings) . . . 23
   John 23
Simmons
   Bessie C. 105
   Christian 110
   Elva F. 109
   Gail C. (Alexander) 110
   Gregory Scott 110
   Hazel (Thompson) 110
   Helen 110
   Horace Greely 110
   James Gale 110
   John P. 104
   Lyda (Alexander) 110
   Nancy M. (Landes) 104
   Raymond Alexander 110
   Sarah J. (Landes) 105
   William M. 105
Simonton
   Eleanor 130
Simpson
   Dennis Harold 38
   Harold 38
   Mayfred E. (Dukes) 38
   Ronald Paul 38
Singers Glen, Va. 41, 42
   Singers Glen Cem. 42
Sioux City, Iowa 87, 110
Sise
   Peyton (Bird) 60
Skelton
   Margaret Elizabeth 40
Slate Hill, Md. 116
Slate Hill, Pa. 116, 117
Smedley
   Rena 67
Smith
   Ann 34, 98
   Betsey 99
   Billy D. 31
   Cathy S. (Bayless) 32
   Dungale S. (Lankaitis) 31
   Helen 2
   Henry 10
   Jackie Eugene 32
   James 99
   John 99, 125
   John M. 16, 99
   Julia 105
   Julia M. (Stancliff) 32
   Margaret B. 120

Mary Ann 98
Michael Jay 32
Nancy 99
Polly 99
Robert Washington 125
Roberta Marie 31
Sarah 16, 99, 104
Sarah T. (Alexander) 125
Thomas 98, 99
William 99
Willis 99
Snell
   Dorothy (Northup) 112
   Paige 112
   Ralph 112
Snow
   Jacqueline 60
Society of the Cincinnati . . . 126
Somers
   Sarah Vitura 86
Somerset Co., Md. . 1, 2, 4-10,
     12, 15, 18, 57, 116, 117,
     121-124, 127, 128, 134, 136,
                     147
   Addition to Hogg Quarter . 11
   Annemessix . . 128-130, 132,
                     146
   Chance 121
   Daintry 7-9
   Fleming's Loss 15
   Golden Quarter 127
   Hogg Quarter 6, 8, 9
   Hungary Neck 9
   Hunting Quarter 6, 7, 9
   Manokin 147
   Manokin Hundred . 121, 122,
                127, 147
   Manokin Presbyterian Church
                       7
   Manokin River 7, 121
   Middle Town 15
   Monmouth 7
   Mt. Hope 10
   Nanticoke Hundred 9
   Pocomoke 146
   Princess Anne 7, 119
   Raphoe 7
   Ripley 127
   Rokiawakin River 7
   The Strand 7
   Trouble 6-9
   Warwick 18
   Whaley's Chance 7
   Wicomico Hundred . . . 7-10
   Wicomoco Creek 6
   Windsor 7
Sordillo
   Carol Ann 86
   Claire A. (   ) 86
   Vincent Frank 86

Sorrells
   Mary F. 113
South
   Hezekiah 138
Southington, Conn. 86
Spanish American War 85
Spaulding
   Barbara 111
Speece
   Conrad 16
   Conrad, Rev. 16
Spiggle
   Doris A. (Huffman) 109
Spotsylvania, Pa. 57
Spring
   John 148
Springer
   Beverly E. (Alexander) . . . 28
   Bobbie Jo 28
   Clarris 28
   Colleen D. (Good) 28
   Florence (Anderson) 28
   Gregory Eugene 28
   James Alexander 28
   James Allen 28
   Kimberly L. (Farran) 28
   Lynly Dawn 28
   Morgan Rene 28
Springfield, Va. 111
Springhill, Va. 114
Springs
   John 119
   Richard 119
   Sarah S. (Alexander) 119
St. John's, Mo. 86
St. Louis Co., Mo. 86
   Shrewsbury 87
St. Louis, Mo. 54, 66-68
   Alexander & Sons 66
   Bellefontaine Cem. 66
   Beredith Realty Co. 66
   Modern Realty Co. 66
   Oak Grove Cem. 68
   Occidental Lodge 66
   Olive Street Bank 66
   Valhalla Cem. 66
St. Paul, Minn. 87
St. Peter's Parish, Md. 149
Stafford
   Alvah M. 2
Stakley
   Mr. 26
Stambaugh
   Betty J. (Monroe) 31
   Christopher 31
   Deanna K. (Delker) 31
   Edwin Emmett 31
   Emmett Hibler 31
   Infant 31
   Irene (McCain) 31

James Steven 31
Janet Louise 31
Joanna (VanSycle) 31
John Charles 31
John Washington 31
Lois Melva 31
Melva O. (Murphy) 31
Paul James 31
Robert Martin 31
Roberta M. (Smith) 31
Virginia S. (Cottrell) 31
Stamford, Conn. 60
Stanardsville, Va. 112
Stancliff
   Julia Mae 32
Stansbury
   Ruth Ernestine 66
Stanton
   George W. 44
   Harriet A. (Alexander) 44
   M.C. 44
   Martha E. 44
   Nancy (Kice) 44
Staunton, Va. . . 16, 43, 47, 54,
    58, 62, 106-108, 113, 115
   Augusta County Independent
    60
   Oak Hill Nursing Home . . . 58
   Stirling 107
   Thornrose Cem. . . 44, 60, 61
   Western State Hospital . . . 44
Steele(e)
   James 129
   Jane 130
   Jean (McCulland) 69
   John 123, 129
   Margaret (   ) 130
   Mary . . . 123, 128, 129, 132
   Mary (   ) 129
   Moses 129
   Nathaniel, Jr. 69
   Sarah 69
Stephens City, Va. 112
Sternhagen
   Melvin 29
   Virginia A. (Guy) 29
Stevenson
   Peter 2
   Thomas . . 116, 129, 136, 146
Stickley
   Elizabeth 104
   Gabriel 104
   Margaret . 99, 104, 106, 111,
     112
   Rebecca (Keller) 104
Stirling Castle 1
Stirling, Scot. 1
Stockdale
   Catherine (Alexander) . . . 113
   Clyde J. 113

Stockton Field, Calif. 34
Stockwell
   Milton 29
   Patsy L. (Guy) 29
Stoddard
   Harriet J. (Guy) 29
   Kenneth 29
Stogdale
   Clyde 115
   Edith (Alexander) 115
Stone Coal Creek 56
Stonewall, Va. 105
Stoughton
   William 9
Stratton
   Thomas 132
Strawbridge
   Thomas 6, 7
Streiber
   Sally 67
Stribling
   Charles R. 58
   Erasmus 16
Stringer
   Alice Margaret 38
   Elmer 38
   Lois (Harris) 38
Stroberg
   Sandra Lynn 109
Stuart
   John A. 43
Stuart, Fla. 114
Stubbs
   Harrison Alexander 66
   Harrison Bailey 66
   Ruth V. (Alexander) 66
   Susan Bailey 66
Stump
   John 140
Sugar Grove, W.Va. 109
Sulivant
   Alie 149
Sullins
   Flossie (Alexander) . . 25, 26,
     28, 33, 36
   Max 33
   Rita 33
   Violet 33
   Walter Leon 33
   Walter R. 33
Sullivan
   Arlo Alexander 26
   Doris 68
   Flora G. (Alexander) 26
   Infant 26
   Orian A. 26
   Thelma Lucille 26
Summers
   George 140

Summerville
   Rhoda 149
Sumner Co., Kan.
   Milvane 33
   Wellington 36
Sumner Co., Tenn. 125
Sussex Co., Del. 8
Swann
   Thomas 141
Swannanoa, N.C. 149
Swansboro, N.C. 114
Swanson
   Alan Garfield 91
   Christopher William 91
Swecker
   Betty J. (Alexander) 107,
     108, 110
   Cara Stuart 108
   Charles Emmett, Jr. 108
   Charles Emmett, Sr. 108
   Gail M. Stuart 108
   Melanie 108
   Stephanie 108
   Suzanne 108
Sweet
   Emma Jane 44
Syranic Lake, N.Y. 112

T

Tafoya
   Esperanza Gertrude 34
Taghboyne Parish, Ire. 2
Talbot
   Thomas 8
Talbot Co., Md. . . . 1, 117, 148,
     149
   Alexander's Chance 149
   Cardiffe 149, 150
   East Ottwell 150
   Highfield's Addition 150
   Irish Freshes 149
   Lowe's Good Luck 149
   St. Peter's Parish . . . 149, 150
   St. Stephen's Parish 149
   Wales 149
Tallahassee, Fla. 109
Tampa, Fla. 87
Tappahannock, Va. . . . vii, 91,
     108
Tarver
   Augustine (Bellier) 33
   Beverly Elaine 33
   Dorothy F. (McCain) 33
   Dorothy Joanne 33
   Ethelred 33
   George Lee, Jr. 33
   George Lee, Sr. 33
   Violet N. (Edwards) 33
Tate
   Hannah (   ) 149

Thomas 149
Tatum
   Gail 88
Taylor
   Amelia N. (Ramsey) 134
   Ann . . . 4, 116, 122, 123, 136
   Comfort (Anderson) 116,
                    127, 128
   Elias 128
   George 116, 127, 128
   Isaac 132
   Jane 125, 132
   Jeremiah 132
   Margaret 148
   Mary . 4, 121, 128-130, 132,
                       134
   Stuart, Rev. 35
   Thomas 150
   William 57
Teed
   Alice Delana 30
Teft
   Bessie M. (Shelley) 94
   Clyde Delose 73, 94
   Emma L. (Alexander) . . . 73
   Ida (Brova) 94
   Ray Delose 94
   Shirley Marie 94
   Wayne 94
Tennessee 56, 87
Tennessee River 134
Terry
   Carolyn Faye 107
   Janet C. (Gibson) 107
   Lawrence Ervin 107
   Norma G. (Alexander) . . . 107
   Randall Thomas 107
   Thomas Nelson 107
Thacker
   Barbara 41
   Barbara (Byrd) 40
   Carl 41
   Catherine (McCrary) 41
   Catherine S. (Caricofe) . . . 41
   Charles S.H. 41
   David 41
   Delbert R. 41
   Donald 41
   Eleanor T. (Alexander) . . 40
   Eliza J. (Adams) 41
   Elizabeth (Blain) 41
   Elizabeth T. (Alexander) . 19,
                      20
   Ella D. (Evers) 41
   Elsie 41
   Emma (Applegate) 41
   Family 40
   Floyd Hubert 41
   Frances ( ) 40
   Frances Elizabeth 41

Goldie R. (Caricofe) 41
Guy Newton 41
Henry 41
Hester J. 41
James Morgan 40
John 40, 41
John Wesley 41
Joseph Byrd 41
Katie (Coffman) 41
Levi J. 41
Lydia Catherine 42
M. Gertrude (Good) 41
Margaret Adaline 42
Martha E. 41
Martha Ellen 41
Mary Ann 40, 41
Mary Virginia 41
Newton S. 41
Norma Jane 41
Norman Robert 41
Peggy 41
Rebecca Caroline 42
Rosa 41
Russell 40
Russell Jennings 41
Samuel Henning 41
Sarah Jane 40
Stephen Hank 41
Virginia ( ) 41
Virginia (Walters) 41
William 19, 20, 40
William Houck 42
The Fork 11
The Strand 7
Theis
   Alexander Albert 67
   Betty Lee 67
   Elizabeth L. (Alexander) . . 67
   Gertrude E. (Bakewell) . . . 67
   Harry S.G. 67
   Virginia Dean 68
Theta, Tenn. 118
Thomas
   Bessie M. (Shelley) 94
   Clarence 94
Thompson
   Elizabeth 98
   Hazel 110
   Richard 128
Thomson
   Margaret 121
Thornton
   Alice ( ) 96
   Brenda K. (Hendrickson) . . 96
   Brett Edward 96
   Garett Evan 96
   George 96
   George Edward 96
   Helen M. (O'Neill) 96
   Ida (Bowles) 87

James Roy 87
Malory 87
Margye A. (McLaughlin) . . 87
Nathaniel 87
Roy Lee 87
Sarah 120
Sherri (Tribble) 87
Terry Ann 87
Thomas Lee 87
Thomas Patrick 96
Throckmorton
   Jane 130
Timberville, Va. 108, 114
Tippicanoe Co., Ind.
   West Lafayette 30
Tokyo, Japan 33
Toney
   John Simms 112
   Lucinda (Alexander) 112
Topeka, Kan. . . 30, 31, 36, 80,
                      86
   Greenwood Cem. 31
   Mt. Hope Cem. 30
   Rochester Cem. 34
   Stone Church Cem. 31
Townsen
   Lisa Faith 112
Townsend
   Linda Gayle 34
   Solomon 11
Traverse City, Mich. 29
Trenton, N.J. 133
Tressco
   Tracey 57
Tribble
   Sherri 87
Trimble
   W.W., Rev. 23
Trotter
   Jane (Alexander) 126
   Mary 133
   Richard 126
Trouble 6-8
Troyer
   Mattie B. 113
Trumbull
   L.H. 26
   Nathan Leonard 26
   Virginia M. (Alexander) . . . 26
   Walter Lynn 26
Tucker, W.Va.
   Mt. Pleasant Cem. 98
Tull
   Eleanor 15, 18, 57
   James 18
   Jonathan 18, 57
   Mary (Fountaine) 18, 57
Turley
   Carolyn J. (Miller) 39

Twillor
  Robert 9
Tyree
  Catharine A. 98
  Elizabeth ( ) 98
  John 98
Tyrell Co., N.C. 148

U

U.S. Congress 119
Ulster, Ire. 2
Underhill
  Barbara 25, 29, 39
  George LeRoy 29
  Irma B. (Guy) 29
Urich, Mo. 96
Utah 80

V

Valley Forge, Pa. 138
Van Buren Co., Iowa 36
Van Collie
  Carol 29
Van Dew
  Leonie 97
Van Lear
  Annie 106
  Emma 111
Vansant
  Annabelle 28
  Ida M. (Peterman) 28
  Lelan 28
VanSycle
  Joanna 31
Vaughn
  Ira 36
  Naomi E. (Vint) 36
  Virginia Lee 36
Vernon Co., Mo.
  Clayton 66
Verona, Va. 108
Versailles, Mo. 81
Victoria, Tex. 81
Vienna, Va. 112
Vines
  Anadel 109
Vint
  Asa 36
  Delilah (Bodkin) 35
  Eli 35, 36
  Elizabeth (McQuain) 35
  Elizabeth A. (Alexander) . . 23
  Eva 36
  Ida May 35
  Ira 36
  John 35
  John W. 36
  Lee 35, 36
  Mary E. (Loch) 36

Mary E. (McCord) 36
Naomi Ellen 36
O'Della 36
William 23, 35
Virginia 5
Virginia Beach, Va. 87
Vogt
  Byron Keith 96
  Keith 96
  Lori D. (Bowes) 96
  Tracy Ann 96

W

Wabaunsee Co., Kan.
  Kaw Twp. 31
Waco, Tex. 2
Wadkins
  Dorothy A. (Dukes) 38
  J.L. 38
Wagner
  Beulah 92
Wakulla Co., Fla. 142
Wales 78, 107
Waley's Chance 7
Walker
  Evelyn 87
  Sarabell 142
  William 142
Walker, William 142
Walker's Creek, Va. . 23, 35-38
Wallace (see Wallis)
  Alexander 121
  Andrew 138, 148
  Ann 121, 122
  Catharine . . . 6-9, 116, 122,
                       137
  David T. 122
  Dorothy 122, 147
  Edward R. 121
  Elizabeth 121, 136, 147
  Elizabeth (Alexander) . . . 4, 7
  Elizabeth (Hart) 121
  Ezekiel 118, 121
  Frances (Young) 121
  George 121
  Grace (White) 121
  Hannah 121
  Isabella 122
  James 121
  Jane . . . 121, 124, 128, 134,
                    136, 147
  Jane (Alexander) 121
  Joannah 120
  John 121, 122
  Joseph 121
  Margaret 121
  Margaret (Connelly) 86
  Margaret (Thomson) 121
  Margery ( ) 121
  Mary 121, 124, 125

Mary (Hollins) 122
Matthew 4, 6, 7, 121
Matthew, Jr. . . . 4, 7, 121, 125,
                    128
Richard 121
Robert 86, 122
Ruth (Alexander) 138
Samuel 121
Sarah 86, 121
Sarah (Alexander) . 121, 125,
                    128
Sarah (McKnitt) 121
Thomas, Sr. 122
William 121, 122
Wallis (see Wallace)
  James, Rev. 144
  Jean B. (Alexander) 144
Walters
  Virginia 41
Walthall
  Flossie 34
  Lena M. 26
  Lena Mae 26, 33
  Mary E. (Diehm) 33
  Samuel White 33
Walton
  Ann (Smith) 98
  Catharine A. (Tyree) 98
  Catherine ( ) 98
  Eli 98
  Elizabeth (Thompson) 98
  Isom 15
  Jane 98
  John Nicholas 98
  John Samuel 98
  Nancy 98
  Nancy (Armstrong) 98
  Nicholas 98
  Rebecca A. (Moore) 98
  Richmond 15
  Richmond T. 15
  Richmond Terril 16, 98
  Samuel 98
  Sarah (Alexander) 16, 98
Wamego, Kan. 31
Wampler
  Bessie 38
War of 1812 . . . 16, 19, 56, 99,
          118, 119, 132, 140
Warbritton
  Flossie (Walthall) 34
  Ray 34
Ward
  Claire Lee 86
  Raymond Lee 86
  Sarah V. (Somers) 86
Wardlaw
  Tibbie 140
Warehouse Point, Conn. . . . 83
Warm Springs, Va. 108

Warren
  Mildred I. (Pippenger) ... 71,
    80, 85, 86, 92, 96
  Tas Manley 92
Warren Co., Ky. 143
Washington
  Gen. 133
Washington Co., Pa. 117
Washington Co., Tenn. ... 133,
    134
  Big Limestone Creek ... 133,
    134
Washington, D.C. . 58, 69, 105,
    113
  D.A.R. Library 117-119, 121,
    131, 135-139
  Grand Lodge 141
  Masonic Cem. 141
  NASA Headquarters 91
Wasson
  Elizabeth H. (Crutcher) ... 68
  Eric Lee 68
  Ron 68
Waterbury, Conn. 109
Waters
  Maria 119
Watson
  A.S. 48
  D.E. 48
Watt
  John Gill, Rev. 57
Watts
  John 141
  John B. 57
Wayne Co., Mich.
  Detroit 95
Waynesboro, Va. ... 1, 15, 19,
    35, 36, 41, 43, 44, 47-49, 54,
    56-58, 60, 63, 65, 68, 69, 71,
    72, 78, 85, 104, 108, 109,
    113, 114
  Alexander Casket & Furniture
    Co. 47
  Augusta Memorial Park Cem.
    .... 44, 59
  Bethlehem Church Cem. . . 44
  C.W. Alexander & Co. 62
  First Presbyterian Church
    59
  General Wayne Motor Inn
    47
  Liberty House Nursing Home
    63
  McCormick Lumber Co. . 62,
    69
  Presbyterian Cem. .. 18, 43,
    46, 47
  Riverview Cem. . . 16, 18, 20,
    43, 44, 46-48, 58-60, 62, 63,
    69

Springdale Cem. 43
T.W. Alexander & Son ... 58,
    62
  Wayne Avenue Presbyterian
    Church 60
  Zion-St. James E.L. Church
    57
Waynesville, Mo. 34
Weatherly
  Anne 9
  Elizabeth 9
  Elizabeth (Robertson) 9
  Elizabeth (Robinson) 8
  James 9
  James II 9
  John 9
  Mary 9
  Rachel 9
  Sarah 9
Welch
  Colleen P. (Corteville) 97
  Joseph Michael 97
  Joseph Theodore 97
Welfinger
  Rev. 107
Wellington
  Donald Eugene 32
  Dorothy D. (Holmes) 32
  Veronica Lynn 32
Wellington, Kan. 37
  Hatcher's Hospital 36
Wellman
  Elizabeth 140
Wells
  Jack 2
  John C. 57
Wellsville, Kan. 34
Welsey, Kan. 37
Wenger
  Hester J. (Thacker) 41
  Infant 41
  Sarah E. 41
  Solomon C. 41
West
  Suzie 81
West Berlin, Ger. 59
West Lafayette, Ind. 30
West Salem, Wisc. 87
Westminster, Md. 106
Wetzel
  Henry, Rev. 104
Weyers Cave, Va. 19, 71, 106,
    107, 109, 110, 114
Whan
  William 140
Wheatley
  Forrest Lee 34
  Phyllis A. (Hirni) 34
Wheeling, W.Va. 72

Wherry
  Jesse 141
White
  Alexander 66
  Amanda 66
  Bertha A. (Evans) 35
  Bettie J. (Duncan) 35
  Donald Dean 35
  Electa M. (Davis) 35
  Ethan James 66
  Gervaise Suzan 32
  Grace 121
  Hannah 124
  Harry Alvin 35
  Homer Gerold . . 23, 26, 35,
    36, 38, 39
  James 134
  James Franklin 35
  Janet E. (Kimball) 35
  John 121, 124
  Leo Alvin 35
  Mark 66
  Mary E. (King) 35
  Mexa E. (Hopwood) 35
  Priscilla (Alexander) 124
  Royden Laverne 35
  Susan B. (Stubbs) 66
White Co., Tenn. 36
Whitesell
  Harrison M. 105
  Sadie (Wine) 105
Whitlock
  C. Augustus 48, 60
  Edith 47
  Edith Rice 60
  Elizabeth 61
  Emma J. (Alexander) . 1, 43,
    48, 60
  Emma Jane 19
  Emma Lottie 61
  Ethel Louise 61
  James A. 61
  John A. 60
  John Cassius 48, 60
  John William 61
  Leola Richardson 60
  Lydia Augusta 61
  Margaret (Laing) 61
  Margaret D. (   ) 60
  Mary (Depriest) 60
  Mary Bessie 61
  Maxwell Bruce 61
  Mrs. C.A. 54
  Mrs. J.C. 54
  Nina Belle 61
  Robert T. 60
  Sarah M. (Alexander) ... 48,
    60
  Willie Bruce 61

Whitmer
  Abraham 42
  Margaret A. (Thacker) 42
Wichita, Kan. 31, 36-39
  Calvary Cem. 37
  Crawford Nursing Home . . 38
  Hillhaven 37
  Hillside Cem. 37, 38
  Maple Grove Cem. 37
  Resthaven Cem. 37
  St. Francis Hospital 37
  White Chapel Cem. . . . 38, 39
  Wichita County Hospital . . 37
Wicomoco Creek 6
Wilburn
  Edith Rugole 34
Wiley
  David 119
  James Oliver 119
  Moses 119
  Susan (Alexander) 119
Wilkes Co., N.C. 144
Wilkinson
  Kelly M. (McLaughlin) 87
  Lee A. 87
Williams
  Adam Scott 67
  Betty (Alexander) 111
  Betty L. (Theis) 67
  Daniel Scott 68
  Elizabeth ( ) 57
  Ella 59
  Henry K. 111
  James 121
  Mark 111
  Michael 111
  Peter 130
  Peter Christopher 68
  Rena (Smedley) 67
  Steve 111
  Thomas 57
  Virginia C. (Davis) 35
  Wallace H., Jr. 67
  William Henry 35
Williamsburg, Va. 69
Williamson Co., Tenn. 149
Willson
  Rev. 23
  Robert 138
Wilmington, Del. . . . 43, 47, 60,
                      130
Wilson
  Adam 129
  Dorcas Amelia 117, 120,
                     143
  Ephraim 6
  Family 47
  John 150
  Margaret 118
  Margaret (Alexander) . . . 148

  Margaret (Jack) 148
  Martha 125
  President 43
  Rev. 43
  Robert 148
  Samuel 144, 148
  Thomas 6
  Thomas, Rev. 6
  Violet Winslow 144
  Zaccheus 125
  Zaccs. 134
Wilson Co., Tenn. . . . 137, 139,
                     140
Wilucki
  George Ernest 66
  Sarah S. (Alexander) 66
Winchester, Va. . . 72, 109, 111
Wine
  Archibald Earl 106
  Bertie (Hoover) 105
  Betty Louise 105
  Caroline V. (Alexander) . . . 63
  Catharine (Good) 105
  Charles Gabriel 105
  Clarence Elijah 63
  Cora (Gladdy) 106
  Daisey P. (Landes) 106
  David Samuel 105
  Dennis H. 105
  Dora (Hulvey) 105
  Dora L. (Hulvey) 105
  George 105
  George David 105
  Ida Ellen 106
  James Harvey 106
  John 43
  John Alexander 43
  John Wendell 105
  Julia F. (Link) 105
  Lois M. 114
  Lucy Anne 105
  Margaret 105
  Margaret A. (Alexander)
       105
  Mary E. (Alexander) 43
  Mary Katherine 106
  Nelson P. 105
  Ora (Landes) 106
  Pollina 43
  Roberta (Hoover) 105
  Sadie C. 105
  Samuel Walter 105
  Sarah 113
  Sarah Ellen 105
  Sarah Margaret 43
  Sharon Barney 114
  Stella C. (Byers) 105
  Virginia (Hudson) 105
Winebarger
  Frances 56

Wineberg
  Lutie 110
Winegar
  Mary 37
Winfield, W.Va. 71
Winn
  Dorothy 59
Winooski, Vt. 109
Winship
  W.L. 94
Winslow
  Dovey Wilson 145
  Jean (Osborne) 145
  Moses 145
Winston-Salem, N.C. 108
Wisconsin 39
Wise
  Lucinda 106
  Sandra 66
Wise, Va. 108
Wofford
  Cecil 26
  Daisy (James) 26
Wonderly
  Eva Louisa 113
Wood
  Carroll 112
  David 99
  David I. 99
  Jennie (Shaw) 112
  John Alexander 112
  John Leigh 112
  John W. 99
  Margaret L. 99
  Maria 99
  Nicholas L. 99
  Rebecca (Alexander) . . . 112
  Rebecca Leigh 112
  Robert W. 99
  Thomas 99
  William L. 99
Woods
  Rev. 81
Woodson
  Emily 71
  Judith Ann 82
Woodstock, Va. . . 40, 108, 109
Woodward Co., Okla. 37
Worcester Co., Md. 1, 18, 122,
                  127, 147
  Addition 127
  Coventry Parish 11
  Daintry 15
  Fleming's Discovery 15
  Freeman's Adventure . . . 127
  Freeman's Discovery . . 11, 15
  Mill Lot 15
  Mt. Hope 11, 15
  Pocomoke 128, 131

Pocomoke Hundred . 15, 16, 98
Providence 11, 15
Sandhill 15
Sheldon's Addition 11, 15
Snow Hill 11, 15
The Fork 11
Warwick 15, 57
Wicomico Hundred 10
World War I 35
Wroe
  Absolem 141
  Eliza 141
Wyandotte Co., Kan.
  Kansas City .. 30, 31, 37, 85, 91, 94, 95
  Rosedale 80

Y

Yadkin River 148
Yankee
  Vanessa 30
Yonkers, N.Y. 65
York Co., Pa. .. 116, 133, 134, 137
  Carroll's Delight 133
  Marsh Creek 133
  Slate Hill 116
York Co., S.C. 132
  Bethel Cem. 137
  Clover 137
Young
  Arthur 121
  Arthur Wayne 110
  Frances 121
  H.W. 114
  Joseph 137
  Kezia (Alexander) 137
  Lena E. 114
  Martha 138
  Martha R. (Ocheltree) ... 114
  Nettie (Alexander) 110
  Rev. 112
  Robert 140
Younk
  Helen I. (Guy) 29
  Walter Richard 29

Z

Zack, Va. 23
Zainie
  Carla D. (Maness) 85
  Kassim 85
Zick
  Beltty L. (Guy) 29
  Joan P. (Guy) 29
  Verle 29
  William 29

Zimmerman
  Jean 29
Zucker
  Cindy Gail 67
  Jennifer Marie 67
  Julie Ann 67
  Nancy (Alexander) 67
  Ronald 67
  Zachary 67

No Surname
()
  Brigett 11
  Hannah 118
  James 11
  John 9
  Sevin 9
  Tandy 125
  Tom 9

Heritage Books by Wesley E. Pippenger:

Alexander Family: Migrations from Maryland

Alexandria (Arlington) County, Virginia Death Records, 1853–1896

Alexandria City and Arlington County, Virginia Records Index: Vol. 1

Alexandria City and Arlington County, Virginia Records Index: Vol. 2

Alexandria County, Virginia Marriage Records, 1853–1895

Alexandria Virginia Marriage Index, January 10, 1893 to August 31, 1905

Alexandria, Virginia Marriages, 1870–1892

Alexandria, Virginia Town Lots, 1749–1801
Together with the Proceedings of the Board of Trustees, 1749–1780

Alexandria, Virginia Wills, Administrations and Guardianships, 1786–1800

Alexandria, Virginia 1808 Census (Wards 1, 2, 3, and 4)

Alexandria, Virginia Death Records, 1863–1896

Alexandria, Virginia Hustings Court Orders, Volume 1, 1780–1787

Connections and Separations: Divorce, Name Change and Other
Genealogical Tidbits from the Acts of the Virginia General Assembly

Daily National Intelligencer *Index to Deaths, 1855–1870*

Daily National Intelligencer, *Washington, District of Columbia*
Marriages and Deaths Notices (January 1, 1851 to December 30, 1854)

Dead People on the Move: Reconstruction of the Georgetown Presbyterian
Burying Ground, Holmead's (Western) Burying Ground, and
Other Removals in the District of Columbia

Death Notices from Richmond, Virginia Newspapers, 1841–1853

District of Columbia Ancestors,
A Guide to Records of the District of Columbia

District of Columbia Death Records: August 1, 1874–July 31, 1879

District of Columbia Foreign Deaths, 1888–1923

District of Columbia Guardianship Index, 1802–1928

District of Columbia Interments (Index to Deaths)
January 1, 1855 to July 31, 1874

District of Columbia Marriage Licenses, Register 1: 1811–1858

District of Columbia Marriage Licenses, Register 2: 1858–1870

District of Columbia Marriage Records Index
June 28, 1877 to October 19, 1885: Marriage Record Books 11 to 20
Wesley E. Pippenger and Dorothy S. Provine

District of Columbia Marriage Records Index
October 20, 1885 to January 20, 1892: Marriage Record Books 21 to 30

District of Columbia Marriage Records Index
January 20, 1892 to August 30, 1896: Marriage Record Books 31 to 40

District of Columbia Marriage Records Index
August 31, 1896 to December 17, 1900: Marriage Record Books 41 to 65

District of Columbia Probate Records, 1801–1852

District of Columbia: Original Land Owners, 1791–1800

Early Church Records of Alexandria City and Fairfax County, Virginia

Essex County, Virginia Guardianship and Orphans Records, 1707–1888: A Descriptive Index

Essex County, Virginia Marriage Bonds, 1804–1850, Annotated

Essex County, Virginia Newspaper Notices, 1738–1938

Essex County, Virginia Newspaper Notices, Vol. 2, 1735–1952

Essex County, Virginia Will Abstracts, 1751-1842 and Estate Records Index, 1751–1799

*Georgetown, District of Columbia 1850 Federal Population Census (Schedule I)
and 1853 Directory of Residents of Georgetown*

Georgetown, District of Columbia Marriage and Death Notices, 1801–1838

*Husbands and Wives Associated with Early Alexandria, Virginia
(and the Surrounding Area), 3rd Edition, Revised*

Index to District of Columbia Estates, 1801–1929

Index to District of Columbia Land Records, 1792–1817

*Index to Virginia Estates, 1800–1865
Volumes 4, 5 and 6*

John Alexander, a Northern Neck Proprietor, His Family, Friends and Kin

Legislative Petitions of Alexandria, 1778–1861

Pippenger and Pittenger Families

Proceedings of the Orphan's Court, Washington County, District of Columbia, 1801–1808

Richmond County, Virginia Marriage Records, 1854–1890, Annotated

The Georgetown Courier *Marriage and Death Notices:
Georgetown, District of Columbia, November 18, 1865 to May 6, 1876*

*The Georgetown Directory for the Year 1830: to which is appended, a Short Description
of the Churches, Public Institutions, and the Original Charter of Georgetown, and
Extracts of the Laws Pertaining to the Chesapeake and Ohio Canal Company*

The Virginia Gazette and Alexandria Advertiser:
Volume 1, September 3, 1789 to November 11, 1790

The Virginia Journal and Alexandria Advertiser:
Volume I (February 5, 1784 to January 27, 1785)

Volume II (February 3, 1785 to January 26, 1786)

Volume III (March 2, 1786 to January 25, 1787)

Volume IV (February 8, 1787 to May 21, 1789)

The Washington and Georgetown Directory of 1853

Tombstone Inscriptions of Alexandria, Volumes 1–4

Virginia's Lost Wills: An Index

Westmoreland County, Virginia Marriage Records, 1850–1880, Annotated

www.ingramcontent.com/pod-product-compliance
Lightning Source LLC
Chambersburg PA
CBHW080611270326
41928CB00016B/3008